People's Diplomacy

THE UNITED STATES IN THE WORLD

A series edited by Benjamin A. Coates, Emily Conroy-Krutz, Paul A. Kramer, and Judy Tzu-Chun Wu

Founding Series Editors: Mark Philip Bradley and Paul A. Kramer

A list of titles in this series is available at cornellpress.cornell.edu.

People's Diplomacy

How Americans and Chinese Transformed
US-China Relations during the Cold War

Kazushi Minami

Cornell University Press
Ithaca and London

Publication of this book was made possible by generous grants from the K. Matsushita Foundation and the Center for Language Education and Cooperation. Thanks to this funding, the ebook editions of this book are available as open access volumes through the Cornell Open initiative.

Copyright © 2024 by Cornell University

The text of this book is licensed under a Creative Commons Attribution-NonCommercial-NoDerivatives 4.0 International License: https://creativecommons.org/licenses/by-nc-nd/4.0/. To use this book, or parts of this book, in any way not covered by the license, please contact Cornell University Press, Sage House, 512 East State Street, Ithaca, New York 14850. Visit our website at cornellpress.cornell.edu.

First published 2024 by Cornell University Press

Library of Congress Cataloging-in-Publication Data

Names: Minami, Kazushi, 1988– author.
Title: People's diplomacy : how Americans and Chinese transformed US-China relations during the Cold War / Kazushi Minami.
Other titles: How Americans and Chinese transformed US-China relations during the Cold War
Description: Ithaca : Cornell University Press, 2024. | Series: The United States in the world | Includes bibliographical references and index.
Identifiers: LCCN 2023039714 (print) | LCCN 2023039715 (ebook) | ISBN 9781501774140 (hardcover) | ISBN 9781501774157 (paperback) | ISBN 9781501774164 (pdf) | ISBN 9781501774171 (epub)
Subjects: LCSH: Exchange of persons programs, American—China—History—20th century. | Exchange of persons programs, Chinese—United States—History—20th century. | Cultural diplomacy—United States—History—20th century. | Cultural diplomacy—China—History—20th century. | Politics and culture—United States—History—20th century. | Politics and culture—China—History—20th century. | Cold War—Social aspects. | United States—Relations—China. | China—Relations—United States.
Classification: LCC E183.8.C6 M557 2024 (print) | LCC E183.8.C6 (ebook) | DDC 303.48/2730510904—dc23/eng/20230905
LC record available at https://lccn.loc.gov/2023039714
LC ebook record available at https://lccn.loc.gov/2023039715

Contents

Introduction	1
1. The Origins of People's Diplomacy	20
2. Trade: A New Open Door	44
3. Science: A Miracle Drug	67
4. Education: To "Change China"	91
5. Tourism: The New Marco Polo	115
6. Sport: Friendship and Competition	138
7. Art: From Mao to Beethoven	159
Epilogue	180
Acknowledgments	191
Notes	195
Selected Bibliography	249
Index	255

Introduction

The relationship between the United States and the People's Republic of China is the most important bilateral relationship of the twenty-first century. This is a truism. The United States is the sole superpower in the world with unmatched military, economic, and cultural resources, whereas China is a rising power, with its influence spreading from Asia to Europe to Africa. No other two countries can shake the world as hard as they can. Many scholars and policy makers warn that the United States and China may be ordained for the so-called Thucydides Trap, a theory that war is all but inevitable when an emerging hegemon challenges an established one.[1] This doomsday scenario seems more plausible than ever as I write this book in the spring of 2020. With the global COVID-19 pandemic exacting enormous tolls from China to Europe to the United States to the rest of the world, Americans and Chinese, be they politicians, pundits, or citizens, point their angry fingers across the Pacific, as if the other side were to blame for their own mistakes and sufferings. Bigotry abounds, and a new cold war is simmering. It is no understatement that the stability of the world depends on whether the United States and China can avoid a tragic repetition of history.

The most important bilateral relationship, however, entails far more than strategic rivalry. The US economy relies on all things "Made in China," while China is one of the largest consumers of American products, as exemplified by over two hundred million iPhone users in that country. Currently, 317,000 Chinese students study at US universities, one-third of the international student body. Over four million tourists traveled between the two countries each year before the pandemic, and so did myriad groups of politicians, professionals, and scholars. Chinese people consume American culture on a daily basis, from Coca-Cola to Hollywood films to NBA games; Americans, too, cherish things Chinese, from porcelain to dumplings to giant pandas. Many of these exchanges suffered serious setbacks in recent years due to the trade war, Hong Kong protest, and COVID-19, some of them probably unrepairable in the near future. Yet, lest war precipitate a complete cutoff, a thick, dense web of networks carrying people, goods, and ideas will continue to enmesh the United States and China, keeping their relationship exceptionally intimate.

But how did it all come about? I answer this question by tracing the origins of contemporary US-China relations to the Cold War—particularly the transformative decade of the 1970s. The Chinese Communist Revolution of 1949 tore down most of the intricate ties that had connected the United States and China for centuries—historians have dubbed them "a special relationship," "a shared history," or "fateful ties"—turning the former World War II allies into "imperialists" and "Red Menace."[2] In the 1950s and 1960s, they collided over Korea, Taiwan, Vietnam, and other parts of the developing world, politically, economically, and militarily. Washington and Beijing maintained a channel of communication in Warsaw, Poland, but their talks hardly bore any fruit during the presidencies of Dwight D. Eisenhower, John F. Kennedy, and Lyndon B. Johnson. The crucible of the Cold War allowed few Americans and Chinese to travel to either country—none under the agreement of their governments.[3] Michel Oksenberg of the University of Michigan aptly wrote that at the end of the 1960s, "Americans were more familiar with the moon than the People's Republic."[4]

All this changed in the 1970s. On February 21, 1972, Richard Nixon became the first US president to set foot in the People's Republic of China (see fig. 0.1). Nixon and his national security adviser Henry Kissinger had a series of meetings with Chinese leaders, including Mao Zedong, chairman of the Chinese Communist Party (CCP), and Zhou Enlai, premier of the People's Republic, which resulted in the Shanghai Communiqué, a defining treatise on US-China relations to this day. It stipulated:

> There are essential differences between China and the United States in their social systems and foreign policies. However, the two sides agreed that countries, regardless of their social systems, should conduct their relations on the principles of respect for the sovereignty and territorial integrity of all states, nonaggression against other states, noninterference in the internal affairs of

Figure 0.1. Richard Nixon and Mao Zedong shake hands at the chairman's residence in Zhongnanhai, Beijing, February 21, 1972.

other states, equality and mutual benefit, and peaceful coexistence. . . . The United States and the People's Republic of China are prepared to apply these principles to their mutual relations.[5]

The Shanghai Communiqué, a symbol of Sino-American "rapprochement," was followed by a stalemate in bilateral relations caused mainly by the thorny problem of Taiwan, or the Republic of China, a US ally controlled by the Chinese Nationalist Party (Kuomintang or KMT).[6] Washington and Beijing finally reached an agreement in late 1978, which allowed the United States to retain unofficial contacts with Taiwan after severing official ties. On January 1, 1979, the United States and China normalized relations, and a few weeks later, Vice Premier Deng Xiaoping toured the United States for nine days. The footage of the new leader of China wearing a cowboy hat at a Texas rodeo near Houston signified an important fact—that the Cold War in East Asia was no more (see fig. 0.2).

Policy makers in Washington and Beijing were the architects of this process, but they were not the carpenters. They set strategies, conducted

Figure 0.2. Deng Xiaoping, wearing a ten-gallon hat, greets the audience at a Texas rodeo, February 2, 1979. Photo by Dirck Halstead/Getty Images.

negotiations, and designed the blueprint for the new bilateral relationship, but they could not build it by themselves. The work was left to Americans and Chinese from various walks of life—businesspeople, scientists, students, tourists, athletes, and artists, among others—who engaged in "people's diplomacy," which I define as a form of diplomacy whereby nonstate actors, independent of, yet often guided by, the state, create informal connections between countries. Through people's diplomacy, they cultivated new ties between the United States and China in the absence of formal diplomatic relations, ties that were tenuous yet crucial. I foreground these people in this book. Who were they? What did they want? How did they accomplish what they accomplished? Drawing on a vast array of US and Chinese sources, I answer these questions to challenge the dominant narrative on Sino-American rapprochement—that US and Chinese policy makers single-handedly turned bilateral relations upside down. They didn't, for it was the people, both American and Chinese, who transformed the distant, strained relationship into what is with us today: a close, durable relationship with unparalleled scope, complexity, and impact.

From Rapprochement to Normalization

Before departing Shanghai, Nixon boasted that his trip to China was a "week that changed the world."[7] The statement was smug but not hyperbolic. Nixon, an anti-communist firebrand, shook hands with Mao Zedong, a self-appointed vanguard of international communism. Newspapers across the world printed the photograph of their handshake at the chairman's cozy den, and suddenly, the Cold War as everyone knew it—a global struggle between the US-led West and the Soviet-led East, capitalism and socialism, democracy and dictatorship, the good and the evil—ceased to make sense.

Geopolitics dictated the process for the historic handshake. In late 1969, Washington began to negotiate nuclear arms control with Moscow through the Strategic Arms Limitation Talks (SALT), angling to preserve a rough parity in the two countries' nuclear capabilities. By reaching out to Beijing, which had become Moscow's archenemy by the late 1960s, the Americans tried to pressure the Russians into accelerating the SALT negotiations. The Nixon administration was also desperate for "peace with honor" in Vietnam. More than sixteen thousand American soldiers died there in 1968 alone, yet Hanoi showed no sign of backing down at the Paris peace talks. The US overture to China, the largest sponsor of Hanoi's war efforts, undermined the North Vietnamese negotiation position, although Beijing refused to sway Hanoi into peace. The China opening in February 1972 helped Nixon achieve the other two diplomatic milestones of his presidency: the SALT agreement in May 1972 and the Paris Peace Accords in January 1973.

Security was also paramount in Beijing's decision to invite Nixon. The Sino-Soviet split, an ideological and diplomatic rift between the former communist brothers since the late 1950s, culminated in a border conflict in March 1969 over the Zhenbao/Damansky Island, located on the Wusuli/Ussuri River, followed by further skirmishes in Xinjiang that August. Moscow dispatched more than a million troops, equipped with nuclear weapons, along the Chinese borders and put them on high alert. Soviet "revisionists" replaced US "imperialists" as China's most dangerous enemy. Mao had no choice but to use the lesser evil to fend off the greater evil, and the Nixon administration, too, opposed a Soviet attack on China, which it feared might lead to Soviet domination of the Eurasian landmass. In addition to the Soviet Union in the north, China was flanked by Japan in the east, India in the west, and the Association of Southeast Asian Nations (ASEAN) in the south, all of them in the US camp. Mao's handshake with Nixon extricated Beijing from this predicament.

Geopolitics occasioned normalization of US-China relations as well. After Nixon's visit, US and Chinese strategic interests diverged, with Kissinger pursuing détente with Moscow and Mao touting his Three Worlds Theory, which divided the world into the US and Soviet superpowers ("First World"); their allies in the developed world ("Second World"); and vast swaths of the developing world ("Third World"), China included, the target of superpower domination and exploitation.[8] In the late 1970s, however, the expansion of Soviet influence in the Persian Gulf, the Horn of Africa, and Southeast Asia, combined with the slow progress at the second round of the SALT negotiations, brought Washington and Beijing closer again. For Zbigniew Brzezinski, the national security adviser for President Jimmy Carter, normalizing US-China relations was a "strategic response" to Soviet "adventurism."[9] So it was for Deng Xiaoping, who launched an invasion against Vietnam, the former Chinese ally turned Soviet client, on February 17, 1979, ten days after his return from the United States. The Soviet invasion of Afghanistan that December killed détente and turned Washington and Beijing into strategic partners.

Domestic politics shaped Sino-American rapprochement as profoundly as did geopolitics. A well-known hawk since his vice presidency in the 1950s, Nixon could travel to China and celebrate it as "a journey for peace," without arousing overwhelming backlash at home.[10] Although the journey earned him a landslide victory in the 1972 presidential election, Watergate soon crippled his presidency. With Congress trying to restrict executive power, President Gerald Ford deemed it almost impossible to acquiesce to Beijing's insistence on the "three principles" on Taiwan—that Washington should abrogate the defense treaty with, withdraw troops from, and severe diplomatic ties with Taiwan—on which hinged normalization of US-China relations. To Beijing's irritation, Pentagon increased its sales of submarines and fighter jets to Taiwan; the State Department permitted the opening of new Taiwanese consulates in the United States; and Vice President Nelson Rockefeller attended the funeral of Chiang Kai-shek, the president of the Republic of China, in April 1975. The Chinese, who dismissed Watergate as "nonsensical," realized that Washington had neither intention nor ability to settle the Taiwan issue. Ford visited China in December 1975, but returned empty-handed.

A similar dynamic was at play in China. The Cultural Revolution, Mao's last revolution that incited uprisings against authority of all kinds, threw the country into violent chaos in the late 1960s, forcing the chairman to deploy the People's Liberation Army (PLA) to suppress the rebels and restore order.

This ebb in China's "continuous revolution"—and the mysterious death in October 1971 of General Lin Biao, Mao's chosen heir, who was rumored to have opposed Sino-American rapprochement—enabled Mao to invite Nixon. In late 1973, however, the Criticize Lin, Criticize Confucius Campaign, ostensibly targeted at the renegade general and the ancient philosopher, empowered a quartet of Shanghai-based politicos, led by Mao's wife Jiang Qing and joined by Zhang Chunqiao, Yao Wenyuan, and Wang Hongwen. This group, later labeled the Gang of Four, chastised those who managed US-China relations, particularly Zhou Enlai and his protégé Deng Xiaoping, as "capitulationists." They reached the pinnacle of power in 1976, with Zhou's death in January and Deng's purge in April. The Gang never held the reins of Chinese foreign policy, but the domestic turbulence they whipped up precluded normalization of relations with the United States.[11]

Leadership transition in both countries broke this impasse in the late 1970s. Drowning in urgent issues, including negotiations for the Panama Canal Treaties, Carter remained uncommitted to recognition of China for over a year. As Brzezinski replaced Secretary of State Cyrus Vance, an advocate of détente, as Carter's main foreign policy adviser, he and his allies such as Vice President Walter Mondale and Secretary of Defense Harold Brown persuaded the president to play the China card against the Soviet Union. Meanwhile, Mao's death on September 9, 1976, followed by the Gang of Four's arrest a month later, ended "the ten years of turmoil" in China since the onset of the Cultural Revolution in 1966. After a brief reign by Hua Guofeng, Mao's handpicked successor, Deng sidelined him in December 1978. He ushered in China's reform era, with the tagline "Reform and Opening-Up" (*gaige kaifang*), through cooperation with capitalist countries, especially the United States. The Taiwan problem never disappeared, but neither Carter nor Deng faced serious trouble at home when they announced the upcoming normalization on December 15, 1978.[12]

Geopolitics and domestic politics catalyzed diplomatic breakthroughs from Sino-American rapprochement to normalization of relations. Scholars—American, Chinese, or otherwise—have amply demonstrated this in the past quarter century.[13] The transformation of US-China relations, however, reached far beyond the relationship between the two governments. By the end of the 1970s, Americans and Chinese had conceived and nurtured new ideas of each other, ideas that would inform bilateral relations from the 1980s onward. These ideas were not as simplistic and hostile as "imperialists" and the "Red Menace" in the 1950s and 1960s, nor were they as glorifying and idealistic as the "special relationship" before 1949. They were complex and dynamic and contradictory. World-changing as they were, diplomatic achievements between Washington and Beijing in the 1970s were prerequisite but not sufficiency for these ideas to emerge after two decades of mutual estrangement. To understand who promoted these ideas and what these ideas encompassed, we need a new analytical thrust: people's diplomacy.

People's Diplomacy

The people—who often go by the name of "nonstate actors" in scholarly writing—shape international relations as much as international relations shape them.[14] They do not represent the state, yet they engage in diplomatic activities with their own capacity to pursue their own interests. Scholars coined "public diplomacy" as an umbrella term for the activities of nonstate actors that are in one way or another regulated by the state, but I use "people's diplomacy" to describe the kind of interactions between Americans and Chinese in the 1970s, because the term captures the agency of the people, instead of generalizing and appropriating them as "the public."[15] Washington and Beijing, too, called these interactions "people-to-people" exchanges or *minjian jiaoliu*.

The United States and China both invested in people's diplomacy during the Cold War, when winning the hearts and minds of people around the world became more important than ever. In 1956, Eisenhower launched the People-to-People Program, consisting of forty committees devoted to cultural and educational exchanges with foreign countries, to build "a true and lasting peace." "If we are going to take advantage of the assumption that all people want peace," he enthused, "then the problem is for people to get together and to leap governments—if necessary to evade governments—to work out not one method but thousands of methods by which people can gradually learn a little bit more of each other."[16] These programs, aimed at combating the Soviet peace offensive, were but one example. The United States Information Agency (USIA), the Central Intelligence Agency (CIA), and the State Department's Bureau of Educational and Cultural Affairs coopted nonstate actors, from movie stars to Olympic athletes to jazz musicians, for propaganda efforts throughout the Cold War.[17] Far from passive, these actors often deployed themselves for their own agendas, as exemplified by nuclear scientists, civil rights leaders, and human rights activists, who pressured the government to pursue arms control, racial equality, and justice and morality, at home and abroad.[18]

The CCP institutionalized people's diplomacy (*renmin waijiao*) soon after the founding of the People's Republic. With the slogan "influence the policy through the people" (*yi min cu guan*), it was intended to achieve two strategic goals. The first was to cultivate informal ties with the capitalist bloc. Beijing mobilized various organizations and individuals, technically separate from the party-state yet indeed dictated by it, to establish contacts with businesspeople, scientists, and journalists in Japan, Western Europe, and the United States, in the hope that these "foreign friends" (*waiguo pengyou*) would lobby their governments to improve relations with China. The second was to expand Chinese influence worldwide. Beijing sent doctors, scientists, and athletes to developing countries in Asia and Africa, often under the auspices of the CCP's International Liaison Department, particularly in the 1960s, when Beijing, Washington, and Moscow jockeyed for leadership in the developing world. Beijing lauded the power of the people—or the masses (*qunzhong*) as it often called them—to enhance China's international status. The "people" partaking in these initiatives were by no means commoners (*laobaixing*); rather, they were carefully vetted individuals with proper background, ideological correctness, and political influence, who understood their diplomatic mission.[19]

Ping-Pong diplomacy is the most prominent example of people's diplomacy in the history of US-China relations. A spontaneous conversation struck up by American and Chinese table tennis players at the World Championships in Nagoya, Japan, in April 1971 resulted in the US team's visit to China, covered extensively by US and Chinese media. This extravaganza made the US and Chinese public receptive to the diplomatic stunts that July: Kissinger's secret trip to Beijing and Nixon's announcement of his upcoming visit. US and Chinese policy makers pledged in the Shanghai Communiqué to cultivate new contacts between the Americans and Chinese to expedite normalization of relations:

> The two sides agreed that it is desirable to broaden the understanding between the two peoples. To this end, they discussed specific areas in such fields as science, technology, culture, sports and journalism, in which people-to-people contacts and exchanges would be mutually beneficial. Each side undertakes to facilitate the further development of such contacts and exchanges. Both sides view bilateral trade as another area from which mutual benefit can be derived, and agreed that economic relations based on equality and mutual benefit are in the interest of the people of the two countries. They agree to facilitate the progressive development of trade between their two countries.[20]

The lack of diplomatic relations necessitated a mechanism that reduced the footprint of the state in administering these "contacts and exchanges." Washington entrusted this task to nongovernmental organizations devoted to fostering ties with China, most notably the National Committee on US-China Relations. Although formally independent of the government, members of these organizations became informal diplomats, who consciously tried to assist normalization of relations through their activities. Beijing, for its part, called up "mass organizations" (*qunzhong zuzhi*)—quasi-nongovernmental organizations serving the broad interests of the masses, such as women's federations, communist youth leagues, and sports associations. Despite their ostensibly "nonstate" outlook, the Chinese party-state controlled nearly all activities of these organizations. The Chinese Table Tennis Association, for instance, could never have invited the Americans to China of its own volition; the ordinance had to come from Mao Zedong. Still, Beijing designated mass organizations as "nonstate," which allowed them to communicate with countries without diplomatic relations with China, including the United States. Washington and Beijing "facilitated" exchange programs between these organizations, negotiating the subjects, timing, and composition, although they usually just endorsed the programs determined through direct and indirect communication between the organizations. Aside from these "government-facilitated" exchanges, proposals and invitations came from sundry groups and individuals, governmental or nongovernmental, making the people-to-people exchanges hard to generalize.

The US and Chinese governments handled these exchanges in distinctive ways. While sanctioning the overall framework, Washington gave considerable autonomy to nongovernmental organizations and refrained from intervening directly, except on rare occasions. With no established routine to follow, these organizations raised funds, negotiated with local hosts, and made ad hoc arrangements to fulfill Chinese requests on itineraries and activities in the United States. Beijing, on the other hand, dominated exchange programs through mass organizations, trying to achieve its diplomatic objectives without showing the heavy hand of the state. Mass organizations had a modus operandi: They solicited broad interests of American delegations, which varied from foreign trade to higher education, agricultural policy to factory management, public health to women's liberation, in order to draft itineraries. Local hosts—communes, factories, schools, hospitals, and local branches of mass organizations, among others—then made concrete arrangements based on the propaganda instruction, issued typically by government ministries, CCP departments, national headquarters of mass organizations, or local government bureaus. American guests could raise specific demands on where to go, what to see, and whom to meet in China, but the hosts often flatly rejected these requests, calling them "inconvenient" (*bu fangbian*).

The calculated distance between the state and nonstate actors, created by the lack of diplomatic relations before 1979, made nonstate actors more instrumental for the state and people's diplomacy more influential for bilateral relations than otherwise would have been the case. While carefully separating itself from nongovernmental organizations, Washington supported them by maintaining regular communication, providing policy briefings, assisting visa applications, and funding many of their programs. With the government's backing, these organizations could maintain and expand their activities throughout the 1970s. "Nonstate" actors in China rarely escaped the control of the state. Most of the organizations and individuals that Beijing designated as "nonstate" were, to varying degrees, part of the state. To cover up this obvious masquerade, Beijing encouraged active participation from the masses, allowing them to plan, implement, and improve activities on the ground. This arrangement fostered their desire for more contact with the United States in ways that state propaganda never could. By letting the Americans and Chinese take initiatives within permissible boundaries, which constantly fluctuated, people's diplomacy unleashed—and framed—the people's visions for the new bilateral relationship.

People's diplomacy, for the most part, was not so much a catalyst for diplomatic breakthroughs as a bellwether of them. Always preoccupied with geopolitics, Kissinger relegated the people-to-people exchanges to "counterpart meetings," separate from his talks with top Chinese leaders. In private, he called China scholars involved in these efforts "chowder-headed liberals" and their emphasis on breaking China's "isolation" "crap."[21] Still, Kissinger promoted these exchanges as a device to symbolize Sino-American rapprochement, particularly in the mid-1970s, when he was striving to palliate the Taiwan deadlock and bolster public confidence in normalization of relations. Accusing Kissinger of "standing on Chinese shoulders" to "reach out to the Soviet Union," Beijing refused to broaden or deepen bilateral contacts before securing Washington's consent to the "three principles" on Taiwan, and the people-to-people exchanges seemed to have lost momentum.[22] Only when Washington and Beijing decided in mid-1978 to move toward normalization of relations did they substantially expand exchange programs, which signaled an ever-closer relationship and consolidated popular support for the normalization in both countries.

In this book, I argue that the historical significance of people's diplomacy lay not in its direct impact on policy making, but in the new interests it engendered between the United States and China. The Americans and Chinese had reservations about exchange programs. Reeling from the terror of the CCP dictatorship, many Americans questioned the virtue of empowering the regime that had jailed hundreds of thousands of intellectuals and starved tens of millions of people. For the Chinese, the closer they were to the center of the party-state, the more rigorously they preached against the corruptive influence of US capitalism seeping into China. These misgivings notwithstanding, most Americans and Chinese eventually supported, or at least accepted, normalization of relations, because they believed that a closer relationship would advance their interests, be they economic, cultural, or educational. China's market, youth, and history enticed Americans firms, universities, and travelers, while US preponderance in science, technology, and sport enthralled Chinese scholars, companies, and athletes. The people-to-people exchanges birthed these interests and rendered them tangible for the US and Chinese public.

By forging these interests, people's diplomacy incubated new ideas about US-China relations, which had been impregnated with Cold War hostility for over two decades. Patrick McCurdy, editor of *Chemical and Engineering News*, wrote in 1972:

> How our scientists, engineers, physicians, industrialists, economists, and journalists handle themselves in China, how their counterparts act in this country and how both peoples react and relate to each other's representatives will be critical in shaping a true détente.... We are now in the tone-setting stage in which individual citizens will be largely responsible for converting present rather tenuous connection into the durable fabric of understanding and mutual benefits. Insensitivity or insincerity, or, on the other hand, empathy and forthrightness will form impressions that will endure no matter what the party lines.... The growing number of Chinese connections gives those involved individual leverage of potentially awesome dimensions. We hope they use it wisely.[23]

They certainly did, changing the ways in which Americans and Chinese perceived each other as well as bilateral relations at large. No longer was China "Red Menace" for Americans, and the United States "imperialist" for Chinese. Americans reimagined China as a country of new opportunities, irresistible because of its prodigious potential, while Chinese reinterpreted the

United States as an agent of modernization, capable of not only enriching their country, but also turning their lives around. These images convinced people on both sides of the Pacific that engagement, not containment and isolation, should be the new guiding principle for US-China relations.

The 1970s: A Decade of Disruptions

People's diplomacy was a creation of its time, for Americans and Chinese involved in it were operating within the broader context of disruptive changes, many of which they themselves were creating. The 1970s was a decade of "interdependence." A series of events in the previous decade—the Sino-Soviet split, French recognition of China (1964), French withdrawal from the North Atlantic Treaty Organization (NATO) military command (1966), West German Ostpolitik (*eastern policy*) toward Eastern Europe, and the Prague Spring (1968)—obscured the bipolar world order that had long defined the Cold War. Meanwhile, burdened by the Vietnam War and Great Society social programs, challenged by Western European and Japanese competitors, the United States ceased to be the sole economic superpower in the world, a fact accentuated by the fall of the Bretton Woods system in August 1971 and the Oil Shock of 1973. No one or two countries ruled the emerging multipolar world, politically or economically. "If we do not get a recognition of our interdependence," warned Kissinger, an eloquent proponent of this new order, "the Western civilization that we now have is almost certain to disintegrate."[24] Interdependence, Kissinger and many like-minded thinkers envisioned, demanded participation by China, a country with a population of 800 million, or one-fourth of humanity.[25]

The 1970s was also a decade of "globalization." Merchants, missionaries, and migrants had mediated this historical process since the Age of Discovery, but it entered the popular lexicon in the 1970s, when nonstate actors of all kinds moved across national boundaries in record numbers. They formed transnational "civil society," with shared resources, ideas, and norms, complicating the traditional understanding of what constituted international relations. Never before did the world seem so small and so connected, and the line between the spheres of activity for state and nonstate actors so blurred. These perceptions were sharpened by salient phenomena symptomatic of globalization, such as the rise of multinational corporations, the internationalization of higher education, and the expansion of global mass tourism. China had been largely left out from these developments, but as Joseph Levenson of the University of California, Berkeley, predicted, China was about to "join the world again on the cosmopolitan tide," which was reaching its shores just as it opened the door to the United States and the capitalist world.[26]

These transnational currents were paralleled by domestic tumults in both countries. In the United States, the Cold War consensus—that the government should fight against communism everywhere, no matter the economic, military, and moral cost—unraveled due largely to the Vietnam War. This led to an outburst of various social movements that challenged conventional norms in postwar America, such as the antiwar movement, the civil rights movement, the women's liberation movement, the gay rights movement, and the antinuclear movement. The uncertainties and anxieties these movements addressed and aroused prompted countless Americans to accept, and in some cases crave, more contact with China, a country that seemed to offer a socialist remedy to their capitalist ailments. In 1981, sociologist Paul Hollander deplored as intellectually uncritical and morally skewed these left-leaning individuals who considered China a "good society."[27] His account, ironically, attested to the appeal China held for various segments of American society in the 1970s.

This appeal soon vanished, though. The rise of conservatism, which climaxed in the presidency of Ronald Reagan, repelled the progressive tide of the 1960s and 1970s.[28] Americans were no longer students of Chinese socialism in the 1980s; instead, they were, in the words of sociologist Richard Madsen, "missionaries of the American dream," who believed that "American liberal values were universal," and "having been exposed to them, Chinese society would eventually adopt them." The new connections with China, argued Madsen, allowed Americans to stop questioning their government, society, and culture and "to believe once again that they still had something to teach the rest of the world."[29] Few displayed such an explicit missionary mentality, and most Americans simply wished to maximize their diverse interests through contacts with China. Yet these interests indeed begot certain expectations, or stakes, in what China would become in the future.

The domestic shifts in the United States pale in comparison to the upheavals engulfing China in the 1970s. The deteriorating health of Mao Zedong and Zhou Enlai intensified the power struggle between Deng Xiaoping and the Gang of Four. More than six years after his purge at the beginning of the Cultural Revolution, Deng was restored to vice premiership in March 1973 and tasked with helping Zhou to rectify the political, economic, and social excesses of the Cultural Revolution. After the Fourth National People's Congress in January 1975, Deng implemented wide-ranging reforms to achieve the so-called four modernizations (*si ge xiandaihua*) in agriculture, industry, science and technology, and national defense by the year 2000. Deng's programs, supported by Mao and Zhou, enlisted limited yet considerable assistance from capitalist countries, the United States included. This made the Gang livid. Desperate to perpetuate the political atmosphere that facilitated their ascent, they rallied their allies nationwide to decry Deng's reforms as "great poisonous weeds" (*da ducao*). When Deng alienated Mao in late 1975 by declining to endorse the Cultural Revolution, the aging chairman let the Gang prey on him.[30] Deng was purged again in April 1976 in the maelstrom of the Criticize Deng Campaign, and his reforms fell by the wayside.

The Gang of Four, however, was a spent force without Mao's patronage. Soon after their arrest on October 6, 1976, the *People's Daily* printed for the first time the late chairman's famous speech at the CCP Politburo in 1956, titled *On the Ten Major Relationships*. Its tenth point, on "the relationship between China and other countries," underscored the importance of "learning the strengths of all peoples and all countries."[31] A few months later, Hua Guofeng rolled out ambitious plans to modernize the economy through foreign technology imports. Hua's proposed purchases of equipment, services, and whole plants through massive loans were nonetheless impractical and reckless, so much so that they were later derided as "the Western-Led Leap Forward" (*yang yuejin*), a reference to the Great Leap Forward (1958–1962), a rapid industrialization campaign in which some 45 million died of famine, torture, and overwork. Hua's inexperience, as well as his unwavering loyalty to his predecessor evident in the "Two Whatevers" (*liang ge fanshi*) thesis—that he would uphold whatever decisions Mao made and whatever instructions Mao gave—guaranteed Deng's rise. Rehabilitated in July 1977, the vice premier espoused not only pragmatic plans for modernization, but also reevaluation of Mao's legacies, particularly the Cultural Revolution. Deng replaced Hua as the supreme leader of China at the Third Plenum of the Eleventh CCP Central Committee held between December 18 and 22, 1978. The CCP extols this moment as the beginning of Reform and Opening-Up.[32]

Such were the historical distortions prevalent in Deng Xiaoping's hagiographies. The Third Plenum was not a watershed between two distinctive eras, but a culmination of gradual changes across China in the 1970s that took various forms, from technological updates at the factory to curriculum adjustments in the classroom to increasing competitiveness at the gymnasium. Reformist officials encouraged these changes as enthusiastically as the population embraced them. Nowhere was the Chinese people's thirst for change more pronounced than at Tiananmen Square in Beijing on April 5, 1976. A day after the Qingming Festival, a traditional day of mourning, tens of thousands of Beijing residents protested the removal of the displays commemorating Zhou Enlai's death, until they were dispersed by security forces. The Gang of Four imputed the incident to Deng, but it indicated popular disapproval of Mao and his policies.[33] By the time revolutionary committees (*geweihui*), the institutional foundation of the Cultural Revolution, began to disappear across the country in late 1977, the momentum for reform had already taken deep root in almost all corners of society. The prolonged birth of Reform and Opening-Up coincided with the prolonged death of the Cultural Revolution.

The unfolding of people's diplomacy dovetailed with these developments—by design, not by chance. Although Beijing prioritized building ties with capitalist countries that had normalized relations with China in the early 1970s—Canada, Italy, Britain, Japan, West Germany, and Australia—no country rivaled the United States in its ability to assist China's modernization. China's domestic shifts promoted people-to-people exchanges with the United States despite the lack of diplomatic relations; and these exchanges, in turn, accelerated China's pursuit of reform by channeling US influence in many ways. This synergy became visible only in the late 1970s, and historians, both Chinese and non-Chinese, put the blame for this delay almost squarely on the Gang of Four, the most convenient scapegoat. They did oppose, obstruct, and subvert improvements of relations with the United States, but the rise and fall of the Gang was only part of the larger shift from Mao's China, a country championing class struggle, to Deng's China, a country preaching economic development. To a significant extent, this shift—China's "second revolution" as sinologist Harry Harding phrased it—depended on US-China relations.[34]

The historian Akira Iriye suggested more than four decades ago that scholars analyze "the culture-power relationship." He defined it as "the relationship between a country's cultural system and its behavior in the international system," mediated by nonstate actors trying to project their values, ideals, and interests onto the diplomatic conduct of their country.[35] Historians have since studied this relationship extensively, but not in the context of US-China relations from rapprochement to normalization.[36] This is an unfortunate omission, given the magnitude of disruptions in the "culture-power relationship" in both countries—but particularly in China. Many Americans and Chinese latched onto the new international and cultural systems in the 1970s, as they engaged in people's diplomacy.

Outlines of Chapters

I begin by telling how US-China people's diplomacy commenced. Chapter 1 examines the new ideas for bilateral relations that emerged in both countries in the 1960s. American scholars, activists, and politicians launched a national campaign to reconsider US policy in Asia and reestablish informal contacts with China, while Chinese propaganda portrayed contrasting images of the US government and the American public, vilifying US involvement in Vietnam on the one hand and applauding antiwar protests on the other. Although the Vietnam War and the Cultural Revolution foreclosed any diplomatic breakthrough in the late 1960s, these new ideas portended a drastic shift in bilateral relations in the next decade.

The following chapters explore the six areas of people-to-people exchanges in the 1970s that were most impactful in reshaping US-China relations. Chapter 2 focuses on trade, spurred by China's economic potential and modern US technology. American businesspeople, especially those in the National Council for US-China Trade, tried to cultivate the vast China market through the new "open door," beholding it as an elixir for their economic hardships. This idea, based on a historical myth, remained influential despite the stagnation of bilateral trade in the mid-1970s. Meanwhile, the China Council for the Promotion of International Trade, which assisted Chinese companies and negotiated with American firms, sought ever more eagerly to import US technology. US and Chinese business interests converged in the late 1970s, with the advent of China's economic reform.

Chapter 3 discusses scientific exchanges. Initially aimed at sowing the "seeds of friendship," they became a "miracle drug" for Chinese modernization and US-China relations. Viewing science as a common pursuit of humanity detached from ideology, American scientists, particularly those belonging to the Committee on Scholarly Communication with China, strove to rebuild contacts with Chinese colleagues dating back to before 1949. Chinese scientists, for their part, promoted scientific exchanges with the United States through the Science and Technology Association of China, as a lever to depoliticize and reform Chinese science. Scholars in both countries resumed institutional cooperation even before normalization of relations, as China embarked on a scientific renaissance.

Chapter 4 analyzes educational exchanges, fueled by American and Chinese ambitions to "change China," albeit in different ways. Competing for talent markets worldwide, US universities wished to reconnect with Chinese students, the backbone of bilateral relations before 1949. Bent on nurturing human capital for modernization, Deng Xiaoping agreed to resume student exchanges with the United States in late 1978. The decision dazzled Chinese students, victims of the "revolution in education," the radical egalitarianism that had afflicted Chinese education during the Cultural Revolution. Their enthusiasm to overturn their misfortunes through the new opportunity abroad caused an English fever and a study abroad craze in urban China.

Chapter 5 surveys American tourism in China, which reinvented Maoist dystopia as a popular destination of mass tourism. Viewing American travelers as a prime target of propaganda, Chinese hosts, including the China International Travel Service, arranged group tours to highlight "the superiority of socialism" over capitalism. These tourists, from incredulous journalists to the gullible members of the US-China People's Friendship Association, discussed different impressions of Chinese socialism, juxtaposing it against American capitalism. When tourism became a tool to earn foreign currency in the late 1970s, Beijing portrayed China as the exotic Middle Kingdom, an orientalist image that attracted far more American tourists than did socialism.

Chapter 6 studies sports exchanges. Despite the slogan "friendship first, competition second," sports matches spawned rivalry—and respect—between the two countries. Viewing sport as a political device, the All-China Sports Federation instructed Chinese athletes to display goodwill, often by intentionally losing points, at exhibition games organized with the National Committee on US-China Relations. The competitive mentality of American athletes and fans, who coveted victory as a manifestation of the nation's vitality, nonetheless provoked subtle rivalry on the field. As athletics became an essential element of a modern Chinese nation, Chinese athletes and fans reconsidered the United States a powerful rival to learn from and outplay.

Chapter 7 investigates cultural exchanges. The political qualities inherent in American and Chinese art, particularly classical music and revolutionary ballet, caused friction over programs coordinated by the National Committee and Chinese groups like the China Central Philharmonic Orchestra. Chinese musicians and music lovers, however, showed much excitement for the reintroduction of classical music in China, a "bourgeois pastime" prohibited by Jiang Qing since 1966. Following the end of Cultural Revolution art, symbolized by Jiang's arrest, Chinese artists imported Western art, from music to literature to film, as a source of cultural modernization, a twin to economic modernization, while turning Chinese art into commercial entertainment to earn foreign currency.

I conclude by showing what people's diplomacy created between the United States and China, which revealed itself most clearly in the aftermath of the Tiananmen Square Massacre on June 4, 1989. The bloodshed antagonized policy makers in both countries and traumatized those who had been building mutual ties since Nixon's 1972 visit. These ties nonetheless survived Tiananmen—and soon grew exponentially—because many Americans and Chinese deemed them just too important to sacrifice at the altar of their political faiths. The United States and China were bound together, not by the myth of the "special relationship," but by threads of interest that would become only harder to break. And they remain so to this day.

Chapter 1

The Origins of People's Diplomacy

In the late 1950s, John K. Fairbank, the dean of Chinese studies in the United States, sat in his office at Harvard University, relieved and anguished. McCarthyism had spared him, but the witch hunt left the field ravaged and the American public allergic to China. The "fear and ignorance" toward China would "lead only toward disaster," Fairbank wrote. "Now we both have to learn to live on the same planet."[1] To this aim, he and many of his colleagues relaunched public debate on China, and large foundations with pre-1949 ties to that country, including Ford, Carnegie, and Rockefeller, offered financial help despite the charged atmosphere. "God damn it we're going to support China Studies," resolved Ford program director John Howard.[2] By the end of the 1950s, China scholars had regrouped themselves, aided by the Council on Foreign Relations and other organizations. These scholars were airing such bold ideas as reduction of trade embargo, admission of China into the United Nations, and acknowledgment of "two Chinas," to "live on the same planet" with the People's Republic.[3]

Scholars were hardly alone in espousing this vision. Heeding their counsel, high-ranking officials in the Kennedy administration, Secretary of State Dean Rusk included, proposed relaxation of travel restrictions for American journalists and considered grain sales to alleviate the massive famine in the aftermath of the Great Leap Forward, despite the public preference to "let them starve."[4] In December 1963, the assistant secretary of state for Far Eastern affairs Roger Hilsman declared an "open door policy" toward China, emphasizing that "the way back into the community of man is not closed."[5] The Chinese wouldn't budge, though. Mao Zedong stated in his conversation with a Chilean delegation in June 1964: "We need not rush to solve these small problems [of trade and journalistic exchanges] before we solve the big problem [of Taiwan]."[6]

The specter of nuclear holocaust awakened many Americans to the China problem. On October 16, 1964, two years after the Cuban Missile Crisis, China detonated its first nuclear bomb in the Taklamakan Desert in Xinjiang. Beijing's statement that it would "never at any time or under any circumstances be the first to use nuclear weapons" mollified US policy makers, but not the public.[7] That the bomb fell into the hands of someone who, unlike the Russians, exhibited no dread of nuclear war rattled every American concerned about peace.[8] Many citizens wrote letters to the White House, offering a range of suggestions on nuclear China, from issuing an ultimatum before attacking its nuclear facilities to negotiating the abolishment of nuclear weapons with it.[9] They understood that China's bomb, as O. Edmund Clubb of Columbia University wrote, "ushered the world into a perilous era of new dimensions," such that Americans could "no longer safely ignore 'the China problem'."[10] The *Saturday Evening Post* editorialized:

> It would be matter enough for concern if 700 million people were being systematically taught to hate America—that and no more. Now, however, the paranoiac leaders of Communist China have an atomic bomb . . . nothing in world affairs will ever again be quite the same. The fateful clock . . . is now ticking inexorably close to possible world disaster. . . . The U.S. can no longer postpone the scrapping of that patchwork crazy quilt—full of internal contradictions—which is misnamed a "China policy." We must replace it with a coherent policy worked out by the coolest and ablest brains at our command. . . . Unless Communist China can be brought within the framework of a dependable system of international guarantees . . . the world may face a new kind of aggressive Hitlerism, its madness reinforced a million times by nuclear power.[11]

By the end of 1964, China was a cause célèbre. Many anti-CCP, pro-KMT organizations, most notably the Committee of One Million against the Admission of Communist China to the United Nations, the mainstay of the so-called China Lobby, insisted on the continuation of the current policy. Contrariwise, church groups, women's organizations, and academic circles, as well as some celebrity figures like scholar-diplomat George Kennan and singer-actor Frank Sinatra, discussed new approaches, often viewing China as an indispensable piece in nuclear disarmament.[12]

For average Americans, however, China was an obscure subject with stereotyped images. According to a nationwide survey by the University of Michigan in December 1964, 28 percent of Americans did not even know that a Communist government ruled the mainland; 40 percent did not know about the "two-China" problem; and yet 86 percent believed that the United States should be concerned about China.[13] *CBS Reports* confirmed America's "confusion, ignorance, and anxiety" about China. In a series of door-to-door interviews in Los Angeles and Long Island, one interviewee, asked about his knowledge of China, muttered, "It's a deep dark secret," while another, on the possibility of trade, bewailed, "We should not deal with gangsters. They'll shoot you." CBS correspondent Marvin Kalb lamented that Americans had lived in "a world of stereotyped clichés about China" for so long that its reality "slipped past us, like disturbing shadows in the night." "It may be another fifteen years before we as a nation and a people can deal with China," Kalb commented. "But the question is: Must we wait that long to talk about China?"[14]

As it turned out, Americans and Chinese did not wait for another fifteen years before resuming mutual contacts, and this chapter explains why. Scholars have studied the efforts of the Kennedy and Johnson administrations to reconsider China policy, rendered stillborn by the Vietnam War and the Cultural Revolution.[15] Few, however, have explored the changing debates and sentiments among the US and Chinese public. The first section of this chapter analyzes the activism of the National Committee on US-China Relations, which elevated the China problem, once considered taboo, to national prominence and convinced the informed public of the necessity of a new policy. The second section discusses the contrasting Chinese views of the US government as "imperialists," poised to invade China from Vietnam, and of the American people as allies against it. The third section focuses on the onset of people's diplomacy, arguing that as Sino-American rapprochement unfolded in the early 1970s, these new ideas on bilateral relations lubricated the launch of the people-to-people exchanges.

The New China Lobby

In June 1964, former US ambassador to Italy Clare Booth Luce, wife of Henry Luce, the media magnate who had spearheaded the China Lobby in earlier decades, gave a commencement speech at St. John's University in New York. "China will account for half the population of the whole world," she hyperbolized. "We must soon find ways of living at peace with half the human race, or your generation will know nothing but endless war in the Orient."[16] Luce was alluding to the simmering war in Vietnam. Less than two months later, on August 10, 1964, Congress passed the Gulf of Tonkin Resolution, which conferred unlimited war power on the Johnson administration, paving the way for the sustained bombing of North Vietnam and the stream of US ground troops into South Vietnam. Luce also underscored China's potential. In the 1960s, American officials and scholars increasingly viewed China as a major world power struggling to fulfill its potential.[17] The nascent rise of China transfixed many, including political scientist Hans Morgenthau, who would soon endorse recognition of China, although he predicted that it would remain "a weak and fragile giant" due to the population size.[18] Still, the giant was powerful enough to precipitate a second Korean War in its southern backyard, possibly a nuclear one.

The prospect of war chilled countless Americans, particularly Quakers. Fiercely opposing the Vietnam War, peace activists in the American Friends Service Committee (AFSC) joined China scholars to organize various activities aimed at raising public awareness of the China problem, such as large conferences featuring academics, businesspeople, journalists, lawmakers, and government representatives. Cecil Thomas, an associate peace education secretary of the AFSC's San Francisco chapter, and Robert Scalapino, an Asia specialist at the University of California, Berkeley, held the first such conference at UC Berkeley on December 9, 1964, attracting well over a thousand attendees. When the Quakers and sinologists held the second conference in Washington the next April, "many, if not a majority," on the floor "felt that the time had come for a change in US policy toward China," according to Barbara McLennon of the League of Women Voters, one of over forty nongovernmental groups invited.[19] Overtaken by a tide of similar conferences, numbering over a hundred in 1965 and 1966, Thomas, Scalapino, and several eminent figures in academia and industry began to contemplate a national organization to advance their endeavor.[20]

Congress further riveted the public to the China problem in early 1966. The hearings at the Senate Foreign Relations Committee, chaired by J. William Fulbright, brought together policy makers and scholars of all political hues to reexamine US policy toward China. In the course of the lengthy hearings from February to March, "containment without isolation," a term coined by A. Doak Barnett of Columbia, emerged as a powerful idea. While acknowledging the importance of curtailing Chinese influence in Asia, Barnett advised the government to break Beijing's international isolation, the root cause of instability in the region, by granting admission to the UN, cultivating unofficial contacts, and extending diplomatic recognition in due course.[21] The China Lobby wasted no time rebutting this proposal. Walter Judd, former representative from Minnesota and leader of the Committee of One Million, spurned China's admission to the UN as "illegal" and "immoral," while former senator from Arizona Barry Goldwater, the godfather of the 1960s conservative movement, bashed the entire Fulbright hearings as a "naked and unabashed propaganda show."[22] The China Lobby viscerally sensed the threat posed by "containment without isolation."

The concept struck an emotional chord with millions of Americans who watched these hearings on television. Many of his academic colleagues, as well as citizens familiar with the China problem, profusely acclaimed Barnett's speech as brave and wise, but countless others reviled it. A group of high school students from Georgia, for instance, sent essays—apparently a group project in a government class—all of which opposed rebuilding contacts with China. "It is only common sense," wrote one student, "that if one has a cancerous growth in his body, he cuts out the infected part to prevent the spreading; he certainly does not graft the cancer to other parts of his body."[23] One college student in California wrote the most scathing letter. Mocking Barnett as a "mouth-piece [for China]," "poor simp," and "simple minded jerk," she blared, "We kids should be teaching you, instead of vice versa."[24] As retired journalist Archibald Steele observed, Americans "on the whole" welcomed "a public reappraisal" of China policy, but McCarthyism cast a long shadow over the process.[25]

By mid-1966, "containment without isolation" had become a near-consensus in Washington. A number of officials in the National Security Council (NSC), the State Department, and the Defense Department surmised that a more forthcoming attitude toward the issues of travel restrictions, trade embargo, and UN representation might mitigate Beijing's hostility.[26] This line of thinking informed Lyndon B. Johnson's televised speech to the American Alumni Council on July 12, 1966. While stressing "firmness" against China, the president maintained that "reconciliation between nations that now call themselves enemies" was "essential for peace in Asia." "For lasting peace can never come to Asia as long as the 700 million people of mainland China are isolated by their rulers from the outside world."[27] Johnson continued throughout his presidency to make peace gestures and take small steps to reduce travel and trade restrictions as avowed in this speech.

The time was ripe for Cecil Thomas, Robert Scalapino, and their allies to launch an institutional platform for their activism. On June 9, 1966, the National Committee on US-China Relations was founded, with Scalapino as the chairman and Thomas as the executive director. Its invitation-only membership consisted of a panoply of influential figures in academia, business, religion, and public affairs, all committed to public education on the China problem. "The rising American interest over China's role in international affairs has created an increasing demand for objective and analytical information about China," Scalapino stated at a news conference.[28] The names on the board of directors—from Doak Barnett to David Hunter (deputy general secretary of the National Council of Churches) to Daniel Koshland (former CEO of Levi Strauss)—showed the group's inclination toward the establishment on the East Coast and the West Coast. Funded by the Ford and Rockefeller Foundations among others, the National Committee was a nongovernmental organization by definition. Yet some of its members, including Edwin Reischauer (Harvard historian and the former ambassador to Japan) and James Thomson Jr. (former NSC staffer now at Harvard), had served in the government; others, such as Fairbank, Scalapino, and Barnett, were advising the State Department through the China Advisory Panel. They lent the group credibility and influence. With a membership increasing from ninety to two hundred in a couple of years, the National Committee emerged as the most prominent organization for US-China relations.

The National Committee readily found its market in the informed public.[29] It supplied teaching packets to hundreds of teachers, students, corporations, women's groups, religious associations, and government officials requesting information on China.[30] To offer balanced knowledge of China for community leaders around the country, the National Committee initiated a China Seminar Program, organizing about 130 public events between 1966 and 1970, in which scholars, policy makers, and journalists discussed a range of topics on that country, from culture to history to politics. Harvard University, for instance, hosted a three-day seminar in July 1967, featuring its noted Asia specialists—John Fairbank, Abraham Halpern, Dwight Perkins, and Edwin Reischauer. ABC and CBS reported on this event, with Fairbank's featured remark: "People all over the country are making efforts [to understand China]. We heard from all sorts of places. China specialists are just a small business in this. . . . We are making an effort, but it isn't big enough." ABC correspondent John Scali applauded the seminar for offering "new and interesting ideas which help awaken the American public . . . to the need to end China's isolation from the rest of the world."[31]

The National Committee also mobilized graduate students to reach out to the larger public. Harvard students in East Asian studies pioneered this effort through a curriculum development project for college and high school teachers, a research bureau to collect and edit China-related resources for public use, and a speakers bureau to send China experts, students themselves included, to deliver lectures at local townhall meetings. Fox Butterfield, a doctoral student of Fairbank's, gave one such talk at the Junior Chambers of Commerce in Greensboro, North Carolina, in February 1967. More than three hundred locals showed up—not only white-collar professionals, but also students and such "blue collar types" as truck drivers and mailmen. The "generally favorable reaction" of the audience, reported Butterfield, attested to "the obvious interest in China and the widespread dissatisfaction with our present China policy."[32] Following Harvard's success, other universities with leading Chinese studies programs, including Michigan, Columbia, and Berkeley, embarked on similar projects.

These activities earned the National Committee public recognition as the most influential advocacy group for "containment without isolation." Although declaring itself nonpartisan, the membership of the National Committee in its formative years excluded most scholars on the right and left, who disagreed with the establishment in Chinese studies, particularly Barnett, Fairbank, and Alexander Eckstein of the University of Michigan. Frank Trager of New York University rightly complained that the National Committee represented "one known point of view"—that the United States should recognize China and drop opposition to its seat in the UN.[33] To turn this "monologue" into a true "dialogue," some scholars opposing "the Barnett-Fairbank-Eckstein gang" sought membership in the National Committee, and three well-known hawks—Franz Michael of George Washington University, Richard "Dixie" Walker of the University of South Carolina, and George Taylor of the University of Washington—gained influence within the organization.[34] In the main, however, the National Committee clearly favored a more flexible policy toward China. It was a new China Lobby.

As such, the National Committee tried to sway policy makers. On February 2, 1968, Johnson met the National Committee leadership—Thomas, Scalapino, Barnett, Eckstein, Reischauer, Lucian Pye of Massachusetts Institute of Technology (MIT), and Carl Stover of the National Institute of Public Affairs—for a discussion on China policy. The White House originally allocated thirty minutes for this meeting, but the president showed "a great interest" and extended it for nearly half an hour, despite other urgent issues at hand, such as the North Korean seizure of USS *Pueblo*, the North Korean guerrilla attack on the South Korean presidential palace, and the Tet Offensive.[35] "We have made a truly major effort to communicate [with Beijing] and to keep our policy flexible," he explained to the China scholars. "We are not hidebound."[36] In response to the president's request, Reischauer, Barnett, and Pye submitted a policy paper about a week later, analyzing options for "a reconciliation between the American and Chinese people" or "at least a tolerable modus vivendi." The list—moderating trade restrictions, promoting cultural exchanges, and admitting China into the UN—amounted to nothing innovative, since many of these measures had been tried by Washington but unreciprocated by Beijing.[37] "It is just that it takes two to play some games," the national security adviser Walt Rostow grumbled, "and [Beijing] does not see it in its interest to play, just now."[38]

Soon afterwards, Dean Rusk, the CIA, and NSC staffer Alfred Jenkins each submitted a policy memorandum on China. They all agreed that the Cultural Revolution had thrown China "in a mess," and "limited accommodation" with the United States would remain impossible until the "post-Mao" leadership emerged. Like the National Committee leaders, Rusk and Jenkins supported reduction of trade and travel barriers. While emphatically opposing China's admission to the UN, Rusk entertained a gradual move to tacit acknowledgment of "two Chinas."[39] Yet Beijing had already proved unresponsive to US overtures, and the Johnson administration had no choice but to wait out the mayhem in China. A December 1968 study prepared for the incoming Nixon administration recommended "no radical change in the near term in our bilateral relationship [with China]; but a readiness to move to a new relationship over the longer term."[40] The National Committee's policy proposal, even if fully implemented, would have come to naught in the late 1960s.

The National Committee, however, succeeded in what it set out to do: raising public interest in China. The success reached an apex in March 1969, at the two-day national convocation in New York, titled "The United States and China: The Next Decade" (see fig. 1.1). This mega event was attended by approximately 2,500 participants, including scholars, congresspersons, and policy makers. To stave off "any charges of partisanship," the National Committee invited speakers from all sides of the political rainbow.[41] William Rusher of *National Review*, a conservative magazine founded by journalist William F. Buckley Jr., for instance, decried "a policy of accommodating

Figure 1.1. Edwin Reischauer (center) speaks at a panel featuring John D. Rockefeller III (left) and Edward M. Kennedy (right) at the National Committee's First National Convocation in New York, March 20, 1969. National Committee on US-China Relations Collection. Courtesy of Rockefeller Archive Center and the National Committee on US-China Relations.

the tottering regime of an aging megalomaniac." The convocation was, in Reischauer's words, "too rich and varied a symphony, too full of discordant opinions as well as complex harmonies of complementary concepts."[42] Its underlying message still seemed obvious, though—that the United States should do something about China.

The National Committee's activism paralleled a shift in public opinion on China, most visible on the question of UN representation. According to Gallup polls, only 7 percent of responders supported China's admission to the UN at the height of McCarthyism in 1954. About two-thirds continued to oppose China's seat until 1966, when the gap began to narrow. On the eve of China's entry into the UN in October 1971, the majority of responders were supportive of it, although few acquiesced to Taiwan's ejection.[43] The National Committee was not solely responsible for this shift, since many other groups, often inspired by the National Committee, discussed the China problem and publicized their positions in national newspaper columns or at local townhall meetings, despite counterefforts by pro-Taiwan forces, often backed by the KMT.[44] The National Committee both reflected and promoted the rise of public interest in a new China policy, which contextualized the famous *Foreign*

Affairs article written by Richard Nixon in October 1967. His most-cited line drew on not only his own wisdom, but also the emerging consensus of the time: "There is no place on this small planet for a billion of its potentially most able people to live in angry isolation."[45]

"The American People Are Good"

As American views of China grew more complex and diverse, so did Chinese views of the United States. Beijing's propaganda machine had taught the masses, from factory workers in the city to peasant farmers in the countryside, to loathe US "imperialists" as a cabal of greedy capitalists who initiated wars abroad to alleviate perennial economic crises at home. Mao Zedong, however, separated the US government and the American people, as the oppressor and the oppressed. "We must draw a distinction . . . between the people of the United States and their government," the chairman wrote in 1945.[46] When British American journalist Felix Greene toured China in late 1963, he witnessed "the deep-seated long-term hostility toward the U.S. [government]," while noting "the warmth of feeling toward Americans on the part of the average Chinese."[47] Greene's experience shed light on the duality in the Chinese perception of the United States.

This duality only got starker from early 1965, when the "Resist America, Aid Vietnam" (*kangMei yuanYue*) campaign swept across China. In response to Washington's decision to bomb North Vietnam, the CCP called on local apparatchiks to organize mass meetings and street demonstrations. Between February 9 and 11, millions of Chinese around the country took to the street to march, shout, and sing against US "imperialists."[48] In Beijing, Mayor Peng Zhen addressed a crowd of 1.5 million gathering at Tiananmen Square, denouncing US "imperialists" as "the deadly enemy of the people around the world."[49] The CCP soon expanded the propaganda to cultural life, organizing photograph exhibits, chorus contests, film viewings, and street performances. They uniformly demonized US "imperialists" and glorified Vietnamese resistance, all with the same chant: "US aggressors get out of Vietnam!" Between August 1964 and May 1965, Shanghai held 78,977 shows of 983 plays related to the Vietnam War in theaters, at work units, and on the street, attended by over thirteen million locals in total.[50] These shows turned the distant war into a tangible reality.

The popular anti-Americanism, both genuine and artificial, helped to enhance the vigilance of the masses. In April 1965, about a month into Operation

Rolling Thunder, the CCP issued a directive to accelerate war preparation in large cities, including air defense programs and citizen militia drills. The Chinese masses should "be prepared to handle the worst-case scenario," in which they would not only suffer US bombings, but also "fight on the soil of our country."[51] About a week later, the standing committee of the Third National People's Congress issued a declaration, urging the masses to support North Vietnam and oppose US "imperialists" "with actual deeds," which would form "sufficient preparation" to send volunteer soldiers, if requested by Hanoi.[52] Local Party committees across the country formulated propaganda strategies based on the CCP directive and the People's Congress declaration. A propaganda guide in Nanchang, provincial capital of Jiangxi, warned: "Their next goal is to invade China. US imperialists' invasion plan includes China."[53] In a bombastic essay in the *People's Daily* that September, Defense Minister Lin Biao championed "people's war," or protracted guerilla war, against US "imperialists," in China and the world over.[54]

The warmongering was not a bluff. Washington and Beijing had reached a tacit agreement by early 1966 that China would refrain from sending combat troops to Vietnam as long as the United States stopped short of invading North Vietnam and bombing Chinese territory.[55] To make this arrangement credible, the Chinese nonetheless had to show clear and visible determination to fight should it be violated. After the Gulf of Tonkin incident, PLA units in the Vietnamese border regions sharply ramped up their force levels and combat readiness, and China began to provide massive military assistance for North Vietnam, including anti-aircraft artillery troops, engineering troops, and other material support. Before a rift with Hanoi caused a sharp decline in Chinese aid in 1969–1970, Beijing sent hundreds of thousands of PLA soldiers to North Vietnam—170,000 in the peak year of 1967—fighting US bombers and assisting Hanoi's war-making.[56] The most conspicuous sign of Beijing's acute sense of insecurity was the so-called Third Front Construction (*sanxian jianshe*), an ambitious project to develop the hinterland and resettle defense industries from littoral provinces, which Chinese leaders feared might be targeted for nuclear strikes.[57] Beijing was trying to avoid war by bracing itself for it. As historian Zhai Qiang argued, invasion of North Vietnam or bombing of Chinese territory would have created "a real danger of a Sino-American war with dire consequences for the world."[58]

The war preparation triggered a war scare. The Chinese masses gave unstinting support to the mobilization campaign in public, as was their wont, but feared in private a repeat of the Korean War, which killed over 200,000 Chinese soldiers. Despite Beijing's efforts to combat the tendency among the population to "worship America, fear America" (*chongMei kongMei*) since the early 1950s, these sentiments had survived, particularly among older generations.[59] They cautioned in the wake of the Gulf of Tonkin incident that should the war spill over into China, they would have to take on the powerful US forces, this time without Soviet assistance. "Modern warfare is all about heavy bombs, as well as nuclear weapons, unlike in the past," one old post office worker mused. "I am a little fearful."[60] Harald Munthe-Kaas, a Norwegian journalist stationed in Beijing, reported in early 1966 that street committee officials were whispering rumors of war, saying that war with the United States was "fast approaching." He also noted that many Beijing residents interpreted the resettlement of professors to the hinterland as a sign of war preparation, although it was, in fact, part of the Socialist Education Movement, aimed at reeducating intellectuals.[61] Many urbanites "cherished peace as desirable" and "advocated peace negotiations," according to one report in Guangzhou.[62] The anti-American fanaticism writ large belied the fear of nuclear annihilation.

Chinese youth embraced that fear, however. Many of them firmly believed in the CCP's depiction of anti-US struggle at home and abroad as the only way to defend Chinese revolution from US "imperialists," Soviet "revisionists," and their collaborators in China—rhetoric that fueled the Great Proletarian Cultural Revolution.[63] As historian Chen Jian argued, the escalation of the Vietnam War gave Mao "much-needed stimulus to mobilize the Chinese population," particularly the youth, for his attempt at revolutionizing the entire society yet again.[64] The Vietnam War and the Cultural Revolution were inextricably intertwined, and being anti-American and being revolutionary were two sides of the same coin. This idea was wrapped up in the Red Guard movement. Intrepid and foolhardy, those revolutionary students lampooned the United States as a "paper tiger," which would recoil at their determination for war. At a December 1966 gathering of a hundred thousand Red Guards and other "revolutionary crowds" in Beijing, student representative Shen Aiqun resolved: "Once the Vietnamese people need [us], once Chairman Mao orders [us], we, the Red Guards, will fight shoulder to shoulder with the Vietnamese people right away."[65] Red Guards were revolutionary soldiers fighting US "imperialists" from afar.

And it was no fantasy. In late 1966, a high school Red Guard in Beijing named Zhao Jianjun secretly hopped on a long-distance train to Nanning, provincial capital of Guangxi, with a clutch of some ten friends. From there, he made his way across the border and joined the PLA forces in Vietnam. Two months later, on January 19, 1967, Zhao became the first and last Red

Guard to die on Vietnamese soil.[66] The news spread quickly among the youth, and many of them wished to follow Zhao's path. Between late 1966 and early 1967, more than two hundred students and workers from twenty provinces and municipalities swarmed the small city of Pingxiang in Guangxi, demanding their passports. Many also wrote letters, sent telegrams, and made calls to the Vietnamese embassy in Beijing to request visas. Frustrated with the diplomatic irritants, the CCP ordered local revolutionary committees to discourage the masses from these actions. While praising the "revolutionary spirit" and "internationalist spirit" of the youth, it decreed that "any disorganized, disorderly behaviors" were "wrong," and students and workers should "go back to their original work units in their hometowns to make a revolution." Only by doing so could they provide "active support" for North Vietnam and the Cultural Revolution.[67] Although Zhao and his admirers hardly comprised the majority, their revolutionary anti-Americanism dominated Chinese views of the United States during the peak years of the Cultural Revolution.

Paradoxically, enmity for the US government fed affinity for the American people. Chinese leaders had long portrayed Americans, particularly the working-class, women, and racial minorities, as victims of the kleptocracy engaging in liberation struggles, which would one day turn into a socialist revolution. In January 1959, Mao wrote to William Foster, leader of the Communist Party USA:

> The Chinese people know that United States imperialism has done many bad things to China and to the whole world as well; they understand that only the United States ruling group is bad, while the people of the United States are very good. Among the Americans, although many of them have not yet awakened, only a tiny part are bad, the overwhelming majority are good. Friendly relations between the Chinese and American peoples will eventually break down the barriers put up by [Secretary of State John Foster] Dulles and his like and develop more extensively with each passing day.[68]

For all his tirade against US "imperialists," the chairman conjured up an image of the American people as allies against the US government.

Beijing befriended as many "awakened" Americans as possible to reinforce this image. Anna Louise Strong, a socialist journalist who resided in China after 1958, was one of the best American "friends." She was a celebrity in China because of her 1946 interview with Mao, in which the chairman chirped that "the American people and the peoples of all countries" should "unite and struggle against" "the US reactionaries and their running dogs."[69] Between 1962 and 1966, Strong published "Letters from China," in which she and other American expats in China, such as former Young Women's Christian Association (YWCA) worker Talitha Gerlach, nuclear physicist Joan Hinton, and CCP member Sidney Rittenberg, lauded Chinese socialism. Strong understood her political use. When Mao met her the third time on her eightieth birthday in November 1965, she gathered that the chairman was trying to tell the world, "Now, while the Washington warlords escalate war and threaten to bomb us, take note of the difference between the imperialist warlord and the American people with whom we must be friends."[70] American voices like Strong's, though mostly falling on deaf ears back home, reverberated in China. When a correspondent at Swedish newspaper *Expressen* interviewed college students in Beijing in 1965, they commented: "[We] should separate the US government and the American people. The American people are good. We are [standing] together."[71]

The Vietnam War won Beijing hundreds of thousands of new American "friends"—antiwar protestors—at least in its imagination. As Chinese leaders sought to rally developing countries, from Cuba to the Congo, Laos to Vietnam, against US "imperialists," they lumped Americans with the oppressed peoples of the world. After the Gulf of Tonkin incident, Chinese media began to print a volley of articles about antiwar demonstrations in the United States. When twenty thousand Americans, led by Students for a Democratic Society, picketed the White House in April 1965, the *People's Daily* published a commentary, titled "The American people have swung into action." It read: "Facts opened the eyes of the American people, making them realize that the interests of the Vietnamese people and the American people are the same and that US monopoly capital and the US government serving it are the real enemies of the American people."[72] Over the next few years, more and more Americans got "awakened."

African Americans were China's most useful "friends." In the 1950s and 1960s, Beijing invited several high-profile Black activists to flaunt racial harmony in China. W. E. B. Du Bois was the most prominent among them.[73] On his ninety-first birthday on February 23, 1959, the civil rights legend gave a booming speech at Peking University. "China is flesh of your flesh and blood of your blood. China is colored, and knows to what the colored skin in this modern world subjects its owner," he clamored. "Come to China, Africa, and look around."[74] Mao doubled down on co-opting African Americans in August 1963, when he made the famous statement of support for the civil rights movement: "The fascist atrocities committed by the U.S. imperialists against the Negro people have . . . revealed the inner link between the reactionary policies pursued by the U.S. Government at home and its policies of aggression abroad."[75] Mao made another statement following Martin Luther King Jr.'s assassination in April 1968, which further illuminated this link. "Racial discrimination in the United States is a product of the colonialist and imperialist system," he averred. "The struggle of the Black people in the United States for emancipation is a component part of the general struggle of all the people of the world against U.S. imperialism, a component part of the contemporary world revolution."[76]

Maoism dovetailed with Black Power. While King and his moderate allies espoused nonviolence, proponents of armed struggle against white supremacy, most notably the Black Panther Party (BPP)—"the greatest threat to internal security of the country," in the words of FBI Director J. Edgar Hoover—devoured Maoism to unite with the Afro-Asian world in their fight against US "imperialism."[77] Black Panthers waved *Quotations from Mao Zedong*, commonly known as "Mao's Little Red Book," to show allegiance to the chairman and hawked copies for a buck at college campuses, for fundraising. Mao projected the image of a model American on Robert F. Williams, godfather of the BPP and author of *Negros with Guns* (see fig. 1.2). While living in exile in Beijing between 1966 and 1969, Williams published his newsletter *The Crusader*, extolling armed liberation struggles in the United States and elsewhere. He adulated China as "the last hope" for African Americans. "Without China, there can be no Black struggle in America."[78] In his speech at a mass demonstration against US "imperialism" in August 1966, William proclaimed in his baritone voice that the time was "fast approaching" when the "good reasonable American" must choose "either to overtly side with American chauvinism and jingoism or to take a resolute anti-imperialist and anti-racist stand that will be a firm basis for a just and lasting world peace." Concluding the speech, he screamed: "Long live the militant friendship between the Chinese and revolutionary American people!"[79]

At the end of the 1960s, Beijing had more American "friends" than ever before. The propaganda mill had set a self-amplifying cycle in motion: The more hostile the US government, the more "friendly" the American people, and the other way around. The contrast between the American "friends" and enemies enabled Chinese leaders and commoners to remain cautiously optimistic about US-China relations during the Vietnam War, even at the height of the war scare. Journalist Edgar Snow's January 1965 interview with Mao illustrated this. Snow was the first foreign journalist to travel to the

Figure 1.2. Mao Zedong signs Robert F. Williams's copy of *Quotations from Chairman Mao Tse-tung* at the National Day celebration in Beijing, October 1, 1964. Robert F. Williams Papers, HS 1091. Courtesy of Bentley Historical Library, University of Michigan.

CCP-controlled areas in Shaanxi Province in 1936, and his book *Red Star over China* offered a sensational eyewitness account of the budding Communist movement. Thirty years later, Mao sounded sober, but not pessimistic: "Naturally, I personally regret that forces of history have divided and separated the American and Chinese peoples from virtually all communication during the past fifteen years. Today the gulf seems broader than ever. However, I myself do not believe it will end in war and one of history's major tragedies." The chairman intoned that "there was hope" for a rapprochement, although he could not foretell when it would materialize. "It would take time. Maybe there would be no improvement in my generation," said Mao. "I am soon going to see God."[80] Little did he know that he would see Richard Nixon before God.

Pinning Hopes on the People

The CCP's Ninth National Congress in April 1969 essentially ended the Cultural Revolution, shifting the country's focus from continuous revolution to economic reconstruction. Desperate to mend China's crippled relations with foreign countries, Mao put the Foreign Ministry back into business, rebuilding the diplomatic corps and reposting ambassadors abroad. After years of hiatus, mass organizations, including the Foreign Ministry–affiliated Chinese People's Institute of Foreign Affairs (CPIFA), were restored or reactivated. Reeling from the Soviet threat in the north, Mao was now ready to respond to US overtures. In a subtle yet dramatic move, the *People's Daily* reprinted Nixon's inaugural address on January 20, 1969 in its entirety. A line stood out: "We seek an open world—open to ideas, open to the exchange of goods and people—a world in which no people, great or small, will live in angry isolation."[81]

Washington did not fail to notice the signal. Soon after taking office, Nixon and his national security adviser Henry Kissinger, along with NSC and State Department officials, implemented a series of new policies—validating US passports for travel to China and allowing foreign subsidiaries of US firms to trade with China, for example—as stepping stones to a diplomatic rapprochement, which Doak Barnett and others were pitching to the White House through letters and meetings.[82] Although polemics on US interventions in Indochina and sporadic mass gatherings against US "imperialists" continued into the early 1970s, Beijing reciprocated US moves by forgoing personal denunciation of Nixon, releasing some American prisoners, and resuming the Warsaw talks in January 1970. When the US invasion of Cambodia caused a suspension of these talks that May, the White House began sending secret messages through Pakistani and Romanian channels to propose a higher-level meeting, unbeknownst to the State Department. In his second annual foreign policy report to Congress in February 1971, Nixon pledged to "carefully examine what further steps . . . we might take to create broader opportunities for contacts between the Chinese and American peoples."[83]

Americans were debating when, not whether, these opportunities would surface. In January 1971, the National Committee on US-China Relations held a two-day roundtable in New York, featuring guest speakers from Britain, Canada, France, and Japan, countries that had cultivated various exchanges with China even before fully normalizing relations. Alexander Eckstein concluded that based on their experiences, Americans could build "de facto cooperative relations" with Chinese in an "active ad-hocery" manner, even without diplomatic relations.[84] The Committee of One Million threatened to sabotage such efforts, but with its core members deceased or retired, it could hardly deploy effective countermeasures. "The [old] China Lobby quietly died some time ago without benefit of an obituary," the *Washington Post* quipped.[85] John Fairbank aptly observed in the spring of 1971 that with the Cultural Revolution essentially over, and Americans itching to get out of Vietnam and build contacts with China, "the time is ripe for China to shift outward again."[86] The question: How to make that shift?

Mao used his old American "friend" as a fulcrum. In the fall of 1970, Edgar Snow made his final trip to China before his death, just before Nixon's visit. The *People's Daily* published a photograph of Snow standing with Mao at Tiananmen Square to observe the October 1 National Day celebration, with the chairman's quotation on the upper-right-hand corner: "The people of the world, including the American people, are our friends."[87] Snow sat with Mao for a long interview on December 18. In a "heart-to-heart talk" as "old friends," the chairman stated: "Today I do not want to make a difference between Chinese and Americans. I am pinning hopes on the peoples of these two countries. I am pinning great hopes on American people. American people will become a great potential force beneficial to the world." Mao continued, directing the conversation to "the most reactionary person in the world." "If Nixon wants to come, I am willing to talk with him. We can agree or disagree. We may or may not fight. He can come as a tourist or as president. In short, anything is fine." Stammering out his words, Mao puffed a cigarette to calm down.[88] Nixon could now come to China, and, by extension, so could any American, progressive or reactionary.

Mao acted swiftly. Before Snow's interview got published, he decided to invite the US table tennis team to China after much deliberation on the interaction between Chinese player Zhuang Zedong and American player Glenn Cowan in Nagoya. "Although the U.S. government is unfriendly to China, the American people are friends of the Chinese," Zhuang beamed to Cowan. "I give you this [silkscreen tapestry of Mt. Huangshan] to mark the friendship from the Chinese people to the American people."[89] Meeting the American visitors in Beijing, Premier Zhou Enlai declared that they "opened a new page in the relations of the Chinese and American people," and "this beginning again of our friendship will certainly meet with the majority support of our two peoples."[90] Ping-Pong diplomacy, recollected Kissinger, created "an international sensation" that "captured the world's imagination."[91] *Time* and *Life* magazines covered the team's travel to Beijing, Shanghai, and

Guangzhou, carrying colored photographs of Chinese people in ordinary life, humanizing them for the readers.[92]

The cascade of Sino-American rapprochement that ensued astonished the American public. Letters of approval and protest deluged the White House, especially after China's admission to the UN on October 25, 1971, the last day of Kissinger's second visit to that country.[93] Nixon took great care to stage his trip to China. A huge entourage of newspaper correspondents, magazine writers, and television reporters followed the president from the Great Hall of the People to the Great Wall of China. Television provided a collective experience for millions of Americans who tuned in to watch what the *New York Times* phrased "TV's biggest show since man reached the Moon."[94] The show was entertaining and convincing. According to a Gallup poll, 98 percent of Americans knew of Nixon's visit to China, and 68 percent accepted his claim that it was "effective" in promoting world peace.[95] The China opening aroused the conservative wrath, not least because the Shanghai Communiqué affirmed Taiwan as "a part of China," but the silver-tongued president won allegiance from key figures like Barry Goldwater and Ronald Reagan by depicting his move as leverage against the Soviet Union.[96] At a banquet in Beijing, Nixon gave a pompous toast: "This is the hour, this is the day for our two peoples to rise to the heights of greatness which can build a new and better world."[97]

Beijing rushed to justify the rapprochement. Soon after the Ping-Pong diplomacy, the CCP distributed a summary of Mao's talk with Snow and requested study meetings across the nation.[98] A propaganda guide in Inner Mongolia celebrated Nixon's visit as China's diplomatic triumph, attributing it to "the long-term struggle of the Chinese and American people against US imperialists."[99] But the logic seemed twisted: Why did Chairman Mao invite Richard Nixon to his house after checkmating him? Some officials at the Bureau of Handicraft Industry Management in Shanghai struggled to "figure out" the chairman's intentions.[100] They were not alone. *New York Times* correspondent Tillman Durdin, the first American journalist permitted into China as an individual in the spring of 1971, reported that Mao's policy "puzzled many Chinese and stirred misgivings in some quarters."[101] Relentless propaganda eventually convinced the masses that Mao, harboring no illusion of peace, invited Nixon to expose the failure of US foreign policy and carry on the struggle against US "imperialists."[102] One factory worker in the tourist city of Guilin said it best: "We cannot carve out ivory out of a dog's mouth. . . . We signed the communiqué, but by no means does it suggest that peace has come . . . [because] the reactionary, invasive nature of US imperialists cannot be changed."¹⁰³ Those with an affluent family background, personal experience with Americans, or radio receivers to listen to the Voice of America illegally might have entertained different ideas in private, but the average Chinese, who had long considered revolution and anti-Americanism one and the same, had to travel farther than average Americans in the mental journey toward the rapprochement.¹⁰⁴

The distinction between the US government and the American people made this journey less agonizing. After Robert Williams left China in late 1969, Beijing found his substitute in the Black Panther Party. Following the summer 1970 visit by prominent Panthers Elaine Brown and Eldridge Cleaver as part of the US People's Anti-Imperialist Delegation, a larger BPP group toured China in the fall of 1971. "It was an amazing experience to see in practice a revolution that is going forward at such a rapid rate," BPP cofounder Huey Newton marveled in his memoirs. "To see a classless society in operation is unforgettable"¹⁰⁵ The Committee of Concerned Asian Scholars (CCAS), a small knot of young Asian studies scholars who criticized the reticence of the academic establishment on the Vietnam War, also visited China in the spring of 1971 and 1972. Everywhere they went, Chinese locals showed "no hesitation . . . in offering us their full friendship," making a "distinction" between the US government and the American people.¹⁰⁶ At a banquet in Tangshan, Hebei, the hosts celebrated this friendship with a special cake with icing spelling out "Down with US imperialism" (*dadao Meidi*).¹⁰⁷ Beijing was anxious to turn more Americans into "friends." The CCP stated in May 1971 that people-to-people exchanges afforded "a good opportunity to mobilize the American masses and bolster their mass leadership."¹⁰⁸

Negotiations for these exchanges were rapidly under way. In response to Nixon's request, the State and Defense Departments and the CIA wrote a policy memorandum on the "next steps" toward China in May 1971, which recommended scientific and cultural exchanges.¹⁰⁹ During Kissinger's October 1971 visit, the NSC staffers Alfred Jenkins and John Holdridge submitted to Zhou Enlai's aide Xiong Xianghui a twenty-five-point exchange proposal, covering sport, science, and journalism, among other subjects. Xiong welcomed the proposal, while cautioning that these programs should be conducted on a "private," "non-governmental" basis due to the lack of diplomatic relations.¹¹⁰ During Nixon's visit, Kissinger emphasized that the people-to-people exchanges, though unable to "change objective realities," were still "important" because they could "symbolize" Sino-American rapprochement "in some concrete way that the American people can understand."¹¹¹ By then, proposals for exchanges involving scientists, companies, or orchestras were pouring into the White House and the National Committee. "There's a fantastic mystique. I have been amazed!" National Committee Chairman Alexander Eckstein rejoiced. "There's an incredible amount of curiosity, goodwill, and sympathy."[112]

Washington hurried to steer the nascent exchanges away from Chinese propaganda. A policy paper written by an interdepartmental study group a month after Nixon's trip charged that Beijing was trying to use these exchanges to "increase pressures for establishment of formal diplomatic relations on [its] terms" and "improve [China's] image and mute criticism [in the United States]." It behooved Washington to "open up channels of communication . . . which will slowly build pressures to open up Chinese society" and "provide the American public with a more realistic view of China and sustain public support for our China policies." The State Department urged the White House to "facilitate" the exchange programs through "umbrella organizations" with more influence on public opinion, more balance in political stance, and more eagerness to cooperate with the government than the BPP or the CCAS.[113]

The National Committee was a natural choice. In April 1972, it hosted the return visit by the Chinese table tennis delegation, jointly with the US Table Tennis Association. John Scali, now a special consultant to Nixon, provided logistical support, including security, while minimizing the government's presence in the process. The ping-pong tour was a stellar success, portending the expansion of exchange programs. Scali later proposed to "rule out" the National Committee as an "umbrella organization" because he rated its leadership "inept, emotional, and predisposed to criticize" US foreign policy, particularly in Vietnam.[114] Yet the White House had already made up its mind. Addressing the National Committee membership that May, Assistant Secretary of State for Educational and Cultural Affairs John Richardson Jr. promised to "respect the people-to-people nature" of the exchanges and put the National Committee at the helm. "It is not for me to tell you what the role of the National Committee will be," said Richardson. "You will construct that role for yourselves."[115] Three weeks later, the National Committee, along with the Committee on Scholarly Communication with the People's Republic of China, which specialized in scientific exchanges, drafted a joint position paper, proposing specific subject areas, ranging from language education to youth leadership to gymnastics, based on public impact.[116]

Beijing dithered. The National Committee, in fact, had submitted exchange proposals for the Chinese People's Institute of Foreign Affairs at least twice, in April 1971 and March 1972, both unanswered by the Chinese.[117]

They were deeply suspicious of the National Committee, an elite organization led by China scholars, many of whom had, in one way or another, espoused a "two-China" solution to the Taiwan problem. In the next several years, Beijing would profile the National Committee as a "semi-official" organization, with a "non-governmental façade" yet "intimate ties" to the government, staffed by "CIA personnel" snooping for intelligence and "China hands" with "complex" "political backgrounds."[118] In a nutshell, the National Committee looked like a representative of the government, not the people. The Chinese gave in by that fall, only after Washington gave the National Committee and the Committee on Scholarly Communication a "laying on of hands," or an endorsement as "effective intermediaries" between the US government and the American people.[119] The National Committee leadership traveled to China in December 1972, with a new exchange proposal for the CPIFA, the Chinese People's Association for Friendship with Foreign Countries, and the All-China Sports Federation.[120] Eckstein returned convinced that Beijing was "seriously interested in gradually expanding contacts in a step-by-step fashion."[121]

Kissinger traveled to China in February 1973 for the fifth time in eighteen months. With the war in Vietnam over, the Chinese were more cordial than ever, and Kissinger later reported to Nixon that the former adversaries had now become "tacit allies."[122] As a token of this "alliance," Washington and Beijing agreed to establish liaison offices in the capital of each country in the coming May. From then on, US and Chinese officials no longer had to communicate through a secret channel in Paris. American visa seekers, who had flooded the Chinese embassy in Ottawa, Canada, were also redirected to the Chinese Liaison Office in the Mayflower Hotel near the White House. The people-to-people exchanges were ready to take off.

The Liaison Offices marked both a beginning and a culmination—a beginning of the sustained exchange programs and a culmination of new ideas on US-China relations that began to take shape in the 1960s. In the United States, the movement to calibrate China policy, led by the National Committee, created a new "open door constituency"—to borrow historian Michael Hunt's term—that supported expansion of unofficial contacts with China.[123] In China, the conceptual gap between the US government and the American people generated a space for a new US policy, aimed at "influencing the policy through the people." These ideas informed the US and Chinese statesmen who negotiated Sino-American rapprochement. As Mao stated, "the world changed [Nixon]," as much as Nixon changed the world.[124]

In the early 1970s, US views of China were undergoing tectonic changes. Americans were putting down pamphlets on Beijing's secret plans for world domination and picking up books like CCAS member Mark Selden's *The Yenan Way in Revolutionary China*, Barbara Tuchman's Pulitzer Prize–winning *Stilwell and the American Experience in China*, and British writer Han Suyin's *The Morning Deluge: Mao Tse-tung and the Chinese Revolution*.[125] Some were resentful and fearful. Walter Judd launched the Committee for a Free China as the last stand of the old China Lobby; Taiwan advocates, often with Dalai Lama supporters, organized anti-Chinese demonstrations in large cities; and Southerners inundated their representatives with letters expressing "deep concern" over Chinese subversion.[126] Many of these activities were orchestrated with the KMT, under the Premier of the Executive Yuan Chiang Ching-kuo, which vowed to counter the "large-scale cultural united front" of the "Communist bandits" by marshalling its allies, particularly among Chinese Americans, for its own "people's diplomacy" (*guomin waijiao*).[127] In mid-1973, the KMT, in cooperation with the anti-communist John Birch Society, launched a mass petition campaign targeted at local government offices, with the message: "Cut the Red China connection."[128] Yet the tide was too great to overturn. According to Gallup polls, Americans who saw China favorably more than doubled between May 1972 and April 1973, from 23 percent to 49 percent, while those who saw China unfavorably plummeted from 71 percent to 43 percent.[129] Among adjectives that Americans used to describe the Chinese people, "hard-working" doubled from 37 percent in 1966 to 74 percent in 1972, while "ignorant" (24 percent), "warlike" (23 percent), and "sly" (20 percent) were replaced by "intelligent" (32 percent), "progressive" (28 percent), and "practical" (27 percent).[130] It was a drastic makeover.

China scholars stood sober in this tide. With Beijing hammering home the importance of solving the Taiwan problem before expanding bilateral exchanges, the rapprochement, as Doak Barnett anticipated, was "a gradual, cautious process of mutual accommodation," which would take "much of the coming decade."[131] The public was exhilarated nonetheless. In the wake of Nixon's visit, National Committee staffer Arne de Keijzer found that enrollments in Chinese studies and language classes increased steeply at college campuses across the nation, causing a shortage of instructors.[132] To slake the public appetite and rein in unwarranted optimism, the National Committee ratcheted up public education efforts, most notably the Bay Area Chinese Education Project (BAYCEP) at Stanford and the Project on Asian Studies in Education (PASE) at Michigan, until it transferred these functions to the Asia Society's China Council in 1975. By then, the public euphoria had all but died out.

Chinese views of the United States were about to change, too, albeit slowly. The CCP announced in March 1972 that the Shanghai Communiqué "only set the guidelines on principle" for the people-to-people exchanges.[133] The Chinese people, leaders and commoners, had little idea what would transpire out of these exchanges. When Americans came in greater numbers, the Chinese first applied the only yardstick at their disposal: whether the guests were "friends" or not. When Maud Russell, a former YWCA activist in China, revisited the country in the winter of 1972 and saw a traditional puppet show in a public theater, a five-year-old boy sitting nearby whispered, "Down with US imperialists." When his mother told the boy that she was an "American friend," he gave Russell a milk candy, which made her "extremely happy," according to a Chinese report.[134] Soon, however, the Chinese encountered Americans of different political stripes, defying the dichotomy of "friend" and "nonfriend."

John Fairbank returned to China in June 1972, over a quarter century after his departure in 1946. Having advocated "two Chinas" in various forms, the Harvard sinologist was no American "friend," but the Chinese hosts graciously guided him across the country. The trip was a mixed bag. Fairbank applauded the "miraculous" changes in the countryside and appreciated "the human warmth of personal contact," while heeding the regimentation of society and the ravages of the Cultural Revolution. In his trip report in *Foreign Affairs*, Fairbank argued that the Chinese had "the better of the argument" over whether Washington or Beijing was responsible for the mutual isolation in the past twenty years.[135] Not many Americans and Chinese cared about such a question any more. Now that the "fear and ignorance" between the two countries that Fairbank bemoaned in the aftermath of McCarthyism had thinned, if not dissipated, the million-dollar question was what the new bilateral relationship held for the future.

Chapter 2

Trade

A New Open Door

The imagined wealth and prosperity of China awed the world for centuries—particularly the United States, whose commercial vessel *Empress of China* sailed to Canton in 1784, six months after the War of Independence. Shepherded by Secretary of State John Hay, Americans marched through the "open door" into the China market at the turn of the twentieth century, which boasted over four hundred million customers.[1] The door suddenly shut in 1949. Washington, along with its allies, imposed an embargo on China far more severe than the restrictions against other socialist countries set by the Coordinating Committee for Multilateral Export Controls (COCOM). Beijing resented this "China differential" as a remnant of foreign discrimination. China imported technology and grain first from the Soviet Union and Eastern Europe, and then, particularly after the collapse of Sino-Soviet economic cooperation in 1960, from capitalist countries that had eased trade restrictions after the 1953 Korean Armistice Agreement, such as Australia, Britain, Canada, France, Italy, Japan, and West Germany.[2] While touting self-reliance as its unique economic model, China under Mao Zedong was never isolated from the world economy.[3]

American businesspeople gazed wistfully at the China market in the mid-1960s, now with eight hundred million customers, as China's trade with the capitalist bloc surpassed that with the socialist bloc. Edwin Neilan, chairman of the US Chamber of Commerce, commented that a growing number of member companies reckoned China "one of the major markets of the world."[4] Historical connections with the Pacific made this trend particularly visible in

California. According to Governor Edmund Brown, "many hard-headed businessmen" in his state speculated that trading with China would be "beneficial."[5] Alexander Eckstein of the University of Michigan, who presided over a trade study group organized by the National Committee on US-China Relations in the late 1960s, criticized the US embargo as "ineffective in economic and political terms," although Sino-American trade, even if resumed, was "likely to be of rather modest proportion."[6] *Industry Week* magazine's survey found that a considerable portion of American companies were eager to trade with China by the time Washington lifted the embargo on June 10, 1971. To divert their attention to the Taiwanese economy, which would balloon seven-fold in the 1970s thanks to foreign direct investment, the KMT sponsored a forty-page advertisement in the *New York Times* in 1972, titled "Free China is alive and well," while lending financial and logistical support for Chinese American business selling Taiwanese products.[7] These efforts hardly diminished the traction of the mainland, however. China might turn into "a helluva market," glowed George Dillon, president of Airco.[8]

The Shanghai Communiqué encouraged "progressive development of trade" between the United States and China. Over the next several years, Washington and Beijing wrestled with diplomatic roadblocks, including China's frozen assets and US private claims, US export controls on strategic goods, and US quotas on Chinese textile exports—with little progress until after normalization of relations.[9] To promote trade under this precarious situation, the White House decided to create "a prestigious, private Sino-American Trade Council," through which it could wield influence.[10] In March 1973, Secretary of Commerce Frederick Dent prodded senior executives from such major corporations as Chase Manhattan Bank, Hewlett-Packard, Westinghouse, Boeing, and Cargill into forming what would soon be named the National Council for US-China Trade. It was presided over by Christopher Phillips, a diplomat who had just served as deputy representative to the UN. With a membership quadrupling from 154 to over 600 in six years, the National Council provided counseling and library services for American traders, sponsored information sessions and business symposia, and published the bimonthly magazine *China Business Review*. It also became a point of contact with the China Council for the Promotion of International Trade (CCPIT), a mass organization negotiating business with foreign firms, as well as China's state-controlled foreign trade companies (FTCs).[11] The National Council incarnated the emerging US strategy to reduce government intervention overseas and deploy multinational corporations to secure economic interests around the world.[12]

The China market attracted countless Americans due to the economic woes of the 1970s. The Arab oil embargo in October 1973 exacerbated the scourge of stagflation, while growing competition with the Western Europeans and the Japanese enervated US firms. Beijing's hefty orders in 1972 alone—$2.3 million for one RCA satellite communication ground station; $150 million for ten Boeing 707 airplanes; and $18 million for three hundred thousand tons of corn—came as an auspicious sign.[13] When more and more Americans arrived in China in search of business, they resembled, in the words of John Alioto, CEO of Pacific Far East Line, "a man who has been starving for some time."[14] Frederick Dent cautioned the National Council membership, presciently, that the China market would not be "a panacea for our economic difficulties."[15] Sino-American trade grew from virtually zero to about $3 billion by the end of the decade, but it remained only a trickle of the total US trade volume ($400 billion in 1979). As had been the case for centuries, however, the future, not the present, of the China market captivated Americans.

Chinese businesspeople across ranks—bureaucrats at the Foreign Trade Ministry, officials at the CCPIT, and representatives of the FTCs—were ready to trade with the Americans. Although Beijing cut back foreign trade by 15 percent between 1966 and 1969 in a bid for self-sufficiency, stagnant economic growth, particularly in agriculture, prompted Chinese leaders, Mao included, to abjure autarky. The trade volume bounced back from $4 billion in 1969 to $14.6 billion in 1974.[16] A month after Richard Nixon's visit, the Foreign Trade Ministry circulated an urgent notice, declaring the resumption of Sino-American trade "on the basis of equality and mutual benefit."[17] The Chinese were trying to kill two birds—economic and political—with one stone. At the National Foreign Trade Work Conference in January 1973, Vice Premier Li Xiannian forecast a "considerable" increase in trade, which would accelerate economic development. He then added: "From the viewpoint of diplomacy, we often trade with capitalist countries first and then establish diplomatic relations."[18] Beijing had done so with Canada, Italy, Britain, Japan, West Germany, and Australia; now it turned to the United States.

No one could fathom in 1972 what, how, and how much the United States and China would be trading in the next few years. By 1979, however, the idea that economic access across the Pacific would one day accrue a fortune on both sides underpinned bilateral relations. This chapter explains the rise of this idea. The first section analyzes the initial market euphoria, particularly in the US business community, which soon evaporated due to the political and economic realities of Sino-American trade. The second section focuses on Chinese imports of US technology. Beijing's hunt for modern technology, the key to "catch up" with the world, helped US firms rediscover the China market, which seemed to have disappeared. The third section examines the economic normalization between 1978 and 1980, including America's approval of most favored nation (MFN) and China's go-ahead to joint ventures, which convinced Americans and Chinese of the convergence of their economic interests. Although Washington and Beijing guided bilateral trade through diplomatic channels, this conviction was conceived and promulgated by American and Chinese businesspeople who, against all odds, placed their bets on the embryo of Sino-American trade.

The Myth of the Great Market

American businesspeople itched to enter the China market. The Shanghai Communiqué was followed by a stream of books, articles, and consulting services on how to start doing business with China, many of them offered by amateur China experts.[19] The National Council's founding symbolized and magnified this trend. At the council's inaugural annual meeting on May 31, 1973, Chairman Donald Burnham, a Westinghouse tycoon, proclaimed:

> I am hopeful that, by the time this program today is completed, each of you will be formulating in your minds how your organization can begin to take advantage of this new "open door" to China. . . . The existence of this Council is, of course, no guarantee of success for any one of its members. But businessmen don't expect guarantees—just opportunities. I believe we are facing one of the most exciting opportunities any of us has ever encountered in our business careers—the opportunity to participate in a vast new market of great potential. . . . What real businessman can resist that kind of opportunity?[20]

The "real" businessmen never even tried to resist it. In November 1973, the National Council sent its first mission to Beijing to establish a working relationship with the CCPIT. The Chinese assured them of steady progress in bilateral trade, provided that it was based on "equality and mutual benefits." The CCPIT chairman Wang Yaoting predicted "a bright future" for US and Chinese firms, while Li Xiannian called trade "one of the important ways toward improved [diplomatic] relations."[21] The National Council and the CCPIT agreed to exchange delegations of US corporate leaders and Chinese foreign trade officials, creating an important channel of business negotiations. US companies flocked to the new open door to China. General Motors, Ford Motors, and Westinghouse, for instance, showered the chief of the Chinese Liaison Office Huang Zhen with lavish receptions when he toured their factories near the Great Lakes in late 1974. A First National Bank of Chicago representative even boasted to Huang that the bank had canceled the launch of a Taipei branch to prioritize the mainland.[22] At the National Council's second annual meeting in June 1974, Christopher Phillips asked the restless crowd of members to emulate Chinese "patience and persistence" in doing business with China.[23]

America's hunger for the China market was matched by China's thirst for the American market. To earn foreign currency and expand political influence, Beijing made concerted efforts to export to the capitalist world—advertising products, improving packaging, conducting market research, subsidizing export industries, and holding exhibitions at home and abroad.[24] "If our exports to you are smaller than Taiwan's, how can we liberate Taiwan?" Zhou Enlai shrieked to the Canadian prime minister Pierre Trudeau in 1973.[25] Factories around the country were encouraged to buttress production of export commodities.[26] Japan was China's largest trading partner, but Beijing eyed the United States as a future jackpot. When the US dollar became a floating currency in early 1973, Foreign Trade Minister Li Qiang, with China's economic masterminds Li Xiannian and Chen Yun, established an interdepartmental group that studied the global currency markets, including the Eurodollar markets.[27] In February 1974, the Foreign Trade Ministry's International Trade Research Center, which aided the group and generated dozens of studies on the capitalist economies, asserted that China should cash in on the economic crisis in the capitalist bloc—the "great chaos under heaven"—by bolstering exports.[28] The United States, hard hit by stagflation, was the prime target. The Research Center's March 1974 study advised on leveraging the American lust for the China market to sell back consumer goods like textiles, foodstuff, and handicrafts, tripling or quadrupling the trade volume in the next couple of years.[29]

The mirroring market ambitions of the Americans and the Chinese crossed paths at the China Export Commodities Fair, a biannual trade fair in Guangzhou, commonly known as the Canton Fair (see fig. 2.1). After Zhou Enlai took down banners with political slogans like "The Canton Fair is an important place to promote Mao Zedong Thought," it gradually reverted to a place for haggling between FTC representatives and thousands of for-

Figure 2.1. A machine tool exhibition at the Spring 1974 Canton Fair. The slogan on the wall reads: "Go all out, aim high and achieve greater, faster, better and more economical results in building socialism!" U.S.-China Business Council Records, Gerald R. Ford Presidential Library.

eign merchants, which accounted for more than half of Chinese exports in the early 1970s.[30] Beijing invited forty-two Americans to the fair for the first time in the spring of 1972, and the number mushroomed over ten times in three years. The Americans fought through the hubbub and eagerly bought clothes, carpets, liquor, fireworks, and folk toys, among other items, partly because a small buy at the Canton Fair might lead to a sizable sell later, as in Boeing's case. "There is tremendous opportunity for sales in China," said David Buxbaum, president of May Lee Industries, a small New York-based company specialized in the China trade. "If we let it go by, someone like the Japanese who are very aggressive will take it."[31] To cultivate the American market—which held the greatest "potential" for Chinese goods in "premodern or modern history," according to one fairgoer—the Chinese not only gave American newcomers "preferential treatment" over their competitors, but also requested lectures on the wholesale system, retail marketing, and Food and Drug Administration (FDA) regulations.[32] The Chinese export items, including the baggy, drab, unisex "Mao suit," became popular among hard-core fans in large cities and college campuses. Beijing gushed about this "China fever."[33] As both sides got accustomed to their respective trade practices, the United States became China's second-largest trading partner in 1974, with the total volume nearing one billion dollars.

US policy makers and scholars harbored little optimism nonetheless. They expected bilateral trade to remain "infinitesimal in terms of our total economy," in Henry Kissinger's sober words.[34] The Departments of State and Commerce, as well as the CIA, all pointed to Beijing's principles of self-reliance and balanced trade as major constraints.[35] Trade mattered politically, not economically. Kissinger lectured Nixon in mid-1972 that the importance of Sino-American trade lay not in "the intrinsic economic value," but in "the political and psychological dimension"—that is, trade helped to maintain the momentum for larger bilateral relations.[36] Most China scholars concurred that American companies overestimated the size of the China market.[37] The eight hundred million avid customers "may be more of a mirage than a reality," argued Alexander Eckstein in March 1972.[38] His prophesy was on the mark. Bilateral trade plummeted from $933.8 billion in 1974 to $462.9 million in 1975 to $345.4 million in 1976, while US exports free-fell from $819.1 million in 1974 to $303.6 million in 1975 to $135.4 million in 1976. The China market vanished like a mirage.

And it was not a blip. The plunge derived, above all, from China's economic realities. The agricultural surplus, as well as grain deals with Canada and Australia, obviated grain imports from the United States, which accounted for over 70 percent of the total US exports to China in 1974.[39] More fundamental were China's balance-of-payments problems. As the global recession suppressed Chinese exports, and the runaway inflation in the capitalist bloc raised the prices of import commodities, China registered an unprecedented trade deficit of $600 million in 1974. The US trade surplus against China (over $700 million in 1974) was even larger than that. To propitiate the Chinese, the National Council organized dozens of small import-oriented members into an importers committee in the spring of 1974, but it helped little due to Beijing's unfamiliarity with the US market; unavailability of export products; and inexperience in designing, packaging, and quality control.[40] The State Council of China warned in mid-1975: "If this trend continues, we need to stop all the imports one day. Once it happens, it will have a very bad impact [on our international reputation]."[41] The American market, too, evaded the Chinese like a mirage.

Politics shaped the 1975–1976 slump as much as economics. On the US side, MFN—a status that allows one country the same trade privileges enjoyed by any other country—politicized Sino-American trade in 1973–1974, when the Nixon administration was trying persuade Congress to grant MFN to the Soviet Union as part of détente. Senator Henry "Scoop" Jackson and

Representative Charles Vanik, both enraged by the oppression of Jews in the Soviet Union, added an amendment to Title IV of the Trade Act of 1974, which blocked MFN to any country that denied its citizens freedom to emigrate. China took the stray bullet. Businesspeople, scholars, and policy makers all decried the Jackson-Vanik Amendment for jeopardizing Sino-American trade by undermining the principle of "equality and mutual benefit."[42] Christopher Phillips remarked at a congressional hearing that the lack of MFN, an act of "hypocrisy" in the Chinese eyes, rendered bilateral trade "extremely difficult" when the China market created "a major opportunity for American exporters."[43] The National Council issued a resolution in April 1975, urging Washington to discuss "a comprehensive trade agreement" with Beijing, including MFN, to address the current "unacceptable conditions."[44] The lack of diplomatic relations, however, precluded such an agreement.

Beijing deemed the Jackson-Vanik Amendment more of a political affront than an economic barrier. Chinese officials repeatedly expressed displeasure over the lack of MFN, but never openly coveted it. Mao told Kissinger in November 1973: "So long as the Soviet Union doesn't get it, that would be enough."[45] The Chinese had little reason to be solicitous, since the absence of MFN curtailed Chinese exports to the United States by only 16 percent, according to the State and Commerce Department estimates.[46] The issue rankled, though. On many occasions, the Chinese imputed the trade imbalance with the United States to the tariff status. At a February 1976 meeting with Phillips, Zhang Jianhua, commercial counselor at the Chinese Liaison Office, called his attention to "the fact of life" that American businesspeople often ignored—politics and economics were inseparable. "Where you have two [separate tariff] columns, you have a [China] differential," he roared.[47] The Jackson-Vanik Amendment, though not directly responsible for the shrinkage of bilateral trade, eroded the delicate political foundation on which rested nascent Sino-American trade. That foundation eroded even further when the stalemate over Beijing's "three principles" on Taiwan sapped the momentum in bilateral relations. When Kissinger proposed to negotiate solutions to some economic issues, most notably the assets and claims problem, as a sop before Gerald Ford's December 1975 visit to China, Deng Xiaoping showed "total lack of responsiveness."[48] Politics was the key for bilateral trade, and Beijing made sure American businesspeople knew it. When Phillips visited China in the summer of 1976, the Chinese made "no effort to conceal the view that the amount of trade and its rate of growth [were] related to diplomatic recognition."[49]

On the Chinese side, the strife between the Gang of Four and senior statesmen like Zhou and Deng spilled over into foreign trade. The Gang pummeled the Foreign Trade Ministry for economically pauperizing and politically demoralizing the country by practicing "foreign currency in command" (*waihui gua shuai*), not "politics in command" (*zhengzhi gua shuai*). The Gang, for starters, pressured foreign trade officials into withdrawing traditional handicrafts, a major export commodity, at the spring 1974 Canton Fair, to honor the spirit of the Criticize Confucius Campaign.[50] Their outcry grew louder with the onset of the Criticize Deng Campaign in late 1975. The Gang mobilized their puppet Shanghai Municipal Foreign Trade Office to excoriate the Foreign Trade Ministry and FTCs for permitting foreign currencies in payment, forgoing the "Made in China" (*Zhongguo zhi*) stamp, and lowering the prices of export goods, to sell as much as possible during the global stagflation.[51] Unnerved by the public opprobrium, the ministry and the FTCs sent a joint delegation to Shanghai in July 1976 to deflate the tension. It backfired. According to the Shanghai Trade Office's account, the delegation failed to hold back their frustration when the circular discussion over the virtue of earning foreign currency lingered for days.[52] Emboldened, the Shanghai Trade Office pledged to "wage a battle" to "fully uncover the revisionist line within us and completely eliminate it."[53] Its several members traveled to Beijing a few weeks later and put up big-character posters at the buildings of the Foreign Trade Ministry and the CCPIT, accusing them of abetting Deng's "revisionist line" and threatening to occupy the ministry with one thousand minions. Minister Li Qiang and other officials bit their tongues in fear of further retaliation.[54]

The showdown between the Foreign Trade Ministry and the Shanghai Trade Office was a microcosm of the larger tension over foreign trade since 1949—the tension between ideology and profit. On the one hand, the Chinese considered foreign trade an economic front of the political struggle against capitalist countries. When foreign merchants tried to raise the prices for chemical fertilizers in 1974, for instance, the State Council insisted on increasing domestic production to achieve self-sufficiency. "Foreign capitalists presume that we need them," it blared. "They are very arrogant."[55] The United States was the greatest villain. The Foreign Trade Ministry, in official documents, called foreign trade "one important field of our struggle with the United States" and the Canton Fair a place to confront, maneuver, and co-opt American businesspeople.[56] The ministry contended that Chinese merchants could and should outcompete the Americans in the "price struggle," as the global economic crisis further exposed "the decadent, declining, dying imperialist nature" of the US economy, hidden under "the veneer of prosperity."[57]

This ideological rhetoric coexisted with a pragmatic desire for profit, particularly among rank-and-file trade officials. As early as 1973, factories in the Pearl River Delta region experimented with compensation trade—in which foreign companies provide capital and equipment for production, and the host country repays them with finished goods—with American entrepreneurs in Hong Kong.[58] Despite the official policy of "forming a united front against foreign merchants," local FTC branches and international ports, including Shanghai, Guangzhou, Tianjin, and Fujian, also engaged in "three competitions" (*san zheng*) for more goods, more market shares, and more customers, often by keeping new products secret, striking larger deals than planned, and exporting more at lower prices than their rivals.[59] These officials cared little about ideology. Even some members of the Shanghai Trade Office showed fatigue over the prolonged campaign against the Foreign Trade Ministry in the summer of 1976. "Now that the ministry delegation has left, the fall Canton Fair is about to start, and trade statistics has been reported, it is about time for our campaign to end," they groaned.[60] China's foreign trade policy—a hodgepodge of the Maoist ideology, the principles of self-reliance and balanced trade, and the growing yen for foreign currency—was making a screeching din.

For the moment, however, the nosedive in Sino-American trade dispirited American businesspeople, and the reassurances by scholars and officials seemed futile.[61] Julian Sobin of Sobin Chemicals, one of the core members of the National Council, lamented that the political struggle in China made the prospects of bilateral trade "very iffy." "I'd hate to make my livelihood out of China trade . . . especially now," he clucked.[62] The National Council vice president Eugene Theroux, a frequent traveler to China, shared with the Chinese his concern about the pessimism in US business circles, evident in the National Council's declining membership, but he found no recourse. "The rightward lurch at the time was so strong, and antipathy to business with foreign companies so profound" that the Foreign Trade Ministry was derided as the "Ministry of National Betrayal," recounted Theroux.[63] At the spring 1976 Canton Fair, Americans concluded deals worth only $20 million, down from $40 million a year before.[64] US firms walked through the new open door in the early 1970s, believing that they were entering a vast market that could aggrandize their wealth soon enough—only to find a tiny market wanting in purchasing power and political stability. Many of them stayed in the China market, feeling as if they were clinging to a myth.

To Catch Up with the World

The Americans were in for a long game, determined to bide their time until the myth transfigured into a full-fledged reality that Beijing envisioned: a market for technology exports. Articulating how to achieve the "four modernizations" at the opening session of the Third National People's Congress in December 1964, Zhou Enlai intoned, "We cannot walk the old path of technological development [that other countries have walked], crawling little by little behind them. We must break the regular procedure and strive to adopt modern technology."[65] Years later, Chinese leaders put the premier's words back into action. In January 1973, the State Planning Commission proposed the "Four-Three Plan" (*Si-San Fang'an*) to import modern technology worth $4.3 billion from capitalist countries, the second-largest such project since the Sino-Soviet cooperation of the 1950s, which was promptly approved by the CCP leadership.[66] Beijing mimicked capitalist practices—accepting middle-term credits up to five years, first from Japan and then from Western Europe, for example—in financing 250 large import projects between 1973 and 1977, in chemical fertilizer, chemical fiber, petrochemistry, coal and mining, meteorology, and offshore drilling, among others. These projects included some fifty sets of complete plants, many of them for export products, in which foreign engineers worked with Chinese colleagues to facilitate technology transfer.[67] In his May 1974 talk with the former British prime minister Edward Heath, even Mao Zedong, the evangelist of self-reliance, championed technology imports: "We shall be very glad to have your help."[68] Self-reliance carried the day as political rhetoric, but this concept now ennobled Sinicization of foreign technology, socialist or capitalist.

Despite their preference for imports from countries with which they had diplomatic relations, the Chinese let drop many hints of their hankering for American technology. "The U.S. is very developed and very advanced, while China remains a developing country," Li Xiannian conceded to the National Council delegation in November 1973. "China [has] a great deal to learn from the outside world."[69] Shortly afterwards, Pullman Kellogg announced mammoth contracts worth $200 million to build eight large-scale ammonia plants in China, the biggest nonagricultural deal before 1978.[70] The US business community was jolted. While putting all importers under one umbrella committee, the National Council created a committee for each export industry, the petroleum committee largest among them, which arranged delegations to/from China and organized seminars to discuss how to sell computers, machine tools, or oil rigs. Before 1978, about four hundred

Chinese technicians visited the United States to receive training at Boeing, Pullman Kellogg, Caterpillar, and other firms, and scores of Americans stayed in China to administer complete plant projects.[71] Dwight Perkins of Harvard predicted in 1973 that Beijing's desire for technology would dwarf its obsession with self-reliance. "In the end," he wrote, "China will buy what it wants on economic terms, and politics won't affect this much."[72]

Premier Zhou Enlai and Vice Premier Deng Xiaoping tried to set technology imports as the kingpin of China's economic strategy. Following Zhou's reaffirmation of the "four modernizations" at the Fourth National People's Congress in January 1975, Deng drafted a twenty-point blueprint for industrialization that summer, titled "Some Questions on Accelerating the Development of Industry."[73] "It is by the adoption of the most advanced technologies that the industrially backward countries catch up with the industrially advanced countries in the world. We must also do the same," it read. "Every department and every industry must know the world's advanced level and map out plans and measures for catching up with and surpassing it." The twenty points even preached joint oil ventures in the East and South China Seas to pay for technology imports. Beijing would invite foreign oil companies into its territorial waters, allow them to produce offshore oil, and sell it to the oil-hungry capitalist bloc—a scheme that Beijing rebuffed in public as a violation of its energy sovereignty.[74] Deng's bold suggestions garnered widespread support. In 1975 alone, China achieved 13.1 percent increase in steel production, 18.8 percent increase in oil production, and 39.2 billion yuan (about $20 billion) investment in construction.[75] Joint ventures remained off limits for the moment, but the vice premier was winning what the State Planning Commission called "one hard, tough battle, as well as a key battle," for technology imports.[76] "To catch up with the world" became the refrain of Chinese speeches and writings.

Deng's economic reform was anathema to the Gang of Four. They waged a semantic battle against it by naming technology imports "crawlism" (*paxing zhuyi*), "capitulationism" (*touxiang zhuyi*), and "national betrayal" (*maiguo zhuyi*).[77] In February 1974, Corning's glass snails, a token of friendship given to Chinese visitors, piqued Jiang Qing's ire. She reviled them as an insult and opposed further cooperation with Corning, delaying the imports of color television technology for several years.[78] A few months after the "Snail Incident," a 10,000-ton long-distance cargo ship named *Fengqing* returned to Shanghai from its successful voyage to Europe. Galvanized by this historic achievement, Jiang and her acolytes lambasted Zhou and Deng for purchasing foreign vessels, and only Mao could sideline this "Fengqing Incident" in late

1974. The Gang mounted a fierce counteroffensive against Deng's twenty points in 1975 and 1976. They not only mobilized their student and worker allies to block it from getting enacted, but also charged it as a "poisonous weed," a "revisionist" plot to "accelerate the restoration of capitalism."[79] Gang-incited political rallies and factional infightings pervaded factories around the country between 1974 and 1976, including large steel plants at Wuhan and Anshan, which lowered morale, hindered production, and alienated foreign engineers.[80] The Gang could only slow down technology imports, however. An installation of West German and Japanese steel production equipment in Wuhan Iron and Steel Company, the largest technology imports at the time, for instance, made headway between 1974 and 1978, with only a one-year delay.

The miscarriage of Deng's twenty points hardly daunted American executives. Alexander Eckstein estimated in 1974 that US exports of machinery, transportation equipment, and other high-tech products to China would reach $450 million by the end of the decade, with their proportion in the total exports quintupling from 6 percent in 1973 to 30 percent in 1980.[81] Businesspeople saw a silver lining on the horizon. When the Chinese petroleum engineering delegation demonstrated keen interest in US oil technology in late 1975, Phillips observed, "If the Chinese want something bad enough and can only get it in this country . . . they'll probably buy it willy-nilly."[82] His optimism seemed warranted. Upon return from China in June 1976, Graham Marx, president of G. A. Gray, commented that its machine tool industry, like other industries, fell a quarter century behind the United States, offering a promising export market.[83] At a conference on China's oil industry in Houston, energy experts also underlined China's dual potential as "hardware buyers" and "know-how buyers."[84] The Americans were angling to sell everything they could—plants, machines, tools, and knowledge to get them working.

Hua Guofeng came to power at this critical juncture. At a national industrial conference in the spring of 1977, the new chairman lauded Daqing oilfield in Heilongjiang, the largest Chinese oilfield and the lodestar of self-reliance since its 1959 discovery, for "absorbing some foreign technology without walking the old path." He then pledged to build "some ten more Daqings" before 1985. Newspapers around the country printed his words.[85] "Ten Daqings" aside, Hua's ambitious goals for the Sixth Five-Year Plan (1980–1985), which passed the first session of the Fifth National People's Congress in March 1978, included 400 million tons of grain (270 million tons in 1977), 60

Figure 2.2. A reception during the CCPIT's visit to Washington, September 9, 1977. Left to right: National Council President Christopher Phillips, Secretary of Commerce Juanita Kreps, CCPIT Chairman Wang Yaoting, National Council Chairman William A. Hewitt, Vice Chief of the Chinese Liaison Office Han Xu. US-China Business Council Records, Gerald R. Ford Presidential Library.

million tons of steel (26 million tons in 1977), 250 million tons of oil production (94 million tons in 1977), and construction of 120 large-scale industrial complexes that required colossal investment equivalent to the total amount since 1949.[86] All these numbers soon proved "naïve" and "unrealistic," as historian Ezra Vogel wrote, but Hua consummated what Zhou and Deng had set out to do: destigmatizing technology imports.[87]

The Chinese now sought US technology more candidly and boldly than ever before, as symbolized by the CCPIT's three-week tour of the United States in September 1977 (see fig. 2.2). Visiting industrial complexes and company laboratories across the country, the CCPIT chairman Wang Yaoting drew a distinction between self-reliance and "self-seclusion," and articulated his hope to tap US technology to "speed up" Chinese modernization. "The U.S. is somewhat advanced in technical equipment and technology," he stated. "With this in mind, we have the interest to visit your country."[88] Wang did not forget to pinch the Americans in the sore spot. He claimed at a meeting with Representative John Brademas that "closer collaboration in the fields of technology [trade]" must be based on "further improvements of political relations," which hinged on the Taiwan problem.[89]

China's renewed foreign trade activism brought the China market back to life. In 1977, a large volume of articles, studies, and interviews appeared in the United States that foresaw more business opportunities in China. Eckstein, one of the leading voices, argued that China would maintain at least 5 percent annual growth in trade in the next decade, since it needed technology imports as "a marginal but essential input" for industrial development.[90] In a dramatic speech at the National Council's June 1977 annual meeting, Holger Hansen, general manager of East Asiatic Company, predicted that China, on its way toward becoming "an economic and trading super-power" by the end of the century, would soon enter "a new stage in its economic development," offering an "opportunity" for American companies to sell "equipment and know-how."[91] No longer rueful, Julian Sobin also speculated about "a significant role for American industry" to play in China's "staggering" efforts for the "four modernizations."[92] Eugene Theroux was transfixed by "an unprecedented situation" in the world economy. "There's a labor force of one-half billion people out there that has yet to be unleashed, and we don't know where it's going," he stammered. "My best advice is to exercise patience and perseverance and stay in the game and see what happens."[93]

Beijing went on a technology shopping spree from 1978. Its imports from the United States skyrocketed from $171.3 million in 1977 to $820.7 million in 1978 to $3.8 billion in 1980, while the exports quintupled from $200.7 million in 1977 to $1.1 billion in 1980. China's total imports also increased, albeit at a slower pace, from $7.2 billion in 1977 to $19.6 billion in 1980, registering a whopping deficit of $4.5 billion in three years. Beijing incurred debts in sundry forms, including long-term loans up to ten years from foreign banks, a new policy promoted by Vice Premier Gu Mu after his extensive tour of Western Europe in mid-1978.[94] The CCP reissued Deng's twenty points in April 1978, with ten new items added to the original text. The new thirty points, enacted that summer, stipulated: "While maintaining self-reliance, we must diligently study good things of foreign countries, import . . . modern technology and equipment we urgently need, and make the foreign serve China."[95] By the year's end, Beijing signed a mega deal with Nippon Steel of Japan, worth over $2 billion, to build a giant steel mill in Baoshan, near Shanghai.[96] As Beijing sent out more and more business delegations overseas, Phillips mused that the Chinese saw "nothing inconsistent between a policy of self-reliance and acquiring foreign technology, foreign equipment."[97]

When trade culture changed in China, so did factory culture. Most Chinese factories were using outdated Soviet equipment, often imported from Eastern Europe in the 1960s, but technology imports from the capitalist bloc in the 1970s gradually compelled them to adjust their operation. As Jan-Olaf Willums, a petroleum researcher at MIT, realized in mid-1976, Chinese factories were shifting from "a Russian technology way" to "a Western technology way."[98] This shift contoured one of the ten new clauses in the thirty points, which knocked down a taboo in Mao's China: material incentives in the workplace. On October 24, 1977, Vice Premier Yu Quili, China's economic guru, announced a 10 to 15 percent raise for some 46 percent of the entire Chinese workforce (64 percent of nonagricultural workforce), for the first time since 1963. The CCP further dumfounded the population in January 1978, when it revived pecuniary rewards—higher salaries and cash bonuses—for workers in high-tech industry who scored an exceptional success in Sinicizing foreign technology.[99] The next month, the CCP dismantled revolutionary committees at factories, consisting of cadres, rebels, and soldiers, and reinstituted veteran managers to restore discipline and boost production. The lure of money, not the cachet of a model worker, further drove factory workers to adopt new technology later that year, when Beijing liberalized import regulations for US goods.[100] Technology now wielded political power to accelerate China's opening to the capitalist world.

The United States, however, remained, in Eckstein's words, "a residual supplier [of modern technology] not needed in normal times," which accounted for only 7.4 percent of Beijing's technology imports between 1972 and 1977. The Michigan sinologist estimated that Sino-American trade would "necessarily be erratic, sharply fluctuating and devoid of a firm, systematic, and fully institutionalized footing" before normalization of relations, a view shared by the Carter administration.[101] American businesspeople, including Phillips, had speculated that for all its political importance, the Taiwan problem would not prevent Beijing from buying US technology that it considered essential. They were right. Beijing continued to trade with US firms with membership in the US-Republic of China Trade Council—it only whined that these firms "hurt the feelings of the Chinese people."[102] But the rules of the game were changing, and fast. Having normalized relations with China much earlier, Japan and Western European countries concluded large trade agreements worth billions of dollars in 1978. With Beijing shunning US suppliers when alternative sources were available, the lack of diplomatic relations threatened to put them at greater disadvantage than ever before. American businesspeople drooled over the China bonanza while loathing the tether of politics.

The Economic Normalization

The US business community was growing impatient. Just as inflation was coming back, American companies were losing to the Japanese and the Western Europeans in the China market, partly because US export controls created endless delays in licensing technology exports, which also irritated the Chinese.[103] The National Council submitted a policy statement to the White House in June 1977, urging it to recognize the People's Republic and level the playing field for American traders.[104] It found sympathetic ears in the Carter administration. The national security adviser Zbigniew Brzezinski and the science adviser Frank Press wished to relax export controls on China—put in the same category as the Soviet Union and its Eastern European allies since 1972—as a strategic move against Moscow. Later that year, they not only persuaded Jimmy Carter to expedite advanced technology exports to China, especially offshore equipment and large computers, but also prescribed relaxation of defense-related technology transfer in a policy memorandum drafted for the president. These moves, Brzezinski and Press explained, would serve US interest by making China "a check on Soviet power, influence, and freedom of action."[105] For the first time, trade became a strategic agenda in US-China relations.

Brzezinski's ascent as Carter's main adviser paralleled Deng Xiaoping's rise as China's de facto leader. Between fall 1977 and spring 1978, Deng met dozens of Americans, from Associated Press board of directors to Senator Henry Jackson to United Press International reporters, delivering the familiar message: China would import modern technology from the United States, but Sino-American trade could reach its fullest potential only after normalization of relations.[106] After Brzezinski and Deng agreed to launch normalization negotiations in their May 1978 meeting, Beijing began to accept high-ranking US officials to discuss economic cooperation on the governmental level. Press started off with a large science and technology delegation in July, to which Deng said, "We want to use your capital, your equipment, and your technology and to repay you with our own products."[107] Secretary of Agriculture Robert Bergland came next in early November. "While repeatedly emphasizing their determination to remain self-sufficient and independent, [the

Chinese] look to the U.S., almost naively, as holding the key to their objectives for modernizing their agriculture," reported Bergland.[108] Secretary of Energy James Schlesinger traveled later that month and proposed joint energy projects, which would afford "potentially lucrative commercial opportunities for U.S. industry."[109] Michigan sinologist Michel Oksenberg, now Brzezinski's man Friday on China at the NSC, observed that the Chinese had "embarked on a strategy to modernize China by turning to the West," contrary to the policy of "leaning to one side (the Soviet Union)" in the 1950s. Deng's China was "leaning to one side again—this time our side."[110]

With normalization in the offing, US firms scrambled to the China market. In the spring of 1978, some 240 businesspeople—three times the seat limit—applied for a Department of Commerce seminar on the China trade.[111] "A tremendous explosion" of business interest engulfed the United States, and hotels in Beijing were "absolutely jammed" by corporate representatives, many of them American, according to a Midwestern newspaper.[112] At the fall 1978 Canton Fair, Americans sold $110 million, and Chinese $55 million, a total volume more than eight times the $20 million at the spring 1976 fair.[113] The National Council exchanged about twenty delegations with China in 1978, a sharp increase from previous years, in such areas as mining, petrochemistry, construction equipment, and food processing. "Next year will bust this wide open," the National Council vice president Stanley Young enthused in November, "unless there are unforeseen political complications."[114] The news of normalization all but obviated such a caveat. George Clark, Citibank's senior vice president, envisaged that China would "come on the way Japan came on after World War II," that is, rapid industrialization based on cooperation with the United States.[115] In an interview with the *China Business Review*, Secretary of Treasury W. Michael Blumenthal, former National Council chairman, cautioned that "the [trade] numbers . . . will not go into the sky" overnight, but companies were already lining up to cultivate what the *New York Times* called "American industry's most promising new frontier," now with a staggering one billion customers.[116]

Sino-American economic relations hardly normalized when diplomatic relations did. Washington and Beijing had yet to work out a pile of knotty problems, including assets and claims, US government credits, US export controls, Chinese textile exports, and most important, the absence of MFN—a "stigma of second-class status" as Secretary of Commerce Juanita Kreps phrased it.[117] They began negotiating a comprehensive trade agreement, including MFN, soon after the normalization. During his US tour, an exultant Deng conveyed his "anticipation" that Sino-American trade "should not be lower than" Sino-Japanese trade, which surpassed $6.7 billion in 1979.[118] Like Ford, however, Carter hesitated to grant MFN to China before the Soviet Union. Many in the White House and Congress urged a "China tilt," and Beijing bewailed the delay in economic normalization.[119] The president stood fast nonetheless. Only after sending the SALT II agreement to Senate in June 1979 did Carter issue Executive Order 12167 to exempt China from the Jackson-Vanik Amendment and designate it as a "friendly nation" eligible for MFN.[120] "In effect," recalled Brzezinski, "for the first time, the explicit decision to decouple China MFN from Soviet MFN was made."[121] A few weeks later, the US ambassador to China Leonard Woodcock and Foreign Trade Minister Li Qiang signed a trade agreement in the Great Hall of the People, which granted MFN to China. Congress ratified it on January 24, 1980, and the agreement went into effect on February 1, a year and a month after the normalization of relations.

By then, American companies were rushing to the new open door in record numbers. The Department of Commerce was inundated with phone calls and mail inquiries on the China trade, while the National Council and other business groups organized seminar after seminar across the country, hosting several hundred executives at a time.[122] The repeated message, as a Department of Commerce guide put it, was: "It takes time and patience to enter the China market successfully."[123] Recognizing China's need for debt financing, American bankers were as anxious to lend as manufacturers were to export. David Rockefeller, chairman of the Chase Manhattan Bank, previously known to the Chinese as "the head of US monopolies," which carried out "economic and cultural invasion" against China before 1949, vividly recalled in his memoirs the moment when his company became the first US bank to operate in the People's Republic: "The door to China had swung open, and Chase was waiting on the other side as American companies began to walk through it."[124] As newspapers reported China deals almost every day, some analysts warned that "the China boom" might turn into "a China bubble," but the opportunity seemed to trump the risk by a large margin.[125] Paul Marer of Indiana University's Kelley School of Business commented, "To say that many of our largest multinationals are willing and eager is an understatement."[126]

The China market was bound to be a small market, given Beijing's chronic shortage of foreign currency. Fearing the deleterious impact of mounting loans on its international credibility, Beijing doubled down on its export strategies—compensation trade, import substitution, and processing trade—with initiatives emanating from local governments. Shanghai, which produced more than one-fifth of China's export goods, took the lead, as if to shake off the Gang of Four's stigma. In late 1977, for instance, the city proposed to open factories in Hong Kong, assemble semifinished products there, and export finished products to the United States and other capitalist countries in order to evade high tariffs.[127] In a letter addressed to Hua Guofeng, Shanghai also wished to use compensation and processing schemes to export more high-end products, particularly electronics, while simultaneously bolstering sales in textiles and handicrafts.[128] Quietly dropping Mao's Three Worlds Theory as the tenet of foreign trade, the city later decided to cede the "Third World" market to the "Four Little Dragons" of Asia—Hong Kong, Singapore, South Korea, and Taiwan—and focus on penetrating the Japanese, European, and American markets.[129] Chinese traders grew increasingly aggressive—and creative—in selling their products.

No amount of exports could earn enough foreign currency to satiate Beijing's investment appetite, and Chinese economic planners decided to cut a deal with "foreign devils." Departing from plant and equipment purchases in the previous decades, Beijing embarked in 1978 on joint ventures, Deng's brainchild, sanctioning direct involvements of foreign firms in construction and development projects, particularly in the field of energy. It, for instance, invited oil companies around the world to conduct geological surveys in the East and South China Seas, with an eye on joint ventures for the exploration and development of offshore oilfields, estimated to be enormous—an unprecedented move that astounded American oilmen.[130] Controversy ensued, as the old guard like Li Xiannian and Chen Yun warned against economic predation and moral degradation at the hands of foreign capitalists, and many workers expressed chagrin at performing labor for them.[131] Joint venture, however, was the only way to cover the lack of capital, technology, personnel, and management know-how. On July 8, 1979, Beijing rolled out China's first joint venture law, written in a language so obscure that it puzzled foreign businesspeople as much as it reassured them. The piece of law nonetheless pointed to the direction China was heading, as a harbinger of the Special Economic Zones that started to spring up in the next month.

With the economic normalization, the American people attached new meanings to Chinese goods. In late 1979, when the Second Oil Shock pushed the inflation rate over 13 percent and precipitated another round of recession, cheap foreign products made by cheap foreign labor sounded attractive. Christopher Phillips framed "Made in China" as "one means of helping keep prices down—a welcome prospect for American consumers" at a time of widening economic inequality.[132] Many spurned such an idea. US manufacturers, particularly in the textile industry, dreaded Chinese goods as a death blow to their businesses and the working class in general, already in steep decline in the 1970s.[133] Washington and Beijing agreed in July 1980 on the levels of Chinese textile exports to the United States, which amounted to $200 million, half of the total exports, but the American debate on the flood of Chinese products was just beginning.[134] "Made in China" was far from a mere production label; it was a political symbol with contested meanings.

The Chinese people embraced Sino-American trade, associating it with the "four modernizations." The jargon itself thrilled few. When a local television crew interviewed some factory workers in Shanghai, the most affluent city in China, they whimpered that the stresses of urban life and years of political struggle had left them little time and energy to modernize anything.[135] To mobilize the masses once again, the CCP gave them consumer products, many of them imported from capitalist countries or produced with capitalist technology. In early 1979, Shanghai held an exhibition of imported daily commodities, including washing machines, refrigerators, and radios, attended by a sea of crowds.[136] Later that year, Beijing hosted the first national light industrial commodity fair, in which eight hundred thousand shoppers spent 31.3 million yuan (about $20.9 million) for the "four news"—new goods, new kinds, new colors, and new packages.[137] Nothing beat color television, which superseded wristwatches, radios, and bicycles as a new status symbol. As the *Washington Post* reported, "in what appears to be a consumer revolution in China," people sought "with almost capitalistic fervor" a television set, which cost a year's salary for an average worker, to watch sports and films.[138] As commercial advertisements replaced political slogans on billboards, consumerism—largely contained in the Friendship Stores in the 1970s, where only foreigners and officials could shop—was taking urban China by storm.[139] The Chinese knew that the United States was sponsoring the "four modernizations" and that the "four modernizations" made them better off.

The myth of the vast China market collapsed under the weight of reality after 1980. US exports to China exceeded $5 billion for the first time in 1988, out of the total exports of $320 billion, while US imports from China reached $12 billion in the following year, doubled in three years, and has snowballed ever since.[140] The timeless American dream of "selling a billion toothbrushes to China" had long been dead, with the Chinese turning that dream on its head.[141] US multinationals were far from woeful. Their investment in China, particularly its construction, energy, and transportation industries, increased from roughly $380 million in 1985 to over $3 billion in 1994, bankrolling Reform and Opening-Up and profiting handsomely from it.[142] Not that it was smooth sailing. Coming from divergent business cultures, the American and the Chinese constantly wrangled with each other, as detailed by journalist James Mann's study on the auto joint venture Beijing Jeep.[143] Yet the potential of bilateral cooperation was never lost on them. The United States and China were beginning to morph into an integrated economic creature of immense size, soon to be named "Chimerica."[144]

Chimerica was conceived in the womb of American and Chinese imaginations in the 1970s. Blind to the counterevidence stacked against them, American businesspeople proselytized the myth of the China market and turned it into "ammunition," as Christopher Phillips put it, to win a "constituency," inside and outside Congress, in support of recognition of China.[145] Phillips later boasted, rightfully, that despite the Carter administration's "generally uncooperative attitude" and "complete lack of interest," the National Council "did galvanize a significant part of the American business community," convincing countless companies that trading with China would one day make them rich.[146] Sino-American trade, with its trifling sum, was "really a minor part of the process of [diplomatic] normalization," as recollected by NSC staffer Robert Hormats.[147] Still, the imagination it sparked felt like a reality for many.

The Chinese views of bilateral trade were much more contentious and contradictory. Beijing encouraged Chinese traders and engineers to "make connections with foreign capitalists" and "make friends with foreign technicians," to accelerate economic cooperation.[148] The Chinese, however, couched their policy within the familiar ideological framework. "Because of overproduction, [foreign capitalists] need to find markets abroad to solve difficult problems [at home]," Vice Premier Fang Yi theorized at an internal meeting in late 1978. "The biggest market is China, and they dare to invest capital in China."[149] This tension between the old and new economic thinking signaled trouble ahead, just as China set out to write the long saga of Reform and Opening-Up. At the turn of the 1980s, American businesspeople gaped at labor unrests across China fomented by soaring inequality, which bore ominous resemblance to the Solidarity movement in Poland, and the massive cancellations of technology imports and joint projects—"the great write-off," in the words of sinologist Barry Naughton—aimed at offsetting the unrestrained spending in the previous years.[150] China specialist Kenneth Lieberthal's prediction nonetheless held out in the business community: "Taking everything together, it still seems likely that China will remain committed to modernization and to foreign trade as an indispensable element in the effort."[151]

If Americans were troubled by the fate of China's reform, they were awestruck by the implication of China's rise. "Will China, with one-fourth the world's population, develop into a superpower in the decade ahead, with increased ability to challenge U.S. power and policy?" Warren Phillips, president of Dow Jones, wondered in late 1972.[152] *Washington Post* columnist Robert Samuelson wrote a day after the diplomatic normalization that it "pales" beside China's decision to end "one of the great hibernations of modern history." "Should China follow the development pattern of its Asian neighbors . . . the world economy will have undergone a facelift of unimaginable proportions," he marveled. "And what that will do to world politics, no one knows."[153] Not many businesspeople asked these types of questions, as they saw opportunities, not risks, in the rise of China. One businessman who had just returned from China in the summer of 1977 said it best:

> Reflecting back on China . . . [the two-week trip] has truly been an experience of a lifetime. . . . Is capitalism better than communism for these people? Capitalism tried (with miserable failures) from 1911 to 1949. Now . . . they don't have much but at least they are not starving. But the people live in poverty by our standards and are far from being brought up to our level. China definitely wants to trade with the U.S.—you get the definite idea they consider the U.S. as a better ally than Russia. After being in China I definitely favor establishing diplomatic relations with them and opening up trade. They say the Chinese are the greatest little independent businessmen in the world—start trading with them and who knows what will happen.[154]

Less than a decade after the end of the US embargo, Americans and Chinese were increasingly obsessed with Sino-American trade. They could now hardly imagine a future without it.

Chapter 3

Science

A Miracle Drug

The power of knowledge riveted China to the West since the time of the late sixteenth century Jesuit missionary Matteo Ricci. From the early nineteenth century, American missionaries, from the physician Peter Parker to the translator William Martin to the educator Edward Hume, imported Western science to modernize China. Having unified the country in 1928, the KMT sent hundreds of scholars and students to the United States every year, and these US-trained scientists, upon return, conducted advanced research at universities and laboratories, including the Republic of China's premier institute Academia Sinica. Although the majority of the five thousand Chinese scholars and students stayed in the United States after 1949, more than one-fifth decided to go home, many out of a patriotic calling. Scores of them staffed the newly founded Chinese Academy of Sciences (CAS), including nuclear physicist Deng Jiaxian and aerospace engineer Qian Xuesen, heroes of China's "Two Bombs, One Star"—an atomic bomb (1964), a hydrogen bomb (1967), and a satellite (1970). As historian Zuoyue Wang wrote, those who stayed "transnationalized" American science, and those who returned "Americanized" Chinese science.[1]

American scientists bemoaned the loss of contact with Chinese colleagues, and vocally so after the end of McCarthyism. In late 1964, the Pacific Science Board of the National Academy of Sciences (NAS) held two meetings in New York, in which scholars of humanities and sciences, including the president of the American Council of Learned Societies (ACLS) Frederik Burkhardt, the president of the Asia Society Kenneth Young, and the Harvard sinologist John Lindbeck, discussed the possibilities of exchanging publications, holding conferences, and arranging mutual visits with the Chinese. They urged the NAS to set up "an office to facilitate non-governmental scientific and scholarly relations" with China. Their statement read:

> The lack of an organized and systematic effort on the part of American scientists and scholars may have led to lost opportunities to determine the full range of possibilities for establishing fruitful intellectual encounters between Chinese and Americans. On our side, at least, private individuals and private institutions should not act or fail to act in such ways that the door remains locked and cannot be opened to some acceptable encounter.... Although the Chinese regime may continue to restrict scholarly associations and exchanges, now may be an appropriate time to test the intentions of [Beijing] and to begin probing more fully and continuously than we have her willingness to allow responsible scholarly discourse, even on a limited basis.[2]

Following these recommendations, the NAS, along with the ACLS and the Social Science Research Council, created the Committee on Scholarly Communication with China (CSC) in October 1966.[3] Funded by large foundations like Carnegie, Ford, and Rockefeller, this small band of fewer than twenty scholars prescribed scientific exchanges to cure the ailing US-China relationship.

The CSC embodied the two forces that were reshaping science in America: privatization and globalization. Agitated by the militarization of their profession during the Vietnam War, countless American scientists demanded separation of science and the state, a sentiment that fed into the radical Science for the People movement.[4] In response, US policy makers encouraged private sector investment in research and development, while promoting international cooperation to address transnational issues, most notably environmental problems.[5] Richard Nixon gave a speech at the UN General Assembly in 1970, titled "Global Challenges—The New Dimension in Foreign Affairs." He vowed to "view our preeminence [in basic research] as an asset to be invested in building effective partnerships with other nations to create a world pattern of free sharing of scientific and technological knowledge," something essential to confront global challenges.[6] China should not be left out of this pattern. Science could "transcend national boundaries" and "contribute to international understanding," the NAS president Philip Handler stated. Sino-American scientific exchanges would accelerate "the pace of understanding and the growth of knowledge so that they may sooner be applied for the benefit of all mankind."[7] Scientists were spreading US influence around the world by creating a transnational network of knowledge.

Mao's China was a far cry from the scientists' dreamland that it promised to be. After the Anti-Rightist Campaign of 1957 turned more than three hundred thousand "intellectuals" into "class enemies," the Cultural Revolution further disrupted Chinese science. Peasants, workers, and soldiers with little scientific knowledge wrested control of research institutes across the country, prosecuting, beating, and killing some scientists while sending others to farms and factories to eradicate their "elitism." As the recent scholarship uncovered, "mass science"—mobilizing the masses to conduct scientific experiments—brought new discoveries and innovations to such disciplines as chemistry, entomology, seismology, and meteorology, but heavy emphasis on applied science halted progress in theoretical science, particularly physics and mathematics.[8] Invoking self-reliance, Beijing stopped sending scholars to international conferences, while ignoring the requests by the Americans to visit the Chinese Academy of Sciences, as the CAS itself came under attack by Red Guards.[9] The Science and Technology Association of the People's Republic of China (STA), a mass organization for scholarly exchanges, ceased all activities.[10] Chinese scientists were growing intellectually ravenous. They had hardly begun to restore authority in their universities and laboratories in the early 1970s before they returned to international conferences, attended lectures by foreign visitors, traveled abroad in research missions, and devoured the knowledge of their colleagues.

Sino-American scientific exchanges resumed against this backdrop. In May 1971, a month after Ping-Pong diplomacy, Beijing granted visas to two American biologists and Vietnam War opponents, Arthur Galston of Yale and Ethan Signer of MIT. The two were rushed through research institutes in Beijing and Shanghai in a couple of weeks. After the trip, they gushed about "a lot of important scientific information of which we are unaware," including acupuncture, and touted the "mutual benefit" of scientific exchanges. "Chinese scientists admire us as the world leaders in science and they would be glad to accept advice and help if given in the right way," they commented.[11] Galston and Signer's visit was returned by two delegations from China in the winter of 1972, one of doctors and the other of physicists and engineers, cohosted by the CSC. Bei Shizhang, director of the CAS Institute of Biophysics, who led the latter group, stated at a farewell banquet in San Francisco: "New seeds of friendship have now been sown . . . between the scientists of the two countries. These seeds are sure to grow fast and bear rich fruit."[12] For Bei and his colleagues, the "rich fruit" meant scientific progress.

Around the same time, the CAS vice president Wu Youxun told Alexander Eckstein, vice chairman of the CSC, that the Chinese "should learn from the advanced experience of foreign countries and make it serve China." "Therefore," he said, "exchanges of scientific delegations [with the United States] may be expected to increase in the future."[13]

The "seeds of friendship" soon sprouted, and by the end of the decade, they had grown into something more powerful than friendship. Some China scholars called it a "miracle drug"—a stimulant for Chinese modernization and a tonic for US-China relations. This chapter analyzes this mutation.[14] The first section explores the initial debate over the nature of scientific exchanges, with scientists in both countries searching for substance in their largely symbolic interactions. The second section focuses on a controversy involving social scientists in US delegations, symptomatic of a larger tension between the American and Chinese ideologies of science. The third section focuses on the expansion of scientific exchanges in the late 1970s, when Washington and Beijing deployed science as an important catalyst for China's modernization and normalization of relations. Policy makers in both countries facilitated the germination of the "miracle drug," but it was scientists who watered its growth despite political difficulties.

Scientific Tourism

Galston and Signer blazed a new trail of scientific exchanges with China. Following their trip, dozens of articles about Chinese sciences, particularly medicine, appeared in professional journals, while the Committee on Scholarly Communication received hundreds of letters from scientists hoping to (re)build contact with Chinese colleagues.[15] The Americans were anxious to launch formal exchange programs. In May 1971, the CSC staff secretary Anne Keatley, traveling in China with her husband and the *Wall Street Journal* writer Robert Keatley, met Zhou Enlai and submitted a letter from the National Academy of Sciences, prompting the Chinese Academy of Sciences to embark on "the task of re-establishing the intellectual ties that, for so long, characterized the relations between the scholars of China and of the United States."[16] Zhou assured Keatley that despite "lack of preparation," scholarly exchanges would "surely and gradually increase."[17] Keatley flew to Ottawa that summer and winter to deliver two more similar letters to the Chinese embassy in Canada, but they were left unanswered.[18] Beijing apparently preferred the Federation of American Scientists (FAS), a group with no ties to the government, to the CSC, a sister organization of the government-affiliated NAS. When a FAS delegation toured China in mid-1972, Pan Chuntong, chief of the CAS foreign affairs team, proposed to make the FAS an exclusive host, not a cohost with the CSC, for China's first science delegation.[19] As John Holdridge of the NSC suspected, Beijing's flip-flops probably reflected "divergencies of opinion" over how to conduct scientific exchanges with the United States.[20]

These divergences soon narrowed. The CSC chairman Emil Smith, a biochemist at the University of California, Los Angeles, led the first CSC delegation to China in May 1973 to discuss scientific exchanges with the Science and Technology Association. The STA chairman Zhou Peiyuan, a prominent US-educated physicist and president of Peking University, was tepid nonetheless. He called mutual scholarly visits "good" "in principle," but underscored the lack of diplomatic relations as a serious constraint.[21] The CSC and the STA did agree on exchanging about a dozen groups yearly, but the "government-facilitated" mechanism gave Beijing a veto. Still, the CSC rejoiced at the opportunity to "increase American understanding of Chinse society and values" and "advance toward international scientific cooperation" by "institutionalizing" and "expanding" scholarly exchanges with China. The CSC and the STA would exchange 572 researchers in fifty-seven delegations between 1973 and 1977. Although about three-fourths of American scientists who traveled to China in this period did so through ad hoc arrangements with various Chinese hosts, the CSC-STA line provided the only established channel of scholarly communication.[22]

American and Chinese scientists had asymmetric interests, which made scholarly exchanges imbalanced and embattled from the beginning. The Chinese were narrowly interested in applied science, and more than half of the STA groups visited commercial factories and laboratories using advanced technology in computers, lasers, or hydraulics, while shunning institutions of basic research. The operation reeked of industrial espionage, as some hosts complained. The Chinese wrote lengthy technical reports detailing their findings upon return, which were circulated for public use. The espionage allegation, regardless of its validity, engendered fatigue and misgivings among the hosts, including MIT and Bell Laboratories. One company representative predicted that "the more [Chinese] delegations that come to the U.S., the more difficult it will be to get companies to accept visits" "unless [they] receive something of equivalent value in return." Chary of losing the commercial edge, the National Bureau of Standards even ordered the CSC to nix the industrial automation delegation three days before its arrival in the fall of 1975.²³ The Americans, on the contrary, were broadly interested in fostering cooperation in such fields as biology, seismology, epidemiology, geology, chemistry, and archaeology, while not expecting to learn much new information during their visits. They grumbled that the Chinese escorted them to over a dozen schools, laboratories, and factories in a matter of a few weeks—just like the Chinese proverb "viewing flowers from horseback" (*qi ma guan hua*)—while rejecting further cooperation afterwards. American scientists satirized their experience as "scientific tourism."

The CSC prodded Washington to fix the problem. Smith sent a letter to Henry Kissinger before his November 1973 trip to China, asking the secretary of state to negotiate longer-term research visits "at a high governmental level."²⁴ But the White House had reservations. Aware of Jiang Qing's criticism of Sino-American scientific exchanges, NSC staffer Richard Solomon had warned Kissinger in the previous summer that exchange programs involving "China's scientific and academic communities" might be adding to Zhou Enlai's "political vulnerability." Solomon promised to make the CSC "sensitized to the larger interest that is being served by exchange programs" and "discourage any uncoordinated approaches" to Beijing—but his words failed to sway the CSC, which believed that advancing scientific exchanges could assist Zhou.²⁵ During Kissinger's visit, Arthur Hummel, acting assistant secretary of state for East Asian and Pacific affairs, did propose longer-term visits in agricultural research, earth resources surveying, and language study to Lin Ping, director of the Foreign Ministry's American and Oceanic Affairs Department. "This will be possible," Lin replied flippantly, "once the conditions are right."²⁶ The message was clear: The conditions were not right. In the summer of 1974, Qian Dayong, political counselor at the Chinese Liaison Office, told Alexander Eckstein that "the only difficulty" in scientific exchanges was that the Americans were "pressing us for longer term exchanges." "This is not practical and possible at the present time," he stated.²⁷

Chinese officials proved less unrelenting toward their compatriots. Chinese American physicists Yang Zhenning (Chen-Ning Yang) and Li Zhengdao (Tsung-Dao Lee), the 1957 Nobel Prize laureates at Stony Brook University and Columbia University, returned home in July 1971 and September 1972, respectively, for the first time since they had left China in 1946. Yang and Li, like many of their colleagues, praised China's scientific achievements, extolled the "serve the people" ethic among Chinese scientists, and promoted public interest in China through talks and writings.²⁸ Yang and Li were different from most foreign-national scientists visiting China, because they could make their critical voices heard by Chinese leaders. In his talk with Zhou Enlai in July 1972, Yang lamented the neglect of theoretical research and scarcity of international exchanges. The premier nodded in concurrence and forwarded his suggestions to Zhou Peiyuan, who did not fail to understand what was expected of him.[29] That October, the STA chairman penned a controversial article in the *Guangming Daily*, urging scientists around the country to strengthen theoretical research. "Science (*li*) and engineering (*gong*), applied and theoretical, both need to be emphasized," it read. "We should not focus on one and neglect the other."[30] Li made similar points in May 1974. After visiting Fudan University in Shanghai, he argued that China should pay more attention to basic research and nurture young talent for theoretical science. Li later met Premier Zhou Enlai, Vice Premier Deng Xiaoping, and Chairman Mao Zedong, and his words mesmerized them all.[31] Out of nationalism and internationalism, Yang and Li made themselves China's most influential science advisers at the time (see fig. 3.1).

Yang Zhenning, Li Zhengdao, and hundreds of other Chinese American scientists electrified their colleagues in China, still suffering from the shackles of the Cultural Revolution. Unlike other Americans, they were often

Figure 3.1. Yang Zhenning (right) discusses science policy with Mao Zedong (center right), Zhou Peiyuan (center left), and Zhou Enlai (left) in Beijing, July 17, 1973. Courtesy of the CN Yang Archive, the Chinese University of Hong Kong.

allowed to spend months in research institutes, hold many lectures, work with local scholars, and sometimes coauthor research papers in Chinese journals.[32] Yang, for instance, collaborated with Fudan mathematician Gu Chaohao for about ten days in 1974, publishing articles in *Fudan Journal* and the CAS's *Scientia Sinica*. He even invited Gu to Stony Brook University as a visiting scholar, an offer that would materialize in five years.[33] Chinese Americans rekindled Chinese passion for theoretical research, particularly in high energy physics, owing much to Yang and Li. Yang—who invited three Chinese scientists to a high energy physics conference in New York in 1973, the first Chinese attendance at a scholarly conference in the United States—detected "profound changes of outlook" in physics and mathematics in China, caused by the "stimulation" of "better up-to-date knowledge of developments abroad." He noticed that while "the majority of the Chinese population" supported Sino-American exchanges, scientists and engineers showed greater enthusiasm due to "the observation that communication with the United States is beneficial to Chinese development in science and technology."[34] As Ren Zhigong (Chih-Kung Jen), a noted physicist at Johns Hopkins University and frequent traveler to China, wrote in late 1975, there was "a slow revival of interest in basic science studies."[35]

Ren's comment reflected Deng Xiaoping's reform of the Chinese Academy of Sciences that year. Based on the vice premier's conviction that "the Academy of Sciences is an Academy of Sciences, not an Academy of Cabbage," the CAS's ten-year development plan drafted in March 1975 foregrounded the two agendas that the academy had been promoting since the summer of 1972: balanced investment in applied and theoretical research, and scientific exchanges with developed countries.[36] That July, Deng tasked Hu Yaobang, vice president of the CAS, with consulting the academy staff to write a blueprint for an overhaul, which Hu and other officials like Hua Guofeng completed in August. As summer turned into fall, the vice premier and his aide Hu Qiaomu studied and revised Hu Yaobang's report. On September 26, Deng finished drafting "The Outline Report on the Work of the Academy of Sciences." It stipulated: "There is no denying that, compared both with the requirements of socialist construction and with the advanced levels in the world, the current strength and level of scientific research in our country lag considerably behind." One way to "catch up" with the world was to "develop basic science so as to lay a solid theoretical foundation."[37] Deng was even more outspoken in a private conversation with Hu Yaobang. He criticized political commitments imposed on scientists as the "largest waste" "drawing back" China's scientific standard and went on to insulate science from class struggle: "Science and technology are a productive force, and scientists are workers."[38]

The Gang of Four took umbrage at Deng's science reform. In *Peking Review*, Zhang Chunqiao denounced it as a sign of "bourgeois restoration," which would prompt scientists to "scramble for fame and gain" as they allegedly did before 1949. Deng was trying to engineer a revisionist China, raged Zhang, where "the satellites went up to the sky while the red flag fell to the ground."[39] After Deng's purge in April 1976, the "Outline Report," like the twenty-point economic reform, was labeled a "poisonous weed" and reviled by all, including a handful of the Gang's followers in the CAS—although "the resistance" against these figures was reportedly "very strong."[40] Scholarly exchanges once again became a risky business. At a June 1976 symposium of science and technology centers nationwide, a welding technician at an oil refinery mill in Shanghai lambasted Deng and his associates, who "only cherish foreigners, foreign equipment, and foreign methods." "We should not blindly worship foreigners," he thundered.[41]

The fate of the "Outline Report" paralleled the CSC's fleeting hope to scrap "scientific tourism." When the first STA delegation visited the United States in September 1975, Zhu Yonghang, the vice chief of the CAS's foreign affairs team, remarked that the STA would soon be able to fulfill the CSC's request for longer stays at fewer sites.[42] Encouraged, the CSC sent another letter to Kissinger before Gerald Ford's trip to China that December, arguing that exchange programs "should be expanded to include longer visits and more in-depth programs."[43] The secretary of state was not so sure. By then, he knew that Beijing would "try to sustain the relationship at its current level by limiting cultural and scientific exchanges to present levels," due to the stalemate over Taiwan.[44] "Contrary to many of my compatriots," a frustrated Kissinger told Foreign Minister Qiao Guanhua in Beijing, "I believe China lived 2,000 years without cultural contact with America and can live another 2,000 years without contact with America." Qiao retorted, "Logically speaking, the argument about expanding exchanges before normalization is not tenable."[45] The double whammy of the Gang of Four and the Taiwan deadlock bore down on Sino-American scientific exchanges.

American scientists were running out of patience. Adding to the bickering over longer stays, they became dissatisfied with the numeric disparity between the US and Chinese delegations. Between 1972 and 1975, the STA sent twenty groups to the United States, while the CSC sent only fourteen to China, because Beijing refused several proposed groups. The STA justified this disparity by reasoning that the government-facilitated exchanges as a whole, including those administered by other organizations, remained numerically balanced.[46] To the Americans, the logic was flimsy at best, bogus at worst. The CSC sensed mounting discontents among hosting institutions with the lack of Chinese reciprocity.[47] When the STA endorsed only five out of seven US delegations proposed for 1976, the CSC decided to postpone two out of seven Chinese delegations scheduled for that year, to maintain a numeric parity.[48] The State Department bewailed the CSC's decision as "unfortunate." US officials, Kissinger included, deemed it detrimental to the symbolic value of scientific exchanges, which they hoped would camouflage the diplomatic impasse. Scientists, however, pursued substance, not the symbol, in scholarly communication with China. "The symbol is paramount," wrote Mary Bullock, an associate for the CSC, "but the symbol lacks substance."[49]

The CSC remained confident, though, that they would soon find substance. Frank Press, an MIT geophysicist and the new CSC chairman, gave a cheerful speech at an American Philosophical Society's symposium in October 1976. While dismissing "scientific tourism" as "superficial," he envisioned that China would eventually accept substantive exchanges with the United States. "There are 900 million Chinese people with a government interested in scientific and technological development," Press stated. "They certainly will soon operate at world levels in many fields. They need access to our universities and laboratories to proceed efficiently with their development." He saw "strong motivations for both sides," since American scientists were equally eager "to know the new generation of Chinese scientists and to establish friendly relations." Press concluded with an encouraging note: "I believe exchange programs will develop and the years ahead will be exciting ones."[50] Sino-American scientific exchanges remained largely symbolic for a couple more years, limited to cursory tours, guest lectures, and exchanges of journals, books, data, specimens, and plants, but the substance that would accrue once the political barriers were removed kept scientists in both countries committed to a freer flow of knowledge. Still, however, they had to come to terms with each other on a fundamental question: Just how free should it be?

The Social Science Crisis

The scholarly open door animated China scholars in the United States. The CSC-STA scheme now allowed them to study Chinese society and culture in China—not from Taiwan or Hong Kong—through the lens of science. Frederic Wakeman, a leading sinologist at UC Berkeley, commented that participants in scientific exchanges were "perforce exposed to a range of issues and a depth of perception that don't always appear to simple 'tourists' to China."[51] Natural scientists welcomed social scientists into their groups, because social scientists could provide larger sociopolitical context to their discipline-specific findings. Elated by the opportunity previously denied him, Victor Li, a Columbia law professor, wrote that China scholars, "by virtue of their expertise and professional commitment," had "a special role to play in the work of developing better understanding" between the United States and China. "China specialists can, and indeed must . . . apply our special understanding and commitment to influence the course of [bilateral relations]," he avowed.[52]

The CSC repeatedly proposed delegations in humanities and social sciences, in which the Americans could learn most. These requests were also intended to balance out Chinese visitors inundating industrial sites in the United States, thereby allaying the frustration of local hosts. The STA accepted few such delegations, however, since it considered social sciences academically irrelevant and politically dangerous. During the Cultural Revolution, Maoist theorist Chen Boda attacked the social science community in China as "full of ghosts and monsters," asserting that there was "no point" in studying Chinese language and that history was "useless."[53] To add to this perception, the Committee of Concerned Asian Scholars and the Federation of American Scientists tipped the Chinese hosts, perhaps out of professional rivalry, that some established "China experts" in the United States had the CIA's backing.[54] Beijing had no reason to be welcoming toward them. When the ACLS president Frederik Burkhardt extended an invitation to a Daoism conference in Japan in the fall of 1972, the CAS returned a scathing rebuff: "Here we would solemnly warn you that if you dare to play any schemes or tricks, we will certainly smash your dog head."[55] As Zhou Enlai told the CSC leadership in May 1973, social sciences in China were in "a period of struggle, criticism, and transformation." "I have found we need a stage of preparation," the premier faltered. "Perhaps later we can consider [exchange programs in these fields]."[56]

The CSC responded by launching the China Scholar Escort Program. For each natural science delegation, it assigned at least one China scholar, based on disciplinary match, who served as an interpreter, as well as an analyst who informed the group of the sociopolitical background of Chinese science. China scholars jumped at the opportunity. It gave them a "sense of reality" for their research and "a union card" that granted them "personal assurance and public credibility," according to one scholar. "Seeing the system in operation . . . has helped me make real in my mind what I had hitherto approached only through the written world." Upon return, China scholars often spoke at conferences to spread their firsthand observations of Chinese society, and their colleagues consumed them eagerly. John Thomas of the Harvard Institute for International Development, who participated in a seminar on Chinese agriculture, for instance, raved about gaining, "for the first time, a basis for understanding agriculture and rural development in China."[57] China scholars also wrote scholarly articles based on their fieldwork. The *China Quarterly*, a leading journal in Chinese studies, published about fifty "Reports from China" between 1972 and 1979, many of them written by recent scholar escorts.

The STA frowned upon the presence of social scientists in CSC groups. With language ability, expert knowledge, and intellectual curiosity, China specialists often vexed the hosts, consciously or unconsciously, by their bold, brusque, impolite behaviors. When a 1973 delegation in early childhood studies attended the Shanghai Philharmonic Orchestra's concert in Guangzhou, Michigan sociologist Martin King Whyte griped about "too many restrictions" on Western music, including Beethoven, which he knew was banned at the time.[58] Philip Kuhn, a renowned historian at the University of Chicago, who joined the 1974 botany delegation, repeatedly requested meetings with Chinese historians with precarious status, including Zhou Yiliang, who was later accused of supporting the Gang of Four.[59] Roy Hofheinz of Harvard, who accompanied an earthquake delegation around the same time, took numerous photographs of what the Chinese considered embarrassing sights, including a sign in Beijing saying—accurately—"Peking Man's bones were lost by Americans."[60] Nearly denied a visa due to his alleged acts of espionage in 1945, Frederick Mote of Princeton, a "sly" escort to the 1974 linguistics delegation with keen interest in the Criticize Lin, Criticize Confucius Campaign, submitted two letters of self-defense, both returned to him by the hosts.[61] The STA remained patient with social scientists despite their faux pas. During the STA's September 1975 visit to the United States, Zhu Yonghang accentuated the difficulties stemming from special arrangements necessitated by China scholars. His tone was calm nonetheless, according to the CSC staff director Anne Keatley, as if to say "see what we've done for you lately," instead of "this has got to stop."[62] The STA chairman Zhou Peiyuan even held out hope for US delegations in Chinese studies, stating that Chinese scholars were beginning to engage in "new activities" in social sciences.[63]

Then came the shocker. In June 1976, the counselors at the Chinese Liaison Office Xie Qimei and Cha Peixin submitted to Keatley a fuming statement by the STA regarding two China historians, Lloyd Eastman of the University of Illinois and Ramon Myers of the Hoover Institution, who had both accompanied a wheat studies delegation the last month. It charged that they "openly engaged in political pronouncements against us" and "attacked leading members of our central committee, including even Chairman Mao." "They have seriously hurt the feelings of the Chinese people," the statement blasted. "We feel the utmost indignation." The STA proclaimed that the incident rendered it "difficult" to accept "such non-specialized personnel" in natural science groups in the future.[64] Eastman and Myers brushed off these allegations. A Chinese report did mention their provocative attitudes, but nothing amounting to an assault on Mao.[65] A couple of incidents in Shanghai, the Gang of Four's bastion, stuck in Eastman's head nonetheless. When a local guide asked him to compare Taiwan with the mainland, he candidly described the higher living standard in Taiwan.[66] On another occasion, Eastman was ambushed by local cadres who riddled him with sensitive questions "in an exceedingly pushy way," which he felt "terribly irritating and exhausting."[67] Keatley and other CSC members gathered that it was a ploy to kill the China Scholar Escort Program. Frank Press responded to the STA's statement in "a very low key way," offering a brief apology without acknowledging its accusations.[68] It worked, and hardly a further word was heard from the STA on the matter.

The controversy lingered into the fall, however. Soon after the Eastman-Myers incident, William Skinner, a Stanford anthropologist, withdrew from a steroid chemistry delegation scheduled in September. Having been expelled from China after the 1950 Communist takeover of Sichuan, Skinner had no stomach to be a "test case" on the heels of the June incident. David M. Lampton of the Ohio State University, a young expert on China's health care system, filled in for him as an "unsullied" scholar escort.[69] In August, Cha Peixin called CSC staffer Patricia Tsuchitani to deliver a new message from the STA: Since Lampton's expertise was "obviously different" from the group's focus, it could not accept him unless he served as a full-time interpreter. The Americans choked. Not only was Lampton a specialist on China's natural science policy, he was also hardly the first social scientist to accompany a natural science delegation. Most recently, the UCLA sociologist Ralph Turner, who chaired a major NAS study on earthquake prediction, had escorted an earthquake delegation that June. If Turner qualified, so did Lampton. Keatley deemed the STA's request "unacceptable" and advised the CSC leadership to cancel the entire group should Lampton be excluded.[70] The heated case came to a strange close a couple of weeks later. Keatley designated Lampton as an interpreter as demanded, but the STA prepared two interpreters of its own.[71] In October 1976, the steroid chemistry group, Lampton included, toured China without a hitch, as the first CSC delegation after Mao's death. Tsuchitani concluded that the STA, in essence, acquiesced to the scholar escorts.[72]

The feud over social scientists was no petty squabble. The timing of the two incidents implied, albeit without evidence, that the Gang of Four and their stooges contrived them to obstruct US-China relations. At a deeper level, however, lay a fundamental problem embedded in scholarly exchanges—that is, the Americans and Chinese had different ideas on science. The CSC pursued an ideal of free exchange of knowledge. Scientists should have individual autonomy in undertaking research and communicating ideas without government intervention. The STA demurred, since it viewed science as a business of the state, not individuals. Scientists can conduct themselves only within the confines set by the state. When the two ideas met, they clashed. In late 1975, the Foreign Ministry and the Foreign Trade Ministry warned that US agencies in Hong Kong orchestrated "cultural penetration" against China by sending the CAS, mass organizations, and Chinese universities books and periodicals that touted the political and economic "superiority" of the American system. The State Council also maintained that "class enemies at home and abroad" engaged in "sabotage, espionage, and corruption" against China by importing foreign publications. As a result, all foreign materials addressed to individuals were confiscated by customs, and the members of Chinese delegations overseas were prohibited from bringing back social science publications, except those published in Hong Kong and Macau and those written by communist organizations abroad.[73] The ideological chasm between American science and Chinese science underlay the social science crisis of 1976—and it would never quite disappear, even after normalization of relations.

The arrest of the Gang of Four in October 1976 seemed to usher in a sea change. As the crusade against them swept across the country, scientists catalogued their wrongdoings. Zhou Peiyuan wrote that the Gang had attacked theoretical research despite Mao's endorsement of Yang Zhenning and Li Zhengdao's suggestions, while the *People's Daily* implicated them in hundreds of thousands of deaths caused by the magnitude 7.6 earthquake that hit

Tangshan, Hebei, on July 28, 1976.[74] Peking Radio was now loudly beating the drum for theoretical research, and in early 1978, *Goldbach's Conjecture*, novelist Xu Chi's biography of the mathematician Chen Jingrun, who, by dint of hard work, published world-class research on the eponymous conjecture during the Cultural Revolution, made him a national hero. Scientists openly called into question the philosophy of "mass science." At a CAS forum in March 1977, Yan Jici, an eminent French-trained physicist, stated that scientists "must apply themselves to their special fields of study if they are to make any contributions at all." "What's wrong with being a specialist?" he boomed. "We should strive to be specialists, or better still authorities."[75] No longer a "poisonous weed," Deng Xiaoping's "Outline Report" was revived as "a sweet flower" and adopted as an official policy in June 1977, a month before the comeback of its author.[76]

It was time to bury "scientific tourism." In June 1977, the CSC leadership paid its second visit to China since 1973 and submitted a series of requests to the STA, including student exchanges, lecture tours, and one-month stays at fewer sites. While valuing these proposals "in principle," Zhu Yonghang told Mary Bullock, now a staff director at the CSC, that "scientific tourism" was more appropriate before normalization of relations. Zhou Peiyuan also remarked that one-month visits to fewer sites were "difficult to implement concretely," as long as the "three principles" on Taiwan remained unfulfilled. Miffed, the NAS president Philip Handler threatened to veto Chinese delegations in advanced technology should the Chinese maintain their stance, but the STA chairman remained "stiff and uncompromising." "The [Chinese] tone was negative, and our reaction one of general dismay and even hopelessness," recollected Wakeman, who attended the meeting. "Whatever scientific and technical promise the exchanges may hold for the Chinese, foreign policy considerations remain paramount."[77] Zhou was apparently "not a scientist being used as a tool," but "a hard line member of [the] upper establishment."[78] He wouldn't budge, reasoned Handler, unless Secretary of State Cyrus Vance made headway on the Taiwan question in his upcoming visit to China that August. In a letter to Vance, Handler explained his "clear impression" that with "some improvement" in bilateral relations, "commensurate modification and expansion of the exchange program might become possible."[79] To his disappointment, Deng Xiaoping later censured Vance's position on Taiwan as a "retreat" from his predecessor's.[80]

The ground was shifting slowly, though. At five universities and twenty-five research institutes the CSC visited in June 1977, Chinese scientists, who were sitting quietly in the back seats during the meetings just a few years before, had grown "more relaxed, more outspoken, and direct," according to Bullock. It was "a real change of mood," set off by the renewed vigor for the "four modernizations."[81] Contrary to Zhou Peiyuan's snub, Chinese scientists began later that year to discuss long-term research collaboration with American colleagues and organize more seminars and lectures with them.[82] All this heralded a paradigm shift—from an old system, in which science was part of the struggle against class enemies, to a new system, in which science was a common endeavor of humanity. Scientists could now pursue freer exchanges of ideas with foreigners to facilitate modernization, without violating party canons such as self-reliance. A "renaissance" of science was on the rise in China, the CSC reported.[83]

Toward the Spring of Science

Deng Xiaoping was the patron of the renaissance. In early August 1977, just a couple of weeks after his late July rehabilitation, the vice premier chaired a series of meetings on science and education, in which he claimed that science should be "the forerunner" of modernization. "There is little scientific research now," he grunted. "We should let scientists do research."[84] Following this instruction, the CAS formulated the basic science development plan that September, setting specific goals for 1985 in seven natural science disciplines. It summarized that as "a developing socialist country," China should "strengthen basic scientific research" through foreign exchanges, so that "a substantial portion" of Chinese science could "catch up with the world's modern standards" by the end of the century.[85] To enshrine this goal in China's national agenda, Deng whipped up a propaganda campaign for the National Science Conference, scheduled for the next spring. In August 1977, the conference preparation team led by the CAS vice president Fang Yi instructed schools, factories, and communes to organize events to celebrate science and technology.[86] Youth was the prime target. Elementary and secondary schools in Shanghai, for instance, held a "science and technology week" that November, in which students attended lectures, experiments, and excursions with professional scientists to nurture a sense of mission for the "four modernizations."[87] Everyone knew that something important was going to happen.

On March 18, 1978, six thousand scientists and officials from across the nation gathered at the Great Hall of the People to attend the largest science conference in Chinese history, which lasted for two weeks. Due partly to the propaganda efforts, the conference received from the public more than five thousand letters, hundreds of books and articles, and even secret recipes for traditional Chinese medicine.[88] In an incessant flow of speeches, Hua Guofeng famously pledged to "enhance the standard of scientific culture of the entire Chinese population."[89] Nothing stood out more than Deng's opening speech, however. Guo Rifang, a CAS staffer who assisted the vice premier in the preparation of this speech, remembered that although one CCP Central Committee member criticized the "low" "Marxist-Leninist quality" of the original draft, the political wordsmith peremptorily told him not to "change a single word."[90] In a high-pitched voice, Deng not only endorsed scientific cooperation with foreign countries, but also proclaimed, this time openly, that science was a "productive force," and scientists were "workers"—a statement that lifted the class stigma that had been thrust on intellectuals since 1949.[91] The entire floor was on fire. Some participants said in relief: "From now on, we can work freely."[92] When the conference ended, Chinese science had transfigured into a practical tool for modernization, separate from politics. At the closing ceremony, Guo Moruo, the aging president of CAS, encouraged the exuberant audience to embrace "the spring of science."[93]

Chinese scientists basked in the spring warmth. After the National Science Conference, scholars began to voice their "fatigue" over the requirement to devote one-sixth of their working time to political activities, asserting that after a decade of "darkness and dilapidation," Chinese science "should develop now." "Time is valuable," they snapped. When cadres at research institutes asked scientists to write a political report, many of them did so pro forma, with a quick retort: "Please don't ask me next time." Cadres reported a sense of "helplessness," as scientists spent more and more time emulating the mathematician Chen Jingrun and less and less beating the dead horse that was the Gang of Four. Some even took to flouting the official line on politics and ideology, averring that they "dread" another Cultural Revolution and that capitalism had "some superiority" over socialism.[94] "Red science"—the idea that scientists should be "both red and expert"—was moribund, and they no longer had to sacrifice professionalism at the altar of political correctness. It was a time of redemption for millions of intellectuals.

The spring of science portended a summer of scholarly exchanges. In his October 1977 conversation with Charles Yost, a scholar-diplomat at Princeton and chairman of the National Committee on US-China Relations, Deng acknowledged "the big gap between China and the advanced countries of the world, especially in science and technology." He hoped to import modern science from the United States as "the common inheritance of mankind," although the scale of scientific exchanges would be "quite different" after normalization of relations.[95] At the beginning of 1978, Chinese scientists began substantive correspondence with American colleagues on a personal basis, exchanging papers, data, and charts.[96] Soon, a growing number of Chinese scholars traveled to the United States by invitation of universities, scholarly associations, and professional societies, while American scientists, Chinese Americans in particular, were hosted by an increasingly diverse array of organizations in China, "with little central coordination."[97] "In spite of the continuing absence of formal diplomatic ties, there are many signs that indicate that we are entering a period of new openness in Sino-American scholarly relations," Mary Bullock enthused. "New institutional patterns may emerge."[98]

Beijing's unbridled ambition for scientific modernization alerted American scholars and policy makers. In May 1978, Roy Hofheinz, Dwight Perkins, and Lucian Pye told Samuel Huntington, a Harvard scholar now at the NSC, that Chinese leaders worshipped modern science as a "miracle drug," which would "effect great results" once imported from France, West Germany, Japan, and the United States, without recognizing "the need to have scientific processes take root in their institutions and become self-generating." "Hence," they predicted, "the results of the importation of Western science are likely to be disappointing."[99] The CIA concurred, calling Beijing's "exceedingly ambitious" science development plan "a kind of Chinese Christmas list."[100] As charged, the Chinese coveted modern science as a cure for their self-admitted backwardness at the dawn of the reform era. They realized, however, that it was prolonged medication, not an instant remedy, and their writings and speeches hammered home the importance of Sinicizing Western science. The medication should start now. By declaring science devoid of "class nature," Deng legitimized foreign scientific cooperation and unleashed scientists to hunt down the "miracle drug."[101]

The Carter administration dangled the "miracle drug" to entice the Chinese into strategic cooperation. Unlike Kissinger, Zbigniew Brzezinski and Frank Press, now Jimmy Carter's science adviser, recognized substance in scholarly exchanges—as a lever to tilt bilateral relations against Moscow. They believed that American scientists should explore the "very great" potential of scientific cooperation with China, which would serve "our national interest."[102] In July 1978, Press himself led a delegation of fourteen top science officials to Beijing, to send "an immediate and strong message to the Soviet Union."[103] He submitted a broad proposal for longer-term exchanges, intensive seminars, training programs, and joint projects involving such government agencies as the National Aeronautics and Space Administration,

Figure 3.2. Deng Xiaoping and Frank Press discuss science and technology cooperation in Beijing, July 19, 1978.

the National Science Foundation, and the National Institutes of Health. "The time has come to develop government-to-government contacts in the sciences," Press insisted.[104] Deng's eyes lit up, as he latched onto the chance to learn from the country "in the forefront of science and technology in the world." "We would like to invite more scientists and technicians and engineers and scholars [from the United States] to help us for longer periods and . . . in a wider scope," he pleaded. "We would like to ask all of you present to give us your help" (see fig. 3.2).[105] That October, a Policy Review Committee chaired by Press formulated concrete action plans for scientific cooperation, aimed at "exerting influence on [China's] future domestic and international orientation and, perhaps, moderating Soviet foreign policy conduct."[106] Three weeks later, Presidential Directive 43 set cooperation in energy, education, space, agriculture, medicine, geoscience, and commerce as an official US strategy toward China.[107]

Never had scientific exchanges fared so prominently in US-China relations. When Mary Bullock visited China in August 1978, three weeks after the Press delegation, the CAS representative Feng Yinfu advocated "penetrating" exchanges involving scientists of all generations; the STA representative Huang Kunyi proposed a range of new exchange formats, including mutual visits of senior scholars for a few months, to "turn our scientific tourism into a more substantive exchange program"; and Qian Hao, a staffer at the STA and the recently reestablished State Science and Technology Commission, which coordinated research around the country, indicated interest in a joint symposium by the NAS and the CAS. When Bullock asked if NAS's ties to Taiwan posed any problem, Qian answered, "In the past that was the case, but now I am not entirely sure."[108] That same month, Chinese physicists participated in an international conference on high energy physics in Tokyo, despite Taiwanese attendance. Responding to solicitous reporters, Zhu Hongyuan of the CAS Institute of High Energy Physics intoned three times: "Taiwan is a province of China. As fellow countrymen, we are pleased to attend the same conference."[109] In late 1978, the Science and Technology Commission and the Foreign Ministry set a new guideline for scholarly exchanges with capitalist countries, urging research institutes to arrange visits directly with foreign counterparts, to lift the burden off the embassies. Without noticing the irony, Beijing banned "scientific tourism" by Chinese scholars while abroad.[110]

Sino-American scholarly cooperation hit a milestone in November 1978, when the board of directors of the American Association for the Advancement of Science (AAAS), the largest organization of scientists in the world and the publisher of *Science* journal, toured China for three weeks. Edward David, former science adviser for Nixon, noted: "In [Beijing], the weather is chilly; there is ice on the ponds in the mornings and winter is coming. But there is the air of spring among scientists, teachers, and intellectuals."[111] They were "the happiest people we found in China," the AAAS executive officer William Carey recounted. "They are frank in admitting backwardness, and direct in asking for any help or knowledge that we can share." Peppered with questions during his lectures in Beijing and Shanghai, Carey wrote that although China had "a long way to go to recoup the time and talent lost" during the Cultural Revolution, "the desire and determination to reach parity" with developed countries seemed "clear."[112] The AAAS and the STA reached an agreement on a number of joint programs, including lecture tours, journal exchanges, and collaborative projects to popularize science among the Chinese public. Less than two weeks after the delegation's departure, Washington and Beijing agreed to recognize each other. It seemed like a political side effect of the "miracle drug."

The "period of struggle, criticism, and transformation" for social sciences in China was winding down as well. In May 1977, CAS's Department of

Philosophy and Social Sciences was reorganized into the Chinese Academy of Social Sciences (CASS). Under the leadership of Hu Qiaomu, former editor of the *People's Daily*, the CASS redefined social sciences, once deemed useless and dangerous, as a set of disciplines that could guide modernization. The fall of 1978 was a late spring of social sciences. In September, Hu chaired the preparatory meeting for the National Planning Conference on Philosophy and Social Sciences, scheduled in March 1979. "Without philosophy and social sciences, there would be no scientific socialism or the Chinese Communist Party or the People's Republic of China," Hu declared at Beijing Capital Theater, the meeting venue. Social sciences were "very necessary" for navigating social changes in the reform era, and "their missions were very manifold."[113] In the next month, the CASS published a lengthy article in *Historical Research*, China's premier history journal, which highlighted the potential of social sciences to play an "indispensable part" in the "four modernizations."[114] With the help of foreign scholars, social sciences, economics in particular, would soon become another "miracle drug," on par with natural sciences, which fueled Beijing's market reform in the 1980s.[115]

Social sciences ceased to be a forbidden sanctuary in Sino-American scholarly exchanges. During the CSC's June 1977 visit, the Chinese told Bullock that the CASS would make it "easier to accommodate social science interests [in exchange programs] than in the past."[116] When three sinologists in the delegation—Frederic Wakeman, Roy Hofheinz, and Albert Feuerwerker of the University of Michigan—later toured historical research institutes, Wakeman marveled at the sight of Chinese historians, many of whom had identified history as "the science of class struggles" just three years before, now reading books written by Western scholars. "I am struck by the promise of what is to come," he wrote.[117] Wakeman was probably astounded by what actually came in the spring of 1978, when Beijing allowed several American social scientists, led by Paul Pickowicz of UC San Diego, to conduct an extensive household survey in a small village in Hubei. They interviewed as many as six hundred villagers, the first such undertaking by foreigners since the leftist Swedish scholar Jan Myrdal's research in the early 1960s.[118] Chinese scholars craved Western social sciences. "Many foreigners have now surpassed us in the study of Chinese history," the noted historian Gu Jiegang begrudged. "Now is the time to greatly activate our international academic exchanges."[119]

Sino-American scientific cooperation took off as soon as bilateral relations normalized. On January 31, 1979, Carter and Deng signed a broad science and technology cooperation agreement in Washington, along with separate agreements on high energy physics, agriculture, and space.[120] In the coming months, Washington and Beijing reached agreement after agreement, in environmental sciences, astronomy, botany, chemistry, and paleontology, among other fields, all overseen by the US-China Joint Commission on Scientific and Technological Cooperation.[121] American and Chinese scholars began to fly incessantly across the Pacific. The CSC and the STA launched the Senior Scholar Program that summer, sending fifteen American scholars to Chinese research institutes in the inaugural year, while American scientists, particularly Chinese Americans like Yang Zhenning, Li Zhengdao, and another Nobel Prize–winning physicist Ding Zhaozhong (Samuel C. C. Ting), invited Chinese colleagues to their labs as visiting professors and research students. In the spring of 1979, the veteran diplomat and CASS vice president Huan Xiang led China's first delegation of social scientists to the United States, to survey religion, law, history, management, and international affairs. Bullock was "just stunned" by their interest in these topics, inconceivable in the past.[122] The heavy dose of the "miracle drug" drove the Chinese to want more and more. The prominent sociologist Fei Xiaotong, a member of Huan's group, said: "Our visit actually did nothing but open the door. Even the prelude has not been finished."[123]

Sino-American scholarly exchanges broke so much new ground in 1978 and 1979, but they pale in comparison to what unfolded in the next decade. As the 1979 science and technology agreement was renewed twice in 1984 and 1989, the original three agreements snowballed to 29 protocols—from high energy physics to cancer epidemiology, marine sciences to hydraulic engineering—involving more than two dozen US governmental agencies.[124] Scholarly exchanges in social sciences flourished as well, but Beijing never lowered its guard against American social scientists. In early 1981, when Steven Mosher, an anthropology PhD student at Stanford, who had conducted research in a remote village in Guangdong, published his findings on abortion in a Taiwanese journal, Beijing imposed a temporary moratorium on long-term fieldwork by foreigners.[125] The Chinese ambition for modern science never waned, however, as evident in the colossal science and technology development plan enacted in March 1986, dubbed the 863 Project.[126] By the late 1980s, China had become the largest US partner for science and technology cooperation, and science and technology cooperation had become the largest item among government-to-government programs between the two countries.

US and Chinese policy makers negotiated these developments, but they were predicated on the idea shared by American and Chinese scientists in the 1970s—that scientific exchanges should bring substance to bilateral relations. In a 1976 compendium of essays by policy makers and scholars, Doak Barnett and Albert Feuerwerker wrote that scholarly exchanges between the CSC and the STA provided "tenuous ties" that signaled "common interests" between the United States and China.[127] Scientists in both countries defined the "common interests" in many different ways, from rebuilding scholarly contacts prior to 1949 to incorporating China into global science to accelerating Chinese modernization. So powerful were these interests that many scientists, particularly Chinese, saw scientific cooperation as preordained. Oblivious to the sinuous path in the 1970s, a veteran STA official remarked in 1996: "In the end, the interaction proved to be a natural trend that no one could stop."[128]

American scientists had doubts about that. They remained divided over the morality of aiding the regime with a record of denying freedom of ideas and suppressing countless intellectuals. The division showed itself in the "Letters & Comment" section of *Mechanical Engineering* journal. Hunter Rouse of the University of Iowa led a delegation of engineers to China in the summer of 1974 and published two field reports in that journal the next spring. Lauding Beijing for freeing its people from "starvation, exploitation, venereal and other diseases, beggars and thieves, and rape," Rouse wondered "what Americans would give to be equally free from crime, unemployment, strikes, and inflation!"[129] A verbal brawl broke out. A reader fumed that "all clear thinking engineers" should be "ashamed" of Rouse as a member of the engineering profession. "Does Professor Rouse really believe that a rational American would trade any part of traditional Western freedom and moral norms for the beehive philosophy of Mao and Chou En-lai?"[130] Rouse fired back, attributing the "phobia" to "Shades of Joe McCarthy and John Foster Dulles."[131] So did many others. Defending Rouse's piece, an engineer delineated what the majority of readers seemed to have settled for: "While we must never forget the past, we cannot and must not let the past distort our perception of the present, without an understanding of which no future is possible at all."[132] The fracas shed a small light on the rift that had pervaded American academia since McCarthyism.

The prospect of China's scientific modernization held American scholars spellbound. In 1967, years before the first American and Chinese scientists traveled across the Pacific, Philip Abelson, editor-in-chief of *Science*, wrote that China, with "substantial natural resources and a tremendous human potential," would "soon" become a great power." "Will mainland China then be a menace to all mankind, or will she return to a long tradition of noninterference in the affairs of others?"[133] Abelson's question lingered in the heads of American scientists. Edward David wrote about his "mixed feelings" upon return from China, on the eve of normalization of relations:

> One cannot help but admire and respond positively to the smiling scientists and engineers one meets there. One is startled by the ambitious plans for modernization but dubious about their execution. One sees the common interests of China and the United States, but is concerned [whether] a Chinese course can be held long enough to achieve common objectives. Beyond all this, however, there is no doubt that we have witnessed over the past 6 years a major change on the world scene—the opening of China to the West. The dimensions of the change are not yet fully apparent. As they emerge, we will find that there are new fundamentals. It is significant that the Chinese place science and technology in the forefront of these.[134]

The symbolic "seeds of friendship" sown earlier in the decade had grown into an irresistible "miracle drug." American scientists continued to debate whether it would cure China's backwardness or exacerbate the pathology of communism. Yet such a concern hardly held them back from prescribing it to advance the US-China relationship.

Chapter 4

Education

To "Change China"

Americans and Chinese have always tried to harness the power of education to "change China."[1] With the help of Yale College graduate Yung Wing, the Qing dynasty sent 120 students to the United States as China's first Educational Mission in 1872. A quarter century later, Edmund James, president of the University of Illinois, wrote to President Theodore Roosevelt, "The nation which succeeds in educating the young Chinese of the present generation will be the nation which . . . will reap the largest possible returns in moral, intellectual, and commercial influence." The United States should control China, James asserted, with "the intellectual and spiritual domination of its leaders."[2] Concurring, Roosevelt launched "American-directed reform in China" in 1908, by appropriating the Boxer Rebellion indemnity for a scholarship fund, which brought tens of thousands of Chinese students to US universities in the next four decades.[3] American missionaries and philanthropists, meanwhile, built institutions of modern education in China, with American ideals of liberal education, college autonomy, and academic freedom. Educational ties seemed to be remaking China in the American way, until 1949.

The CCP broke these ties and eviscerated their legacies. It overtook Yale-in-China's Yali School and renamed it "Liberation Middle School"; nationalized Peking Union Medical College, vilifying it as a symbol of US cultural imperialism created by the Rockefeller Foundation; and dismantled Yenching University, presided over by China-born missionary John Leighton Stuart for over a quarter century, with its professors and properties reallocated to Peking University and other institutions. Russians replaced Americans as teachers. Beijing sent more than eight thousand students to the Soviet Union between 1951 and 1964, while reorganizing universities, US-style "elite" institutions for intellectuals, into Soviet-style "mass" institutions for peasants and workers, with the pedagogical focus shifted from theoretical knowledge to practical skills.[4] As higher education spread into the countryside during the Great Leap Forward, the number of universities in China skyrocketed from 229 in 1957 to 1,289 in 1960, and student enrollments from 441,000 to 962,000.[5] The expansion of educated youth fueled the Cultural Revolution, in which students charged teachers, professors, and administrators with deploying examinations as "weapons" to suppress their revolutionary spirit. Red Guards turned the college campus into a battleground, until Mao Zedong dispatched PLA troops in 1968, closed universities in large cities, and sent millions of high school graduates "down to the countryside."

When Chinese universities began to reopen in 1970, "revolution in education" took them by storm. The Science and Education Group in the State Council, China's top education bureaucracy before the restoration of the Ministry of Education in January 1975, abolished entrance examinations and introduced new admission requirements: at least two years of work experience after secondary school and a letter of recommendation from a supervisor, usually reserved for students with peasant-worker-soldier backgrounds. The new university offered a travesty of higher education. The curriculum duration was reduced by one or two years by minimizing courses irrelevant to technical training; students were required to spend months working in communes and factories; and peasants and workers were frequently called up to teach short courses or write new textbooks. Departing from the Chinese pedagogical tradition centered around lectures, university officials experimented with such pragmatic activities as class projects, take-home examinations, and problem-solving tasks. As universities morphed into factories, factories were turned into universities. Following Mao's July 21, 1968, instruction to emulate the training program at Shanghai Machine Tool Factory, factories around the country set up their own schools to spawn technicians and engineers, allegedly better than college graduates. Official college enrollments bounced back from 48,000 in 1970 to 565,000 in 1976. By then, however, 15,000 "July 21 universities," as well as 7,500 "May 7 colleges," local government-run agricultural training camps in the countryside, were teaching over 1.7 million students.[6]

Many Americans were transfixed by the revolution in education. Even before Richard Nixon's visit to China, a booming literature existed on this topic, since scholars and educators found parallels at home. In the early Cold War, particularly after the Sputnik Shock of 1957, American education became increasingly divided between the educational reformer John Dewey's progressive tradition and the rising tide of conservatism, and the division manifested itself along many lines, such as the New Deal, homosexuality, and desegregation. This split was further complicated in the late 1960s by the campus crises caused by antiwar protests and mounting youth problems, especially unemployment.[7] The reformers' solution was to make education more egalitarian and more career-oriented. Transcending the Equal Educational Opportunities Act of 1974, they put into practice a welter of new and old ideas—open door schooling, de-schooling, free school, school without walls, to name a few—to make schools and colleges less elitist and less hierarchical. They also introduced shortened undergraduate curriculums, work-study programs, student-centered classrooms, vocational training, and internships, to make higher education less detached from the real-life needs of college graduates.[8] To the reformers, China seemed like a vast laboratory of progressive ideals, and tours of universities and schools became a signature activity for visitors to China.

Americans flocked to Chinese universities for another purpose: restoration of educational ties. The 1965 Hart-Celler Act abolished the national origins quotas on immigration and cleared the way for countless international students and scholars, particularly Taiwanese, Hong Kongese, and then mainland Chinese, to flood college campuses in the coming decades. Internationalization of higher education and the rising public interest in China combined to ignite a desire for educational exchanges. One study from the early 1970s revealed that most of the 165 universities surveyed favored exchange programs with China.[9] The National Committee on US-China Relations, the Committee on Scholarly Communication with China, the Council on International Educational Exchange, the Institute of International Education, and the National Association for Foreign Student Affairs were all discussing the subject, while the Committee of Concerned Asian Scholars, the American Friends Service Committee, and the Federation of American Scientists submitted concrete proposals when they sent groups to China in the spring of 1972.[10] These proposals did not solicit a positive response, but student exchanges became an important item on the agenda for both educators and policy makers. Richard Solomon of the NSC commented in mid-1972 that student exchanges would promote bilateral contacts "in a sustained and orderly manner."[11]

Not until the end of 1978 did Sino-American student exchanges come into operation. Behind this slow process was a fierce debate on education in China, between egalitarianism and meritocracy, revolution and counterrevolution—a debate on how to "change China." This chapter foregrounds it. The first section focuses on the early negotiations on student exchanges, which mirrored the violent pendulum swings in China's education policy. The second section analyzes the counterrevolution in education, which climaxed after Mao's death, through the lens of a controversial subject: English. The third section examines the agreement on student exchanges between Washington and Beijing, which drove American educators to China's student market and Chinese youth to a new life in the United States. The resumption of student exchanges was more than a diplomatic achievement; it was a collective answer of Americans and Chinese to the question of how to "change China."

Revolution and Counterrevolution in Education

Chinese universities intrigued some and appalled others. Those leaning to the left, many of them supporting education reform at home, tended to eulogize Chinese education, just as John Dewey eulogized Soviet education in the 1920s.[12] The Committee of Concerned Asian Scholars, for instance, waxed lyrical about the system that nurtured "a graduate whose skills can immediately be used in solving society's problems," while hundreds of students, teachers, and administrators who traveled to China wrote a spate of similar panegyrics in sundry media outlets.[13] In contrast, China scholars and other skeptics saw universities as "a disaster area." The National Committee delegation in December 1972 felt "depressed" by their visits to China's leading universities—Peking, Tsinghua, Fudan, and Zhongshan—which they found "open only in token respect." "Young politicos, devoid themselves of education and spouting only ideological jargon," briefed the group, as professors "sat silent . . . and appeared to be cowed, broken men."[14] When they were ventriloquized to speak, they sounded like "the most subdued area of the society, the most controlled and the most cautious."[15] Over a year later, Jan Prybyla of Pennsylvania State University still reported "the impression of paralysis, of a slow and painful digging out from a holocaust."[16]

The prospects for student exchanges seemed dim, but not hopeless. When the National Committee leadership broached the topic on several occasions, it triggered mixed reactions from the Chinese. Vice Foreign Minister Qiao Guanhua gave Alexander Eckstein the soon-to-be standard response: The risk of harassment by Taiwanese students made student exchanges a nonstarter before the opening of the Chinese embassy in the United States. Chinese officials were less stiff in private. Some admitted the benefit of sending students for language training overseas; others promised to study the feasibility of student exchanges, especially after the Vietnam War.[17] During Henry Kissinger's February 1973 visit, Zhang Wenjin, a senior official in the Foreign Ministry, declined Columbia University's offer of English language classes for Chinese students, but left a promising note: "I think in the future our students will eventually go into the U.S., and it is my hope that it will not take a long time."[18] From late 1972 onward, Beijing began sending dozens of students to Britain, France, West Germany, Canada, Australia, and Japan, primarily for language training, while reopening the Beijing Language Institute for international students.[19] Some American students, mostly of Chinese descent, also spent a few weeks to months at Chinese schools through ad hoc arrangements.[20] Soon, US universities were looking into the possibility of educational exchanges, although most of their proposals were turned down.[21]

The National Committee assisted the gradual comeback of US universities to China. In November 1974 and April 1975, it sent out two delegations consisting of presidents and chancellors from dozens of universities and colleges with strong interest in China, including the University of Michigan, Rockefeller University, and Stony Brook University. The goal of these groups was twofold: to evaluate the revolution in education and discuss student exchanges. At Chinese universities, delegation members acknowledged that the emphasis on practical training had "a very familiar ring to an American educator" and seemed "both understandable and laudable." Those who had presided over the campus wars in the late 1960s were particularly impressed. They commended the "law and order" on the Chinese campus and reacted with a twinge of envy to the solidarity between teachers and students, who, despite their disregard of individual talent, looked confident in their ability to modernize the nation.[22] Roger Heyns, former chancellor of UC Berkeley, compared the "sense of common purpose" in China with "a fragmented society of isolated and self-centered individuals" in America: "The Chinese people show very little evidence of the gnawing self-doubts . . . the sheer loss of morale and of confidence in fellow men and in institutions that characterize not only the United States but also much of the Western world."[23]

On balance, however, the American administrators were unflattering in their assessment of the revolution in education. The "damper" on individual talent, bewailed by many Chinese professors in public and private, would prove "very damaging," one trip report read, since it made intellectuals as "incapable" as "the traditional ivory-tower literati."[24] The University of

Michigan president Robben Fleming presented the most fundamental critique in a commencement address at the University of Florida, titled "The Price of Freedom." "Inherent in the Chinese system is an almost complete subjugation of the individual to the needs of the State," he professed. Despite all the shortcomings, "in the last analysis our system respects the wishes of the individual and refrains from imposing a decision by the State." "Freedom has its price," Fleming concluded with an implicit censure of the student protests. "The real price of freedom for an individual is a deep and abiding concern for others, so that freedom is never irresponsible nor callous."[25] The audience was vociferous. According to Fleming's own account, some "self-elected radical students" ridiculed his criticism of China, while "a responsible local citizen" gave him "obvious approval."[26] The American debate over China's revolution in education was a continuation of the smoldering campus politics.

The university delegations found Chinese officials guarded yet reassuring about educational exchanges. When Heyns sounded out Deng Xiaoping on "long-term visits" by American and Chinese teachers in November 1974, the vice premier replied that such visits "can be considered." "In the past, many students went from China to the United States to study," he said, adding a laugh line: "Would you take me as a student?"[27] Heyns later wrote to Kissinger, advocating exchanges of teachers, particularly in Chinese studies.[28] The April 1975 delegation handed a proposal for student and faculty exchanges to Minister of Education Zhou Rongxin, who rejected it on the spot as "premature," but sounded far from dismissive. The United States and China were "friendly nations," he stated, which, by inference, deserved deeper educational ties.[29] Some US officials, including the chief of the US Liaison Office George H. W. Bush, were hopeful that Beijing might accept student exchanges, especially in language training, during Gerald Ford's trip that December.[30] In an October meeting with Philip Habib, assistant secretary of state for East Asian and Pacific affairs, the Foreign Ministry representative Lin Ping nonetheless brushed off the idea as "not practical."[31] That the diplomatic stalemate over Taiwan hindered educational exchanges had become a common knowledge by then, because the Chinese kept giving the cold shoulder to a growing list of US proposals.[32] The Ministry of Education's guideline for hosting university groups was quite simple: "Regarding proposals for scholarly exchanges, we can listen, but make no specific commitment."[33]

The fuzziness in Chinese attitudes toward student exchanges was shaped by the fuzziness in the politics of education. Alarmed by the quality of new college graduates, Zhou Enlai and his allies tried to roll back the revolution in education, particularly in admission and curriculum. Following his July 1972 talk with Yang Zhenning, the premier instructed the Science and Education Group to initiate education reform to nurture talented youth. "This matter cannot be delayed anymore," he bristled.[34] In April 1973, the State Council decreed the restoration of examinations in physics and chemistry as part of the college admission process. Emboldened, more and more universities took to administering "curricular tests" (*wenhua kaoshi*) to measure applicants' literacy and numeracy, and to matriculating secondary school graduates without a stint at communes and factories in such fields as science, foreign language, and fine arts, to maximize their potential.[35] While calling these practices "wrong," the 1974 college admission guideline stipulated that universities should accept new types of students—those from bourgeois backgrounds showing "truly good performance" and those who "can be educated well"—provided that the peasant-worker-soldier students retained "privileged" access to higher education.[36] Deng carried on the education reform in 1975, with the help of Zhou Rongxin, chosen by Zhou Enlai as minister of education over Chi Qun, the leading figure in the Science and Education Group. Bent on restoring entrance examinations in all subjects and reducing vocational training in the curriculum, Zhou Rongxin went on a lecture tour of universities around the country that summer. Everywhere he went, he preached counterrevolution in education.[37]

The Gang of Four and their student underlings fulminated. Viewing the education reform as an assault on their power base, the Gang turned the curricular test on its head. In June 1973, Zhang Tiesheng, a twenty-two-year-old production brigade leader in Liaoning, scored only six points on physics and chemistry. He wrote a litany of complaints on the back of his near-blank test sheet: "Frankly speaking, I cannot accept those leisured bookworms that do not work.... The examinations were monopolized by university nerds like them." A few weeks later, the vice chairman of the Liaoning Provincial Revolutionary Committee Mao Yuanxin, Mao Zedong's nephew and the Gang's ally, ordered the *Liaoning Daily* and the *People's Daily* to publish Zhang's jeremiad as an implicit criticism of Zhou Enlai.[38] Commentaries in support of Zhang appeared in dozens of outlets, including in the CCP's flagship journal *Red Flag*.[39] After the "blank examination incident," Zhang was not only admitted to college, but also elected into the Standing Committee of the Fourth National People's Congress.

In late 1975, Tsinghua University emerged as the next battlefield for the educational civil war. Liu Bing, the CCP's first vice secretary at the university, submitted two letters to Mao Zedong in August and October, blasting Chi Qun and Xie Jingyi, chairman and vice chairman of the university revolutionary committee, for their arrogance and autocracy.[40] Mao was not sympathetic. Having grown wary of Deng's "readjustment" reforms, he responded by ordering Liu to hold campus-wide discussions on education. With the Criticize Deng Campaign flaring up, students quickly turned these discussions into a mass rally against the vice premier. In December, the revolutionary committees at Peking University and Tsinghua University published a joint article in *Red Flag*, titled "The orientation of the revolution in education must not be tampered with." This well-circulated piece railed against Deng and Zhou Rongxin for promoting a "revisionist education path" and brought their reform to a complete halt.[41] Four months later, on April 13, 1976, Zhou Rongxin died after prolonged interrogation at his own Ministry of Education. That was six days after Deng's purge.

The Gang of Four's triumph was tactical, not strategic. The higher education overhaul initiated by Zhou Enlai and accelerated by Deng Xiaoping reverberated at schools around the country, stirring the yearning of countless teachers and students for better education. They became increasingly vocal about their annoyance at campus politics and the long hours required outside the classroom that interfered with their study and research. The Hubei Provincial Bureau of Education, for instance, reported a "reversion" to the "old path" of faculty leadership at Wuhan University, where professors told the workers' propaganda team (*gongxuandui*), a group of cadres that had been overseeing universities since 1968, to "mind their own business" in "politics" and let them "lead" in "research." Li Guoping, chair of the Mathematics Department, bellowed at them: "Is the Mathematic Department yours or mine after all?"[42] Wuhan University was no exception. Professors at other universities, particularly the older generation who abhorred the workers' propaganda teams, openly disobeyed their instructions and touted the importance of theoretical knowledge.[43] An Australian student at Shanghai Normal University named Ann Kent wrote that once higher education was "extensively modified and rationalized" by Deng and Zhou Rongxin, there was "a silent consensus amongst the professional establishment" not to allow the students to wrest back control of universities.[44] Unlike *Red Flag*'s depiction of students as the vanguard of the revolution in education, many of them were just swimming in the changing current. David Zweig, a Canadian student at Peking University, recollected that "there was a change in the air" during the 1975 education reform, and few students opposed it until the Criticize Deng Campaign engulfed the campus.[45] The political typhoon only disguised the waning of the revolution.

As Chinese education vacillated between revolution and counterrevolution, the desire for student exchanges with the United States germinated. Professors who deplored the disorientation of higher education looked to educational exchanges as a way of jump-starting the training of young talents necessary for modernization. In his tour of five Chinese universities in early 1974, the Penn State president John Oswald heard "many expressions of hope that there would be more groups from America."[46] The National Committee's university delegation in November 1974 also noted the "aspiration" of Chinese professors and administrators for longer visits by American and Chinese scholars, and a senior researcher at the Chinese Academy of Sciences told Merle Goldman of Boston University, who accompanied the group, that China should send students to the United States for advanced training.[47] The Chinese probably noticed the dialectic between the revolution in education and student exchanges: Only when Chinese education shifted its priority from the political elites to the intellectual elites could student exchanges be reinstated. Many articles continued to appear in the United States that saluted China's revolution in education, but the writers seemed to have missed this dialectic, surmising that student exchanges would automatically follow when Washington and Beijing worked out the Taiwan problem. In reality, diplomatic recognition and counterrevolution in education were *both* essential for student exchanges. The former seemed far off in the mid-1970s, but the latter did not.

From Revolution to English

For the Chinese who were hoping to restore educational exchanges with the United States, English was an elephant in the room. Granting that the political barriers disappeared in time, language would still hobble Chinese students, who, unlike American students in Taiwan, could only take classes in their home country, few of them taught by foreigners. English was the most frequently taught foreign language in China, especially after the decline of Russian in the early 1960s, but the quality of English education had plummeted. A 1962 report estimated that due to the shrinking number of classes and the declining quality of textbooks, the level of English among high school graduates had fallen three years lower than before 1949.[48] The State

Council decided to reinvest in foreign language education by almost tripling the number of foreign language schools, from fourteen in 1964 to about forty in 1970. This plan was soon scrapped. When foreign language schools resumed enrolling students in the early 1970s, they were tasked with rewriting dictionaries with peasants and workers to eradicate "serious capitalist perspectives" in original editions and assigned to work units in the countryside after graduation, which hardly required any language expertise.[49] One student exclaimed that the purpose of learning a foreign language was "to support the world revolution, definitely not to suck around behind the butt of foreigners!"[50]

Such a hemorrhage of talent could not go on for too long—particularly when Beijing needed more language specialists, including interpreters, translators, and teachers. At the 1971 National Education Work Conference, representatives from foreign language schools made a case for rigorous curriculums, bordering on the battered theory that "foreign language is exceptional" (*waiyu teshu lun*). "This thing called language is not something we can easily master," they pleaded. "We need to work hard for it."[51] Universities in Beijing and Shanghai soon began to invite British, Canadians, and Australians to teach short-term intensive English courses, although they were instructed to use *Peking Review* and other jargon-ridden writings.[52] Regardless of the textbook contents, foreign language turned Chinese students outward. When the US linguistics delegation toured China in the fall of 1974, students at Shaanxi Normal College "were very excited to hear 'real Americans' speak and could not have been warmer and friendlier."[53] Even Mao picked up some English before Nixon's visit—his favorite words were "law and order" and "anti-Mao."[54]

The Gang of Four glowered. Recognizing the tension between foreign language education and the revolution in education, they tried to turn back the tide by sensationalizing the death of a fifteen-year-old female middle school student in Henan, named Zhang Yuqin. In July 1973, she committed suicide after getting rapped on the knuckles by class teacher Yang Tiancheng for writing on the back of her English test: "I am Chinese. Why study English? Even without ABC, I am still a revolutionary."[55] Jiang Qing and her sidekicks like Chi Qun and Xie Jingyi idolized the girl as a young revolutionary martyr, who, just like Zhang Tiesheng, resisted the return of elitism in education, for which foreign language was partially to blame. Yang was sentenced to two years in prison.[56]

Zhang Yuqin's suicide was a tragedy, but the popular enthusiasm for English barely suffered from it. On March 1, 1972, two days after Nixon left

Shanghai, Shanghai People's Radio Station revived an elementary English program, which had stopped since 1966. The program contents were loaded with ideology, and the first lecture called English a "weapon" to fight class enemies around the world. But the listeners—the main targets were engineers and teachers—seemed interested simply in learning the language, often in study groups.[57] In the first week of the program, Shanghai Radio received 417 letters from inside and outside the city, many of them requesting a slower pace of teaching.[58] The first edition English textbook sold one million copies in six months, ten times more than the pre-1966 total, and hundreds of letters continued to inundate Shanghai Radio every month, praising the program yet demanding improvements.[59] Beijing People's Radio Station (Peking Radio) followed Shanghai in broadcasting English lessons, which Zhou Enlai commended as "extremely influential."[60] American travelers often noted the eagerness of Chinese commoners, particularly youth, to study English by listening to the radio.[61] Many of them kept tuning in to English even in the heyday of the Gang of Four, but their motivation to study rose "unprecedentedly high" after the Gang's October 1976 arrest. Between 1977 and early 1978, Shanghai Radio received five thousand letters from the masses of listeners, many of them requesting more beginner lessons. Due to the limited supply, some English enthusiasts waited in line from 3 A.M. to buy the reprinted textbooks.[62] The overwhelming reactions by the listeners implied an orchestrated campaign to promote English, but the ease and speed with which it took hold signified a genuine aspiration among the population to learn the language.

As English came to prime time, the revolution in education came undone. In a November 1976 article in the *Guangming Daily*, the Ministry of Education pilloried Zhang Chunqiao and his Shanghai clique for distorting Mao's teachings and wreaking havoc on Chinese education.[63] Hua Guofeng, however, dragged his feet for months, while universities continued to waste young talents. Deng Xiaoping was fidgeting in exile. "We cannot achieve modernization if we rely on empty talk," he told his close associates in May 1977, pledging to inculcate "respect for knowledge and talent" in the CCP leadership.[64] The vice premier sprang into action soon after his rehabilitation, at an August meeting on science and education, attended by dozens of leading officials and scholars. "This century has twenty-three years left," Deng intoned. "Where should we begin if we were to achieve the four modernizations and catch up with the world's modern standard?" Everyone nodded in assent to his answer: "scientific research and education." "We lack scientific workers now," he chirped. "We should run universities well."[65]

Deng was determined to expel "intellectuals without intellect," who had been dominating universities for years. He later snorted: "Alas, they were such a disaster!"[66]

The result was a sweeping reform of higher education. On October 21, 1977, the first national college entrance examination since 1966 was announced for that December. When the word reached a remote village in Inner Mongolia, a thirty-year-old "sent-down youth" named Ma Bo was so "overjoyed" that he barged out of his cabin and plunged into the snow—and no doubt he was not the only one who did that.[67] There were 5.7 million applicants competing for 273,000 spots, with the average acceptance rate of 4.8 percent. The enormous need for examination papers was met by halting the printing of the fifth volume of *Selected Works of Mao Tse-tung*.[68] A series of other decisions followed in short order—retrenching vocational training, reinforcing theoretical teaching, and assigning human and financial resources to the eighty-eight "key universities." Around the same time, workers' propaganda teams left college campuses; Zhang Tiesheng, the poster child of the revolution in education, was reprimanded as "a committed, red-handed anti-revolutionary"; Yang Tiancheng, who was held responsible for the suicide of his student, was exonerated; and *Red Flag* repudiated Chi Qun's infamous "two estimates"—that the pre-1966 education was bourgeois education and that all those educated before 1966 were bourgeois intellectuals.[69] These developments sealed the fate of the current college students endowed with political capital, who took on new college students armed with intellectual talent in the spring of 1978, and proved no match. British scholar Robin Munro, then at Peking University, wrote that "the ghost of the Cultural Revolution . . . has now at last been laid to rest."[70]

American educators were dumbfounded by the backlash against the revolution in education—China's educational "Thermidor" in David M. Lampton's words.[71] The delegation of US state education leaders, sent by the National Committee days after the announcement of the college entrance examination, gasped at the list of reforms that kept getting longer during their stay. "Even Sputnik didn't prompt such a quick change in American schools," the Massachusetts commissioner of education Gregory Anrig commented. Those in the group who admired the revolution in education chose to discount the reality. In her posttrip speech at the University of Illinois, the assistant secretary of education Mary Frances Berry, a staunch advocate of education reform, extolled what remained of the extreme egalitarianism and pragmatism in Chinese education as "the future of American education." "The Chinese experience may not, in every instance, be directly applicable here. But the direction of their overall policy . . . should, I believe, represent our basic direction."[72]

Berry's speech quickly caught fire. Albert Shanker, head of the American Federation of Teachers, felt "deeply disturbed" by the belief that the United States had "much to learn from a totalitarian system whose educational philosophy is anathema to the free world," while *New York Times* writer William Safire criticized the assistant secretary of education's distaste for examinations, asserting that testing was not "anti-poor," but "pro-student."[73] Berry and other progressives kept calling it "premature" to mourn the death of China's revolution in education, but as *Washington Post* correspondent Jay Matthews wrote, Deng's "cold-blooded rejection of egalitarian rights . . . in favor of test results" was "enough to warm the heart of the most conservative member of an American school board."[74] Many educators in the United States applauded Deng's education reform because they were also leaving government-induced egalitarianism for market-based meritocracy to ward off what they feared as an imminent collapse of higher education—a process consummated by the Reagan administration.[75] China's new education policy seemed like a coda to the prolonged struggle over the future of American education.

In April 1978, a month after the National Science Conference, the National Education Work Conference ushered in the spring of education. In his opening speech before hundreds of officials and educators, Deng identified teachers as "workers" and quoted Mao's words that "the main task of students is to study." He also defended examinations with a fitting analogy: "An examination of product quality is a necessary process to guarantee the level of factory production."[76] Education Minister Liu Xiyao, Deng's right-hand man, urged the attendees to remodel their institutions to extract "excellent talent" from the "broad pool" of the youth. "This is an honorable yet onerous mission given by history," he boomed.[77] Universities across the country, large and small, began to revise curriculums, accept thousands more students, and appropriate funds to renovate research and teaching facilities. The Ministry of Education aimed to produce 4.5 million college graduates between 1978 and 1985, more than a half of the 8.9 million between 1950 and 1978—a goal reached a few years later than expected.[78] When Lawrence Cremin, a leading historian of education at Columbia Teachers College, led another delegation of local education leaders to China that summer, Chinese teachers, professors, and administrators asked for their advice, admitting that the revolution in education was "a radical error of affirmative action."[79] Paul Salmon, executive director of the American Association of

School Administrators, cautioned that the "new educated elite" might destroy all facets of the egalitarian society China had striven to build since 1949.[80] Deng was happy to take that risk.

The Chinese, however, could not extract talent that did not exist, as was the case in foreign language. The December 1977 college entrance examination in English consisted of such simple questions as "Are you a Red Guard?" "What day comes after Sunday?" and "What are the full names of our Party, our country, and our army?"[81] Most students botched them up nonetheless. Only 2.3 percent got passing scores in Shanghai, and nearly half of all test-takers in Xiangyang District, Hubei, turned in a blank test sheet. When many high school graduates turned out to be "foreign language illiterates," who needed to learn the Latin alphabet in college, Chinese officials customarily blamed the Gang of Four for the cumulative product since 1949.[82] At the August 1978 National Forum on Foreign Language Education, attended by 235 representatives from over eighty schools, some veteran teachers lamented that the foreign language skills of high school graduates had declined to a level below first-year middle school students in 1964. Worse still, only 30 percent of middle-aged scholars could read foreign publications, and even fewer could participate in international exchanges. Foreign language, which should wield "great influence" on Chinese modernization, was in fact the weakest link.[83] The forum issued "a few opinions on strengthening foreign language education," which proposed the obvious—building foreign language schools, improving curriculums, and revising teaching materials—but the country was racing against the clock.[84]

The only quick fix was to outsource foreign language education. In addition to relaxing the restrictions on foreign films and novels for educational use, Beijing invited more language instructors from overseas in the late 1970s to train Chinese teachers and students, especially in English.[85] Yet the classroom was too small to educate all the necessary talents in foreign language. In a symbolic move, Beijing stopped jamming the Voice of America (VOA) in October 1978.[86] The CCP Propaganda Department took care to "allow but not encourage" the masses to listen, but many did regardless.[87] Over 2,500 letters of support arrived at VOA's Hong Kong division by the year's end, from as far as Xinjiang.[88] By tuning into VOA, listeners could, for the first time, not only learn English, but also hear news stories from around the world as the Americans told them, without government censorship. It was part of a normative shift. Beijing was now determined to nurture educated youth with professional skills to accelerate modernization, not with political resolve to bolster the peasant-worker-soldier trinity. The Chinese would do anything to achieve that goal—hiring foreign teachers, unjamming foreign radio, or sending students abroad. The counterrevolution in education knocked down one of the two obstacles for student exchanges with the United States.

The Road to Student Exchanges

American hopes for student exchanges bounced back with the rise of Hua Guofeng. In May 1977, Philip Handler and Eleanor Sheldon, presidents of the National Academy of Sciences and the Social Science Research Council, respectively, sent a joint letter to Zhou Peiyuan, chairman of the Science and Technology Association, proposing to negotiate student exchanges as part of broader scholarly cooperation between the two countries. "To achieve fuller understanding between our two peoples requires that we begin to live and study together," it read.[89] A month later, when Handler traveled to China with the delegation of the Committee on Scholarly Communication with China, Zhou and the STA representative Zhu Yonghang reiterated the official line, calling student exchanges "most difficult" before settling the Taiwan problem. The ravages of the revolution in education, Zhou further explained, left few students and scholars who met the "necessary criteria" for study abroad—youth, health, knowledge, and language.[90] Even as the counterrevolution in education unfolded that fall, Zhou never wavered.[91] When a group of US state education leaders toured China, local hosts were instructed to refuse any proposal for student exchanges.[92] As the national security adviser Zbigniew Brzezinski told Jimmy Carter, student exchanges were predicated on diplomatic recognition.[93]

Zhou Peiyuan's rock-hard attitude belied Beijing's ambition to send students abroad, which was rising alongside the political status of Deng Xiaoping, an exponent of student exchanges.[94] At the National Education Planning Forum in November 1977, Vice Education Minister Yong Wentao, Deng's man, proposed to start preparing for student exchanges as "an important component of foreign affairs work."[95] Less than two weeks later, the STA sent a group of senior Western-trained university administrators to the United States, hosted by the National Committee for a month. As this "lively, questioning group" toured universities from coast to coast to survey US higher education, from admission to curriculum, organization to funding, testing methods to job placement, they listened eagerly to school representatives preaching student exchanges.[96] The visit resulted in a detailed report, to be circulated at the spring 1978 National Education Work Conference. It suggested that Beijing send "senior scientific workers" or "talented youth" to the United States, while inviting American scholars to China—without mentioning the Taiwan problem at all.[97] The Ministry of Education was planning to send 1,300 to 1,500 students overseas before 1980 and five thousand before 1985.[98] Deng took exception. At a June 23, 1978, meeting at Tsinghua University, China's top university in science and engineering, the vice premier insisted on "sending tens of thousands [of students], not fewer." It would be "worthwhile" no matter the cost, he bawled. "Even if a hundred out of a thousand students run away . . . we still have nine hundred left."[99] Beijing soon began discussing student exchange agreements with Japan, Britain, France, West Germany, Australia, and Canada, to reach its new goal of sending out three thousand students by the year's end and ten thousand by 1979.[100] The United States was next on the list.

When Brzezinski and Deng agreed to initiate normalization talks in May 1978, the second roadblock to student exchanges was lifted. Then, the STA, the Chinese Academy of Sciences, and Chinese universities moved quickly. When two American scholars—the Harvard biochemist Paul Doty and the MIT chairman Howard Johnson—visited CAS that July, Deputy Secretary General Qin Lisheng proposed exchanges of the most promising young students and scholars.[101] Harvard and MIT set up special committees to work out concrete issues involved in accepting Chinese students, such as admission, language, cultural adaptation, and, most important, "reciprocity" in gaining access to Chinese resources in the social sciences.[102] Also in July, Stanford sent a delegation of security studies scholars, led by sinologists John Lewis and Douglas Murray, who elaborated on the formal exchange proposal Stanford had submitted to the STA that March. Qin welcomed exchanges in "basic sciences" (physics, chemistry, or biology) and "technical sciences" (computer science, semiconductors, or civil engineering), while promising to accept Chinese-speaking American students and scholars to China.[103] It was a small price to pay for American nurturing of Chinese human capital.

Just as Harvard, MIT, and Stanford—closely followed by several others—were setting up their own enterprises in China, US and Chinese policy makers were beginning to negotiate government-sponsored student exchanges.[104] During Frank Press's July visit, the CAS vice president Fang Yi proposed, as part of scientific cooperation, to send five hundred students to the United States by the end of 1979. It was a "pleasant surprise," the chief of the US Liaison Office Leonard Woodcock recounted. "This was completely beyond our expectations . . . Everybody was excited."[105] Deng reaffirmed to Press that he was "in favor of" sending Chinese students to the United States and would likewise "welcome" American students to China. "It might be that we will send more [than five hundred]," he added.[106] Press and Deng agreed that a Chinese delegation would pay a return visit to the United States in the fall to sign a formal agreement on student exchanges.

Washington and Beijing had no time to waste. Upon his return, Press commissioned the National Academy of Sciences and the National Science Foundation (NSF) to write a policy paper on student exchanges, and NAS assigned this task to the Committee on Scholarly Communication with China, which had been contemplating the topic with other governmental and nongovernmental organizations for several months. Their talks had yielded one consensus: The United States should seek "reciprocity" by securing the rights of American students and scholars to receive language training and conduct social science research in China.[107] In late August, the CSC convened a meeting of representatives from twenty-five universities and five educational institutes—of which at least eight were already negotiating with the Chinese—to finalize the policy paper. They blithely believed that the "rich educational ecology" in the United States would accommodate the needs of Chinese students.[108]

The preparation was more hectic in China. On the plus side, student exchanges met little resistance. At a September meeting of diplomats and officials stationed abroad, participants praised Deng and Fang's "unprecedented" decision, contending that sending students to universities with Taiwanese enrollments would *not* constitute "two Chinas." They encouraged Chinese students to mingle with American students, "interact with capitalist society," and "face the world and brave the storm," while discouraging romance as a distraction.[109] On the minus side, English remained an obstacle. When the selection process for study abroad commenced in August, Chinese officials found themselves in a barren field, such that nearly 80 percent of test-takers got failing scores, and the Ministry of Education lowered the passing score for the written test from sixty to fifty points out of a hundred.[110] Beijing rushed to organize English boot camps for hundreds of students as they prepared for the departure.

Zhou Peiyuan came to the United States in October 1978 to finalize the agreement on student exchanges. His delegation, consisting of top scholars and officials, first stopped at San Francisco and Los Angeles to discuss individual deals with UC Berkeley, Stanford, UCLA, and the California Institute of Technology, all of which proved "more than willing" to accept

Chinese students with or without a government agreement. Zhou was emboldened before flying to Washington. At the negotiation table with the NSF director Richard Atkinson, he demanded that Chinese students be separated from Taiwanese students on campus and prohibited from reading newspaper and magazine articles on Taiwan. The "heated and emotional outpouring," unexpected and bewildering for the US side, precipitated "an impasse" and made Atkinson "pessimistic" about the agreement. Zhou, however, was apparently firing what the Chinese termed an "empty cannon." He stopped mentioning Taiwan on the next day and soon signed an informal understanding on student exchanges, which went into the formal agreement on science and technology cooperation on January 31, 1979.[111] It stated that in the initial year, China would send five hundred to seven hundred students to the United States, to be hosted by nearly a hundred institutions, and the United States, under the aegis of the CSC, would send sixty to China. The government of the sending country would provide financial support for the students, which foreshadowed financial trouble for Beijing.[112] What mattered, however, was to send as many students to the United States as fast as possible.

On December 27, 1978, four days before diplomatic normalization came into effect, the first cohort of fifty Chinese students arrived in Washington. All of them were "visiting scholars" in natural sciences, with an average age of forty-one, who had received university education before the Cultural Revolution.[113] By then, some schools—Stanford and UC Berkeley, for example—had already begun to host Chinese students through university-to-university arrangements (see fig. 4.1).[114] These students, and the thousands who followed in the next couple of years, lacked proficiency in language and culture. Some nervous ones asked on the plane whether there were grain coupons (*liangpiao*) in the United States.[115] Ignorance about the foreign land coexisted with fantasy in the minds of Chinese youth itching to get out of China. The state had kept them hog-tied for decades, controlling where they were born, schooled, employed, and likely buried. They wanted to recapture their future when the unreachable star that was America suddenly seemed within their grasp. Hu Chengli, an undergraduate student at Northwestern Polytechnic University, personified this raw desire. He sent a letter to the MIT provost Walter Rosenblith in January 1979, petitioning for a two-year scholarship at the university, hailed in China as the world's number one in science and engineering. Written in "rather elementary" English, as he admitted, Hu's letter evinced a determination to resort to all means available to study in the United States: "Excuse me, sir, can you tell me how

Figure 4.1. Zhu Naigang, Dong Yunmei, Shi Zanxing, Yuan Zhuan, and Ren Shangyuan arrive at Stanford on November 14, 1978, a month and a half before the arrival of the first group of government-funded students. *Stanford Campus Report* 9, no. 9 (1978): 1. Courtesy of Stanford News Service.

much [the tuition is]? All right? Please answer me. I am sorry to trouble you."[116] For the first time in their lives, millions of Hus could dream.

American students seldom felt the same level of hankering for China, but they also yearned to study China on the ground, not from the classroom in Taiwan. In September 1978, the US International Communication Agency, an amalgam of the United States Information Agency and the State Department's Bureau of Educational and Cultural Affairs, designated the CSC to administer the National Program for Advanced Research and Study, to send about a dozen students and scholars to China in early 1979. When the CSC announced the fellowship competition that October, the due date for applications was less than a month away.[117] On February 23, 1979, seven graduate students in Chinese studies—accompanied by John Jamieson of UC Berkeley, the first "Resident Scholar" at the US embassy who oversaw American students in China—arrived in Beijing for testing and placement at Beijing Language Institute (see fig. 4.2). The "confused elation" upon arrival was quickly overtaken by the demands of daily life in China. As one student wrote, the Americans had to adjust to "spartan living" in the freezing winter, as heating and hot water were available only for a few hours a day. They

Figure 4.2. Zhou Peiyuan, John Jamieson, and the first group of US students gather at Beijing International Club, February 24, 1979. Photo by Li Shengnan of Xinhua News Agency.

did not regret coming to China, though. Unlike a few years earlier, international students could freely travel to different cities and roam local streets, riding the world-famous "Forever" bicycles and "rubbing elbows and everything else" on crowded buses.[118] That was exactly what the Americans hoped for. John Pomfret, an undergraduate at Stanford in the second cohort of exchange students, reminisced that he gained "a better idea of what it was like to be Chinese."[119]

Legions of university presidents and chancellors visited China in 1979. By the year's end, Stanford, UC Berkeley, Harvard, MIT, Columbia, UCLA, Stony Brook, Wisconsin, Michigan, and Pittsburg, among others, were exchanging students with Chinese universities. For many schools, it was a long-overdue reunion. Oberlin College, for instance, restored ties with Shanxi Agricultural University and Taiyuan Engineering Institute, descendants of its sister school, Ming County Middle School, which was disbanded in 1951.[120] The Americans were keen on both assisting the "four modernizations" and gaining access to academic resources in China. When the chancellor of UC Berkeley Albert Bowker met Zhou Peiyuan in the spring of 1979 to complete an agreement with Peking University, he expressed his desire, shared by most university administrators, to send out American students in social sciences in return for accepting Chinese students in natural sciences. UC Berkeley professors who accompanied Bowker later visited leading universities in east and south China, including Nanjing, Fudan, and Zhongshan. After meeting junior faculty, these scholars did not mince words: "We think that your education system should not produce such [poor] talents." They proposed that each department at "key universities" send one scholar to the United States every year to narrow the "big gap" between China's outsize ambition for modernization and its (lack of) resources. "Exchanging scholars would be very beneficial," they asserted. "The gap of backwardness might disappear very quickly." The Chinese did not seem offended.[121]

US universities were engaging in global talent competition in China. With the last generation of postwar baby boomers graduating in the next few years, the domestic pool of college students was projected to shrink drastically, adding to the financial trouble created by budget cuts. Similar trends characterized higher education in other developed countries as well.[122] China stood as "the world's last great untapped market . . . for students," as Patrick Maddox and Anne Thurston, sinologists at Harvard and the National Committee, respectively, put it.[123] Far more important than the tuition revenue, Chinese students could also provide high-quality human resources, especially in physics and mathematics. US universities had all but exhausted the human capital of other countries, including Taiwan, from which the best and brightest had fled to the United States in hundreds of thousands in the form of immigration since 1965. Chinese students were the next wave of academic labor force—or what was widely criticized as "brain drain" from developing countries. "Americans' love affair with China continues . . . because the quality of students that come is so high," one professor raved. "These kids come with the sole purpose of study. They do 100 percent—150 percent—of what they're asked to do."[124]

That was because Chinese students were desperate. Constantly mobilized, manipulated, and martyred in the clutches of Mao's China, they finally found a way out in study abroad. English seemed like the passport. In her famous memoir *Life and Death in Shanghai*, Nien Cheng, a former Shell Oil employee who had undergone harsh criticism and torture during the Cultural Revolution, noted "a terrific vogue" of English after the normalization of US-China relations:

> When I went to the public park to join a class for *taijiquan* exercise in the mornings, I saw young people on the benches, on the lawn, and in the pavilions reading English textbooks or spelling English words aloud. The daily English lessons broadcast by the Voice of America became very popular. The young people boldly purchased powerful radio sets and tuned in. . . . As the

government took no action to stop this trend, even people not learning English began to listen openly to the Voice of America broadcasts. To listen to foreign broadcasts had always been taboo in Communist China.... Now people not only listened to the Voice of America but discussed what they heard openly.... Now when I met the schoolchildren who used to yell, "Spy, imperialist spy!" at me, I was greeted with "good morning" or "good afternoon."[125]

The "English fever" was part of the euphoria among urban youth, who embraced study abroad not only because they wanted to modernize the nation, but also because they craved upward mobility. It was a game changer.

Chinese students kept coming in greater torrents. According to the Institute of International Education, the number of Chinese students at US universities, most of them specializing in science and engineering, soared from 1,000 in 1979 to 2,770 in 1980 to 8,140 in 1983, making the United States by far the largest host country.[126] Chinese leaders tried to limit the growing outflow of "self-funded" students, sponsored by families, relatives, and friends, who numbered seven thousand in 1983, but the attempt was soon aborted since Beijing's tight budget necessitated more of them.[127] In 1989, the number of Chinese students reached 33,390, surpassing the pre-1950 total of 30,000, and mainland Chinese replaced Taiwanese as the largest group of international students in the United States. Meanwhile, hundreds of American students and scholars, particularly in the humanities and social sciences, visited Chinese universities every year in the 1980s, although most of them received short-term language training instead of conducting long-term fieldwork. Some US universities went beyond student exchanges and made greater commitments in China, as epitomized by the Hopkins-Nanjing Center for Chinese and American Studies, a pioneering joint educational venture that took off in 1986.[128] China was "the country of the future" for the Johns Hopkins president Steven Muller.[129] And so was the United States for Chinese students and officials.

The restoration of Sino-American student exchanges was a strategic decision made by Washington and Beijing, but it was contoured and conditioned by the American and Chinese debates on education in the 1970s, in which meritocracy trounced egalitarianism. Desiccated by the revolution in education, Chinese students gorged themselves at the trough of new opportunities in the United States. In his bestseller *Chinese Students Encounter America*, author Qian Ning conducted hundreds of interviews to analyze the "study abroad craze" at the turn of the 1980s, when word spread that self-funded students were eligible for study abroad. Even those living in small towns in the countryside set their minds on flying to the United States, to leave behind the "inertia" that beset Chinese education, and to start all over again with a clean slate. "This discovery of the New World was one of the most important events in China in the eighties," wrote Qian. "That generation of China's youth was no less passionate and courageous than [Christopher] Columbus."[130]

Not everyone in the New World welcomed Chinese students. Many conservative lawmakers and university board members questioned the wisdom of training them, particularly in advanced technology. This was where the "change China" mentality kicked in. As Maddox and Thurston argued, based on extensive interviews with school officials, few tried to *make* Chinese students "more like us" as Edmund James insisted in 1906, but many surmised that they would naturally *become* "more like us" as they assimilated to American culture.[131] One university administrator envisioned: "Eventually . . . they have enough exposure to different things [in this country] that their eyes are opened and they are curious." "Just the viewpoint they learn here helps China modernize," a professor who recruited many students from China gushed. "Their viewpoint about Western life, about how research is conducted—all this creates pressure on the government to change."[132] Such was a pipe dream that Americans had subscribed to for many decades. A few thousand students could do little to "change" a stiff, senile behemoth like the Chinese Communist Party, only 4 percent of its forty million membership possessing college degrees in the mid-1980s.[133]

The "change China" rhetoric unnerved Chinese officials nonetheless. They feared what many American educators expected—that exposure to American culture might turn Chinese students into advocates of American values such as freedom, democracy, and individualism. The "Western fever" among urban youth, who fancied Western lifestyle and clothing, seemed to confirm this fear at the dawn of the reform era, when Beijing faced mounting youth problems, a blowback from the Cultural Revolution. School officials tried tirelessly to discredit the appeal of Western culture. A high school principal in Shanghai, who had recently returned from the United States, convened a school assembly to criticize the moral decadence in American society and urged students to learn from the negative example.[134] At a similar gathering at Wuhan University, two professors who had studied in the United States in the 1940s enumerated the failures of American capitalism—rampant unemployment, high prices, rising tuition, astronomical medical bills, or inadequate social welfare.[135] These events conveyed the same message: Only socialism can save China.

It hardly persuaded Chinese students in the United States. According to a Hong Kong newspaper, more than a thousand of them applied for asylum between 1978 and 1981, almost 10 percent of the entire group.[136] With about one-third of Chinese students remaining in the United States after their studies, student exchanges became a double-edged sword for Beijing, which suspected that Washington was plotting "peaceful revolution" (*heping yanbian*) against it by indoctrinating Chinese youth.[137] On the East Coast and the West Coast, CCP representatives tried to police the students by holding regular meetings and hosting periodic visits by government officials, but to little effect.[138] The disarrayed, fractured democracy movement in North America incarnated Beijing's worst nightmare. Thirty-four-year-old Wang Bingzhang, a government-sponsored medical student at McGill University, who founded the Chinese Alliance for Democracy and launched the *China Spring* journal, commented in 1982: "I think that medicine can cure only a few patients; it cannot cure diseases of a nation."[139] When Beijing let loose the Chinese students, they did not stop at studying for the "four modernizations," as instructed. No longer tethered, they went on to engage with the question that would become only more contentious: How to "change China"?

Chapter 5

Tourism

The New Marco Polo

Since a Venetian merchant narrated *The Travels of Marco Polo* in the thirteenth century, travelogues have shaped and reshaped Western views of China. Samuel Wells Williams, one of the first American missionaries to China, pioneered this genre of literature in the United States with the 1848 publication of *The Middle Kingdom*, while Arthur Henderson Smith's *Chinese Characteristics* later became a standard text among Westerners.[1] By the early twentieth century, American newspapers had many correspondents in China, carrying regular news stories on war, famine, and revolution—themes woven into such bestselling novels as Pearl Buck's *The Good Earth* and Alice Tisdale Hobart's *Oil for the Lamps of China*.[2] Yet Americans still relied on travelogues for information that media rarely covered. Journalists Agnes Smedley and Anna Louise Strong, for instance, offered glimpses into the Communist movement in the 1920s and early 1930s, when few Americans foresaw the CCP's rise to prominence.[3] Edgar Snow's *Red Star over China* changed all that in 1937. The first eyewitness account of the CCP's success in Yan'an after the Long March convinced millions of readers, from the United States to Europe to China, to see Mao Zedong as a powerful leader remaking the country from within.[4] By 1949, American journalists were prophesizing a revolution that would echo the world over.[5]

Mao killed American journalism in China. Upon taking power, the CCP promptly ousted most American reporters, forcing the US public to rely on Chinese news agencies, including Xinhua News Agency and Radio Peking, and foreign media such as Reuters (Britain), Agence France-Presse (France), and the *Globe and Mail* (Canada). Beijing left the door ajar, occasionally allowing American "friends"—those with favorable views of the CCP—into its territory and deploying them as a propaganda tool.[6] Edgar Snow and British-American writer Felix Greene were among the best "friends." When they visited a few times in the late 1950s and 1960s, the Chinese took them around the country, feting them, pampering them, and securing their positive impressions of Chinese socialism. Blinded to reality, Snow and Greene bordered on becoming China apologists, producing books and films that masked China's inconvenient truths, including the massive famine during the Great Leap Forward.[7] The American public wanted facts on the ground. When the Eisenhower administration upheld its travel ban in response to Beijing's surprise invitation to eighteen American reporters in August 1956, the *New York Times* and the *Washington Post* editorialized that it should be lifted to ensure "freedom of the press and freedom of knowledge."[8] Their efforts to send correspondents to China never bore fruit, and more than two decades passed without a single American journalist freely reporting from China.

American journalism returned to China with the US table tennis delegation in April 1971. The media coverage of its adventure in Beijing, Shanghai, and Guangzhou whetted the curiosity of Americans, who were traveling internationally in record numbers. When Beijing started to issue hundreds of visas to Americans—while allowing only a small number of Chinese to travel to the United States for family reunions—they used such dramatizers as "pilgrimage" and "odyssey" to capture their excitement and trepidation and delirium for a voyage to terra incognita behind the bamboo curtain. Essayist Susan Sontag poeticized her emotions before her 1973 trip to China: "I am taking one small suitcase only, and neither typewriter nor camera nor tape recorder. Hoping to resist the temptation to bring back any Chinese objects, however shapely, or any souvenirs, however evocative. When I already have so many in my head."[9]

The Chinese Liaison Office was quickly "swamped" with countless visa applications, but most of them were rejected partly due to China's limited capacity to accommodate foreign travelers.[10] In principle, all American visitors to China—the number swelled from several hundred to tens of thousands in a few years—were to be accompanied by English-speaking guides, of whom there were only two hundred at most in late 1973, according to travel writer Susan Dryfoos. In the early 1970s, Beijing allocated about 60 percent of visas to Chinese Americans, many of whom did not need English-speaking guides; 35 percent to those involved in government-facilitated exchange programs; and only 5 percent to the rest—old "friends" and new "friends," leftists and rightists, the politically motivated and the intellectually hungry—who traveled under the broad category of "tourists."[11] Most of them were not "tourists" in the dictionary sense, who traveled abroad to spend holidays. Rather, they were journalists, professional and amateur, for they visited China to understand the alien society, some more critically than others, and share their findings at home. They were new Marco Polos in Mao's Middle Kingdom.

The Chinese were ready to welcome back foreigners in the early 1970s, after years of xenophobia. Beijing began to accept tourist groups from the Soviet Union and other socialist countries in 1956, and later from some non-communist countries, to expand political influence and earn foreign currency, but these tours ground to a halt with the onset of the Cultural Revolution. Red Guards denounced China Travel Service (CTS) and China International Travel Service (CITS), state-owned tour operators, for their "foreign connections," while taking hostage Canadian, French, Japanese, Norwegian, and Swedish journalists to block their dispatches.[12] The turmoil subsided only in 1970, when Zhou Enlai validated tourism as "a political mission" to gain "sympathy," but not "foreign currency," from foreigners. The March 1971 National Tourism Work Conference concluded that tourism was "part of foreign affairs work," aimed at shoring up China's international image. Beijing began to reopen more and more sites and cities to foreigners, including the Forbidden City (1971), the Yan'an Revolutionary Memorial Hall (1973), and Guilin (1973). Between 1971 and 1977, the number of foreigners admitted into China through the China Tourism Enterprise Administration (CTEA), a government agency that ran CTS and CITS, increased twenty-fold from 1,600 to 32,000, and its foreign currency earnings almost 120-fold from $119,000 to $14 million.[13] For Chinese leaders, tourism was as much a political mission as it was an economic mission.

Historians have explored American tourism, particularly in Europe and Latin America, as part of US cultural diplomacy, often criticized as intended at "Americanization" or "cultural imperialism."[14] Quite the contrary, American tourism in China was part of *Chinese* cultural diplomacy, which capitalized on what historian Judy Tzu-Chun Wu called "radical orientalism," a tendency among left-leaning Americans who "idealized the East and denigrated the West."[15] This chapter concerns the formation and unraveling of this tendency in American perceptions of China. The first part analyzes Beijing's tourism policy in the early and mid-1970s, which simultaneously pursued propaganda and profit. The second part examines the literature of

American travelogues in China, in which quixotic narratives gave way to critical ones as Beijing tightened its grip on American visitors. The third part explores a turnabout in China's tourism policy in the late 1970s, when Deng Xiaoping promoted commercial tourism, and Americans reimagined China as a tourist destination. Beijing tried to control how Americans thought about China by manipulating the new Marco Polos. It failed, because Americans—and many Chinese as well—had their own agendas.

Politics and Economics of Chinese Tourism

"To see is to believe" (*bai wen bu ru yi jian*) encapsulated the essence of Beijing's tourism policy. Instead of tooting their own horn, Chinese hosts were instructed to exhibit specific aspects of workaday life to convert a foreigner into a "volunteer propagandist" of Chinese socialism.[16] "We do not request any foreigner to accept the thinking of the Chinese people," Mao avowed in 1970. "If they see how many wrong lines our Party had to correct before gradually walking up to the right path . . . they should be able to understand."[17] In China, travelers were most often hosted by CTS, CITS, the Chinese People's Institute of Foreign Affairs (CPIFA), and the Chinese People's Association for Friendship with Foreign Countries (CPAFFC), depending on their rank and interest.[18] These organizations issued a propaganda directive to be studied and implemented by foreign affairs teams at local host units, varying from communes to factories, universities to hospitals, women's federations to model prisons, Children's Palaces (childcare centers) to May Seventh Cadre Schools (reeducation labor camps). Foreigners were yoked together in small groups, shackled by inflexible itineraries, and chaperoned by Chinese guides almost anywhere, anytime. Following Mao's slogan "remember the past bitterness and contrast it with the present sweetness," these guides juxtaposed the CCP's post-1949 achievements to the KMT's pre-1949 disasters, the post-1966 breakthroughs to the pre-1966 stalemates. In doing so, they tried to nudge foreigners into a voluntary, not forced, conclusion that the CCP made China better.

Beijing's socialist propaganda targeted not only foreigners, but also the Chinese masses. Commoners from all walks of life regularly received training to master the art of being "neither humble nor arrogant" (*bu bei bu kang*) in receiving foreigners, a process designed to rekindle their revolutionary vigor. The Foreign Affairs Office of the Shaanxi Provincial Revolutionary Committee, which escorted scores of tourist groups every year to the ancient capital of

Xi'an and the revolutionary capital of Yan'an, stated that their work was not a "burden," but a "promoting factor" for domestic politics.[19] Socialist propaganda even penetrated into the Chinese household. In one family in Shanghai, home lessons on Mao Zedong Thought—a family pastime often flaunted to foreigners—convinced a young boy to join the Little Red Guards. When the study session stalled for two weeks, he complained to his mother, "We should do well what we show to foreign guests."[20] The story might be exaggerated or fabricated, but tourism in China embodied Mao's adage that "foreign affairs promote domestic affairs" (*waishi cu neishi*).

The Chinese meticulously prepared for foreigners, based on their classifications. Edgar Snow, for instance, was pigeonholed as a "friendly bourgeois writer" and a "middle-class Westerner," whose knowledge of China "falls far behind" the reality and needed updating, according to the Foreign Ministry's 1970 propaganda instruction.[21] Snow was not hard to please. Following Mao's 1971 remark that "some people on the right can come as well," Beijing also accepted foreigners "on the right," a broad category that encompassed almost anyone who harbored skepticism about Chinese socialism.[22] *New York Times* reporter James Reston, one of the few American journalists admitted into China in mid-1971, was one. He called Mao Zedong Thought "a new religious belief" while dining at a restaurant, and his guide promptly pontificated about its "scientific truthfulness."[23] When words failed to proselytize, the Chinese resorted to stagecraft. Acupuncture, practiced by millions of "barefoot doctors" during the Cultural Revolution, was the headliner. When Reston had acute appendicitis in Beijing, doctors at the Anti-Imperialist Hospital gave him an appendectomy combined with acupuncture, which released him from the pain (see fig. 5.1).[24] Huashan Hospital in Shanghai also staged acupuncture anesthesia shows for Reston, to fix his "biases of the Western capitalist class." An oilfield engineer greeted him in the middle of a brain surgery, reciting Mao's quotations without showing any agony. "I have been feeling very good," he later said to the *Time* reporter, "because Mao Zedong Thought armed my brain."[25] An acupuncture fad followed Reston to the United States.

Beijing took pains to provide comfort as best it could. The Chinese, for instance, paid close attention to the hygiene of hotel rooms and the quality of meals served, seeing them as essential components of the tourist experience.[26] They also tried to keep travelers from undergoing anything discomforting, except such unavoidables as culture shock, homesickness, and occasional food poisoning. Few people lost personal items in China. In March 1974, for example, a janitor at the Peace Hotel in Shanghai found the

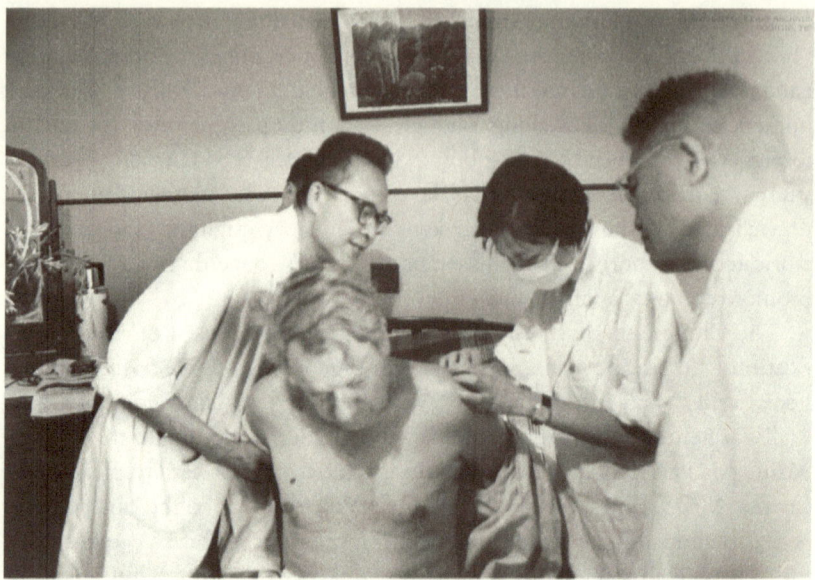

Figure 5.1. James Reston receiving medical treatment in China. Sally Reston Papers, Record series 26/20/121, box 2, courtesy of the University of Illinois at Urbana-Champaign Archives.

ID and cash of Joyce Kallgren, a political scientist at UC Berkeley, after checkout, and they were immediately delivered to her. "This is very important," rejoiced Kallgren. "We cannot do this in the United States, but you can do this in China."[27] Soon, many tourists learned to leave the hotel door unlocked. Beijing found it more difficult to hold in the reins of the Chinese masses. Countless foreigners reported incidents where they were stalked and surrounded by a horde of curiosity-seekers who wanted to take a glimpse of them. Local governments made constant efforts to discourage onlooking (*weiguan*), but it never quite disappeared throughout the 1970s and beyond.[28]

China's tourism policy took a sharp turn when it suffered a humiliating blow by Italian film director Michelangelo Antonioni. Seeing him as a more reputable Felix Greene, Beijing invited Antonioni to spend five weeks in China to shoot a documentary film titled *Chung Kuo* (*China*), released in December 1972. About a year later, Chinese officials started to slash *Chung Kuo* as a mockery of China. They deemed Antonioni's realist shots of everyday life in China, aimed at humanizing its people, an intentional act of demeaning Chinese socialism.[29] Beijing was particularly outraged by the film's depictions of political meetings as a product of government coercion, not mass political consciousness; and the Nanjing Yangtze River Bridge as a symbol of poverty manifested in the barracks nearby, and not of infrastructural mastery. The *People's Daily* reviled *Chung Kuo* for its "deep-seated hatred for China" and "viciously distorted scenes and shots," while Jiang Qing bashed Zhou Enlai's invitation to Antonioni as "not only failure, but also treason."[30] Fearing a repetition of *Chung Kuo*, Chinese guides exercised enhanced vigilance over foreigners who took pictures of "backward scenes." Isabel Hilton, one of the first British students in China, one day went to Haidian District, a quiet area on the outskirts of Beijing, to photograph everyday life. No sooner did Hilton start to take pictures than a local cadre walked up to her and asked why she "deliberately" came to the "backward, run down part of Beijing" to take "an anti-Chinese photograph." The surrounding crowd, growing in numbers, shouted "little Antonioni" at Hilton and demanded she give up the camera film. She had to oblige.[31]

Beijing suspected tourists of being potential spies. The fear was not ungrounded—the CIA, for instance, was creating an extensive intelligence network from the US Liaison Office under the leadership of James Lilley, future ambassador to China.[32] At the March 1975 National Tourism Work Forum, Luo Qingchang, China's intelligence guru and director of the CCP Investigation Department, stated that tourism was "a very important political work" in "carrying out the struggle against the enemies."[33] So paranoid were the Chinese, they raised their eyebrows at almost anything. When a group of foreigners traveled on a long-distance train, some requested to sit on the "hard seats" with commoners, not on the "soft seats" reserved for them. "These kinds of people usually understand Chinese language, and some of them have a close relationship with the embassy," one guide later reported. "They carry tape recorders with them and can hear anything in the hard seat car."[34] Beijing was desperate to detect a second Antonioni on the prowl, and anyone could be one. Accustomed to roaming the streets, reading local newspapers, and talking to strangers, most foreign travelers were just curious. In Mao's China, however, being curious was not always seen as being friendly. Beijing later imputed the xenophobic atmosphere at the time to the Gang of Four, but it was deeply embedded in Maoist tourism.[35]

Equally grave was the Chinese fear of ideological demoralization. Foreign tourists carried a "strong capitalist lifestyle" that might "entice and corrode us," warned Yang Gongsu, a career diplomat at the Foreign Ministry and head of the CTEA. They touted "freedom, democracy, and high standard of living," measured by the number of automobiles and televisions. Beijing dreaded moral corruption from capitalism as much as its material allure, for Chinese guides reported a number of cases in which foreigners flirted with them. Some female Japanese travelers, for instance, devoted a "fan club" to their "tall and handsome" male guide, a typical capitalist act of personal idolatry. Male tourists accosted female guides more often, some writing "love letters," others resorting to more explicit means. Holding a female guide's hand, one traveler whispered, "My wife has not been with me for a long time, and I need your comfort." Strangely enough, Chinese guides often considered these acts of libido "friendly," which perturbed their superiors.[36] Chinese officials felt alarmed that personal intimacy involved in tourism might undermine the moral integrity of Chinese society. They soon forbade guides from developing a romantic relationship with tourists—but who knows if it worked.

Beijing, however, kept accepting more tourists and opening more cities and sites. For all the drawbacks, tourism served China's strategic goals. Politically, it was a platform to put into practice Mao's Three Worlds Theory, which divided the world into the US and Soviet superpowers, their dependent allies, and developing countries resisting superpower domination. At the 1975 National Tourism Work Forum, attendees argued that to rally the world against the two superpowers, Beijing should inspire "Second World" guests, "uncertain about their future and in emotional agony," with socialism as a new socioeconomic model, and "Third World" guests, most of them from decolonized countries, with self-reliance as a principle for nation-building.[37] Economically, tourism was a goose that laid the golden eggs of foreign currency. While bearing the cost of travel for a small number of "invited" guests, Beijing profited from the growing number of "self-funded" guests. The CTEA's foreign currency earnings ballooned from $119,000 in 1971 to $3.73 million in 1974, a year in which it introduced a new price system for foreign tourists to boost the revenues.[38] Yet the goose was still a gosling, and the golden eggs were cursed with stigma. To further promote tourism, Beijing had to reconcile its political and economic goals.

A creative solution surfaced: an "economy class" for self-funded "lower- and middle-class" tourists. The CTEA classified foreign tourists into three categories, depending on their political and economic attributes. The "lower-class" were left-leaning people with relatively low socioeconomic status, including students, teachers, and blue-collar workers; the "middle-class" were those in the political center, with relatively high socioeconomic status, including professors, doctors, news reporters, and businesspeople; and the "upper-class" were the rich and powerful, including lawmakers and corporate executives, assumed to be right-leaning. Among the thirty-eight thousand tourists the CTEA accepted between 1971 and 1975, 87 percent were "lower- and middle-class," and only 13 percent were "upper-class rightists"[39] The Foreign Ministry reasoned that by offering a 30 percent discount on flights inside China and cutting the daily travel fees by half, from $40 to $20, the "economy class" would attract more "lower- and middle-class" tourists, contributing to both political and economic goals in tourism. The Pandora's box was opened. The "economy class" implied not only commercialization of tourism, but also class exploitation of foreigners, antithetical to the ideal of classless society. Facing pushback from the Gang of Four's followers, the Foreign Ministry framed the "economy class" as part of "public diplomacy" toward "lower- and middle-class" foreigners. Since most of them came to China to study Chinese socialism, they should need little comfort, luxury, and fanfare—posh hotels, fancy meals, and lavish banquets. "We can attract the broader masses of [tourists] . . . if we establish the economy class," Vice Foreign Minister Ma Wenbo claimed.[40]

This logic hardly stood the test of reality. Due to the high cost of international travel, a trip to China, even with a modest reduction of expenses, remained out of reach for the vast majority of foreigners who could possibly be categorized as "lower- and middle class"—take the two regular China tours offered in the United States for example. *The Guardian*, a radical weekly newspaper, offered a three-week tour of China biannually at $1,929 per person after discount—today's equivalent of $11,000—when a similar package tour of Europe cost as low as $700. The US-China People's Friendship Association (USCPFA), a nongovernmental organization for grassroots exchanges with China led by pro-China figures like William Hinton, the author of *Fanshen*, arranged two dozen tours each year, with a slightly more prohibitive price tag.[41] It would be a bit of a stretch to call tourists who could afford such a trip "lower- and middle-class." Yet Luo Qingchang disavowed "foreign currency in command, money in command [of tourism]." "We are not tour guides in capitalist society," he asserted.[42] In December 1975, the Foreign Ministry and the Civil Aviation Administration rolled out the "economy class" to "expand our political influence" worldwide.[43]

The "economy class" aggravated the tension in tourism that it tried to mask. As feared by Chinese officials, the capitalist nature of the industry aroused the desire of rank-and-file tourism workers for material riches. Angling to "make a profit in one grab," Chinese guides and guards followed foreigners into theaters and restaurants in droves, watching shows for free and demanding liquor when dining. Host organization officials who accompanied foreign groups often found it harder to cater to the demands of local tourism workers. When nine Japanese tourists visited a university fishery brigade in

Tianjin, guides joined them for lunch and dinner. The group consumed an enormous amount of seafood, including more than eighty-eight pounds of shrimp, which cost 300 yuan, nearly half of the average annual salary of an urban worker. Each guest paid two yuan per meal; the rest was for CTS to cover. Chinese drivers also scrounged their share. They devoured the pricy three-yuan meals, with soda and beer, as they drove between tourist destinations. If they ran out of food or beverages, they could refuse to take the guests to the next stop. Stealing was rampant. Tourism workers pocketed 90 percent of cigarettes prepared for foreigners in reception rooms and airport lounges.[44] Some guides even disguised themselves as overseas Chinese to shop at Friendship Stores.[45] "All you have to care about is whether [the guests] eat well, live well, and play well," according to tourism workers in Guilin.[46] Money, not Mao Zedong Thought, was clearly in command.

For these covetous tourism workers, politics mattered little. They flouted the official goal of winning over "lower- and middle-class" foreigners, particularly from the "Third World." Although proscribed from taking tips or receiving gifts from travelers, guides, guards, and drivers drooled to make pocket money by regaling rich tourists from developed countries, not "poor friends" from developing countries. Tourism workers even classified their guests into "A, B, and C," based on their economic merit. They preferred "invited" guests assigned by government ministries or mass organizations over "self-funded" tourists assigned by the CTEA, because the former meant more luxury with less labor. One driver explained that he had to drive a large van for "self-funded" guests from early morning to late at night without sumptuous parties and meals, whereas he could drive a small taxi for "invited" guests only from 9 A.M. and enjoy banquets in the evening. "Foreign guests hosted by CITS do not count as foreign guests," lampooned one tourism worker. "Even if we do the hygiene work in a sloppy manner, it is no problem." Chinese officials found "problems on all sides." "This is very dangerous," they warned. "We should be alerted."[47]

Chinese tourism in the late Mao years was a chimera, feeding on socialist propaganda and foreign currency, which were poisonous to each other. It was destined to be short-lived. The "economy class" accelerated its demise by eroding the edifice of the Three Worlds Theory, supposed to be "in command" of tourism, and putting mounting pressure on tourism workers, who demanded material incentives and swindled the system. What was happening in the tourism industry was a microcosm of what was happening in the country at large—an unwinding of Mao's China. With that, American images of China changed dramatically.

American Travelers in New China

As often analogized, Richard Nixon's trip to China was a moon landing.[48] The last man left the moon in December 1972, but more Americans thronged to China. In April that year, the *New York Times* correspondent Tillman Durdin became the first American journalist visiting China individually, followed by dozens in the next few months. Professional journalists were joined by amateur journalists, from scholars to students, politicians to activists, executives to housewives. These travelers created a vast literature on China in the 1970s, which Australian sinologist Stephen FitzGerald labeled a "cathartic outpouring" of "ephemeral travelogue."[49] Some of them provided informative analysis, others offered little more than impressionistic commentaries. Some hailed Chinese socialism, others questioned, criticized, and ridiculed it. Some simply tried to convey the realities of China, others wished to import facets of Chinese society. Despite the variety that defied generalization, a trend emerged in this literature in the mid-1970s—a shift from romantic, uncritical accounts to dispassionate, critical ones.

Nothing endeared China to more Americans than its people. Travelogues put a human face on the Chinese masses, who had long been portrayed by US media as brainwashed, emotionless drones that only listened to Mao Zedong's words. "It wasn't the politics but the people that affected me," one tourist wrote. "I saw that a person living in China loves and laughs and cries and needs friends and values family, the same way we do in this country."[50] Beijing trained the masses to act simple, diligent, and reserved in front of foreigners. "Still," commented Susan Dryfoos, "this abstemiousness does not bespeak a nation of puritanical puppets."[51] She was referring to students walking arm in arm with friends on the street or couples hugging each other in the park at night. If language stood in the way of communication, Polaroid cameras helped. When *Newsday* publisher William Attwood gave locals their snapshots, it "melt[ed] people's reserve right away."[52] As Durdin wrote, the "whole society suddenly becomes human and more understandable" after a tour of China.[53]

China's socioeconomic system transfixed many Americans, who believed, often naïvely, in the policies, statistics, and stories presented to them. In the fall of 1972, the Federation of American Scientists sent the prominent economists Wassily Leontief, John Kenneth Galbraith, and James Tobin to China. After two weeks of travel and study, Leontief marveled at the "almost unbelievable" achievements in communes and factories. "It works" was his assessment of the Chinese economy.[54] Galbraith also came back with "no serious doubt" about China's "highly effective economic system." "The Chinese economy isn't the American or European future. But it is the Chinese future," he wrote. "And let there be no doubt: For the Chinese, it works."[55] While calling China "miserably backward and poor," Tobin noted the availability of consumer goods and the lack of involuntary unemployment, something unseen in other socialist economies. He lauded the absence of "urban pathologies" rampant in the United States—beggars, idlers, derelicts, peddlers, vendors, litter, thefts, and diseases—which would "astound and delight" the mayor of New York.[56] These commentaries were only a trickle in a stream of books, articles, and interviews favorably comparing standards of living in China before and after 1949.

Owing much to propaganda, many Americans came to behold Chinese socialism with awe. During the *CBS Special Report* in August 1971, James Reston gushed about Chinese efforts to "change the character of people." "I don't think anything in the Soviet revolution or even in our own compares in magnitude with trying to change a quarter of the human race," he commented.[57] Reston, like many others, eulogized the sense of purpose and the spirit of youth exhibited by the Chinese people, akin to the frontier spirit, once the hallmark of the American people. "This country is engaged in one vast cooperative barn-raising," he later wrote. "They work at it night and day . . . against a background of sights and sounds that tend to make Americans outrageously nostalgic and even sentimental."[58] Mao's China was as exotic as it was familiar. Losing confidence in an increasingly individualistic, unequal, and unhealthy America in the 1970s, travelers like Reston romanticized the society that valorized what they seemed to have lost—altruism, egalitarianism, and collectivism. They spotted them everywhere in China, from mass education to gender equality, low crime rates to the remedial prison, *taijiquan* exercise to affordable health care, often without acknowledging their complexities. Many Americans—from biologist Arthur Galston to Black activist Unita Blackwell to actress Shirley MacLaine—were willing to believe in the message Chinese propaganda was delivering: The United States was a rich country with poverty, and China was a poor country with richness.[59] "Radical orientalism" was in full swing.

Most Americans, however, would balk at paying the price for Chinese socialism: freedom. Foreigners were appalled, for instance, when Chinese college students, asked about their future aspirations, invariably answered that they would contribute to the state by following its orders. "Can individuality and creativity continue to be contained . . . in a nation with such a rich cultural heritage?" David Rockefeller of the Chase Manhattan Bank wailed.[60]

To counter such "capitalist thinking," Beijing defined the Chinese meaning of freedom: The CCP—Mao Zedong, more precisely—freed the Chinese people from the evils of feudalism, imperialism, and revisionism, and the experience of the triple liberation should inspire them to devote themselves to the collective, not the individual, thereby accepting the mission assigned by the state.[61] The Chinese freedom was a negative, not positive, freedom— freedom from the past travails. As such, it was a tough sell to the Americans. Leontief eloquently explained: "Not unlike food, freedom is a source of direct personal satisfaction, but it is also an indispensable condition of health and normal growth. After a long period of malnutrition, the appetite may disappear. But . . . first a few and then many of the individual organs show signs of debility, and the system as a whole gradually begins to malfunction and to lose its capacity for healthy growth."[62]

The more Beijing harped on the superiority of Chinese socialism, the more riven Americans became over it. While lavish banquets, effusive toasts, and countless handshakes entertained and moved some, the mundane itinerary, full of monotonous, didactic lectures by cadres and unstimulating excursions to tourist sites under the watchful gaze of guides, frustrated and disillusioned others (see fig. 5.2). Eminent writer Barbara Tuchman noted a "curious mixture of exaggerated privilege and strict control" in China. "The effect of all this gracious attention was not so much to make one feel oneself an object of friendship as of manipulation."[63] The *New Yorker* reporter Orville Schell felt a "coldness" and "absence" in a rash of stilted discussions with officials, in which they responded to any question outside the script with a studied silence. "We may have at last managed to get physically inside China, but . . . we were in so many ways irrevocably still on the outside," he bemoaned.[64] The fog of propaganda and the lack of transparency in China even turned some left-leaning Americans, who came anxious to learn about Chinese socialism in motion, into staunch anti-communists.[65]

Nothing shown to foreigners was entirely genuine in China, even if it seemed so. When the CBS crew stayed in Shanghai for two months to film *CBS Reports* on the city, the reception team mobilized thousands of locals to ward off a second *Chung Kuo*. In a small district called Zhangjiazhai, residents concurred that they should not exhibit their "wholly objective" life in a "laissez faire" manner. When the Americans came, they put on work clothes to toil in, no matter how hot and humid it was.[66] The finished program featured Shanghai commoners in a simple yet elegant style, reading newspapers, singing songs, and playing Chinese chess, just as they wanted to portray themselves.[67] In January 1976, the Central Broadcasting Administration and the

Figure 5.2. A Chinese guide gives a lecture in July 1971 to members of the Committee of Concerned Asian Scholars in Yan'an, as they take notes on the stone table; Anna Louise Strong met Mao Zedong here on August 6, 1946. Reprinted with permission of Paul G. Pickowicz. Courtesy of the University of California San Diego Library.

Foreign Ministry ruled that foreign films shot in China should "fit the real image of New China," as determined by the state.[68] The *New York Times* aptly wrote that there was "no spontaneity" in China, for everything was "meticulously organized . . . rehearsed, and staged."[69]

Beijing even tried to sway American reporting on China from afar. It distrusted major US media corporations, partly because more than a dozen of them signed a petition in late 1971 to oppose the expulsion of two prominent Taiwanese correspondents from the UN.[70] These corporations soon reached agreements with Xinhua to exchange news stories, photographs, and footage, but Beijing ignored their proposals to have correspondents stationed in each country. The Chinese were also outraged by the *New York Times*. They frequently filed complaints against its stories and editorials, some of them hinting at "two Chinas," while demanding withdrawal of anti-CCP advertisements sponsored by pro-KMT Chinese Americans. Citing the freedom of press and advertising, the *Times* stood fast, knowing that the adamancy would cost the company what possibility it had for a permanent bureau in Beijing.[71] In early 1974, the Chinese Liaison Office mailed the *People's*

Daily's opprobrium of Antonioni to the press, as a warning against the "well-planned anti-China sentiment" fomented by it.[72] Beijing then began to restrict visas to US correspondents. Contrary to the robust reporting from 1971 through 1973, few newspersons were admitted into China in 1974, except in Henry Kissinger's entourages. As a result, American travelogues became dominated by members of the USCPFA's local chapters in New York, Chicago, Los Angeles, Honolulu, and other major cities—ordinary citizens with much curiosity about China yet little capacity for critical analysis, who were committed to outreach activities after the trip. They sang the praises of Chinese socialism in the USCPFA's monthly journal *New China*.

China scholars loathed what Douglas Murray called a "visa culture" bearing down upon them.[73] They often self-censored their writings and speeches upon return from China in the hope of securing a second visa in the future. "Certain scholars whose careers hinge on heavy accessibility do have inhibitions about what they say," Robert Scalapino observed. "It is . . . a very delicate question."[74] It was particularly so after the Chinese blocked a delegation of Harvard sinologists in the fall of 1973, when John Fairbank published a book review on China's labor camps in the *New York Review of Books*.[75] Beijing's visa policy proved counterproductive because it alienated countless Americans already vexed by the raft of articles written by incredulous travelers who went "to China, with love," saw it through "rose-tinted glasses," and found no "warts," as critics put it.[76] Peter Berger, a sociologist at Rutgers University, deplored "the sudden collapse of all critical faculties into a veritable orgy of gullibility," while James Grant, a young writer at *Barron's* magazine, slammed "learned ostracism" of uncritical scholars who indulged in "the myth of the New China."[77] "The bitterness that separated our two countries in the 1950s has ended, but so too has the 'Marcopoloitis' that paralyzed American critical faculties in the early 1970s," Harvard law scholar Jerome Cohen blared. "True détente must be based not on emotional mood-swings but on accurate understanding."[78]

Beijing's failure to control US public opinion was laid bare by Edward Luttwak, associate director of the Washington Center for Foreign Policy Research at Johns Hopkins University, who toured China with the former secretary of defense James Schlesinger in the fall of 1976. In a show of respect for Schlesinger's vocal anti-Soviet attitude, Beijing granted his group rare access to Tibet, Xinjiang, and Inner Mongolia, and did not cancel or postpone the trip despite Mao's passing. Luttwak never returned the favor. Not one to slant his views, he later published a scathing travelogue in the conservative magazine *Commentary*, titled "Seeing China Plain," in which he exploited every opportunity to discredit the CCP's rule in Inner Asia. In Tibet, he noted a local official rattling off "move," "go," and "faster" in the Tibetan language, without knowing how to say "please" and "thank you." Luttwak reprimanded American travelers deceived by Chinese propaganda. "How could our intellectuals and our journalists . . . fall into the very same trap [as they did to the Soviet tourism policy in the 1930s]?"[79] "Seeing China Plain" met backlash. Audrey Topping of *National Geographic*, whose positive report on Ürümchi in 1975 was lambasted by Luttwak, wrote that "he didn't read my articles any plainer than he saw China."[80] Most readers, however, admired his outspoken criticism of China. One of them praised the article as "magnificent," while charging that "the utter irresponsibility" of unsuspecting tourists was "indeed a scandal."[81]

Mao's death on September 9, 1976 offered a moment of reckoning for the new Marco Polos. In reexamining the chairman's legacies, some contrasted "Old China" with "New China," while others highlighted the catastrophes he inflicted upon the Chinese people.[82] Perhaps most influential in shaping the tenor of this debate was the Belgian sinologist Pierre Ryckmans. After a six-month stay in China in 1972, he penned *Chinese Shadows*, translated into English in 1977 under the pseudonym Simon Leys. By detailing the devastation of the Cultural Revolution and the horrors of Mao's totalitarianism, Ryckmans tore apart the rosy picture of China drawn by the plethora of Western travelogues.[83] Though embroidered with exaggerations, his account validated many Americans who griped about "pervasive Chinese secrecy, rigidly planned tours, and their inability to approach common people."[84] By the summer of 1977, when John Fairbank wrote a glowing review of *Chinese Shadows* in the *New York Times*, the Sinophilic literature had become passé.[85] So had "radical orientalism," as exemplified by the lagging membership and internal strife of the Committee of Concerned Asian Scholars.[86] With the age of self-doubt in the United States and the age of abstemiousness in China both winding down, Americans were less inclined to believe that they had something—anything—to learn from China. Michel Oksenberg rejoiced in mid-1977: "Clearly, the bloom is off the China rose."[87]

"Foreign Currency in Command"

In November 1977, the CCP's foreign news periodical *Reference News* published an article written by a tourist from Hong Kong. He made a list of suggestions to address the shortcomings in China's tourism industry, from the shortage of hotels to the low quality of food, unprofessional staff to unhygienic bathrooms, unavailability of souvenirs to lack of air conditioning. "In my personal view," he wrote, "China can make very rapid progress [in tourism] if it is determined to follow these steps." The "four modernizations" would incur an enormous cost, the writer pointed out. "Then, why not take this ready-made money?"[88] The article presaged Beijing's new tourism policy. That April, the CTEA had issued a report on tourism, blaming the Gang of Four for everything wrong about it—xenophobic tendencies, lack of foreign currency earnings, hedonistic guides, and even traffic accidents.[89] In doing so, the CTEA cleared the way for a leap in the tourism policy, from "politics in command" to "foreign currency in command."

"Foreign currency in command" meant making tourism profitable. The August 1977 National Tourism Planning Forum, attended by foreign affairs cadres around the country, declared that earning foreign currency for the "four modernizations" was "the mission of tourism." The number of tourists in China seemed "very disproportionate" to its "international prestige." Among the 21,100 tourists the CTEA received in 1976, only 1,400 were Americans, a tiny 1.6 percent of over 90,000 visa applicants in the United States.[90] The CCP soon set the 1978 target at one hundred thousand tourists, more than tripling the 1977 total, while adding fifty cities and regions, including Kunming, Chongqing, and Chengdu in the southwest, to the list of forty-six already open to foreigners.[91] Beijing wished to learn the capitalist ways of tourism as well. In the spring of 1978, the managing director of CITS Yuan Chaojun led a delegation of fifteen officials to the United States. Sponsored by Pan American World Airways (Pan Am) and other corporations, the group crisscrossed the country as tourists, visiting the Statue of Liberty in New York; the Johnson Space Center in Houston; and Hollywood, Disneyland, and Universal Studios in California. Yuan seemed impatient to build a flourishing tourism industry. "People all over the world, including the United States, want to visit our country," he glowed at a banquet in New York.[92]

The door to China swung wide open in 1978. The number of tourists quadrupled, and Beijing earned $263 million in foreign currency.[93] Yet complaints piled up fast, too. Tourists reported a glut of embarrassing incidents—mice biting holes in their socks, surly hotel staff refusing to help them out, or hotel dishes that had declined to the pre-Cultural Revolution standard.[94] The shortage of guides and interpreters reached an alarming level. Zhao Jianguo, head of CITS's Beijing branch, was "most concerned that the reputation we have worked so hard to achieve may now be somewhat damaged." As freelance writer Marie Ridder wrote, a trip to China was no longer "a sought-after privilege" for foreign "friends." Since Beijing was now competing for "the tourist dollar" by appealing to "a different clientele"—"the hard-core tourist, the spoilt traveler"—hotels should provide "toilets that work, mattresses without lumps, [and] air conditioning when the temperature is over 100 degrees."[95] The July 1978 National Tourism Work Forum discussed these issues, vowing to enhance the service quality and train more guides.[96]

The bottleneck in the tourism industry was the shortage of hotels. Hotels designated for foreigners were chronically overbooked in the 1970s, and tourists in search of bed and breakfasts were often whisked to a nearby city, from Beijing to Tianjin, for instance. The Chinese, however, lacked the capital and know-how to build and manage modern hotels that could handle the new wave of tourists. An entrepreneurial solution dawned on Deng Xiaoping in October 1978, when he said, "We can use foreign capital to build hotels!"[97] His idea quickly materialized. The next month, Beijing signed a $500 million agreement with Intercontinental Hotels, a subsidiary of Pan Am—hitherto the biggest business deal with a US counterpart—mandating it to design, build, and manage a chain of five or six luxury hotels in Beijing, Shanghai, Guangzhou, and other major cities, equipped with bars, bridge tables, and billiard halls. Each of these hotels was projected to bring in as much as $55 million in annual foreign currency revenue, one-fifth of the tourism industry's total foreign currency earnings in 1978. Intercontinental was even allowed to raise capital in stock markets overseas on behalf of the Chinese government, which boasted an excellent credit score thanks to the long-standing tradition of balanced budget.[98] Electrified by the deal, Hyatt, Western, and Hilton soon entered into negotiations with Beijing.[99] Suddenly, hotel business seemed like a fat goose laying golden eggs.

Beijing also set its eyes on overseas Chinese capital (*qiaozi*). "Some overseas Chinese are very patriotic," said Deng. "We can use them."[100] Lu Xuzhang, director of the Overseas Chinese Travel Service, who worked for the State Council's task force on building hotels with foreign capital, negotiated with 120 businesspersons from over twenty countries in 1978 and 1979, many of them overseas Chinese in the United States, Hong Kong, Macau, and Singapore. In 1979, the State Council approved the first six joint venture hotels, including two in Beijing built with Chinese American entrepreneurs: Jianguo Hotel (with Clement Chen Jr.) and Great Wall Hotel (with C. B. Sung). Jianguo Hotel, which went into operation in 1982, would repay the loan in four years and generate massive revenue worth almost eight times the construction cost in ten years.[101] In late 1978, Lu also invited famed

Chinese American architect I. M. Pei to a tour of China, which led him to design Fragrant Hill Hotel in Beijing.[102] Tourists in China no longer had to worry about sleeping in a hotel dining hall.

Beijing's hunt for foreign currency did not stop at building hotels. In February 1978, the Ministries of Light Industry, Commerce, and Foreign Affairs wrote a joint report on the souvenir industry, long vilified for "exporting culture." The sales of tourist gifts in 1977, mainly guide maps, postcards, and pin badges, remained a meager $21.1 million due to the lack of production capacity, product variation, and souvenir shops. The report asserted that the sales should grow by leaps and bounds from $63.4 million in 1978 to $250 million in 1980 to $790 million in 1985, with the prices maximized to "increase the national income as much as possible."[103] Later that year, the Ministry of Light Industry requested an investment of over $200 million in production, wrapping, and marketing of souvenirs, soon approved with an additional $90 million. The State Council further dictated that all major hotels and tourist destinations should set up gift shops, citing the case of Dongfang Hotel in Guangzhou, where a gaggle of three hundred tourists bought artifacts worth $160,000, almost emptying the showcases.[104] A year later, the Zhaoling Mausoleum Museum in Xi'an proudly reported that in the first half of 1979, it earned $27,000 in foreign currency, about $10 per visitor.[105] Money was now the sole yardstick of success in the tourism industry.

Beijing ceased to trumpet the superiority of socialism around the same time. William Hinton, who revisited China with his daughter Carma in 1977, lamented that the pro-China literature in the United States, to which he himself had contributed, lost a "mass base" of support due to its "deceitfulness."[106] Other American "friends" found China's English-language periodicals not only dull, but also mendacious. *China Pictorial* and *China Reconstructs*, two magazines widely available in the United States, often featured peasants and workers toiling in "very beautiful clothes," for example.[107] Socialist propaganda had failed. In November 1978, the Shanghai Municipal Propaganda Department sketched a blueprint for China's new propaganda strategy, targeted at the "vast middle-class" tourists, who "hardly understand China" and "harbor suspicion against socialism." "[We should] let tourists witness how splendid and magnificent China's rivers and mountains are, how much emphasis China places on archeological work, and how well China repairs and conserves famous historic and cultural sites," the document read. "This kind of propaganda is more effective" than spouting Maoist spiels at the uninitiated, which Hu Yaobang, director of the CCP Propaganda Department, dismissed as "playing the harp to a cow."[108] The new propaganda policy was tantamount to no propaganda. Tellingly, in the spring of 1979, Beijing officially stopped distributing to foreigners "Mao's Little Red Book," an inspiration for a generation of radicals around the world.[109]

The US tourism industry pounced on the opportunity they had long been waiting for—an opportunity for commercial tourism in China. The Pan Am president Najeeb Halaby recognized China's "ultimate tourist lure" as "a truly little-visited, off-the-beaten-track destination" in 1970; American Express and several other travel companies developed and advertised China tours in 1971 and 1972, without permission from Beijing, for which thousands applied; and Eric Friedheim, editor of *Travel Agent* magazine, who joined Ethiopian Airlines' inaugural tour of China in 1973, applauded its "limitless" "tourist potential."[110] Before mid-1977, however, a voyage to China remained out of reach for most aspiring tourists. Only a fraction of them could afford the two-week tours offered by Japan Airlines and Ethiopian Airlines, priced at about $4,000, or luxury cruise lines that cost as much as $35,000—today's equivalent of $170,000. A Greek cruise liner *Aquamarine* appealed to some typical orientalist stereotypes in advertising "a frustratingly brief but fascinating kaleidoscope of irrigated paddies, oriental gardens, swarms of bicyclists, men and women with shoulder-poles, pigtailed girls in Mao jackets, doll-like children, and friendly greetings everywhere."[111] Despite the high price tags, these tours sold fast, carrying hundreds of Americans across the Pacific each year. Unlike the new Marco Polos, these tourists wrote little about China.

A trip to China continued to be an entertainment for the rich, but not just for the superrich. In the summer of 1977, Beijing reached an agreement on package tours with Pan Am. Under this agreement, Pan Am carried American tourists directly to Hong Kong, not via Tokyo or Addis Ababa, and a train took them into China from there, making the travel far more efficient than before. Dreading the influx of tourists, Beijing barred Pan Am from publicly advertising these tours, and Pan Am mailed the brochures only to its frequent customers. In four days, 120 signed up at the price of $2,400, and the wait-list reached the limit of eight hundred. In 1978 alone, the Pan Am tours brought two thousand Americans to China, about one-tenth of all American tourists.[112] By the time Washington and Beijing normalized relations, at least two dozen organizations operated similar two- to three-week tours of China, priced between $2,000 and $4,000, all of them selling out quickly.[113]

These package tours fell short of pleasing Deng Xiaoping. Although Japanese tourists outnumbered Americans by a large margin, the vice premier reckoned the United States "the biggest source of customers in tourism" and sought a direct airline that could save tourists a layover in Hong Kong. "Profit is not only a commander, but also a general!" Deng shrieked, turning to Pan Am again for "a non-governmental format" to establish direct air links. Despite the misgivings of other officials, he even insisted on designating Pan Am as CTS's "agent" in the United States, who would bring in "tens of thousands" of tourists every year. "We should open this gate to the United States," resolved Deng. In October 1978, he broached this idea to the Pan Am president William Seawell, who offered to terminate the Taiwan route in return for a China route.[114] Beijing and Pan Am reached a direct commercial airline deal in the summer of 1979, legalized a year later by the civil aviation agreement between Washington and Beijing. On January 7, 1981, China's Boeing 747 "Jumbo Jet" flew from Beijing to New York, by way of Shanghai and San Francisco, with 139 passengers on board, marking the first direct commercial flight between the two countries.[115]

The advent of mass tourism diversified what a trip to China meant for Americans. While scholars, journalists, and pundits continued to visit China to observe, analyze, and assess the country in transition, tourists saw it as the Middle Kingdom, the new frontier of international tourism. English-language guidebooks on China, of which only a handful existed in the mid-1970s, started to appear in bookstores, cataloguing all kinds of tourist activities.[116] Shopping was king. In the words of Nina Hyde, fashion editor of the *Washington Post*, China was "a shopper's paradise." "If you are . . . looking for inexpensive, unique and therefore sure-to-be noticed items, shopping in China is a ball," she wrote, referring to ping-pong paddles, Mao jackets and hats, and laundry bags with Chinese characters. "The best way to shop in China is to keep your eyes open fulltime and pick up items where you see them."[117] The new American tourists, both women and men, were as energetic and inquisitive and rapacious as were the new Marco Polos—although they were looking for very different things.

Mass tourism also changed the ways in which American travelers and Chinese commoners interacted with each other. Toward the end of the 1970s, Beijing prohibited guides from meddling with tourist behavior, including hanging out in the city, photographing "backward" scenes, and talking to locals, assuming that they could impress more foreigners by minimizing control and manipulation.[118] Now as more than half of American visitors came to China as tourists, their conversations on the street were no longer policed, at least as closely as before.[119] When the playwright Arthur Miller and his wife and photographer Inge Morath were wandering around in a narrow alleyway in a traditional *hutong* district in Beijing, they encountered an old man, who stared at them in wonder and delight. "Imagine! Finding you people here, right out on the *street*! And being able to speak to you like this!" he sputtered in English. "We've been hounded for years, you see . . . this awful fear and hatred of foreigners . . . [but] here we are! And we can talk about anything at all!"[120] Nothing seemed off-limits. Some Chinese asked about Jimmy Carter's concept of human rights; some mentioned Mao's complicity in the Cultural Revolution; and others dubbed China "Asia's Gulag Archipelago."[121] These outbursts of candor, still rare as they were, contrasted with the political gibberish Americans had been hearing for a long time.

Tourism in China was a booming business in the 1980s. The number of American travelers to China—hovering at about 20 percent of all foreign visitors—doubled between 1980 and 1984, from 100,000 to 210,000, and so did foreign currency earnings in the tourism industry, from $617 million to $1.1 billion. By 1988, more than three hundred thousand Americans were visiting China every year.[122] Beijing turned American orientalism on its head, using it as a device to monetize tourism. In 1980, CITS published the first edition of *The Official Guidebook of China*. With colorful maps and photographs—from the Forbidden City in Beijing to the Grand Canal in Suzhou to West Lake in Hangzhou—it provided a compendium of practical information about visa application, payment methods, and public transportation, as well as hotels, restaurants, shops, and tourist sites in more than eighty cities across the country. "China is an exciting and fascinating country," the preface read. "Hopefully this Guidebook will convey the unique qualities of excitement and mystery that have captivated the traveler to China since the days of Marco Polo."[123]

The flow of tourists remained one-sided. By the end of the 1970s, few Chinese had traveled to the United States outside government-facilitated exchanges, except some correspondents. The president of Xinhua's UN branch, Zhang Haitao, published a book based on his visits to more than thirty states spanning six years, while a delegation of media personnel in the summer of 1978 produced a series of articles in the *People's Daily*. By way of introducing America to the readers, they all applied Marxist theories to analyze its economic decline and social unrest.[124] As more journalists, scholars, writers, and family members traveled to the United States in the 1980s, a small literature of the personal travelogue began to take shape. Authors noted their wonders about the abundance of everything—cars, food, music, sex, jeans, computers, skyscrapers, taxes, drugs, fatties, schizophrenia, newspapers, automation, politeness, cleanliness, and friendliness. Novelist Ru Zhijuan wrote: "America is heaven for some, hell for others; it's a pioneer of the Western civilization for some, a seductive witch with . . . irresistible mysterious charm for others. In short, it's like a maze."[125] The Chinese portrait of the United States has become only more complex and contradictory ever since.

American perceptions of China in the 1980s were characterized, to some extent, by a backlash to Beijing's abortive attempt to control them in the previous decade. China was a mirror, onto which Americans projected their best dreams and worst nightmares in the era of "radical orientalism." When the era unraveled, the mirror warped. Americans who stayed in China for months and years in the 1980s—journalists stationed in major cities, English teachers at universities, or China scholars conducting fieldwork—rediscovered various aspects of China, from rural poverty to unwieldy bureaucracy, human rights abuses to the horrors of the Cultural Revolution, in their own terms, not the ones imposed by the Chinese. As Stanford sinologist Harry Harding observed, a growing number of Americans were returning "from China with disdain," most succinctly epitomized by the title of a 1982 article written by an English teacher: "China Stinks."[126] The pendulum swung fast from admiration to contempt, adulation to patronization, one set of biases to another. China changed much, but so did Americans.

Many "new China hands" were trying to maintain balance. A. M. Rosenthal, executive editor of the *New York Times*, who traveled to China in May 1981, was one. "It is not sentimental to say that you simply cannot be an American in China for more than a few days without feeling you are in friendly territory," he wrote, after having a pleasant chat with Shanghai locals in front of billboards of the upcoming "American film week." Yet he had trouble reconciling that impression with "the decades of distaste" he felt for the "authoritarianism or totalitarianism," still visible in many corners of society.[127] Rosenthal, like most Americans, was sure of one thing: "Dengism is certainly better than Maoism, substantially." "We should not pretend that small freedoms are full liberty," he mused, "but if we can do anything to encourage Deng in the direction of freedoms, then let us do so."[128] In the era of mass tourism, Americans had much space to articulate their hopes and fears about the future of China. And there was hardly anyone to censor them.

Chapter 6

Sport

Friendship and Competition

Avery Brundage, the former president of the International Olympic Committee (IOC), famously stated that "politics has no place in sports."[1] Contrary to this naïveté, sport has always been a continuation of politics by other means—particularly so during the Cold War. Following the Soviet entry into the Olympic Games in 1952, the East-West rivalry replicated itself on the field, where athletes from the capitalist and socialist blocs competed to demonstrate the ability of their systems to produce the stronger body. When the sense of national decline engulfed the United States in the 1970s, sport was at the forefront. At the 1972 Munich Olympics, the Russians dealt a heavy blow to the Americans by winning seventeen more gold medals, including in men's basketball. The Munich fiasco reignited a question that had haunted American officials, coaches, and athletes for decades: Can a totalitarian state with government control on sport produce better athletes than a free state with decentralized amateur sport?[2] "Winning is very important. Maybe more important than ever," Gerald Ford, a former football star at the University of Michigan, wrote in *Sports Illustrated*. "I don't know of a better advertisement for a nation's good health than a healthy athletic representation."[3]

Unlike the United States, China was a "sick man of East Asia." Bent on shedding this ignominious image, the KMT promoted athletic competition and physical exercise to make the population stronger and healthier, while sending athletes to international sporting events, including the 1932 Olympic Games in Los Angeles, China's Olympic debut, to stimulate nationalism at home and gain recognition abroad. The CCP inherited these goals. With the mantra "friendship first, competition second" (*youyi di yi, bisai di er*), the State Physical Culture and Sports Commission, led by General He Long, facilitated sports exchanges with the Soviet Union and Eastern Europe in the 1950s to learn new techniques, and with developing countries in the 1960s to buttress Beijing's leadership among them.[4] "Friendship first" masked China's long-held desire to excel at international competitions, until the Cultural Revolution crushed it. Mao Zedong and his disciples accused the Sports Commission of monopolizing sport with a coterie of elite athletes and erecting "an independent kingdom" with the ethos "competition first, friendship second." He Long died under house arrest; diplomats like He Zhenliang, chief negotiator of Chinese representation with the IOC, were imprisoned; and table tennis coaches and players, including Fu Qifang, Jiang Yongning, and Rong Guotuan, committed suicide. To uproot elitism in sport, the PLA, under General Lin Biao, assumed control of the Sports Commission in 1968. China's national teams stopped training in 1966 and withdrew from all international events until 1970.[5]

Ping-Pong diplomacy catapulted China back to the international sports scene. The thirty-first World Table Tennis Championships in Nagoya, China's first appearance in a major international competition since 1966, marked the beginning of new sports diplomacy, aimed at recouping the country's reputation tarnished during the Cultural Revolution. Beijing bestowed this task upon the Sports Commission, which was freed from military control in February 1972. In 1974 alone, it exchanged 172 groups of 3,200 athletes with eighty countries, 70 percent of them in the "Third World," while spending more than a million yuan to send out coaches, players, and sports equipment as part of foreign aid.[6] The golden rule of Chinese sport was "friendship first, competition second." Rather than showing off athletic competence, Chinese players were required to embody political comraderies, often by intentionally losing games. Before the 1971 Nagoya Games, for instance, Zhou Enlai promised Pyongyang that the Chinese would yield to the North Koreans in men's singles and doubles. Starving for victory after a long hiatus, the ping-pong players contravened the order and defeated the North Koreans, lowering their ranking below the South Koreans. Zhou later chastised the entire team for winning four gold medals in seven events and sent veteran diplomat Han Nianlong to Pyongyang to offer Kim Il-sung an apology.[7] Beijing was eager to lose the game to win the politics.

The spectacle of Ping-Pong diplomacy convinced US officials and scholars of the diplomatic utility of sport. After Richard Nixon's visit to China, the US government tasked the National Committee on US-China Relations with managing cultural exchanges, and the National Committee, in cooperation with the All-China Sports Federation, a mass organization for sports exchanges, arranged more than a dozen sports groups to/from China before 1979. As the program director Douglas Murray explained, the National Committee planned these exchanges "to enhance public opinion" on bilateral relations in both countries.[8] Such thinking was shared by US policy makers, particularly at the State Department's Bureau of Educational and Cultural Affairs, who had been leveraging sport to win the hearts and minds of the world.[9] Washington embraced sports exchanges with Beijing as a symbol of rapprochement and a "door-opener" to facilitate more substantive contacts in the future.[10]

"Friendship first," however, did not bode well with American athletes. Weaned on the axiom "winning isn't everything; it's the only thing," many of them found friendship matches with the Chinese strange at best, "awful" at worst, as one table tennis player said after the 1971 tour of China.[11] If the ostensible display of friendship did not discomfit American athletes, they were alerted by what they suspected was hidden under it. The Americans were better than the Chinese in almost all sports save for ping-pong, but many players and coaches noted China's athletic potential in the 1970s, visible in militarization of sport, the rise of sports academies, and the will of Chinese athletes to learn. As the Chinese returned to international games in greater numbers, the *Washington Post* warned about the challenge they might pose to US "dominance" in the future.[12] American athletes wished to promote friendship with future Chinese rivals—by winning, not by losing.

The 1970s was a decade of sports nationalism for both the United States and China. While Americans were battling the mentality of decline, Chinese were slowly coming out of what historians Xu Guoqi and Andrew Morris called "an aberration" and "an interregnum" in Chinese sports history, in which Beijing truly prioritized friendship over competition.[13] This chapter writes these developments into the history of US-China relations. The first section looks at the coexistence of friendship and competition in sports exchanges in the early 1970s, which enabled Chinese athletes to show goodwill and learn techniques simultaneously. The second part examines sports nationalism in China, pent up during the Cultural Revolution but uncorked by superior American athletes, especially the 1975 track-and-field delegation. The third section analyzes the process in which competition subdued friendship in the late 1970s, when Americans and Chinese, be they athletes, coaches, or spectators, reckoned each other with rivalry and respect. Washington and Beijing seldom paid much attention to sports exchanges, but the prominence of exhibition games, broadcast by radio and television, made them a unique venue in which the American and Chinese people fostered new ideas on bilateral relations.

"Friendship First"

Ping-Pong diplomacy enshrined the amalgam of sport and politics in Chinese foreign policy. No one personified this amalgam better than Zhuang Zedong, the three-time table tennis world champion who approached Glenn Cowan in Nagoya. He wrote in June 1971: "Yes, we are a table tennis delegation, not a friendship delegation. . . . [But] if we were to simply play table tennis and return with seven trophies, how meaningful would that be. . . . [If] we carry out a friendship mission . . . and conduct people's diplomacy, our influence would be different!" Chinese athletes, argued Zhuang, should become "foreign service officers who do not work at the Foreign Ministry."[14] The National Sports Conference that summer affirmed "politics first, technique second" as the canon of China's sports diplomacy, and his lofty political ambition made Zhuang an eminent athlete-diplomat for the next several years, leading Ping-Pong diplomacy around the world.[15]

Zhuang's most important assignment was the April 1972 return visit to the United States, as part of the tour of the Americas. The delegation of thirteen players visited Detroit, Williamsburg, Washington, New York, Memphis, Los Angeles, and San Francisco in eighteen days, holding five official matches and five friendship matches, televised to over ten million Americans, which made the group far more visible than Taiwan's ping-pong tours in 1971 and 1972.[16] Mindful of their diplomatic mission, the Chinese attended a banquet at the White House despite the US bombings of North Vietnam, as instructed by Mao.[17] They also behaved with poise and aplomb throughout the trip, not only on the court, but also at an automobile assembly plant, a children's hospital, and the houses of ordinary Americans whom they visited, despite the cacophonous shouts of anti-China, pro-China, and anti-Vietnam War demonstrations that trailed them along the way.[18] Though disturbed by the anti-communist reverend Carl McIntire's placard saying "Mao Killed More Christians Than Hitler Killed Jews," Zhuang kept his cool and praised the performance of his opponents in Memphis: "We warmly congratulate your progress."[19] US media highlighted friendly encounters between the Chinese players and Americans from all strata of society. Many of those who believed in the grim depiction of Chinese sport by a defected table

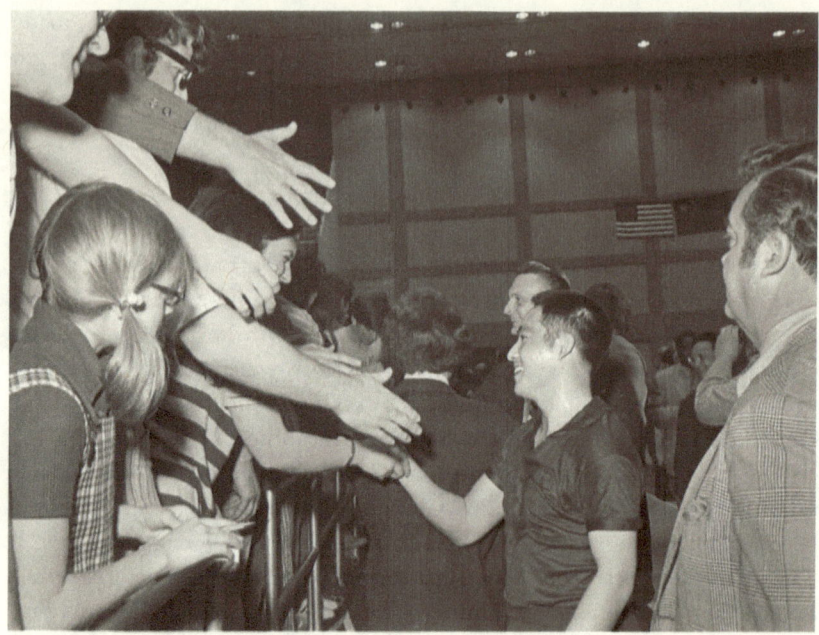

Figure 6.1. Zhuang Zedong shakes hands with spectators in the stands after a friendship match at the College of William and Mary, April 16, 1972. Photo by Qian Sijie of Xinhua News Agency.

tennis player in *Reader's Digest*—"Agony and desperation are the rewards of achievement in Mao's athletic factories"—probably changed their minds (see fig. 6.1).[20]

Friendship gleamed particularly bright at the 1974 Asian Games in Tehran. Iran had helped China replace Taiwan in the Asian Games Federation in the previous year, the first of a series of such takeovers in international sports organizations. The CCP vice chairman Wang Hongwen, member of the Gang of Four, instructed Team China to "help the host country when possible," while the CCP leadership dictated, "Do not use strength to bully the weak. Give up the championship." CCP representatives who accompanied the delegation kept their eyes peeled for perfect occasions to lose. They ordered the water polo team to lose to Kuwait, which helped Iran win the championship; the women's basketball team to lose to Japan, which blocked a South Korean gold; and the entire team to walk out of matches with the Israelis to show solidarity with the Arabs.[21] Thanks partly to Chinese friendship, Iran ranked second in the medal tally, only after Japan.

"Friendship first," however, was far more difficult to implement than it sounded, for manipulating the game required superior technique. Chinese players, in other words, should be capable of losing in a way that celebrated friendship, instead of embarrassing themselves or disgracing the opponents. Zhou Enlai expounded in the summer of 1971: "If you want to win 'friendship', you need to have some competence. . . . We can let the opponents win only when we have the competence to defeat the opponents. If you do not have the competence to defeat the opponents, [yet] still say you let them win, they will disagree. If you let them find out [that you are losing purposely] by casually making mishits, it is not friendship first, either; it is 'disrespect first.' If you still say 'friendship first', it is a joke, then!"[22] This problem loomed larger than ever in the early 1970s, when the Chinese began to take on West Germans in soccer, Japanese in volleyball, and Americans in basketball. Only superb technique could warrant friendship with them.

Not many could pull off such a stunt. After the Cultural Revolution, China retained relative strength in table tennis, track and field, gymnastics, swimming, and weight lifting, but fell far behind the world standards in most other sports. While castigating the "big country chauvinism" exhibited by the table tennis players in Nagoya, Mao decried that the "ability" of Chinese athletes was "not high at all," except in ping-pong. They had "nothing else to boast about," he groaned.[23] Zhou also lamented the weak national teams in volleyball and basketball and ordered them to hone their skills.[24] When Beijing's invitations for international practice matches in volleyball met rejection after rejection, even Jiang Qing, a protagonist of "friendship first," croaked to the volleyball team: "You are too incompetent. You hurt the self-esteem of the people of our country!"[25] To nurture world-class athletes in five years, Beijing reinstated national championship games in the "five major ball games" (volleyball, basketball, soccer, badminton, and table tennis) in 1972; the Sports Commission's flagship periodical *New Sports* also resumed printing in 1972, featuring new techniques, strategies, and trends in international sport; and the 1973 National Sports Conference even discouraged young athletes from having relationships and getting married.[26]

Chinese athletes far preferred hard training on the court to hard labor in the countryside. When the CCP statement came out that "if we can perform as well in all of the five ball games as in table tennis, we can be more active in foreign affairs, with more influence," the Shanghai Municipality's second volleyball team latched onto it and sent an open letter to the Party leadership in the fall of 1973. Hitting all the rhetorical marks—from "catching up with the world" to "serving Chairman Mao's revolutionary diplomatic line" to "receiving the training of the Great Proletarian Cultural Revolution"—they proposed intensive training programs to defeat Japan, the "Oriental Witches," in two years.[27] To protect athletes like them from political quicksand, the Sports Commission invoked Mao's instruction to "draw a line" between "big country chauvinism" and "winning glory for the nation."[28] The arbitrary line seemed to be shifting rapidly.

A mosaic of friendship and competition characterized China's sports exchanges with the United States. The strength of American athletes rendered intentional losing almost impossible, and the Chinese had to rely on spontaneous yet conspicuous goodwill gestures to underscore friendship. For the gymnastics delegation that toured the United States in May 1973, an ideal opportunity arose when the music tape for the floor performance by fifteen-year-old Nancy Theis got garbled at the exhibition meet in Madison Square Garden, attended by fourteen thousand spectators. After some moments of unnerving hush, Chinese piano accompanist Zhou Jiasheng played the music for her. When Theis finished her performance as planned, she and her coach took Zhou onto the stage as the audience gave him a warm round of applause. Zhou's quick-witted tact, televised across the United States and reported back to China, became one of NBC's best sports news scenes in the decades to come.[29] As *Sports Illustrated* described, Madison Square Garden was "one large warmhearted Smile Button."[30] "They're so friendly, I hate to look at this as a competition," said Marshall Avener, a gymnast from Penn State. "We've really been close. They are probably the friendliest, warmest bunch of people I've competed against."[31] Little did she know that the Chinese team, upon return, produced a detailed report on American techniques and published it in the Sports Commission's *China Sport Science and Technology* journal. The report judged that although the gymnasts "scored some success" in the United States, their performance fell "far behind the demand of the Party and the state." It called for more training, more research, and more planning.[32]

American lawmakers, athletes, and sports aficionados were even more obsessed with winning than the Chinese. Amateur sport was being embroiled in a controversy in the United States, which overshadowed the June 1973 swimming and diving delegation to China. Since China was not a member of the International Swimming Federation (Fédération Internationale de Natation or FINA) before 1980, the FINA, along with the Amateur Athletic Union (AAU), prohibited the Americans from competing with the Chinese. Some withdrew from the group, others went to China and swam in different races from the Chinese, as if not competing. The AAU took offense nonetheless. Upon return, the entire delegation—athletes, coaches, and officials—was banished from the AAU and denied membership in all subcommittees of the US Olympic Committee. The red tape incensed Senator James Pearson from Kansas. He thundered on the Senate floor: "Mr. President, we cannot continue to allow these self-appointed sports bureaucrats . . . to interfere with our athletes, or with our foreign policy."[33] Pearson, like many others, had attributed the embarrassing losses and disqualifications in basketball, track and field, and swimming at the Munich Games to the chronic turf war between the AAU, which oversaw US representation in international sport, and the National Collegiate Athletic Association (NCAA), which administered college sports.[34] The petty war continued, as the NCAA banned college athletes from attending some AAU-organized events, including a basketball game with the Soviet Union and an international track meet in Virginia, arousing public outcry.[35] Although the swimming group was later acquitted by the Supreme Court, Pearson saw the incident as just another example of the "endless obstacles facing athletes and development of amateur sports in this country"—obstacles that dragged down Team USA.[36]

International sport was caught in domestic politics in China as well. When two US delegations, one in swimming and diving and the other in college basketball, visited China in June 1973, the Sports Commission organized exhibition matches in Beijing, Shanghai, Hangzhou, and Guangzhou, each attended by thousands, to "promote friendship and expand China's influence on the American people."[37] With much clout in cultural politics, Jiang Qing did not miss this opportunity to flaunt her rising power. Hoping to have a "peek" at the Americans, she suddenly requested a swim meet one afternoon in Beijing, although the swimmers were exhausted from a morning trip to the Great Wall.[38] Jiang made herself even more visible in the basketball games, in which she, along with Wang Hongwen and Yao Wenyuan, sat with the chief of the US Liaison Office David Bruce. She watched basketball with "interest and good humor," whispering to Bruce that she was worried if the Chinese victory over the US women's team, which consisted only of John F. Kennedy College in Nebraska, made the American coach "tense." When the Americans gave Jiang souvenir emblem pins at the post-game meet-and-greet, she rummaged through her pocket, took out some jasmine petals, and handed them over in return. It was a good show of friendship. As Bruce observed, Jiang turned the basketball games, televised nationwide, into "a major political event, with important domestic implications," by which to aggrandize her political stature.[39]

Chinese athletes and coaches were more excited about American skills than about Jiang Qing's presence. With the slogan "make the foreign serve China" (*yang wei Zhong yong*), they were instructed to learn as much as possible at the joint practices and instructional clinics arranged by the Sports Commission, where athletes from both sides shared their techniques. Zhou Xiyang, a member of the diving team, recounted that the lectures by US Olympians "made a key contribution for the Chinese diving team to advance into the world."[40] Chinese men's basketball players seemed "pretty cool" about losing all eight games to the US college all-stars and "grateful to hear criticism and suggestions," according to Kevin Stacom, a guard at Province College.[41] "We admire your American players for they are the best at basketball in the world," said Dong Yiwan, a leading member of the Sports Federation. "We are not of your caliber, but we can advance friendship and learn from your visit."[42] These joint sessions married the two goals of China's sports diplomacy: promoting friendship and improving skills. Yet the former became increasingly subordinate to the latter. Soon after the US swimming and basketball team visits, the Sports Commission published translations of Jack Richards's *New Treasury of Basketball Drills from Top Coaches* and James Counsilman's *The Science of Swimming*.[43] Chinese ambition for victory was simmering under the glow of friendship.

The Triumph of Competition

The tension between friendship and competition drew closer to a breaking point in the mid-1970s. As the vice chairman of the preparatory committee, Zhuang Zedong helped to organize the first Asian-African-Latin American Table Tennis Friendship Invitational Tournament in Beijing in the summer of 1973. "We the people of Asia, Africa, and Latin America have the common mission to . . . oppose hegemony," he stated at the opening ceremony, exuding friendship.[44] Chinese sport soon became entangled in political struggle. Just before the 1974 Asian Games, Deng Xiaoping encouraged Team China to "enhance the standard of athletic technique and strive for good results in competition," contradicting the spirit of "friendship first." Later, the Gang of Four and their supporters nitpicked this statement as evidence of Deng's "revisionist road." Determined to pursue "revolution in sport," they urged athletes to focus on class struggle "even if they underachieve for three years."[45] A 1976 *Red Flag* article, solicited by the Gang, avowed that China should uphold "friendship first, competition second" by "criticizing bourgeois concepts like championship-ism."[46] Having replaced General Wang Meng as chairman of the Sports Commission in 1974 under the Gang's auspices, Zhuang turned ping-pong into a tool for Mao's Three Worlds diplomacy, assisting the second and third Asian-African-Latin American Tournaments in 1975 (Lagos) and 1976 (Mexico City). Friendship seemed to be making a rapid comeback.

The US track-and-field delegation in May 1975 toured China at this critical juncture. The NCAA refused to approve this AAU-authorized group and threatened to disqualify the entire team from all NCAA events for the rest of the season.[47] Later, however, the NCAA dropped its charge, and the track-and-field group traveled to China as the first official US national team. The NCAA's decision might have been influenced by congressional and executive pressure. Undeterred by the AAU and NCAA's opposition, Pearson and his congressional allies were redoubling their efforts for legislation aimed at wresting control of amateur athletes. Gerald Ford was also preparing Executive Order 11868, which he would sign three weeks after the return of the track-and-field delegation, to create the President's Commission on Olympic Sports, tasked with tightening government control over amateur sport and improving US performance at international events.[48]

The diplomatic stakes were also high. In 1974 and 1975, tension over Sino-American cultural exchanges was crackling, which culminated in the indefinite postponement of China's performing arts troupe in late March 1975 (see Chapter 7). The track-and-field delegation, scheduled about a month later, seemed in peril. Mao, however, gave a clear order to his aides: "Do not retaliate [by canceling the track meet]."[49] Ford also wrote a letter to the delegation, recognizing its symbolic role before his own China trip later that year: "As an athlete during my own school days, I know how much participation in sporting competition can contribute to the building of friendship and understanding."[50] American athletes on the track-and-field team were carrying more political weight than they realized.

The Chinese had to exhibit friendship to far superior opponents this time. While missing some of the very best due to schedule conflicts, the US team consisted of sixty-six top college athletes, many of them world-class. Lacking information about Chinese competitors, they had "some anxiety" before departure.[51] Once the team was in China, it disappeared as quickly as the bigger, faster Americans beat the Chinese in ninety-one out of ninety-nine events in eight friendship matches with China's local and national teams in Guangzhou, Shanghai, and Beijing. The Americans were merciless—they would no more have let up against the Chinese than they would have against the Russians. In

Beijing, Dick Buerkle of the University of Rochester lapped four Chinese runners as he dominated the 10,000-meter race. Columbia track coach Irving Kintisch gushed that the group "managed to enjoy itself immensely, while winning everything in sight."[52] The chief of the US Liaison Office George H. W. Bush lauded the overwhelming performance of the American athletes before 250,000 spectators in three cities. It was, in his telling, "far more effective propaganda for the superpower role of the United States than any number of military operations remote from China's borders."[53]

Rarely did sports fans in China have to sit through such an embarrassing streak of losses. To maintain the façade of "friendship first," the Sports Federation used two tactics: "friendship lap" and joint practice. After each event, Chinese and American athletes ran an extra lap on the field, hand in hand with each other, as thousands of spectators cheered for them without showing any grudge (see fig. 6.2). "Throughout the trip, the goodwill poured like Niagara Falls," recounted Kintisch.[54] The "friendship lap" was followed by clinics, in which American athletes and coaches unsparingly imparted their skills and know-how to the Chinese. Chinese runners listened eagerly to the lecture by Deborah Sapenter, a star runner for the 400-meter sprint, while Chinese coaches bombarded the Americans with questions, including about the training method of the javelin thrower Frederick Luke, the bronze medalist at the 1972 Munich Games. The individualized practice of American athletes was an eye-opener for the Chinese, who were accustomed to mass-producing athletes with standardized training. The Sports Commission later circulated a detailed report on American techniques, which concluded that "it is completely possible for us to catch up and surpass the world's modern standards in track and field in a relatively short period of time."[55] There was a good reason for the rush: China was trying to displace Taiwan from the IOC and participate in the 1976 Montreal Games for the first time since its 1958 withdrawal from the Olympics.[56] The bid was unsuccessful in 1976, but most countries supported China's return to the IOC, including Canada, which debarred Taiwan from using the name "Republic of China" in Montreal, triggering its boycott. If Chinese athletes were to compete at the games, they should perform better.

The US track-and-field tour induced a subtle change in China's "friendship first" mentality. Despite the cordial atmosphere, the crushing defeats awakened sports nationalism among Chinese officials. After a particularly one-sided race in Guangzhou, Ni Zhiqin, president of China's Track and Field Association, groaned to UCLA sinologist Richard Baum, an escort to the US team assigned by the National Committee, about the inadequacies

Figure 6.2. American and Chinese athletes run a "friendship lap" after competition at Guangdong Provincial People's Stadium in Guangzhou, May 18, 1975. Courtesy of *Columbia Magazine*.

of training, coaching, and facilities caused by political interference in sport. "With 800,000,000 people, you'd think we could train some runners," he grumbled.⁵⁷ Guo Lei of the Sports Federation also admitted to Baum and other National Committee officials: "We attach importance to these exchanges because our sports development, like our economic development, is in a backward state. It is developing, and we want to overcome our backwardness, but we are quite limited by our material conditions."[58] The Sports Commission instructed each province and municipality to send fifty coaches and officials to the exhibition meets. They were shell-shocked. The Guangdong delegation reported that the meets "aroused the national pride, inspired the fighting spirit, and [made us] determined to . . . surpass the world's modern standard [in sport]." It rated China's track-and-field levels "very incommensurate" with "the high prestige in the world of the great socialist nation with 800 million people."[59]

Such was a shared feeling among athletes and fans as well. After the 10,000-meter race in Beijing, Dick Buerkle found a Chinese runner named Xie Baojiang pensive on a bench. Xie had just broken the national record, but lost to the future Olympian by more than seventy seconds. When Buerkle asked Xie whether he was thinking about his lap times, he beamed, as if to dissemble mixed emotions: "No, I am thinking of friendship."[60] To the Americans, "friendship first" was hocus-pocus. "I know this [result] must be embarrassing for them, and you can tell it hurts, but they keep on clapping," said Buerkle.[61] Although instructed to cheer for both sides, even the spectators could not hold themselves back sometimes. On the final day of competition in Beijing, a Chinese runner in the women's 1,500-meter race caught the lead American runner in the last 400 meters to win the gold medal. Visibly dispirited by the preceding losses, the audience in the stands suddenly rose up and chanted, "Jia you! Jia you!" (Go! Go!) It was a rare eruption of Chinese sports nationalism. Baum wrote in his memoir: "Notwithstanding the debilitating traumas of the Cultural Revolution and other Maoist excesses, Chinese national pride and patriotism were evidently still alive and well, lying dormant, awaiting only a superb performance by a gutsy Chinese athlete to be reawakened."[62]

With the Taiwan problem unresolved, sports exchanges continued to be an important instrument to symbolize Sino-American rapprochement. Yet two Chinese groups hosted by the National Committee—a women's basketball delegation in November 1975 and a men and women's volleyball delegation in October 1976—caused some hiccups. The basketball group held exhibition games at five universities across the United States, including Queens College in New York, which was hosting a Taiwanese women's basketball team around the same time. The National Committee precluded a squabble with the Chinese by persuading Queens College to cancel the Taiwan game.[63] A larger storm was gathering for the volleyball group. Soon after a Taiwanese team participated in a summer 1976 international volleyball tournament in Honolulu, the Chinese Liaison Office demanded the National Committee include some provocative lines in the volleyball group's pamphlet, including a reference to the dreadful state of Chinese volleyball under the "reactionary KMT rule." The National Committee agreed, and quietly deleted them later.[64] The volleyball group encountered further trouble in Pasadena, Texas, where the Ku Klux Klan was rumored to be planning an anti-China demonstration.[65] Worse, a Taiwanese chamber music group was visiting Rice University in Houston, less than fifteen miles from Pasadena, on the same night. The Chinese nevertheless did not cancel the game, content with the assurance that no "two-China" incident would take place.[66] Hua Guofeng's new regime apparently had no intention of jeopardizing the token of friendship with the United States.

Friendship on the surface gave way to competition on the court. During the women's basketball tour, Team China won three out of four exhibition games against individual colleges, while losing to the US College All-Stars, 94–82. Au fait with the Chinese practice of helping the opponents who tripped, one college team decided to commit more fouls than usual to slow them down. By half time, however, the Chinese heeded this tactic and started to jump over the Americans who tripped to make the basket. "All pretense of friendship was dropped," the National Committee program coordinator Jan Berris recollected, "and the spirit of competitiveness led the way to a Chinese victory."[67] The atmosphere of the fall 1976 US gymnastics delegation to China was nowhere near as competitive. Women's national coach Linda Metheny, impressed by Chinese improvements since the 1973 visit to the United States, cautioned nonetheless, "We must do something to promote a stronger developmental program if we are to remain competitive. . . . If the Chinese come out from behind the Bamboo curtain . . . there will be a definite reshuffling of the top powers in world gymnastics."[68]

Competition was trumping friendship. In the spring of 1977, the Sports Commission published a commentary in *New Sports*, articulating the sports policy of the post-Mao era. Overturning almost all the official lines during the Cultural Revolution, it highlighted the importance of winning the championship for "the glory of the nation."[69] This goal seemed set in stone on July 30, 1977, when Deng Xiaoping made the first public appearance after his restoration at a China-Hong Kong friendship soccer game. He once stated: "We were a sick man of East Asia before; from now, we should be a strong man of East Asia."[70] That winter, a member of the cultural affairs office in Red Star Commune near Beijing, named Jiang Lianming, sent an open letter to *New Sports*, which distinguished itself by its candor. Slamming the vacuous political commentaries that filled many pages, Jiang wrote: "When your journal meets the readers, how many of them actually read it? [The editorials] are a waste of pages.... It is better to use these spaces to publish articles [that help us] carry out the spirit of the editorials by concrete deeds."[71] *New Sports* soon retrenched articles on politics and increased the coverage of new techniques, international trends, and world records. As "friendship first" ebbed away, the ambition for competitiveness grew. When the National Committee leadership visited China in October 1977 and discussed sports exchanges with Zhu Ze of the Sports Federation, he seemed more forthcoming than ever. "We wish to learn from you," he said.[72]

Racing to the Championship

The surge of sports nationalism in the United States and China altered the nature of their sports exchanges in the late 1970s. As more and more Americans and Chinese saw sport as a matter of national prestige, a delicate balance of rivalry and respect replaced the strange symbiosis of friendship and competition. After the disappointments at the Montreal Games, where the Russians won fifteen more gold medals than the Americans, the White House and Congress decided to implement far-reaching reform in amateur sport. In November 1978, Jimmy Carter signed the Amateur Sports Act, a piece of legislation that sports historian Thomas Hunt called "a product of a Cold War perception . . . that Soviet dominance on the Olympic fields had a detrimental impact on American prestige abroad."[73] To churn out better athletes, this law mandated the US Olympic Committee to designate a national governing body in each sport, which then selected and trained Olympic athletes without the AAU and NCAA's interference. The Amateur Sports Act marked a watershed between a broad-based Team USA in the early Cold War and an elite Team USA in the renewed Cold War.

Beijing, for its part, redefined sport as a cultural supplement to economic modernization. In November 1977, *New Sports* encouraged its readers to contribute to the "four modernizations" by working out, arguing that the strong, healthy body was essential for a modern socialist nation.[74] International sport became a venue to showcase the new body. Wang Meng, reinstalled as chairman of the Sports Commission after Zhuang Zedong's fall in October 1976, proclaimed to the entire nation through Peking Radio that Chinese sport should "develop at a high speed."[75] The January 1978 National Sports Conference, attended by 1,400 officials from around the country, listed many ways to "catch up and surpass the modern standards of the world," from rehabilitating sports officials to organizing training camps to building new facilities.[76] "Make the foreign serve China" was more relevant than ever—even the national ping-pong team vowed to study new skills from foreigners.[77] The 1978 sports development plan, drafted by the Sports Commission, stipulated that by the end of the twentieth century, China should become "one of the most developed sporting nations in the world," with "first-rate athletic corps" with "first-rate athletic skills." Dominating the medal tally at the Asian Games should be the first step.[78] China lost to Japan in the 1978 Bangkok Games, but won at the 1982 Delhi Games. The Chinese were now vaulting for the medals.

"Friendship first" was ejected not only from the international games, but also from the schoolyard. Chinese teachers and cadres used to police physical education (PE) to ensure that friendship prevailed among students. When Shirley MacLaine led an American women's delegation to a kindergarten in Guangzhou in 1973, they were baffled by kids playing tug of war without a winner or loser.[79] When a group of American educators toured Chinese schools five years later, sports activities were no longer under surveillance. The Americans found "the competition and contact" in the PE class "fierce." "Chinese boys play soccer with a vengeance. Chinese girls engage actively in running and gymnastics activities," one member wrote. "Everyone participates with enthusiasm and competitiveness."[80] That, combined with sports academies, each training hundreds of young athletes, signified China's "mind-boggling" potential in sport.[81]

The rise of sports nationalism coincided with commercialization and globalization of sport. Professional sports leagues in the United States flourished in the 1970s due to the free agent system, skyrocketing salaries, booming ticket sales, and entrepreneurial ownership. Television was the "big daddy" in the process, as the *New York Times* put it. The televised hours of sporting events almost doubled from 787 hours to 1,356 hours in ten years.[82] As sports business matured, it coveted new markets overseas. The Major League Baseball (MLB) pioneered this trend in the 1960s, but the National Basketball Association (NBA) spearheaded it in the 1970s with many exhibition games abroad.[83] Meanwhile, multinational corporations discovered the profitability of international games, with the broadcast revenue for the Summer Olympics soaring from $1.6 million at the 1964 Tokyo Games to $88 million at the 1980 Moscow Games to $287 million at the 1984 Los Angeles Games.[84] Global sport earned the United States not only prestige, but also a fortune. Small wonder that China seemed like a promising market.

Against this backdrop, Sino-American sports exchanges switched gears from amateur sport to professional sport, particularly soccer and basketball. Imported from Europe and the United States at the turn of the twentieth century, they were among the most popular sports in China, on par with table tennis, practiced at schoolyards across the country. China entered the Asian Football Confederation in 1974, won the bronze medal at the 1976 Asian Cup, and returned to the Fédération Internationale de Football Association (FIFA) in 1979, while joining the Asian Basketball Cup in 1975 and dominating it ever since. Soccer, perhaps the most popular sport in the world, all but superseded ping-pong as the star of China's sports diplomacy in 1977 and 1978, when Chinese soccer players toured fifty-two countries, and foreign soccer teams from twenty-four countries visited China.[85] Soccer and basketball were the forerunners of sports commercialization in China, too, along with table tennis, volleyball, and badminton. Even before Beijing launched national leagues of professional sports clubs in the mid-1990s, regional teams in these sports formed semiprofessional leagues in the 1980s, with provincial and municipal governments selling sports lottery tickets.

The New York Cosmos became the first professional sports club to visit China in September 1977. The United States never qualified for the World Cup tournament between 1950 and 1990, but the Cosmos, the 1977 North American Soccer League champion, had some star players on the roster, most notably the Brazilian "King" Pelé, the German "Emperor" Franz Beckenbauer, and the top Italian striker Giorgio Chinaglia—although Pelé was retiring in two weeks. Both teams played hard. "[The Chinese] were all over us physically and we got our egos handed back to us," Cosmos captain Werner Roth commented.[86] After tying the game in Beijing by 1–1, China's national team defeated the Cosmos by 2–1 in Shanghai before an exuberant audience of 50,000, despite a superb free kick goal by Pelé, a household name in China (see fig. 6.3). The victory, wrote *New Sports*, exhibited the country's "ambition and ability" to challenge the world in ball games other than ping-pong. "[We] absolutely can do what foreigners can do," it enthused. "[We] can not only hit the small ball well, but also kick a soccer ball well."[87] When China's national team paid a return visit to New York that October, it tied the friendship game with the Cosmos by 1–1. The audience was frustrated with the lack of tackles, but as NBC sports broadcaster Dick Schaap stated, the game was "a victory for both sides"—the Americans wishing to improve bilateral relations and the Chinese resolved to demonstrate their athletic might.[88]

Figure 6.3. New York Cosmos and Team China players enter the Jiangwan Stadium in Shanghai, September 20, 1977. National Committee on US-China Relations Collection. Courtesy of Rockefeller Archive Center and the National Committee on US-China Relations.

The Chinese rivalry and respect were much more intense in basketball, an American forte. When a Chinese basketball delegation toured the United States in late 1978, the men's team tied the game with Rutgers University at 84–84 after an impressive comeback in the final quarter, thanks to center Mu "Iron Poll" Tiezhu, a 7'6 giant. To the bewilderment of the Rutgers coach, the Chinese declined the usual five-minute overtime to secure the draw, invoking "friendship first, competition second." They were probably trying to save face. When the women's team was trounced by the US College All-Stars by 92–66, one Chinese player whined about their "aggressiveness." "We can't play like the Americans, because if we did, the officials in Asia would make us worry about fouls all the time," she said. The Chinese coach also complained, "The officials don't seem to call the three-second rule when they should, do they?"[89] The Chinese found solace in the spring of 1979, when the US College All-Stars visited Beijing. Although all other teams lost to the Americans, the PLA Bayi Rockets, with Mu, defeated the US men's team twice before an electrified crowd at the Capital Indoor Stadium. As the Rockets defended seconds before the 72–69 win, the announcer shouted: "This is such a key moment!"[90] At the postgame clinic, which was later edited into a detailed booklet, the US head coach Gene Bartow applauded the Chinese progress since he led the college basketball delegation to China in 1973. Bartow, however, identified "basic technique" as the "biggest weakness" of the Chinese players and encouraged them to attend more international games to gain experience.[91]

Deng Xiaoping heard Bartow's advice. In August 1979, he invited the Washington Bullets, the 1978 NBA champion, to Beijing and Shanghai, in response to the solicitation by the owner Abe Pollin. This first NBA team to visit China soundly defeated the Bayi Rockets and the Shanghai Sharks. "The Chinese played a methodical game," recollected star center Wes Unseld. "They were steeped in the fundamentals and could execute, but there weren't a lot of the nuances that we played with, or the speed and the quickness getting up and down the court." Mu Tiezhu—"the biggest pagoda we've seen in China" in the words of the general manager Bob Ferry—impressed the Bullets, but the Bullets dazzled the Chinese, including Sharks center Yao Zhiyuan, father of the future NBA star Yao Ming. Five hundred million Chinese watched the games on television as "hoops fever" swept across the country.[92] Ten years later, China Central Television was airing videotaped NBA games.

The awe inspired by US athletic power infused nationalism in the minds of Chinese sports aficionados. China's sports nationalism had never been extinct even during the Cultural Revolution, but the new sports policy brought it to the surface in the late 1970s, when Chinese fans openly cheered for Chinese players. They snickered at inferior opponents from developing countries and extolled Chinese victories over superior competitors from developed countries, most of all the United States.[93] In June 1978, when the women's basketball team defeated the Americans by 86–83 in a friendship game in Beijing, one of the 18,000 spectators wrote a fan letter: "At the game last night, you played very well . . . defeating the very strong US women's basketball team at one blow. You won the glory for the nation! . . . We the audience felt more excited and inspired than ever. Everyone commended you, saying, 'These girls are good. They lived up to the expectations of the audience!'"[94] The letter evinced a desire, shared by countless sports enthusiasts, to claim China's rightful place in the world as a modern sporting nation.

"Friendship first" died a painful death in 1979, when the Chinese soccer team lost to the North Koreans in the qualifying group stage for the 1980 Moscow Olympics. The Moscow Games, if not boycotted, would be a milestone in China's sports history. In November 1979, the IOC accepted the People's Republic of China as the only representation of China, while allowing the Republic of China to maintain membership as "Chinese Taipei." *New*

Sports celebrated China's entry into the "United Nations of athletes."[95] By then, a desire to host the games in China had taken hold of Deng Xiaoping.[96] Viewing the Moscow Games as an "important but pressing political task," the Sports Commission set an ambitious goal of becoming a top-ten country by winning five gold medals and fifteen medals in total.[97] Beijing longed for a slot in men's soccer, too. Torn between sports nationalism and socialist friendship, it plotted with Pyongyang to tie the game at 3–3. The North Koreans, however, scored one more goal and kept the lead until the end, leaving the Chinese stunned on the field. The truth dawned on them that "friendship first" was an illusion, even between the socialist brothers.[98] From this point on, friendship no longer blinded Chinese officials, athletes, coaches, and fans to the harsh reality in the world of sport.

Nationalism was paramount in international sport in the 1980s. At the 1980 Winter Olympics in Lake Placid, the Americans defeated the Russians in the men's ice hockey tournament, with Mike Eruzione's game-winning goal in the third period—the fabled "Miracle on Ice." A month later, on March 21, Jimmy Carter announced the US boycott of the Moscow Summer Olympics in response to the Soviet refusal to withdraw troops from Afghanistan. Beijing gave unwavering support to Washington and joined the boycott, delaying its Summer Olympic comeback for another four years.[99] Sport was one important element underpinning the US-China strategic partnership after the normalization of relations, until July 1982, when Chinese tennis player Hu Na disappeared during the Federation Cup in California, defecting to the United States the next April. Enraged by the international scandal, Beijing retaliated by canceling all official cultural exchanges with the United States that year, as it also railed against US arms sales to Taiwan. Sport was a continuation of politics by other means.[100]

China's sports nationalism went through the roof at the 1981 Volleyball World Cup in Tokyo. The Chinese women defeated such powerful rivals as the Soviet Union, the United States, and Japan, winning the championship for the first time. Hundreds of millions of Chinese watched the games on television, often with a throng of neighbors, and hailed the female players, especially the main attacker Lang Ping, as national "heroes" (*yingxiong*), a stigmatized title just a few years before. They received over thirty thousand fan letters, and their story was turned into books, movies, and musicals, all of them featuring their arduous training and dogged determination to win the trophy. As anthropologist Susan Brownell explained, the volleyball championship provided "not just a catharsis but also a vindication of sorts" for all the Chinese who suffered during the Cultural Revolution.[101] China was no longer the "sick man of East Asia."

China's Olympic dream came true at the 1984 Los Angeles Games. Thanks partly to the counterboycott by the Soviet Union and its satellite states in Eastern Europe, China won fifteen gold medals, including in women's volleyball, and came in fourth in the medal tally. Yet Beijing was far from complacent. The United States dominated the games by winning eighty-three golds, and the emergence of new stars, such as the gymnast Mary Lou Retton, sprinter Carl Lewis, and basketball icon Michael Jordan, ushered in a new era of US supremacy in global sport. Soon after the Los Angeles Games, the CCP leadership issued a notice, declaring that there was "still a great gap" between China and the world. The Sports Commission then held national meetings on sports strategy and published a report, titled "Chinese Sport in 2000," which pledged that China would nurture world-class athletes in most sports and become one of the top countries in the Olympic medal race by the end of the century.[102] The Chinese zeroed in on the United States.

This mix of rivalry and respect was a product of sports exchanges in the 1970s. China's "friendship first" incantation actually won many friends, including Olympic runner Michael Manley, member of the 1975 track-and-field team, who wrote a letter to the IOC in 1976, urging China's admission. "The fact that the athletes of the world's most populous nation are not included in the world's greatest attempt at promoting friendship through athletics most certainly hinders the objectives of the Olympic Movement," he argued. "The 'friendship first, competition second' motto with which the Chinese have received visiting athletic teams certainly fits in with the Olympic ideals."[103] A few years later, however, "friendship first" fell out of fashion. Just like the United States, China was instilling in its population what Xu Guoqi dubbed a "championship mentality," an obsession with winning gold medals for national prestige, most evident in China's first case of soccer hooliganism in 1985, after a 2–1 defeat to Hong Kong in the qualification round for the 1986 World Cup.[104] The United States was the defending champion of international sport, and China was a rising star. Great power competition was now the name of the game.

Chapter 7

Art

From Mao to Beethoven

Since long before the US Declaration of Independence, art circulated between China, Europe, and North America. Americans indulged in Chinese art in the early twentieth century, when collecting and preserving artworks helped the expansion of their knowledge and influence the world over.[1] Meanwhile, Chinese artists, including the painters Li Tiefu, Xu Beihong, and Lin Fengmian, studied abroad, mostly in Paris and New York, fusing Chinese and Western art upon return. Peking opera singer Mei Lanfang's six-month tour of the United States in 1930, in which he showcased China's traditional drama while befriending American cultural icons like Charlie Chaplin, marked an intersection of globalizing American and Chinese art.

The United States was a cultural superpower during the Cold War, wielding supremacy generated in New York, Hollywood, and elsewhere. While exporting films, concerts, exhibitions, and performances that incarnated esthetic maturation and artistic diversity, Americans consumed foreign culture ever more voraciously, including Chinese culture.[2] To maintain its international legitimacy, Taipei staged cultural shows in the United States that exploited American orientalism. The Republic of China pavilion at the 1964 New York World's Fair, for instance, featured 450 national treasures, as well as the Peking opera, in a building resembling the Imperial Palace in Beijing.[3] These cultural spectacles fed American fascination with things Chinese, even at the crest of Sino-American hostility.

The CCP weaponized Chinese art. At the Yan'an Forum on Literature and Art in May 1942, Mao Zedong famously declared that art should serve politics.[4] Which is to say that art should translate the ideas of the Chinese revolution for peasants in the countryside, most of them illiterate. As the Soviet Union replaced the United State and Europe as the main source of China's artistic inspiration after 1949, socialist realism, characterized by the stark depiction of revolutionary life, dominated oil painting; music, once an elite pastime, morphed into an aural whip to rally the masses; and performing arts troupes, featuring ballets and operas glorifying the struggle of peasants against landlords, traveled extensively, even to remote villages.[5] While deploying Chinese art, including Peking opera, as part of cultural diplomacy, Beijing imposed an embargo on Western art. Yet some Western music, literature, and films reached Chinese audiences through public and private, legal and illegal circulation.[6]

The Cultural Revolution terrorized Chinese art. Under duress by Jiang Qing and her acolytes, cultural officials, including Minister of Culture Lu Dingyi, were battered and purged; renowned artists such as the screenwriter Zhang Haimo, stage director Sun Weishi, and Peking opera singer Xun Huisheng died in disgrace; the prominent novelist Lao She committed suicide at Taiping Lake in Beijing; and valuable artworks representing the "Four Olds" (old customs, old culture, old habits, and old ideas) were vandalized and destroyed. The revolution in art grew so disruptive that the CCP decided in 1970 to dissolve the Ministry of Culture and establish a Culture Group within the State Council to rein in cultural politics. Jiang, a former actress in Shanghai, barred any form of art tagged bourgeois or reactionary or Western, and censored all stage performances but the "model plays" (*yangbanxi*)—five operas, two ballets, and one symphony, originally—which idealized and dramatized the Chinese revolution.[7] These shows, designed to be linguistically and artistically comprehensible for the uneducated, saturated everyday life. Hence the byword: "Eight hundred million people watched eight shows." As some historians have argued, revolutionary art, the model plays included, did not mean "cultural stagnation," because commoners, especially youth in the countryside, cherished it—and many of them still do.[8] Undeniably, though, Jiang monotonized Chinese art, so much so that art producers and consumers in China overwhelmingly embraced the cultural opening to the West in the 1970s.

The model plays became a staple in Sino-American cultural exchanges. A standard itinerary in China included at least one of the two model ballets created by Jiang Qing and directed by a select group of peasants and workers: *The White Haired Girl* and *Red Detachment of Women*. Unambiguously preaching class struggle, they impressed those sympathetic to Chinese socialism, enter-

Figure 7.1. Richard Nixon saw Chinese revolutionary ballet *Red Detachment of Women*, which featured female Communist soldiers in Hainan Island fighting a local landlord, February 22, 1972.

tained those heedless of it, and irked those suspicious of it. An eleven-year-old girl in Kansas, who watched the performance on television, praised it in her letter addressed to Mao as helpful for "know[ing] more about each other," while Richard Nixon and Henry Kissinger, like many others, dismissed these "superficial and artificial" shows as "an art form of truly stupefying boredom." When Nixon saw *Red Detachment of Women* in Beijing, he even had to endure a barrage of sensitive questions by the "abrasive and aggressive" wife of Mao sitting next to him (see fig. 7.1).[9]

China's opening to the West necessitated an alleviation of cultural xenophobia. When Kissinger visited China in October 1971, Zhou Enlai, who detested the model plays, asked the China Central Philharmonic to play a Beethoven for the German-born, the first public concert of Western music in years.[10] Beethoven, wrote Kissinger, was a "symbolism" of Beijing's intention "to modernize . . . to throw off the shackles of China's recent past and to adapt [the] country not only to Western technology but also to an awareness of the Western culture that had spawned it."[11] Jiang Qing flew into a rage. With Yu Huiyong, vice director of the Culture Group, she forced the Central Philharmonic's eminent conductor Li Delun to change the program from the Fifth Symphony, which represented fatalism, to the Sixth, known as the *Pastoral*, since its bucolic tone sounded more tolerable.[12] In the summer of 1972, Jiang told China historian Roxane Witke that "the current tendency to idolize the foreign and revive the ancient in the realm of music is aimed in essence at negating the Great Proletarian Cultural Revolution . . . and reviving the practices of the sinister revisionist line in literature and art."[13] According to Wu De, director of the Culture Group, Jiang tried to use Yu to pull the strings of cultural exchanges with the United States, administered with the National Committee on US-China Relations.[14] The infighting manifested itself in the Chinese response to the New York City Center of Music and Drama's proposal for a Peking opera tour of the United States: "Our model dramas are specially prepared for the appreciation of our working people, not for our enemy and money-scented capitalists like you."[15]

Politics and art were intertwined, and the innocuous outlook of cultural exchanges could not disguise that for too long. The National Committee promoted these exchanges to "create the public mood" conducive to normalization of relations.[16] The political qualities inherent in art, imagined or real, intended or unintended, caused cacophonies nonetheless, particularly in revolutionary ballet and classical music, which Washington and Beijing suspected as trojan horses. This chapter concerns the ebb and flow of this tension. The first part examines China's vacillating cultural politics in the early 1970s, focusing on the fallout of the Philadelphia Philharmonic Orchestra's 1973 visit to China. The second part analyzes the rupture between American and Chinese perceptions of art, epitomized by the postponement of China's performing arts troupe in 1975. The third part shifts attention to cultural exchanges in the aftermath of Jiang Qing's arrest, when Deng Xiaoping imported Western art forms beneficial to China's cultural modernization, while commercializing Chinese culture to earn foreign currency. Throughout the 1970s, cultural enthusiasts in China, particularly music lovers, showed passionate support for the reintroduction of Western art into China, and the post-Mao leadership co-opted it.

The Return of Beethoven

When Beijing embarked on artistic exports to the United States, it had to cater to the cultural taste of average Americans, who sought something spectacular. Acrobatics, a hybrid of China's artistic patrimony and physical skills, was a perfect choice for the first cultural group to the United States.[17]

Cohosted by the National Committee and the New York City Center, the Shenyang acrobatic troupe, consisting of seventy-seven members practicing a range of skills from bicycle balancing to plate spinning to lion dancing, toured the United States for four weeks between late 1972 and early 1973. All the tickets sold out, and the eyes of forty-five thousand spectators—and considerably more ABC viewers—were glued to the show. Clive Barnes, a *New York Times* dance and theater critic, wrote that "to call it sensational would be merely to underpraise it woefully."[18] The tear gas canister thrown onto the stage by a pro-Taiwan group in the Chicago Civic Opera House hardly shook the Chinese performers, as they returned to complete the program after a short interval.[19] Nixon invited the acrobats to the White House, and the cordial atmosphere at the reception seemed to symbolize their success in advancing "the understanding and friendship between the Chinese and the American peoples," as troupe leader Zhang Yingwu stated.[20]

The Shenyang acrobats' success rattled the KMT. To countervail the CCP's "cultural infiltration" into the United States, it recruited recent graduates of Peking opera schools, assembled a National Chinese Opera Theater, and pitched it to American impresarios.[21] With Taiwanese backing of $400,000, Harold Shaw, former associate of the celebrated impresario Sol Hurok, agreed to a three-month tour of the United States and Canada starting in September 1973, with sixty-seven performances in twenty-nine cities. Along the way, the KMT garnered financial, logistical, and promotional support of dozens of overseas Chinese organizations, including Chinese Consolidated Benevolent Associations (*Zhonghua huiguan/gongsuo*), the mainstay of its dominance over diaspora communities in North America. Although the opera company entertained almost ninety thousand, including government officials and business executives, the tour was hardly a sellout, with an average seat occupancy rate of 53 percent.[22] The *Washington Post* dance critic Alan Kriegsman aptly wrote that if the Shenyang acrobats offered "artistic acrobatics," the Taiwan troupe, with titbits of sundry Chinese theatrical traditions, exhibited "acrobatic art."[23] It was chic yet bland to the orientalist taste of American audiences. Unlike the mainlanders, the Taiwanese were not "treated like men from Mars."[24]

Beijing had to import some American culture in return for the acrobats. Zhou Enlai's music diplomacy, justified as "a great political mission to promote Chairman Mao's revolutionary diplomatic line," made classical music one of the few palatable options.[25] In early 1973, the London Philharmonic Orchestra and the Vienna Philharmonic became the first foreign orchestras to hold public concerts in China, playing Beethoven, Brahms, Mozart,

Dvořák, and Haydn—names that bespoke relaxation of cultural politics. After months of waiting, the Philadelphia Orchestra, led by Maestro Eugene Ormandy, received an invitation to visit China that September as the first US cultural delegation. The State Department and the National Committee assisted the orchestra in navigating the entire process. Beijing raised a litany of requests, pressuring the National Committee to select programs "understandable to the Chinese people," which required careful reading of Chinese politics.[26] The Philadelphia Orchestra mostly complied. Upon its arrival, however, Chinese officials suddenly requested Beethoven's Sixth Symphony to be added to the program at Jiang Qing's behest, although Ormandy disliked that symphony, and the orchestra did not even carry the scores. When the Chinese promised to deliver them, the maestro caved in.[27]

The Philadelphia Orchestra's tour was "an outstanding success on all counts—musically, diplomatically, and interpersonally," according to Douglas Murray, program director at the National Committee.[28] The retinue of 105 musicians played four times in Beijing and twice in Shanghai, each time attracting a huge crowd of officials and musicians, as well as a batch of peasants, workers, and soldiers. "There was dead silence during the performances . . . and everybody listened with a force that was almost palpable," the *New York Times* art critic Harold Schonberg wrote. "There was no coughing, no whispering, no shifting around. The feeling of concentration was almost frightening."[29] It was a testament to the passion for classical music, so deeply embedded in Chinese culture that urbanites, particularly in Shanghai, secretly listened to Western music and played Western instruments with trusted friends even during the Cultural Revolution, when music conservatories were closed.[30] As ABC put it, with the Philadelphia Orchestra's visit, American musicians "put a toe into the water of China and found it warm."[31]

The Philadelphia Orchestra left a subtle yet indelible mark on Chinese cultural politics. Attending the second concert in Beijing with Yao Wenyuan, Jiang Qing was engrossed in Beethoven's Sixth and visibly enamored when the orchestra played the Yellow River Piano Concerto, a joint work by her and renowned pianist Yin Chengzong. She gave an unusually warm welcome to Ormandy and his fellow musicians after the concert, handing some bean sprout seeds to each of them. "Our music is like bean sprouts that must grow up and prosper," Jiang quipped.[32] When Ormandy visited the Central Philharmonic a few days later and listened to a run-through of Beethoven's Fifth, Li Delun invited him to the podium to lead the orchestra himself (see fig. 7.2).[33] Before the Philadelphia Orchestra's departure, Hu Hongfan of the Chinese People's Association for Friendship with Foreign Countries even mentioned

Figure 7.2. Eugene Ormandy of the Philadelphia Philharmonic Orchestra leads the China Central Philharmonic to play Beethoven's Fifth Symphony, September 15, 1973. Courtesy of the Kislak Center for Special Collections, Rare Books and Manuscripts, University of Pennsylvania Libraries and the Philadelphia Philharmonic Orchestra.

the possibility of de-politicizing Chinese art to fit the taste of American audiences. Murray foresaw "a major change in Chinese cultural policy."[34] After the Philadelphia Orchestra's concert, Jiang fancied more Western music, allowing the Central Philharmonic to practice some ten Western symphonies for foreign dignitaries and instructing Li to teach her classical music that she deemed politically acceptable.[35] Beethoven was in vogue, momentarily.

The dalliance was short-lived. In late 1973, Jiang Qing soured on classical music due to two factors: Harold Schonberg's scathing critique of the Central Philharmonic and the power struggle with Zhou Enlai. While lauding Yin Chengzong's skills as a piano soloist, the *Times* critic, never much given to flattering, scoffed at the Yellow River Concerto as "movie music" and "a piece of trash," and even quoted the Philadelphia Orchestra musicians disparaging it as the Yellow "Fever" Concerto.[36] The incivilities stoked Jiang's anger, tipping the delicate balance between her admiration and despise for classical music. More fundamental than her fury was a turn of the tide in cultural politics. As the Criticize Lin, Criticize Confucius Campaign flared up, a volley of articles appeared in early 1974 that reaffirmed the class nature of music and railed against the restoration of Western music, advocated by Zhou. A *Peking Review* article, written by Yu Huiyong under a pseudonym, reviled classical music as "weapons to . . . serve the bourgeoisie for seizing and consolidating political power."[37] Jiang, Yu, and their allies were signaling that Western music concerts, a diplomatic necessity, by no means foreshadowed an end of the model plays and the political climate that nurtured them. Beethoven was now reverted to a capitalist composer.

Americans could feel the ripple of domestic tumults in China. In December 1973, the NSC staffer Richard Solomon apprised Kissinger of Beijing's "great reluctance" to engage in further cultural contacts. The Chinese, he explained, showed "little interest" in inviting more cultural groups like the Philadelphia Orchestra to "develop a positive public mood about our new relationship."[38] The mounting pressure on Li Delun confirmed Solomon's concern. In May 1974, Ormandy wrote to Li, requesting information about *The Moon Reflected on Erquan Spring*, a Chinese piece that he wished to play in the United States. Although the State Council's Culture Group had no objection to Ormandy's request, Yu Huiyong forced Li to write a response, in which he criticized himself for the political errors committed in that piece and discouraged the maestro from playing it.[39] Jiang Qing's political clout continued to grow into 1975, as the Fourth National People's Congress anointed Yu as head of the newly restored Ministry of Culture.

The cultural dominion was cracking everywhere, though. In the early 1970s, many painters resumed drawing traditional landscape and bird-and-flower paintings, labeled "black paintings" by Jiang Qing, while an underground art group called Wuming (No Name) held secret exhibitions in Beijing and Shanghai.[40] Miffed by the strictures on foreign novels, Beijing Teacher's College persuaded the municipal revolutionary committee to permit viewings of films based on approved novels, including works by Balzac, Gorky, and Sholokhov.[41] An art school principal in Hubei pledged to "take responsibility" for implementing a "less restrictive" policy, allowing teachers to borrow over two hundred Western music records from the library.[42] When a music school in Shanghai held discussions on how to revolutionize the old curriculum, some opined that "it would be fine not to revise it."[43] In the mid-1970s, "mass cynicism" about the model plays was "widespread," recollected Paul Clark, a New Zealand sinologist then at Peking University.[44] It might have emboldened Deng Xiaoping in 1975 to bewail the model plays as cultural impoverishment and to challenge Jiang Qing's reign over May Seventh Art University, an amalgam of six central art schools in Beijing established in 1973. He had the chairman's support. "There are too few model plays," Mao told Deng in the summer of 1975. "[Artists] cannot bring up their opinions; that's no good. There is a fear of . . . writing plays, novels, poems, and songs."[45] In 1976, Deng was condemned as an "anti-revolutionary, revisionist roader" in art and literature, but journals such as *People's Literature*, *Poetry Periodical*, *Film Art*, and *Fine Arts* resumed publishing, with some articles on Western works.[46]

Given the backlash, it was no surprise that the Gang of Four could not derail Sino-American cultural exchanges from within. Despite the Gang's distaste for traditional art, Beijing sent out a Wushu delegation in the summer of 1974 and an archaeological exhibit from late 1974 to mid-1975, under the slogan "make the past serve the present" (*gu wei jin yong*). The group of forty-three martial arts practitioners, including the future star Jet Li, performed for fifty-two thousand spectators in Hawaii, San Francisco, New York, and Washington, promoting Wushu in the United States, particularly among Kung Fu movie fans.[47] Unsettled by Beijing's growing cultural influence, Taipei tried to arrange a US tour of its performing arts troupe around the same time as the Wushu delegation. Washington, however, rejected Taipei's requested itinerary and assigned twenty security guards to protect the Wushu performers.[48] The archaeological exhibit, sponsored by IBM and other donors, toured Washington, Kansas City, and San Francisco after a year and half travel in Europe and Canada. It carried 385 objects from prehistoric and premodern China excavated after 1949, from the scull of Peking Man to china from the Song and Yuan dynasties to the Terracotta Warriors recently found near Xi'an. More than 1.8 million visited the exhibit, sometimes waiting for hours in line. It was a public relations triumph. The chief of the Chinese Liaison Office Huang Zhen asserted at the closing ceremony in San Francisco, "I believe that . . . friendship between the Chinese and American people will continue to develop."[49]

It was a "friendship" in Chinese terms, predicated on whether someone or something conformed to Chinese political claims. Art was not exempted from this straightjacket. When the National Committee organized on-site educational activities at the archaeological exhibit, including slideshow lectures on Chinese art history, the Chinese Liaison Office compelled it to avoid discussion of controversial topics, especially the Four Olds Movement, much to the indignation of China scholars. The Chinese also tried to bar Taiwanese, South Korean, South African, and Israeli reporters from a press preview at the National Gallery of Art in Washington, which precipitated its cancellation.[50] These incidents, minor as they seemed, shed light on the shaky foundation of Sino-American cultural exchanges in the mid-1970s, when Beijing was trying to do what Washington was doing worldwide in a more low-key manner: mobilizing art to spread political ideas. The Chinese considered anyone and anything that contradicted their ideas "unfriendly." It was Cold War cultural politics in action.

Injecting Politics into Culture

The rift surfaced in the spring of 1975, when the Chinese performing arts troupe was scheduled to tour the United States. It would be the largest group from China since the 1972 ping-pong delegation, featuring a diverse set of performance genres, including revolutionary ballet, Peking opera, classical music, acrobatic dance, and Chinese traditional instruments like pipa. By the summer of 1974, however, Beijing was shunning the National Committee. When the former chairman Alexander Eckstein visited the Chinese Liaison Office in July, the political counselor Qian Dayong deplored US insensitivities that tainted cultural exchanges, alluding to Harold Schonberg's writings. "There are some people in the Liaison Office who question the usefulness of maintaining contact with the National Committee," warned Qian.[51] Two weeks later, the cultural counselor at the Liaison Office Xie Qimei nudged the State Department, albeit unsuccessfully, to assign an organization other than the National Committee to the performing arts troupe.[52] The Chinese kept "foot-dragging and stalling" to "bypass" the National Committee, as Douglas Murray bemoaned.[53] When the US-China People's Friendship Association was founded in Los Angeles that September—some of its core members opposing "public criticism" of China—Beijing sent a congratulatory message and began to groom it as a potential substitute for the National Committee, much more proficient in promoting "friendship."[54] Tension was building quietly.

On March 8, 1975, three weeks before the performing arts troupe's arrival, the Liaison Office made last-minute changes to the program. The National Committee program coordinator Jan Berris noticed that the Chinese slipped into the list a song called "People of Taiwan, Our Own Brothers," which included an incendiary line: "We are determined to liberate Taiwan. Let the light of the sun shine on the island." She winced. Since few impresarios were willing to host the Chinese group, the National Committee received the bulk of funding from the State Department, which made the Taiwan liberation song a guaranteed diplomatic embarrassment. Concurring with Berris, the National Committee leadership urged the State Department and the Liaison Office to resolve the issue. With the program finalized and printed within a week, State's East Asia experts were light-headed.[55] The assistant secretary of state for East Asian and Pacific affairs Philip Habib rushed to the Liaison Office and asked Vice Chief Han Xu to remove the song to avoid "meaningless controversies." Han concluded that the demand violated the "one-China" principle in the Shanghai Communiqué, a view that quickly gained support from the Ministries of Foreign Affairs and Culture.[56] Xie telephoned the National Committee president Arthur Rosen, asserting that since Taiwan was "an integral part of China," it was "only natural" for the Chinese to express "their true feelings" about the island.[57] Given the same response by Han, Habib upped the ante with a de facto ultimatum, calling it "inappropriate" to "inject this [political] issue into a cultural exchange program."[58] The Chinese wouldn't budge. When Kissinger's high hopes that Beijing might settle for something indicating "brotherhood" with Taiwan, but not "liberation" of it, were dashed, the National Committee announced an indefinite postponement of the well-publicized performing arts troupe on March 27—two days before its arrival.[59]

An uproar ensued. The USCPFA read a statement at a press conference, in which William Hinton and others "strongly" protested the postponement, charging that it raised "great questions" about American "sincerity" in cultural exchanges.[60] Within the National Committee, Alexander Eckstein—staying in Australia and not fully informed about the unfolding of events—resented the Chinese move, as well as the group's failure to omit the Taiwan song outright. "If we do not have the integrity and the capacity to conduct realistic and genuinely reciprocal exchanges in a come and take spirit with the Chinese, we have no business being involved," he clamored.[61] Almost all letters to the National Committee and most newspaper editorials supported the cancellation, with an exception of the *Chicago Tribune*, which rebuked US government intervention in art as "patronizing" and "scary."[62] Whoever they blamed, all seemed to agree on one point—that the Taiwan problem now threatened further deterioration of US-China relations. "This rather shaky marriage of convenience has entered the critical post-honeymoon period of agonizing reappraisals," Richard Baum wrote in the *Los Angeles Times*.[63]

The postponement of the performing arts troupe, and Vice President Nelson Rockefeller's attendance at the KMT leader Chiang Kai-shek's funeral three weeks later, infuriated the Chinese. They vented their anger by redoubling propaganda toward foreigners in China. The Shanghai Municipal Revolutionary Committee organized viewings of cultural performances, "People of Taiwan, Our Own Brothers" included, for over two thousand visitors in the city. An internal report noted that most viewers, including dozens of Americans, lauded Beijing's determination to sing the song in the

United States—though probably out of courtesy.⁶⁴ While refraining from canceling the US track-and-field group that May, Beijing torpedoed a delegation of mayors scheduled in September by contesting US sovereignty over Puerto Rico and denying a visa to the mayor of San Juan, Carlos Romero Barceló.⁶⁵ It was a careful face-saving maneuver.

The performing arts troupe incident laid bare the fundamental problem in Sino-American cultural exchanges. There is a chance that the plot was hatched by the Gang of Four to add the Taiwan song to the program, but no hard evidence has so far validated this hypothesis. The crisis arose not so much from the Taiwan song per se as from the discrepancy between the American and Chinese ideas about art, which was accentuated by the song. The National Committee, as well as the State Department, viewed cultural exchanges as a tool to deepen bilateral relations in the absence of diplomatic relations. As such, they should feature artistic representations detached from politics, which appealed to audiences across the broad political spectrum. Beijing took exception. While celebrating cultural exchanges as a way of fostering "friendship," it believed that the "friendship" should foreground political values represented by Chinese art, including the sovereignty over Taiwan. Washington accused Beijing of injecting politics into art, but never had art and politics been separable in Mao's China, spanning over three decades, and not just at the zenith of Jiang Qing's power. This was evident in the fall of 1975, when the aging chairman criticized the mentality of "capitulationism" in the fourteenth-century novel *Water Margin*, an indirect attack on Deng Xiaoping, followed by a wave of commentaries extolling the model plays.⁶⁶ Charging the National Committee of "cultural infiltration," Beijing refused its proposal to increase the number of exchanges in 1976 to recoup the lack of progress on the diplomatic front.⁶⁷ The "realistic and genuinely reciprocal exchanges" that Eckstein espoused had to await new cultural politics to emerge in China.

The Gang of Four's arrest was the first step. Beginning in late 1976, newspapers and magazines were filled with bills of particulars against Jiang Qing, including the late 1977 pieces in the *People's Daily* written by famed novelists Ba Jin and Bing Xin.⁶⁸ Hua Guofeng, however, remained equivocal about cultural politics, making few announcements in that embattled realm. Chinese musicians ran out of patience. Having filed many inquires that went unanswered, Li Delun decided to jump the gun and play Beethoven's Fifth Symphony with the Central Philharmonic at a gala concert on March 26, 1977, commemorating the 150th anniversary of Beethoven's death. It was the first public concert to do so since 1966. The tickets sold out so fast that the

Central Philharmonic added more concerts later in the year. A member of the Shanghai Music Lovers' Association now saw "the light that comes after a period of great difficulty."[69] So did countless others at home and abroad. Norman Lebrecht, a British music critic, watched the broadcast of Li's rendition of Beethoven's Fifth in his hotel room in Hong Kong. Careening down the corridor into the bar, he yelled: "The Cultural Revolution's over!"[70] Five months later, Yu Huiyong's suicide spelled the death of Cultural Revolution art.

Modernization loomed as the new tenet of China's cultural politics. With Deng Xiaoping's help, Huang Zhen, appointed minister of culture in December 1977, abolished May Seventh Art University and restored art and music schools across the country, which immediately began recruiting new students. The Central Conservatory of Music attracted seventeen thousand applicants for only three hundred slots.[71] Huang also rehabilitated purged artists and officials, relaxed regulations on foreign films and traditional performances, and fixed damaged theaters, studios, and concert halls.[72] Zhang Junqiu, a prominent Peking opera singer, recollected that Huang, impressed with his voice after years of hiatus, personally arranged his return to the stage, giving him a "second art life."[73] The *New York Times* correspondent Harrison Salisbury, who met a number of Chinese artists in late 1977, observed that they "were emerging from the shadows" of the Cultural Revolution, "luxuriating in their physical release and in their renewed ability to hold up their heads and perform publicly, to write, to compose."[74] In May 1978, the third national committee of the China Federation of Literary and Art Circles reinstated professional societies of writers, playwrights, musicians, filmmakers, and dancers. Before a crowd of over 340 artists and officials, novelist Xu Chi thundered: "We must strive to modernize art and literature, and contribute to the four modernizations!"[75]

The key was cultural imports. The Ministry of Culture circulated a directive in the spring of 1978, instructing local cultural agencies to examine artistic trends overseas through international exchanges. "Foreign travelers to China offer extremely good opportunities for research and study right at our fingertips," it read.[76] Teachers and students at art schools were now encouraged to attend international art exhibitions and analyze foreign films approved by the ministry, while noted translator Cao Ying vowed to translate more foreign novels into Chinese.[77] Two literature journals that resumed publishing in 1977 and 1978, *Literacy Criticism* and *World Literature*, featured "capitalist" and "revisionist" works, on the pretext of "processing poisonous weeds into fertilizer."[78] Western music returned to urban China as a popular pastime, and instruments, particularly piano, became a new status symbol.[79] The Yellow River Concerto was hissed off the stage. "We all got our fill of that music," Li Delun blurted out. A leading member of the Central Philharmonic triumphantly stated, "We are ushering in a bright spring in the field of art and literature . . . a new tide of socialist art is beginning."[80] In July 1978, Beijing accepted a proposal of Chinese American composer Zhou Wenzhong (Chou Wen-chung) to begin exchanging American and Chinese artists in different genres through the Center for US-China Arts Exchange, soon to be founded at Columbia University.[81] During his four-year tenure, Minister of Culture Huang Zhen established similar cultural exchange agreements with twenty-eight countries.[82]

It was an extraordinary turn of events. Gone were the days when the model plays overwhelmed cultural life in China. They survived, but traditional play, Western music, and classical ballet drove them out of one theater at a time, especially in the cities. "I don't have to go to operas anymore," one guide rejoiced. "I hate opera."[83] By the end of the decade, the Chinese population was even enjoying Charlie Chaplin's *Modern Times* and William Shakespeare's melodramas. The fading of the model plays did not mean that art ceased to be part of politics. It still was, and most contemporary art forms in the West, particularly popular culture, remained largely off-limits. Yet Beijing was now poised to patronize art that modernized Chinese culture, not advanced "friendship" with other countries. It was a whole new cultural politics.

Modernizing Cultural Exchanges

In China after Mao, modernizing culture meant two things: making it sophisticated and profitable. Divorced from each other for almost three decades, these two measurements in art now dovetailed: An art that is sophisticated is profitable, and an art that is profitable is sophisticated. An art that amuses, impresses, and captivates cannot be modern unless it compels the audience to pay for it. During the Cultural Revolution, the Gang of Four, courting peasants, workers, and soldiers, kept theater tickets so cheap, if not free, that any show could hardly be profitable and, by extension, sophisticated, based on this logic. In the late 1970s, the Ministry of Culture proposed to raise ticket prices to pre-1966 standards. For *Swan Lake* performed by the China National Opera and Dance Drama Theater, for instance, it suggested one yuan for the Chinese and four yuan for foreigners.[84] The "new tide of socialist art" entertained the rich, not the poor.

By the same token, a sophisticated art with international recognition should accrue foreign currency. Impressed by traditional sculptures and textiles at the National Art and Craft Exhibit, Deng Xiaoping commented in February 1978 that China should "export more [of these products] and earn more foreign currency." He insisted on improving packaging—more cushioning, for example—to make Chinese artifacts more marketable, a suggestion echoed by the State Administration of Cultural Heritage, as well as the Ministries of Foreign Trade and Commerce, which had been acting like art dealers since the early 1970s, bucking the State Council's Culture Group and selling salvaged artifacts at the Canton Fair and elsewhere.[85] The April 1978 meeting of light industry officials around the country avowed to double the exports of artifacts from $720 million in 1978 to $1.5 billion in 1985.[86] They were doing exactly what Jiang Qing abhorred: promoting "cultural exports" to make a profit.

China's first large-scale cultural export to the United States in the post-Mao era was the performing arts troupe in the summer of 1978, more than three years after its postponement. In April 1975, Jerome Cohen of Harvard told Arthur Rosen that the National Committee should usher in "the Sol Hurok era" in Sino-American cultural exchanges, in which impresarios independent of the government hosted Chinese shows for profit, not for "friendship." American impresarios fell on hard times in the 1970s, however, unable to fill theaters for cultural performances. Few of them, surmised Cohen, would be willing to sponsor large Chinese groups requiring security anywhere they went.[87] He turned out to be a little too pessimistic. Anthony Bliss, executive director of the Metropolitan Opera (MET), saw an "entertainment value" in Peking opera and asked the National Committee in May 1976 to cohost the performing arts troupe. Rosen hesitated, worrying if accepting Bliss's proposal after the wrangle in the previous spring would taint the group's reputation. He reasoned nonetheless that the MET's cosponsorship would dilute the responsibility and that Americans, after all, would not be so easily "brainwashed" by Chinese agitprop as some critics warned.[88]

A shrewd impresario, Bliss was not interested in "charitable giving." The Chinese had to raise all the money necessary for the tour by themselves, which nearly doubled the ticket prices from 1975. Quality control was essential to boost ticket sales. "If they wish to export their culture, they will have to do so on terms acceptable to the importer," asserted Bliss. He even traveled to Canada to check on the Shanghai Opera Company's *White Haired Girl*. To make the show more salable, the National Committee convinced the Chinese to reduce classical music and increase things Chinese, most of all Peking opera. This time, the finalized programs did not include "People of Taiwan, Our Own Brothers." Beijing probably understood what Bliss told Rosen: "If the Chinese start out now with a bad performance, it will be ten years before you could bring a Chinese group again and get an audience."[89] The MET, the National Committee, and the Chinese were all in the same boat, under enormous financial pressure.

The tour was a success for all. The group held thirty stages of music, dance, and opera for the audience of 130,000 in total. It was a "spectacle from the East," Alan Kriegsman marveled. "The Chinese have an extraordinary color sense, quite different from Western sensibilities in the mixture and blending of hues . . . thoroughly consistent and dazzling in design."[90] All tickets sold out at the Wolf Trap Center near Washington, and spectators sought autographs of the performers after the shows, especially composer-pianist Liu Shikun. At the finale on the opening night, the curtain rose four times as the group responded to the applause, which lasted for ten minutes. As the *Washington Post* wrote, it was "a demonstration of close American-Chinese relations, at least in the audience," which included such VIPs as Zbigniew Brzezinski.[91] The performers were as thrilled as the audience. Zhou Xiaoyan, a renowned opera singer nicknamed "China's Nightingale," enthused: "Rise up, the Yangtze River! Rise up, the Mississippi River! I wish the friendship between the Chinese and American people flows on forever like you!"[92] Thanks to television rights, box ticket sales, and donations from major corporations, including Bank of America, Coca Cola, Fluor, and Pan Am, the performing arts tour generated revenue of $280,000.

The Chinese were keen on making more money. Following the Guangdong Performing Arts Company's successful tour of Hong Kong and Macau in mid-1979, Beijing sent forty-six commercially oriented cultural delegations worldwide in the next three years, including a group of Shanghai acrobats to the United States in March 1980.[93] They wished to bring the ace performer: giant panda Wei Wei. Given the "panda-monium" caused by Ling Ling and Xing Xing, who came to the National Zoo as diplomatic gifts in 1972, Wei Wei's trumpet-blowing would be a sensation.[94] The State Council, however, decreed in late 1979 that pandas not accompany cultural delegations overseas, lest their diplomatic value depreciated. The Shanghai Acrobatic Troupe sent a letter of protest, averring that as "a messenger of friendship," Wei Wei could "earn foreign currency for the nation." Should she not perform overseas, it would be "tantamount to holding a 'golden rice bowl' in hand and watching gold drain away like water."[95] In the end, the Shanghai acrobats were spectacular even without Wei Wei. "It was an evening of unparalleled virtuosity," the *New York Times* wrote. "One simply refused to believe one's eyes. Yet it was all real."[96] The ticket sales stagnated nevertheless, and the booking rate in New York remained 30 to 40 percent. Having lost $250,000, Columbia Arts Management decided to terminate the sponsorship contract in the middle of the tour.[97] Chinese art troupes proved utterly unprofitable, both inside and outside China—even unsustainable without government subsidies.[98]

While monetizing Chinese art, Beijing imported the other element of cultural modernization: sophistication. Classical music led the way. Following Andrew Davis's Toronto Symphony Orchestra and Herbert von Karajan's Berlin Philharmonic, the Boston Symphony Orchestra, with the Shenyang-born Japanese maestro Seiji Ozawa, visited China in March 1979, with the sponsorship of Coca Cola, Mobil, Gillette, and Pan Am. Ozawa had traveled to China by himself in the previous year, hosted by Han Zhongjie, associate conductor of the Central Philharmonic, who remembered the "freshness" Ozawa brought to the podium. "His conducting is so passionate and impressive . . . that many music students have made him their idol and imitate his conducting."[99] When Ozawa returned in the next spring with the entire Boston Symphony of 104 musicians, the news spread across the country. To listen to his rendition of Beethoven, Amadeus Mozart, Respighi, and Tchaikovsky, tens of thousands of musicians, teachers, students, and music fans, even from such remote regions as Tibet, lined up for tickets to the four concerts—one in Shanghai, three in Beijing. The stakes were high, not least because the Boston Symphony was the first US cultural delegation since the normalization of relations. At the first night in Beijing, Deng Xiaoping praised it for "enhance[ing] contacts and friendship" between the American and Chinese people.[100]

The Boston Symphony's sound reverberated among music lovers in China. Contrary to the quiet, reserved audience, mostly officials, who received the Philadelphia Orchestra in 1973, the Boston Symphony found a young, enthusiastic audience with little hesitation to show their passion for classical music. The Chinese "listened not out of politeness, but with real intensity," wrote Harold Schonberg. "Almost everybody was leaning forward, drinking in the sound in a sort of mass hypnosis . . . there was a look on most faces that can only be described as rapt."[101] At the grand finale in Beijing, the Boston Symphony and the Central Philharmonic jointly played Beethoven's Fifth Symphony before an exultant crowd of eighteen thousand, and the final encore, John Philip Sousa's *The Stars and Stripes Forever*, met with a thunderous applause (see fig. 7.3). The entire Capital Indoor Stadium was

Figure 7.3. Seiji Ozawa conducts a joint concert of the Boston Symphony Orchestra and the China Central Philharmonic at Capital Indoor Stadium in Beijing, March 19, 1979. Photographer unknown. Courtesy of the Boston Symphony Orchestra Archives.

abuzz with boisterous revelry. The audience basked in the afterglow of Ozawa's music, vying to shake hands with the maestro as he walked out of the hall. *CBS Report* narrated: "Maybe . . . it's the music makers, who are the movers and shakers."[102]

The Boston Symphony pulled off something that government officials never could. With his "arms that speak," Ozawa wielded the power of music to promote China's embrace of Western culture and symbolize the new relationship between the United States and China.[103] "The way the Chinese soaked up the music ... has done more good than anything that can be established through diplomatic channels," the US ambassador Leonard Woodcock raved.[104] Cai Jindong, a young pianist in the audience, personified this. Exhilarated by Beethoven's Fifth, he felt that Ozawa had "rhythm in every part of his body and music in his every movement, as if his body was the music." Cai swooned when the music dynamo came back to China a few months later and led the Central Philharmonic to play Beethoven's Ninth with éclat. "It seems like my entire heart, my entire being, has dissolved into this magnificent, glorious symphony.... Beethoven is unmatchable.... This is real music—its power makes me forget everything."[105] Cai could forget the dullness of the model plays, the stigma attached to Western music, and the Cold War hostility ingrained in revolutionary art. In 1985, he went to the United States to further study classical music.

Cai Jindong's rapture was shared by many. Assisted by the Center for US-China Arts Exchange, violinist Isaac Stern visited China in June 1979 to teach Chinese players, from seasoned ones in their thirties and forties to young ones of school age. Stern found most of them bereft of "color and passion." "With a smile, a joke, a friendly gesture," he gradually enlivened the Chinese, allowing them to express their emotions in music.[106] The film based on Stern's visit, *From Mao to Mozart*, won the 1981 Academy Award for best documentary.[107] It was an apt title: Countless Chinese artists were indeed walking on the path from Mao to Mozart, from revolution in art to modernization in art, often with the help of Americans. It was not a glorious path. In the wake of the Cultural Revolution, many artists had to come to terms with their trauma and suffering, both personal and collective, vividly depicted by the so-called scar literature, which emerged in the late 1970s.[108] American artists prescribed art as medicine to help the healing process.

Art was a major trade item between the United States and China in the 1980s. While Washington and Beijing facilitated many delegations after the cultural exchange agreement on January 31, 1979, corporations, museums, art societies, art dealers, and individual artists imported and exported art in ever more complex ways.[109] On the whole, Chinese sought US cultural products, no longer limited to fine arts, more avidly than the other way around. American cultural icons—Coca-Cola, Pepsi, McDonald's, Kentucky Fried Chicken, Disney, and Hollywood—made their way into China in quick succession, although the process was far from straightforward.[110] Movies created a great fandom in China. During the "American film week" held in major cities in May 1981, millions were enamored of *Singin' in the Rain*, *Shane*, *Guess Who's Coming to Dinner*, *Snow White and the Seven Dwarfs*, and *The Black Stallion*, popular flicks that struck a balance between American cinematic tradition and Chinese cultural politics. When a US film delegation visited China that fall, it found "an enormous market . . . for American movies." "And once again," the members crowed, "we've had a demonstration that American movies are preeminent the world over, admired and wanted by audiences everywhere."[111]

By the end of the 1970s, Chinese art consumers and producers were trumpeting the spring of culture, and Beijing was trying to muffle it. A growing number of bootleg films were circulated privately, often by embassy workers, impinging on the Ministry of Culture's efforts to regulate foreign films.[112] The CCP Propaganda Department warned against the spread of "ugly" photographs of foreign movie stars, with "promiscuous" words written on them, many of which originated from *Southern Screen*, a film magazine in Hong Kong.[113] *Minzhu*—literally translated as "democracy"—emerged as a leitmotif in literature. In late 1978, the Shanghai Writers' Association commented that art should not be regulated, standardized, or hierarchized. Art not only fed on "the atmosphere of *minzhu*," but also offered "one of the weapons for the masses to fight for *minzhu*."[114] Hu Yaobang, head of the Propaganda Department, later counseled that *minzhu* should be guided by the CCP. "You talk about launching amateur magazines," he huffed at a meeting on poetry periodicals. "I don't oppose them, but there should be a limit, shouldn't there?"[115] Undeterred, Wang Ruowang, chair of the China Writers Association, blared in late 1979: "We have the freedom of creation. . . . You [the government] should mind your own business."[116]

Modern art seemed to be the greatest menace to the CCP, because it looked "queer." A Chinese official who accompanied Deng Xiaoping to the National Gallery of Art in January 1979 snapped that modern art was "one modernization we don't need."[117] In the next couple of years, however, groups of young avant-garde artists, including Xingxing (Stars) and Caocao (Grass), set up guerrilla exhibitions of experimental art in Beijing and Shanghai, attracting huge crowds before they were closed by the police.[118] The CCP tried to cut off the supply of inspiration from the United States. When Boston's Museum of Fine Arts held the first American art exhibition at the National Art Museum in Beijing in the fall of 1981, the Chinese made a last-minute request to remove thirteen modern abstract paintings, including Jackson Pollock's. They backed down, though, when US officials threatened to cancel the entire exhibition. Chief Justice Warren Burger proclaimed at the opening ceremony: "The works of art in this exhibition express the American spirit of freedom in which each person can write, paint and do whatever he wants as long as it does not violate the Constitution."[119] In late 1985, the contemporary art giant Robert Rauschenberg held an exhibition at the National Art Museum, featuring, among other things, found objects from his international travels, exotic and mundane. The authority clamped down on similar exhibits by Chinese artists, but the avant-garde art movement was gathering momentum in China.[120]

It was an irony of history. No sooner did Chinese leaders accelerate the cultural opening to the West, did they find themselves agonizing over its consequences. The Propaganda Department dictated in late 1978 that Chinese artists must "absorb the essence [of foreign art] and discard the dregs."[121] It was easier said than done in a country where the kissing scene in *The Slipper and the Rose*, a musical rendition of *Cinderella*, printed on the back cover of *Popular Movies* magazine, aroused a controversy.[122] Beethoven glowed on the stage; rock went underground. The playwright Arthur Miller, dancer Martha Graham, and comedian Bob Hope were lauded; Teresa Teng, "Asia's eternal queen of pop," was banned. *Superman* was shown on screen in 1986; the *Star Wars* trilogy, three decades later. The kaleidoscope of Chinese cultural politics was dizzying. When it seemed to be slipping out of control in late 1983, Beijing launched the Anti-Spiritual Pollution Campaign to disabuse the population, particularly urban youth, of "bourgeois liberalism" percolating into art, literature, and society at large.[123] The three-month crackdown was just the beginning of a struggle that would continue throughout the 1980s, and beyond. As Han Zhongjie of the Central Philharmonic presciently said in 1978, cultural politics in China was "like a pan of water with mud at the bottom." "[Jiang Qing] stirred up the mud and made everything murky," he mused. "It's still not clear. We have to keep thinking about it a lot more."[124]

Epilogue

When the United States and China normalized relations on January 1, 1979, the Americans and Chinese found themselves already tangled up in a raft of relationships, inconceivable less than a decade ago. These relationships were bundled together by threads of new interests, growing in size and number, which generated a new set of images of each other. Americans had reimagined China as a budding customer, an earnest scholar, a zestful student, an inhabitant of the Middle Kingdom, a tenacious athlete, and an exotic performer; and Chinese, for their part, had reinterpreted the United States as an avid investor, a research patron, an enthusiastic teacher, an affluent traveler, a sports star, and a cultural connoisseur. Although the normalization was primarily occasioned by the shared strategic concerns against the Soviet Union, these perceptions warranted a new US-China relationship. As Jimmy Carter stated at a press conference on December 15, 1978, "now our rapidly expanding relationship requires a kind of structure that only full diplomatic relations will make possible."[1]

A sense of realism prevailed in both countries. The majority of Americans approved recognition of China as inevitable, while slamming the administration for forsaking Taiwan.[2] Congress moved swiftly to enact the Taiwan Relations Act of 1979, which guaranteed the continuation of unofficial ties with Taiwan, including arms sales. Chinese hyperbolized the normalization as "a diplomatic atom bomb that shook the Pacific and the entire world." A confluence of factors compelled Carter to recognize China—Chinese struggle against US dominance in the world, US domestic pressure for recognition of China, international competition for the China market, and Soviet expansionism in the developing world—according to propaganda reports. The "diplomatic atom bomb" would one day empower China to "liberate" Taiwan without the use of force, through economic integration, as Deng Xiaoping envisaged.[3] Americans and Chinese were walking a fine line, accepting the new bilateral relationship on the one hand and bracing themselves for future missteps on the other.

The realism on both sides was tempered by euphoria in the public discourse. On the same day that Carter celebrated "a long history of friendship" between Americans and Chinese, the *People's Daily* editorialized that their "traditional friendship" would "undergo further development."[4] The historian Michael Hunt bemoaned "the fatal tendency" of Americans "to project our fantasies beyond our borders." "The time has come," he claimed, "to abandon hopes of resurrecting the special relationship and accept as natural rather than aberrational the problems our largely divergent interests and experiences are bound to create."[5] Hunt was hardly living ahead of his time. In late 1978, Beijing residents began to post big-character posters on the brick wall along Xidan Street in the central city, igniting the so-called Democracy Wall Movement. They aired various political voices in essays, journals, and poems, many of them espousing democracy—or "the fifth modernization" as writer Wei Jingsheng christened it. Though initially supportive of the movement, Deng launched a crackdown in the spring of 1979 and abolished the Democracy Wall by year's end, signaling that the advocacy for "the fifth modernization" had "gone too far."[6] The writing was on the wall, clear and bright.

The rift over Taiwan lingered into the early 1980s. Beijing resented US arms sales to Taiwan, while Washington insisted on the mainland's renunciation of force against the island—an altercation that went unresolved even after the August 1982 joint communiqué stipulated the common desires for gradual reduction of US arms sales and "a peaceful solution" to the Taiwan problem.[7] By 1984, however, Washington and Beijing agreed to disagree over how to crack the Taiwan enigma, and Premier Zhao Ziyang and President Ronald Reagan paid mutual visits in January and April, respectively. The rapport was symbolized by the cover of *Time* magazine on April 30, 1984, titled "China's New Face: What Reagan Will See." It featured a young Chinese man with a gentle smile on his face, posing to the camera against the backdrop of the Great Wall, with a bottle of Kekou Kele (Coca-Cola) in his hand.[8] As *Time* magazine predicted, "the Reagan road show through China" raised "the temperature of the friendship another few degrees."[9] Economic, educational, and cultural ties between the two countries continued to grow in the late 1980s, when the rise of the Soviet leader Mikhail Gorbachev obviated the geopolitical imperative for Sino-American cooperation. The interests accrued from the thriving connections seemed to have outlived the common threat from the Soviet Union as the engine of US-China relations.[10] Visiting Beijing in February 1989, President George H. W. Bush declared that "the prospects for our two countries to advance the relationship have never been greater."[11]

Then, the sky fell. On June 3–4, 1989, at the tragic climax of the democracy movement, the Chinese Communist Party leadership ordered the People's Liberation Army to crush the people demonstrating at Tiananmen Square in Beijing as well as other cities across the country. TV stations around the world repeatedly broadcasted the horrors—a line of soldiers shooting unarmed pedestrians indiscriminately, armored vehicles smashing through barricades and rolling into students and workers, and locals using rickshaws and benches to rush the wounded as well as the dead to the hospital. Stunned, the United States, Western Europe, and Japan imposed economic sanctions and arms embargo on China, while canceling almost all official exchanges. At a press conference on June 5, Bush condemned the violent crackdown on the protestors exercising "basic human rights"—"goals we support around the world."[12] The *People's Daily* shot back, blasting "some US media outlets, especially the Voice of America," for "adding as much fuel as possible" to the "anti-revolutionary turmoil" to incite a "civil war" in China.[13] The cauldron of rage and despair turned US public opinion upside down. According to a Gallup poll in the spring of 1989, 72 percent of Americans viewed China favorably and only 13 percent unfavorably; that summer it was 31 percent favorably and 58 percent unfavorably—and the numbers have never quite recovered since.[14] In the fury of arrests and executions that ensued in China, the old rhetoric of US "imperialism" and Chinese "menace" came roaring back.

Bush rushed to minimize the damage. On July 1—three days after the House of Representatives approved economic sanctions against China by 418–0—the national security adviser Brent Scowcroft and the deputy secretary of state Lawrence Eagleburger made a secret trip to Beijing to sit down with Deng Xiaoping at the Great Hall of the People. Deng was boiling with anger at VOA, and the US government behind it, for "rumor mongering" around the world. "If [the rebels] should succeed in [overthrowing the CCP regime] the world would be a different one," he bristled. "To be frank, this could even lead to war." Deng repeated the word "dignity" to justify the carnage. "I would like to tell you, Mr. Scowcroft, we will never allow any people to interfere in China's internal affairs." Deng also warned that the sanctions put bilateral relations "in a very dangerous state," heading toward a "break up." His counsel was a proverb Beijing often invoked when negotiating the Taiwan problem in the 1970s: "It is up to the person who tied the knot to untie the knot." Scowcroft, patient and scrupulous as he was, defended the US reactions to "the progress" in China. "What the American people perceived in the demonstrations . . . was an expression of values which represent their most deeply cherished beliefs, stemming from the American revolution," he explained. "Americans, naturally and inevitably, respond emotionally when they see these values promoted elsewhere." Deprived of the common Soviet enemy, Washington and Beijing quickly ran out of options to bridge the gap. Bush sent a personal letter to Deng later that month, "out of respect, a feeling of closeness and, yes, friendship," but Deng responded with a firm demand on lifting the sanctions. The gulf seemed too deep to even fathom.[15]

The crucial point of contention was what touched off Tiananmen. Americans saw it as a popular movement, inspired by such prominent dissidents as the scientist Fang Lizhi, journalist Liu Binyan, and writer Wang Ruowang, and fueled by the events in the spring of 1989, including the reformist official Hu Yaobang's death (April 15), Gorbachev's visit to Beijing (May 15–18), and the CCP general secretary Zhao Ziyang's forlorn attempt to pacify the protestors (May 19). Chinese officials, by contrast, viewed the movement as an uprising of a lawless mob—a Cultural Revolution redux—instigated by "counter-revolutionaries" abetted by the United States. *The Tiananmen Papers*, a compilation of top-secret government documents, provenance of which remains debated, contained the Ministry of State Security's internal report on US "ideological and cultural infiltration," dated June 1. It detailed subversive activities by American groups and individuals partaking in "economic and cultural exchanges"—including VOA; the United States Information Agency; the Fulbright Program; billionaire George Soros; sinologist Perry Link, one of the editors of *The Tiananmen Papers*; and "missionaries" disguised as "teachers, businessmen, doctors, and technicians"—all of them using American "civilization" to spread "bourgeois liberalization," which Beijing had long been struggling to fend off.[16] For the old guard, military action was amply justified.

Tiananmen was a punch to the gut for all who had been striving for many years to cultivate ties with China. Most nongovernmental groups criticized the bloodshed and suspended exchange programs, while numerous scholars openly forswore traveling to China in the foreseeable future. Yet few of them wished to resurrect mutual isolation harkening back to the Cold War. On June 5, the National Committee on US-China Relations announced the postponement of its programs with "shock and sadness," but left a positive note: "We look forward to a time when the atmosphere for productive programs will again exist."[17] On that same day, the National Committee adopted a five-point policy statement that it should undertake the following:

- Speak truth about events in China and their consequences for US-[China] relations, as we understand those events
- Stay engaged, for it has been engagement that has contributed to the change which the Chinese people themselves have demonstrated they desire and which Americans applaud
- Recognize that although there may be tough times ahead, China is a big, diverse country in which American interests endure
- Remain true to the Committee's historical mandate to foster thoughtful, balanced, and informed discussion of China policy in the United States
- Look to the future as we recall the past[18]

It was a mix of realism and idealism. While acknowledging the coexistence of interests and conflicts that characterized bilateral relations, the National Committee doubled down on the power of people-to-people exchanges to induce, not force, a gradual "change." Herein lay a ray of hope for a future in which China might embrace what David M. Lampton, then president of the National Committee, would call a "more humane governance."[19] The statement was the American playbook for "engagement."

The National Committee scurried to put the words into action. In early July, it hosted a conference of over forty representatives from business, government, and academia at the Wingspread Conference Center in Racine, Wisconsin. While confessing her "moral agony," Jan Berris, now vice president of the National Committee, commented: "The web of relationship is simply too important not to maintain and strengthen. The question of resuming scholarly activity is when and how, clearly not whether." Two ideas arose as a rough consensus. First, the Americans should register their rage to Beijing before restoring contacts. "You don't want to go back [to China] like little puppy dogs," Berris deadpanned. Second, the Americans should "re-engage" China in an "honest, productive, and non-propagandistic" manner.[20] "One does not want to isolate China," argued Lampton. "One of the pressures that has generated momentum for political change in China has been the connections with the rest of the world."[21] After the conference, Lampton, along with Roger Sullivan, president of the US-China Business Council (renamed from the National Council for US-China Trade in 1988), also opposed further sanctions. "It simply does not make sense to turn off these engines of change and then call for increasing movement toward political change," they reasoned.[22] The National Committee was ready to make a move. "It is our responsibility to continue to keep the channels open," the board of directors resolved that August. "We are a lead organization; people will take their cue from us."[23]

The National Committee took the first concrete step to resume exchanges in early September, when Lampton and Doak Barnett traveled to China in a fact-finding mission. The endless rounds of meetings—numbering fifty-two in two weeks—with groups and individuals in Beijing, Shanghai, and Hong Kong reinforced their impression before Tiananmen: The post-Deng leadership struggle, combined with the woes of inflation, unemployment, and foreign currency shortage, trapped China in "a sustained period of political and economic unrest and change," which destabilized US-China relations. Lampton and Barnett, however, found "strong support" for maintaining contacts, which led them to conclude that exchanges in "professional," "non-ideological" fields would still be "productive."[24] Beijing was beckoning to Americans. In mid-September, Deng met Chinese American scientist Li Zhengdao—his first public appearance with a foreign guest since June 4. The retiring octogenarian assured Li of the continuation of Reform and Opening-Up and asked him to send word back home that anyone, including Chinese students who had signed petitions and joined protests, could "cast off the [mental] burden" and come (back) to China.[25]

In October and November, two of the most prominent peace emissaries traveled to China: Richard Nixon and Henry Kissinger. They had the same agenda—to salvage the US-China relationship by underlining its importance for US and Chinese national interests. Through heated debates with Chinese leaders, the former president drove home his message: "While [Tiananmen] was tragic and inexcusable, it was in the interests of both [countries] for our relationship to continue in spite of it."[26] "A modernizing, unified, and effectively governed China that has good relations with us . . . is by far the preferred solution for advancing American security interests in East Asia," he wrote to Bush upon return.[27] Kissinger—who had earlier criticized the US sanctions in a *Washington Post* op-ed, asserting that Tiananmen was "inevitable" given the level of lawlessness—agreed with Deng on the

186 EPILOGUE

Figure 8.1. Brent Scowcroft meets Deng Xiaoping in Beijing for the second time since Tiananmen, December 10, 1989. Photo by Forrest Anderson/Getty Images.

"common interests" between the two countries, global and bilateral, which included negotiating a release of dissident scientist Fang Lizhi, taking refuge at the US embassy with his wife.[28] Nixon and Kissinger paved the way for a second visit by Scowcroft and Eagleburger in December, this time a public one.[29] Although a heap of issues—including the California representative Nancy Pelosi's proposed bill to let forty thousand Chinese students remain in the United States after the expiration of their visas—continued to rankle, the atmosphere was considerably more amicable than in July (see fig. 8.1).[30] "Please tell President Bush," Deng asked the guests, "there is a retired old man in China, who is concerned about the improvement and development of Sino-American relations."[31]

The thaw made possible the Fourth US-China Dialogue in late February 1990, a forum hosted by the National Committee and the Chinese People's Institute of Foreign Affairs (see fig. 8.2).[32] The four-day dialogue in Beijing brought thirteen Americans representing government, academia, business, and philanthropy into conversation with thirty Chinese, including officials, diplomats, and scholars, the first such attempt since Tiananmen. They clashed over virtually everything. On day one, the Chinese fiercely rebutted the former World Bank president Robert McNamara's advocacy of human rights in China. "Don't impose your values on us," one participant

Figure 8.2. The Fourth US-China Dialogue in Beijing, March 1, 1990. Left to right: National Committee President David M. Lampton, US Ambassador James R. Lilley, National Committee Chairman Raymond P. Shafer, Vice Premier Li Tieying. National Committee on US-China Relations Collection. Courtesy of Rockefeller Archive Center and the National Committee on US-China Relations.

retorted. "Your other aim is to split China and divide its leaders!" On day three, Premier Li Peng, widely seen as the main culprit of the massacre, brushed aside the guests' request for softening Beijing's anti-US rhetoric to help Bush placate Congress. "Frankly," he groaned, "China does not owe the US further debts." On day four, the former ambassador to the United States Chai Zemin rebuffed the prophecy of Harry Harding, then at the Brookings Institution, that there would be "a reversal of verdicts" on Tiananmen one day. "This is by no means a friendly attitude," Chai croaked.[33] For all the signs of a deadlock, the Americans did not leave China crestfallen. As much as the two sides disagreed over ideals and principles, the dialogue revealed the ineluctable fact that the US-China relationship, underpinned by myriad interests that were poised to grow further, was too important to be left to decay. "Americans and Chinese can differ—sometimes seriously— and maintain personal friendships," wrote Harding.[34]

US-China relations went into high gear starting in the spring of 1990. Although the stalemates over the sanctions, the Pelosi bill, and the Fang Lizhi case persisted, the Bush administration approved the sale of Boeing jets and authorized Export-Import Bank credits to China, and Beijing lifted the martial law, released some detainees, and agreed to reinstate the Peace Corps and Fulbright programs.³⁵ Often prodded by the business community, the National Committee and other nongovernmental groups gradually began to restore their initiatives. In the denouement of the Cold War, more and more Americans seemed to accept the rationale that the United States should keep engaging with China to influence its future course. Harding insisted on "keep[ing] the door to China open . . . to maintain contact with those in China who wish to promote change," while Lampton and Raymond Shafer, chairman of the National Committee, wrote: "Now is the time for more engagement, not less."³⁶ A breakthrough came that summer, when a delegation of six Chinese mayors toured the United States by invitation of the National Committee, the first high-profile group from China since Tiananmen. "You have your system of democracy, and we have our system of democracy," the mayor of Shanghai Zhu Rongji—whom many Americans considered China's Gorbachev—stated at a press conference. "But that does not mean we have nothing in common."³⁷

And so began the new period of US-China relations, spanning into the next quarter century, in which Americans and Chinese celebrated common interests, with a full knowledge that they had distinctive political norms. In 2001, Lampton published a book on US-China relations during his ten-year presidency of the National Committee between 1988 and 1997. The title said it all: *Same Bed, Different Dreams (tong chuang yi meng)*.³⁸

More than thirty years have passed since Tiananmen. In retrospect, the United States and China seemed to be destined for a rude awakening. In the United States, engagement gained currency with President Bill Clinton's 1998 visit to China and China's accession to the World Trade Organization in 2001, but the "China threat theory" smoldered in academic and policy circles. In China, the Patriotic Education Campaign, and the rise of the new intellectuals who championed the CCP's authoritarian rule, fed state-led nationalism, manifest in the 1996 bestseller *China Can Say No (Zhongguo keyi shuo bu)*. It erupted in such key moments as the Third Taiwan Strait Crisis (1995–1996), the US bombing of the Chinese embassy in Belgrade (1999), and the collision of a US spy plane and a Chinese fighter jet near Hainan Island (2001).³⁹ The two countries, however, had no major crisis in the next ten years, as many Americans marveled at China's "Peaceful Rise" and entertained some overblown ideas like G-2—that the two superpowers should manage global affairs as a duo.⁴⁰ It was the last sparkle of engagement.

Today, engagement is under heavy fire from all sides. Since Xi Jinping and Donald Trump came to power in 2012 and 2017, respectively, more and

EPILOGUE 189

more politicians, scholars, and pundits in the United States have decried it as a curse that plagued presidents from Nixon to Barack Obama, a curse of ungrounded American hopes that China would liberalize and democratize in time.[41] On July 3, 2019, over two hundred figures in academia, government, and industry, Lampton and Berris included, signed an open letter to the White House and Congress. "With the right balance of competition and cooperation, American actions can strengthen those Chinese leaders who want China to play a constructive role in world affairs," they wrote, sounding the tune of engagement. "Efforts to isolate China will simply weaken those Chinese intent on developing a more humane and tolerant society."[42] Their voices were soon drowned out in the sea of anger in mid-2020, when, according to the Pew Research Center, nearly three-fourths of Americans viewed China unfavorably.[43] Many—not least President Trump—toyed with the concept of "decoupling," that is, separating the United States and China, economically and beyond. Orville Schell of the Asia Society inscribed an epitaph for the American ideal that was falling into oblivion: "Engagement: Born 1972, Died Tragically of Neglect, 2020."[44]

But what is engagement anyway? The term encompasses different meanings for different people depending on their political agenda—an incentive to induce Chinese reform, a euphemism to mask US capitulation, or a ruse to "change China" by making it "more like us." The most common, and fatal, misconception is that engagement is a policy designed and implemented solely by the US and Chinese governments. If so, it would certainly fall prey to the growing distrust between US and Chinese policy makers, burdened by the albatross of superpower rivalry. This book has shown, however, that engagement is something far larger than that—it is an idea conceived and nurtured and sustained by scholars, professionals, and ordinary people from different walks of life, on both sides of the Pacific, who believed that building ties between the two countries would serve their own interests in the future. Significantly, they acted on this idea in the 1970s, when few Americans and Chinese could foretell what bilateral relations after twenty years of mutual isolation would look like. Engagement is a conceptual offspring of people's diplomacy, born through a difficult delivery. And, as Lampton says, its "history isn't over yet."[45]

When will the day arrive when the United States and China will accomplish what Nixon and Mao set out to do in a cold winter half a century ago—building a peaceful and stable relationship despite their differences. This question resonates around the world now, in the summer of 2022, when the blast from the Chinese missile tests near Taiwan, in response to House

Speaker Nancy Pelosi's visit to that island, is shaking US-China relations to the core. This book offers no definitive answer to the question. Nor does it comprise a peace manifesto preaching that mutual contacts will change the politics of bilateral relations. Quite the contrary, politics can easily disrupt these contacts—by banishing American journalists, limiting visas to Chinese students, censoring Hollywood films, or diplomatically boycotting the Olympics, to list some recent examples. Washington and Beijing can kill what they dread as venomous spiders harming their national interests—but the web stays, keeping Americans and Chinese entangled, whether they like it or not. History is clear: The answer to the foregoing question thus depends on what people in the two countries think and do about their contacts, as much as on how policy makers manage diplomatic relations. And the question is *when*, not *if*, they can transform these contacts into a durable fabric of bilateral relations, insulated from political whims—for after all, the United States and China must "learn to live on the same planet," as the American and Chinese people realized a long time ago.

Acknowledgments

People's Diplomacy is a product of my journey from Kyoto to Austin to Osaka, spanning over fifteen years—a journey I would never have been able to make by myself. At every key moment, my mentors, colleagues, friends, and family carried me forward. I thank you all. Without your support, this book would never have seen the light of day.

In Kyoto, Takeshi Sakade, my undergraduate mentor at Kyoto University, guided me—then an economics major—into a career in history. When he led me to student forums in Beijing at the height of anti-Japanese demonstrations in 2010, I was surprised by the hospitality of Chinese participants. That experience first gave me the idea that perhaps ordinary people shape international relations in ways not at all intended by government officials. I would also like to thank Edward McCord and Chris Tudda for sharing the joy of historical research when I spent a semester at George Washington University as an exchange student.

In Austin, I spent a life-changing seven years at the University of Texas at Austin, all thanks to Jeremi Suri, my adviser and friend, as well as his loving family, Alison, Natalie, and Zachary. With his natural ability to encourage and inspire, Jeremi buoyed me up whenever I lost my way. Thank you for being a role model as a scholar and a teacher. I also had the privilege of working with a team of distinguished scholars at UT Austin. Mark Lawrence read my dissertation carefully and offered critical feedback that profoundly shaped this book. Huaiyin Li, with his knowledge and experience, gave me extensive comments on China in the 1970s. Joshua Eisenman played devil's advocate as a political scientist, to test my argument. I also thank Travis Gray and Hu Guangji for their friendship.

In Osaka, Hiroo Nakajima, my colleague at Osaka University, saw a potential in my work, for which I am forever indebted to him. I would also like to acknowledge my hardworking students, particularly Gong Bingyi, Li Yuansheng, Franklin Hernandez, Darren Mangado, Yumi Tabuchi, and Ayumu Hirano, for always keeping me on my toes.

A serious study on China is impossible without supportive colleagues in China. I am grateful to Zhao Xuegong, who welcomed me into Nankai University as a visiting scholar. My research in China would never have been as productive without the mentorship and friendship of Jiang Huajie. He Hui also helped me unsparingly with her knowledge of US-China relations.

I am deeply thankful to Jan Berris and Michael Lampton for sharing with me their insights as chief architects of engagement. Special thanks go to Norton Wheeler, who generously commented on the earlier draft of this book. I also thank the numberless others who lent their hands in myriad ways over the years, at archives, conferences, workshops, and classrooms, in the United States, China, and Japan. I cannot list you all here, but you know who you are.

I must acknowledge Sarah Grossman and Jacqulyn Teoh at Cornell University Press, who always answered my unrestrained line of inquiries at every step of the way. I am also thankful for Benjamin Coates, Emily Conroy-Krutz, Paul Kramer, and Judy Tzu-Chun Wu, as well as the two anonymous reviewers, for recommending this book to be included in the acclaimed United States in the World Series.

I would like to acknowledge the K. Matsushita Foundation for generously supporting the publication of *People's Diplomacy* and the Center for Language Education and Cooperation for making it open access.

I could not have gotten here without the encouragement of my family. An important part of me was shaped by Mutsuko Minami, the most intelligent woman I have ever known, who disliked chocolate because everyone else loved it in postwar Japan. I miss you. Atsuyoshi and Tomoe Imamura gave me unstinting love as I grew up in the beautiful city of Kyoto. To my mother, Naoko, who taught me diligence and perseverance, thank you. To my father, Naoto, who did not rein me in when I decided to pursue the same profession as his, thank you. To my sister, Yuki, whose friendship I always cherished, thank you.

This book is dedicated to my wife, Chen Yumeng—I still call her *Chen xiaojie* (Miss Chen) six years into marriage. She moved with me from Tianjin to Austin to Osaka, globe-trotting that made our life exciting and challenging at the same time. Over the years, she has taught me to slow down sometimes, take a walk around the lake, see the changing colors of the trees, and notice other small things that can enrich our lives. For that, I thank you.

Notes

Introduction

1. Graham Allison, *Destined for War: Can America and China Escape Thucydides's Trap?* (Boston: Houghton Mifflin Harcourt, 2017). See also Aaron Friedberg, *A Contest for Supremacy: China, America, and the Struggle for Mastery in Asia* (New York: W. W. Norton, 2011); Michael Pillsbury, *Hundred Year Marathon: China's Secret Strategy to Replace America as the Global Superpower* (New York: St. Martin's Griffin, 2015); and John J. Mearsheimer, *The Great Delusion: Liberal Dreams and International Realities* (New Haven, CT: Yale University Press, 2018).

2. Michael Hunt, *The Making of a Special Relationship: The United States and China to 1914* (New York: Columbia University Press, 1985); Xu Guoqi, *Chinese and Americans: A Shared History* (Cambridge, MA: Harvard University Press, 2014); and Gordon H. Chang, *Fateful Ties: A History of America's Preoccupation with China* (Cambridge, MA: Harvard University Press, 2015).

3. For notable exceptions, see, Robeson Taj Frazier, *The East Is Black: Cold War China in the Black Radical Imagination* (Durham, NC: Duke University Press, 2014); Madeline Hsu, *The Good Immigrants: How the Yellow Peril Became the Model Minority* (Princeton, NJ: Princeton University Press, 2015); Meredith Oyen, *The Diplomacy of Migration: Transnational Lives and the Making of U.S.-Chinese Relations in the Cold War* (Ithaca, NY: Cornell University Press, 2015); and Yunxiang Gao, *Arise Africa, Roar China: Black and Chinese Citizens of the World in the Twentieth Century* (Chapel Hill: University of North Carolina Press, 2021).

4. Michel Oksenberg, "The Strategies of Peking," *Foreign Affairs* 50, no. 1 (1971): 18.

5. *Public Papers of the Presidents of the United States: Richard Nixon, 1972* (Washington, DC: Government Printing Office, 1973), 376–79.

6. In this book, unless otherwise specified, "China" means the country/regime in mainland China, named the People's Republic of China, and "Taiwan" means the country/regime on the island of Taiwan, named the Republic of China.

7. *Public Papers: Nixon, 1972*, 379.

8. CCP Central Archives and Manuscript Division, ed., *Mao Zedong waijiao wenxuan* [Collection of Mao Zedong's diplomatic manuscripts] (Beijing: Zhongguo zhongyang wenxian yanjiushi, 1994), 600–1.

9. Zbigniew Brzezinski, *Power and Principle* (New York: Farrar, Straus and Giroux, 1983), 204.

10. *Public Papers: Nixon, 1971*, 819–20.

11. For a detailed account of Chinese domestic politics in Mao's last years, see Frederick C. Teiwes and Warren Sun, *The End of the Maoist Era: Chinese Politics during the Twilight of the Cultural Revolution, 1972–1976* (Armonk, NY: M. E. Sharpe, 2007).

12. On the impact of US and Chinese domestic politics on bilateral relations, see Yang Kuisong and Xia Yafeng, "Vacillating between Revolution and Détente: Mao's Changing Psyche and Policy toward the United States, 1969–1976," *Diplomatic History* 34, no. 2 (2010): 395–423; Kazushi Minami, "Re-examining the End of Mao's Revolution: China's Changing Statecraft and Sino-American Relations, 1973–1978," *Cold War History* 16, no. 4 (2016): 359–75; and Pete Millwood, "(Mis)perceptions of Domestic Politics in the U.S.-China Rapprochement, 1969–1978," *Diplomatic History* 43, no. 5 (2019): 890–915.

13. Yang Kuisong, "The Sino-Soviet Border Clash of 1969: From Zhenbao Island to Sino-American Rapprochement," *Cold War History* 1, no. 1 (2000): 21–52; Chen Jian, *Mao's China and the Cold War* (Chapel Hill: University of North Carolina Press, 2001), 238–76; Gong Li, "Chinese Decision Making and the Thawing of U.S.-China Relations," in *Re-examining the Cold War: U.S.-China Diplomacy, 1954–1973*, ed. Robert S. Ross and Jiang Changbin (Cambridge, MA: Harvard University Press, 2001), 321–60; Evelyn Goh, *Constructing the U.S. Rapprochement with China, 1961–1974: From "Red Menace" to "Tacit Ally"* (New York: Cambridge University Press, 2004); William C. Kirby, Robert S. Ross, and Gong Li, eds., *Normalization of U.S.-China Relations: An International History* (Cambridge, MA: Harvard University Press, 2007); Enrico Fardella, "The Sino-American Normalization: A Reassessment," *Diplomatic History* 33, no. 4 (2009): 545–78; Chris Tudda, *A Cold War Turning Point: Nixon and China, 1969–1972* (Baton Rouge: Louisiana State University Press, 2012); Lorenz M. Lüthi, "Restoring Chaos to History: Sino-Soviet-American Relations, 1969," *China Quarterly*, no. 210 (June 2012): 378–97; Wen-Qing Ngoei, *Arc of Containment: Britain, the United States, and Anticommunism in Southeast Asia* (Ithaca, NY: Cornell University Press, 2019), 149–76. For a summary of the Chinese scholarship, see Yafeng Xia and Zhi Liang, "China's Diplomacy toward the United States in the Twentieth Century: A Survey of the Literature," *Diplomatic History* 41, no. 2 (2017): 259–62.

14. For a recent historiographical review on this subject, see Erez Manela, "International Society as a Historical Subject," *Diplomatic History* 44, no. 2 (2020): 184–209.

15. The vast literature on US public diplomacy, broadly defined, in the twentieth century includes Frank A. Ninkovich, *The Diplomacy of Ideas: U.S. Foreign Policy and Cultural Relations, 1938–1950* (New York: Cambridge University Press, 1981); Emily S. Rosenberg, *Spreading the American Dream: American Economic and Cultural Expansion, 1890–1945* (New York: Hill and Wang, 1982); Walter L. Hixson, *Parting the Curtain: Propaganda, Culture, and the Cold War* (New York: Palgrave Macmillan, 1997); Kenneth Osgood, *Total Cold War: Eisenhower's Secret Propaganda Battle at Home and Abroad* (Lawrence: University of Kansas Press, 2006); Laura Belmonte, *Selling the American Way: U.S. Propaganda and the Cold War* (Philadelphia: University of Pennsylvania Press, 2008); Nicholas J. Cull, *The Cold War and the United States Information Agency: American Propaganda and Public Diplomacy, 1945–1989* (New York: Cambridge University Press, 2008); Justin Hart, *Empire of Ideas: The Origins of Public Diplomacy and the Transformation of U.S. Foreign Policy* (New York: Oxford University Press, 2013); and Jason C. Parker, *Hearts, Minds, Voices: U.S. Cold War Public Diplomacy and the Formation of the Third World* (New York: Oxford University Press, 2017).

16. *Public Papers of the Presidents of the United States: Dwight D. Eisenhower, 1956* (Washington, DC: Government Printing Office, 1957), 749–52.

17. Tony Show and Denise J. Youngblood, *Cinematic Cold War: The American and Soviet Struggle for Hearts and Minds* (Lawrence: University Press of Kansas, 2010); Toby C. Rider, *Cold War Games: Propaganda, the Olympics, and U.S. Foreign Policy* (Urbana: University of Illinois Press, 2016); and Penny von Eschen, *Satchmo Blows Up the World: Jazz Ambassadors Play the Cold War* (Cambridge, MA: Harvard University Press, 2006).

18. Matthew Evangelista, *Unarmed Forces: The Transnational Movement to End the Cold War* (Ithaca, NY: Cornell University Press, 1999); Mary Dudziak, *Cold War Civil Rights: Race and the Image of American Democracy* (Princeton, NJ: Princeton University Press, 2000); and Sarah B. Snyder, *Human Rights Activism and the End of the Cold War: A Transnational History of the Helsinki Network* (New York: Cambridge University Press, 2011).

19. Herbert Passin, *China's Cultural Diplomacy* (New York: Praeger, 1962); William E. Ratliff, "Chinese Communist Cultural Diplomacy toward Latin America, 1949–1960," *Hispanic American Historical Review* 49, no. 1 (1969): 53–79; and Gordon Barret, "China's 'People's Diplomacy' and the Pugwash Conferences, 1957–1964," *Journal of Cold War Studies* 20, no. 1 (2018): 140–69.

20. *Public Papers: Nixon, 1972*, 376–79.

21. Memorandum of Conversation, July 19, 1973, *Foreign Relations of the United States* (*FRUS*), 1969–1976, vol. 18, doc. 43.

22. Memorandum of conversation, February 15, 1973, *FRUS*, 1969–1976, vol. 18, no. 8.

23. Patrick P. McCurdy, "Chinese Connections," *Chemical and Engineering News*, December 4, 1972, 3.

24. Interview with Kissinger, October 6, 1974, *FRUS*, 1969–1976, vol. 38, doc. 46.

25. Fredrik Logevall and Andrew Preston, eds., *Nixon in the World: American Foreign Relations, 1969–1977* (New York: Oxford University Press, 2008); Niall Ferguson, Charles S. Maier, Erez Manela, and Daniel J. Sargent, eds., *The Shock of the Global: The 1970s in Perspective* (Cambridge, MA: Harvard University Press, 2011); and Daniel J. Sargent, *A Superpower Transformed: The Remaking of American Foreign Relations in the 1970s* (New York: Oxford University Press, 2015).

26. Joseph Levenson, *Revolution and Cosmopolitanism: The Western Stage and Chinese Stages* (Berkeley: University of California Press, 1971), 55. On "civil society," see Iriye Akira, *The Global Community: The Role of International Organizations and the Making of the Modern World* (Berkeley: University of California Press, 2002), 126–56.

27. Paul Hollander, *Political Pilgrims: Travels of Western Intellectuals to the Soviet Union, China, and Cuba 1928–1979* (New York: Harper Colophon, 1981). The latest edition is Paul Hollander, *Political Pilgrims: Western Intellectuals in Search of the Good Society* (New York: Routledge, 2017).

28. See, for example, Bruce Schulman, *The Seventies: The Great Shift in American Culture, Society, and Politics* (New York: Free Press, 2001); and Thomas Borstelmann, *The 1970s: A New Global History from Civil Rights to Economic Inequality* (Princeton, NJ: Princeton University Press, 2012).

29. Richard Madsen, *China and the American Dream: A Moral Inquiry* (Berkeley: University of California Press, 1995), 161.

30. On Deng's downfall, see also Alessandro Russo, "How Did the Cultural Revolution End? The Last Dispute between Mao Zedong and Deng Xiaoping, 1975," *Modern China* 39, no. 3 (2013): 239–79.

31. Mao Zedong, "Lun shi da guanxi [On the ten major relationships]," *People's Daily*, December 26, 1976.

32. For a more positive evaluation of Hua, see, for example, Frederick C. Teiwes and Warren Sun, "China's New Economic Policy under Hua Guofeng: Party Consensus and Party Myths," *China Journal* 66 (July 2011): 1–23.

33. On popular discontents toward the Gang of Four and Mao, see, for example, Roderick Macfarquhar and Michael Schoenhals, *Mao's Last Revolution* (Cambridge, MA: Belknap Press, 2006), 420–22.

34. Harry Harding, *China's Second Revolution: Reform after Mao* (New York: Brookings Institution Press, 1987).

35. Akira Iriye, "Culture and Power: International Relations and Intercultural Relations," *Diplomatic History* 10, no. 2 (1979): 116.

36. For notable exceptions in recent years, see Mao Lin, "'To See Is to Believe?'—Modernization and U.S.-China Exchanges in the 1970s," *Chinese Historical Review* 23, no. 1 (2016): 23–46; Federico Pachetti, "The Roots of a Globalized Relationship: Western Knowledge of the Chinese Economy and US-China Relations in the Long 1970s," and Priscila Roberts, "Bringing the Chinese Back In: The Role of Quasi-Private Institutions in Britain and the United States," in *China, Hong Kong, and the Long 1970s: Global Perspectives,* ed., Priscilla Roberts and Odd Arne Westad (Basingstoke, UK: Palgrave Macmillan, 2017), 181–203, 303–25. For monographs on this subject to date, see Randall E. Stross, *Bulls in the China Shop and Other Sino-American Business Encounters* (Honolulu: University of Hawaii Press, 1990); Huang Renguo, *Jiaoyu yu zhengzhi, jingji de sanxiang hudong: 1949–1978 nian de ZhongMei jiaoyu jiaoliu* [The triangular relationship between education, politics, and economics: US-China educational exchanges, 1949–1978] (Beijing: Shijie zhishi chubanshe, 2010); and Hui He, *Dangdai Zhongmei minjian jiaoliu-shi 1969–2008 nian* [Contemporary history of US-China people's exchanges, 1969–2008] (Beijing: Kexue chubanshe, 2017).

1. The Origins of People's Diplomacy

1. John King Fairbank, *The United States and China* (Cambridge, MA: Harvard University Press, 1958), 275, 320.

2. Interview with John B. Howard, February 15, 1973, fol. 186, box 36, ser. 4, FA618, Ford Foundation Records, Oral History Project, Rockefeller Archive Center (RAC).

3. See, for example, *United States Foreign Policy: Asia*, no. 5 (Washington, DC: Government Printing Office, 1959); and A. Doak Barnett, *Communist China and Asia: Challenge to American Policy* (New York: Harper and Row, 1960).

4. Report on Changes in Public Attitudes toward Communist China by Samuel Lubell Associates, undated, "China Memos, Vol. I 12/63–9/64 [1 of 2]," box 237, Country File, National Security Files (NSF), Lyndon B. Johnson Library (LBJL).

5. Department of State, *Bulletin*, January 6, 1964, 11–17.

6. CCP Central Archives and Manuscript Division, ed., *Mao Zedong wenji* [The writings of Mao Zedong], vol. 8 (Beijing: Renmin chubanshe, 1999), 380.

7. "Wo guo di yi ke yuanzidan baozha chenggong [Our nation's first successful detonation of an atomic bomb]," *People's Daily*, October 17, 1964, 1.

8. Chen, *Mao's China*, 189–90.

9. Letters, Sidney W. Dean Jr. to Lyndon B. Johnson, October 21, 1964, and Elizabeth Jordan to Johnson, October 20, 1964, "CO50–2 People's Republic of 11/22/63–1/12/65," box CO50–2, Country File, White House Central Files (WHCF), LBJL.

10. O. Edmund Clubb, "The New World Triangle," *Progressive* 28, no. 12 (1964): 17–21.

11. Editorial, "Needed: A China Policy That Makes Sense," *Saturday Evening Post*, November 14, 1964, 86.

12. *Intercom* 7, no. 1 (1965): 44–57; George F. Kennan, "A Fresh Look at Our China Policy," *New York Times Magazine*, November 22, 1964, 27, 140–47; and "The Playboy Interview by Joe Hyams—February 1963," accessed April 1, 2020, https://grcmc.org/node/7392/100-frank-sinatra.

13. Survey Research Center, University of Michigan, *The American Public's View of U.S. Policy toward China* (New York: Council on Foreign Relations, 1964), 5, 6, 10.

14. *CBS Reports*, "The U.S. and the Two Chinas," November 11, 1964, Moving Image Research Center (MIRC), Library of Congress (LOC).

15. Noam Kochavi, *A Conflict Perpetuated: China Policy during the Kennedy Years* (Westport, CT: Praeger, 2002); and Michael Lumbers, *Piercing the Bamboo Curtain: Tentative Bridge-Building to China during the Johnson Years* (Manchester, UK: Manchester University Press, 2008).

16. Editorial, "Let's Open the Doors to China," *Saturday Evening Post*, July 25, 1964, 84.

17. Goh, *Constructing the U.S. Rapprochement*, 46–81.

18. Hans J. Morgenthau, "Peace in Our Time?" *Commentary*, March 1964, 66–69.

19. Report on the National Conference on the United States and China, June 3, 1965, "International Relations, China, 1963–65," box 356, League of Women Voters, LOC.

20. "The National Committee on United States-China Relations, Inc.," undated, fol. 394, box 39, ser. 11, RG 5, FA1187, National Committee on United States-China Relations record (NCUSCR), RAC; and Robert A. Mang and Pamela Mang, "A History of the Origins of the National Committee on United States-China Relations," January 1976, unpublished report prepared for the Christopher Reynolds Foundation.

21. "U.S. Policy with Respect to Mainland China," Hearings before the Senate Committee on Foreign Relations, March 8, 1966, 13.

22. "U.S. Policy with Respect to Mainland China," March 8, 1966, 451; and "Goldwater Rips Inquiry On China," *Washington Post*, April 3, 1966.

23. Letter, Theresa Ceellen to A. Doak Barnett, March 21, 1966, "1966—Correspondence Concerning ADB March 6 Senate Hearings," box 103, A. Doak Barnett Papers (ADB), Columbia University (CU).

24. Letter, Charlotte Platt to Barnett, March 9, 1966, "1966—Correspondence Concerning ADB March 6 Senate Hearings," box 103, ADB, CU.

25. A. T. Steele, *The American People and China* (New York: McGraw-Hill Book Company, 1966), 245.

26. Memo, Robert Komer to Johnson, March 2, 1966, "CO 50–2 China, People's Republic of (Communist China)," box 7, Confidential File, LBJL; "Communist China: Long Range Study," June 1966, *FRUS*, 1964–1968, vol. 30, doc. 161; and memo, Thomson to Rostow, August 4, 1966, *FRUS*, 1964–1968, vol. 30, doc. 173.

27. *Public Papers of the Presidents of the United States: Lyndon B. Johnson, 1966* (Washington, DC: Government Printing Office, 1967), 718–22.

28. Edward C. Burks, "New Group to Spur China Discussion," *New York Times*, June 10, 1966.

29. First Annual Program Summary, May 31, 1967, "National Committee," box 82, John K. Fairbank Papers (JFK), Harvard University (HU).

30. See, for example, National Committee on US-China Relations, *An Annotated Guide to Modern China* (New York: National Committee on US-China Relations, 1967).

31. ABC Scope, The Vietnam War—China Briefing, July 22, 1967, MIRC, LOC.

32. Report on Fox Butterfield's trip to Greensboro, North Carolina, February 28, 1967, "National Comm. for US-China Relations—field staff," box 81, JKF, HU.

33. Letter, Frank N. Trager to Scalapino, July 20, 1967, "National Committee for US-China Relations," box 87, JKF, HU.

34. John Chamberlain, "They Say 'Dialogue' but the Monologue Goes On," *Ironwood Daily Globe*, June 16, 1967; and letter, James D. Elkjer to Scalapino, July 24, 1967, "National Committee for US-China Relations," box 87, JKF, HU.

35. Letter, Scalapino to National Committee members, February 26, 1968, "US-China Relations," box 87, JKF, HU.

36. Memorandum for the Record, February 2, 1968, *FRUS*, 1964–1968, vol. 30, doc. 297.

37. Letter, Reischauer to Johnson, February 12, 1968, "O50–2 People's Republic of 11/22/63–1/12/65," box CO50–2, Country File, WHCF, LBJL.

38. Memo, Rostow to Johnson, February 22, 1968, "O50–2 People's Republic of 11/22/63–1/12/65," box CO50–2, Country File, WHCF, LBJL.

39. Memo, Rusk to Johnson, February 22, 1968, *FRUS*, 1964–1968, vol. 30, doc. 302; Memo, Jenkins to Johnson, February 22, 1968, *FRUS*, 1964–1968, vol. 30, doc. 303; and CIA, "Communist China's Troubles and Prospects," February 22, 1968, "China Vol. 2 CODEWORD [1 of 3]," box 244, Country File, NSF, LBJL.

40. Policy Planning Council, "U.S. Policy toward Communist China," December 1968, "Transition: Policy Planning Council Papers—U.S. Policy toward Communist China," box 50, Subject File, LBJL.

41. Letter, Barnet to Mervyn Adams, November 4, 1969, "N August 1968–June 1969, National Committee on US-China Relations [1 of 2]," box 52, Edwin O. Reischauer Papers, HU.

42. A. Doak Barnett and Edwin O. Reischauer, eds., *The United States and China: The Next Decade* (New York: Praeger Publishers, 1970), 218, 239.

43. George H. Gallup, *The Gallup Poll: Public Opinion, 1935–1971* (New York: Random House, 1972), vol. 2, 1254, 1337–38, 1471, 1569–70; and vol. 3, 1711–12, 1864, 1931–32, 2002, 2183, 2268, 2308.

44. CIA Intelligence Information Cable, March 11, 1966, "China Cables, Vol. VI 3/66–9/66 [1 of 2]," box 239, Country File, NSF, LBJL.

45. Richard M. Nixon, "Asia after Vietnam," *Foreign Affairs* 46, no. 1 (1967): 121.

46. *Selected Works of Mao Tse-tung*, vol. 3 (Beijing: Foreign Language Press, 1953), 322.

47. Memorandum of Conversation, April 23, 1964, "China Memos, Vol. 1 12/63–9/64 [1 of 2]," box 237, Country File, NSF, LBJL.

48. *People's Daily*, February 9, 10, and 11, 1965.

49. "Zhongguo renmin yiding yao jiajin nuli jiaqiang zhunbei jueding zhiyuan Yuenan datui Meidi de zhanzheng tiaoxin [The Chinese people should accelerate efforts to strengthen preparation for decisive support for Vietnamese repulsion of the US imperialists' provocation of war]," *People's Daily*, February 11, 1965.

50. Bureau of Culture, CCP Municipal Committee of Shanghai, "Shanhai shi youguan yuanYue kangMei wenyi yanchu huodong tongji biao [Statistical table of cultural activities related to Aid Vietnam, Resist America in Shanghai]," May 25, 1965, B172-5-999-10, Shanghai Municipal Archive (SMA).

51. CCP Central Archives and Manuscript Division, ed., *Jianguo yilai zhongyao wenxian xuanbian* [Collection of important documents since the founding of the nation], vol. 20 (Beijing: Zhongyang wenxian chubanshe, 1998), 141–45.

52. "Quanguo renmin daibiao dahui changwu weiyuanhui guanyu zhichi Yuenan minzhu gongheguo guohui huyushu de juece [National People's Congress standing committee's decision to support the appeal letter of the Congress of the Democratic Republic of Vietnam],"

April 20, 1965, accessed April 1, 2020, http://www.npc.gov.cn/wxzl/gongbao/2000-12/25/content_5328305.htm.

53. Propaganda Bureau of the CCP Municipal Committee of Nanchang, "Tigao jingti, jiaqiang guofang, quanli zhiyuan Yuenan renmin de kangMei douzheng [Heighten vigilance, strengthen national defense, use full force to support the anti-US struggle of the Vietnamese people]," April 1965, author's personal collection.

54. Lin Biao, "Renmin zhanzheng Shenli wansui: jinian Zhongguo renmin kangri zhanzheng Shenli er shi zhou nian [Long live the victory of people's war: commemorating the twentieth anniversary of the victory of the Chinese people's war against Japan]," *People's Daily*, September 3, 1965.

55. James G. Hershberg and Chen Jian, "Informing the Enemy: Sino-American 'Signaling' and the Vietnam War, 1965," in *Behind the Bamboo Curtain: China, Vietnam, and the World beyond Asia*, ed., Priscilla Roberts (Washington, DC: Woodrow Wilson Center Press, 2006), 193–258.

56. Qiang Zhai, *China and the Vietnam Wars, 1950–1975* (Chapel Hill: University of North Carolina Press, 2000), 131–35.

57. Barry Naughton, "The Third Front: Defense Industrialization in the Chinese Interior," *China Quarterly*, no. 115 (September 1988): 351–86; Zhai, *China and the Vietnam Wars*, 140–46; Lorenz Lüthi, "The Vietnam War and China's Third-Line Defense Planning before the Cultural Revolution, 1964–1966," *Journal of Cold War Studies* 10, no. 1 (2008): 26–51; and Covell Meyskens, *Mao's Third Front: The Militarization of Cold War China* (New York: Cambridge University Press, 2020).

58. Zhai, *China and the Vietnam Wars*, 156.

59. He, *Dangdai ZhongMei minjian jiaoliu shi*, 157–61.

60. CCP Tianjin Municipal Post Office Committee, "Guanyu Meidi qinlüe Yuenan hou wo ju zhigong sixiang fanying qingkuang huibao [Situation report on thought reflections of workers at our office after the US invasion of Vietnam]," August 10, 1964, 3-C-12636–16, Tianjin Municipal Archive (TMA).

61. Telegram, Hong Kong to Dean Rusk, January 10, 1966, "China Cables, Vol. V 10/65–1/66," box 239, Country File, NSF, LBJL.

62. "Sheng jishu jiguan tuanyuan, qingnian dui yuanYue kangMei he beizhan dongyuan de sixiang fanying [Thought reflections of Communist Youth League members and nonmember youth in provincial institutions toward Aid Vietnam, Resist America and mobilization for war preparation,]," 225-5-11-058–070, Guangdong Provincial Archive (GPA).

63. Kazushi Minami, "The Vietnam War, Maoism, and the Cultural Revolution: Propaganda and Mobilization in the People's Republic of China," in *Protest in the Vietnam War*, ed., Alexander Sedlmaier (Basingstoke, UK: Palgrave Macmillan, 2022), 265–91.

64. Chen, *Mao's China*, 212.

65. Shen Aiqun, "Zhi yao Yuenan renmin xuya, zhi yao Mao zhuxi yi sheng ling xia women hongweibing jiu liji yu Yuenan renmin bingjian zhandou [Once the Vietnamese people need us, once Chairman Mao orders us, we, the Red Guards, will fight shoulder to shoulder with the Vietnamese people right away]," *People's Daily*, December 19, 1966.

66. Ji Xiaosong, "Huangdan niandai de chuanqi gushi—Hongweibing touyue guojing yuanYue kangMei jishi [A legend in the absurd years: A story of a Red Guard who secretly cross the border to aid Vietnam and resist America]," *Junshi lishi* [Military history], no. 6 (2004): 54–60.

67. "Zhonggong zhongyang, Guowuyuan, Zhongyang junwei guanyu quanzu hongweibing he geming qunzhong zifa fuYue yuanYue kangMei de tongzhi [Notice from the CCP leadership, the State Council, and the Central Military Committee on restraining Red Guards and

revolutionary workers from voluntarily going to Vietnam to aid Vietnam, resist America]," March 3, 1967, Chinese Cultural Revolution Database (CCRD).

68. Letter, Mao to Foster, January 17, 1959, reprinted in *Peking Review*, February 3, 1959, 9–10.

69. *Selected Works of Mao Tse-tung*, vol. 4 (Beijing: Foreign Language Press, 1960), 97–101.

70. Tracy B. Strong and Helene Keyssar, "Anna Louise Strong: Three Interviews with Chairman Mao Zedong," *China Quarterly*, no. 103 (September 1985): 507.

71. Hunan Provincial Committee Foreign Affairs Office and CCP Changsha Municipal Committee Foreign Affairs Team, "Qunzhong tong waibin tanhua xuanbian," February 1966, author's personal collection.

72. Commentary, "Meiguo renmin xingdong qilai le [The American people have swung into action]," *People's Daily*, April 19, 1965.

73. Taj Frazier, *East Is Black*, 37–71; Keisha A. Brown, "Blackness in Exile: W. E. B. Du Bois' Role in the Formation of Representations of Blackness as Conceptualized by the Chinese Communist Party (CCP)," *Phylon* 53, no. 2 (2016): 20–33.

74. W. E. B. Du Bois, *The World and Africa and Color and Democracy* (New York: Oxford University Press, 2007), 201.

75. Mao Zedong, "Statement Calling Upon the People of the World to Unite to Oppose Racial Discrimination by U.S. Imperialism and Support the American Negroes in Their Struggle against Racial Discrimination, August 8, 1963," printed in *Peking Review*, August 16, 1963, 6–7. See also Ruodi Duan, "Solidarity in Three Acts: Narrating US Black Freedom Movements in China, 1961–66," *Modern Asian Studies* 53, no. 5 (2019): 1351–80.

76. "Statement by Comrade Mao Tse-tung, Chairman of the Central Committee of the Communist Party of China, In Support of the Afro-American Struggle against Violent Repression, April 16, 1968," printed in *Peking Review*, April 19, 1968, 5–6.

77. Robin D. G. Kelley and Betsy Esch, "Black Like Mao: Red China and Black Revolution," *Soul* 1, no. 4 (1999): 6–41; Matthew D. Johnson, "From Peace to the Panthers: PRC Engagement with African-American Transnational Networks, 1949–1979," *Past & Present* 218, suppl. 8 (2013): 233–57; Taj Frazier, *East Is Black*, 108–92; Bill V. Mullen, "By the Book: Quotations from Chairman Mao and the Making of Afro-Asian Radicalism, 1966–1975," in *Mao's Little Red Book: A Global History*, ed., Alexander C. Cook (New York: Cambridge University Press, 2014), 245–65; Hongshan Li, "Building a Black Bridge: China's Interaction with African-American Activists during the Cold War," *Journal of Cold War Studies* 20, no. 3 (2018): 114–52; and Julia Lovell, *Maoism: A Global History* (New York: Alfred A. Knopf, 2019), 266–305.

78. Chinese People's Committee for Defending World Peace, "Waibin qingkuang jianbao [Report on foreign guests] 353," September 30, 1964, C36-2-215–13, SMA.

79. "Speech by U.S. Negro Leader Robert Williams," *Peking Review*, August 12, 1966, 24–27.

80. Edgar Snow, "Interview with Mao," *New Republic*, February 27, 1965, 17–23.

81. "Yi pian juemiao de fanmian jiaocai: Meidi xin toumu Nikesong de 'jiushi yanshuo' [One excellent negative example: The new ringleader of the US imperialists Nixon's 'inaugural address']," *People's Daily*, January 28, 1969.

82. Letter, Barnett to Gabriele Roehrich, February 5, 1981, "Kissinger, 1968–81," box 106, ADB, CU.

83. Department of State, *Bulletin*, March 22, 1971, 334.

84. "Prospects and Problems of Developing Relations with China: A Roundtable Meeting," undated, fol. 146, box 19, ser. 5, RG 4, FA1186, NCUSCR, RAC.

85. Warren Unna, "'China Lobby' Dies Quietly," *Washington Post*, January 24, 1970. See also Jeffrey Crean, "'Nixon Is with Us on China': Raging against the Dying of the Lobby," *Journal of American-East Asian Relations* 26, no. 4 (2019): 368–96.

86. John K. Fairbank, "The Time Is Ripe for China to Shift Outward Again," *New York Times*, April 18, 1971.

87. "Mao zhuxi yulu [Quotation from Chairman Mao]," *People's Daily*, December 25, 1970.

88. Edgar Snow, "A Conversation with Mao Tse-Tung," *Life*, April 30, 1971, 46–48.

89. Nick Mulvenney, "China's Ping-Pong Diplomat Left Out in the Cold," *Reuters*, June 6, 2007.

90. John Roderick, "Chou Says 'New Page Has Opened'," *New York Times*, April 15, 1971.

91. Henry Kissinger, *White House Years* (Boston: Little, Brown, 1979), 710.

92. "China: A Whole New Game," *Time*, April 26, 1971; and John Saar, "The Great Wall Comes Down," *Life*, April 30, 1971.

93. See box 2188–2191, Subject Numeric Files (SNF), Record Group (RG) 59, National Archives and Record Administration at College Park, MD (NARA).

94. John J. O'Connor, "China Show TV's Biggest since Man Reached Moon," *New York Times*, February 18, 1972.

95. George H. Gallup, *The Gallup Poll: Public Opinion, 1972–1977* (Wilmington, DE: Scholarly Resources, 1978), vol. 1, 20.

96. Goh, *Constructing the U.S. Rapprochement*, 215–20. See also Joyce Mao, *Asia First: China and the Making of Modern American Conservatism* (Chicago: University of Chicago Press, 2015), 157–68.

97. *Public Papers: Nixon, 1972*, 369.

98. "Zhonggong zhongyang guanyu zhuanfa 'Mao zhuxi huijian Meiguo youhao renshi Sinuo tanhua jiyao' de tongzhi [A notice from the CCP leadership on distribution of 'Digest of the Chairman Mao's conversation with American friend Snow']," May 31, 1971, CCRD.

99. Department of Political Affairs, Inner Mongolian Autonomous Region Revolutionary Committee, "Xuexi 'Mao zhuxi huijian Meiguo youhao renshi Sinuo tanhua jiyao' de xuanchuan jiaoyu tigang [Outline of propaganda education for studying 'Digest of the Chairman Mao's conversation with American friend Snow']," July 1971, author's personal collection.

100. Shanghai Municipal Handicraft Industry Management Bureau, "Xuexi 'Mao zhuxi huijian Meiguo youhao renshi Sinuo tanhua jiyao' qingkuang [Situations in studying 'Digest of the Chairman Mao's conversation with American friend Snow'], 1," June 7, 1971, B158-3-935, SMA.

101. Tillman Durdin, "China Justifying Nixon Visit for Chinese," *New York Times*, August 20, 1971.

102. Guo Yilin, "The 'Propaganda State' and Sino-American Rapprochement: Preparing the Chinese Public for Nixon's Visit," *Journal of American-East Asian Relations* 20, no. 1 (2013): 5–28.

103. Guilin Municipal Revolutionary Committee Political Work Group Propaganda Team, "Guilin shi xuexi ZhongMei lianhe gongbao de qingkuang [Situations in studying the Sino-American joint communiqué in Guilin]," March 17, 1972, 3-2-199-14, Guilin Municipal Archive (GMA).

104. "China Specialists' Views on Current Potential for VOA Broadcasts to Mainland China," April 3, 1970, "E-270," Office of Research and Evaluation, RG306, NARA; and Yu Wang, "Listening to the Enemy: Radio Consumption and Technological Culture in Maoist China, 1949–1965," *Twentieth-Century China* 47, no. 2 (2022): 154–70.

105. Huey P. Newton, *Revolutionary Suicide* (New York: Penguin Books, 2009), 352. See also Judy Tzu-Chun Wu, *Radicals on the Road: Internationalism, Orientalism, and Feminism during the Vietnam Era* (Ithaca, NY: Cornell University Press, 2013), 107–92; and Sean L. Malloy, *Out of Oakland: Black Panther Party Internationalism during the Cold War* (Ithaca, NY: Cornell University Press, 2017), 163–71, 213–14.

106. Committee of Concerned Asian Scholars, *China! Inside the People's Republic* (New York: Bantam Books, 1972), 67.

107. Xi Chen, "Visualizing Early 1970s China through the Lens of the Committee of Concerned Asian Scholars (CCAS) Friendship Delegations," *Cross-Currents: East Asian History and Culture Review* 23 (June 2017): 223.

108. "Zhongyang zhengzhi ju guanyu ZhongMei huitan de baogao [CCP Politburo's report on the US-China summit]," May 29, 1971, CCRD.

109. NSSM 124, May 27, 1971, "NSSM-124," box H-183, NSC Institutional Files, RNL.

110. Memorandum of Conversation, October 22, 1971, *FRUS*, 1969–1976, vol. E-13, doc 43.

111. Memorandum of Conversation, February 24, 1972, *FRUS*, 1969–1976, vol. E-13, doc. 93.

112. Frank Ching, "China: It's the Latest American Thing," *New York Times*, February 16, 1972.

113. Response to NSSM 148, attached to memo, John Richardson Jr. to Kissinger, March 23, 1972, "SRG Meetings NSSM 148–149 3/31/72 [2 of 2]," box H-61, NSC Institutional Files, RNL.

114. Memo, Scali to Solomon, May 19, 1972, "NSSM 148," box H-189, NSC Institutional Files, RNL.

115. "Remarks by John Richardson Jr.," May 16, 1972, fol. 393, box 39, ser. 11, RG 5, FA1187, NCUSCR, RAC.

116. "Position Paper on Sino-American Scholarly, Educational, and Cultural Exchange," attached to letter, Frederik Burkhardt, Philip Handler, and Ralph W. Tyler to John Richardson Jr., June 7, 1972, "International Relations (IR) 1972 CSCPRC: ACLS-NAS-SSRC Exchange Program: Proposed," National Academy of Sciences Archives (NAS).

117. Letter, Eckstein to CPIFA, March 20, 1972, fol. 116, box 15, ser. 4, RG 4, FA1186, NCUSCR, RAC.

118. "MeiZhong guanxi quanguo weiyuanhui jiankuang [Digest on the National Committee on US-China Relations]," undated, 196-1-568–5, Shaanxi Provincial Archive (SPA); and Foreign Ministry and State Physical Culture and Sports Commission, "Guanyu Mei tianjing dui guanyuan Asi, Peiji liang ren qu fang shi [On Arne J. de Keijzer and Peggy G. Blumenthal, officials in the US track-and-field team]," May 30, 1975, 281-5-160–1, SPA.

119. Memo, Holdridge to Kissinger, August 28, 1972, *FRUS*, 1969–1976, vol. 17, doc. 248; and telegram, Arthur K. Watson to William Rogers, September 23, 1972, "POL CHICOM-US 8-5-72," box 2190, Subject Numeric Files, RG59, NARA.

120. "Possible U.S.-China Exchanges," undated, fol. 116, box 15, ser. 3, RG4, FA1186, NCUSCR, RAC.

121. "Notes from the National Committee," vol. 3, no. 2 (1973): 1.

122. Memo, Kissinger to Nixon, March 2, 1973, *FRUS*, 1969–1976, vol. 18, doc. 18.

123. Hunt, *Making of a Special Relationship*, 5–40.

124. *Diaoyutai dang'an* [Diaoyutai files] vol. 1 (Beijing: Hongqi chubanshe, 1998), 526.

125. Mark Selden, *The Yenan Way in Revolutionary China* (Cambridge, MA: Harvard University Press, 1971); Barbara W. Tuchman, *Stilwell and the American Experience in China, 1911–45* (New York: Macmillan, 1971); and Han Suyin, *The Morning Deluge: Mao Tsetung and the Chinese Revolution, 1893–1945* (Boston: Little Brown, 1972).

126. Fan Zhonghui and Liu Haifeng, *Huang Zhen zhuan* [Biography of Huang Zhen] (Beijing: Zhongyang wenxian chubanshe, 2007), 570; and letter, Brinkley to Nixon, June 28, 1973, "POL 17 CHICOM-US 2-21-73," box 2191, SNF, RG59, NARA.

127. Telegram, Consulate in Boston to the Ministry of Foreign Affairs, May 25, 1972, 11-7-2-3-6, Institute of Modern History Archives, Academia Sinica (IMH). See also Jaw-Ling Joanne Chang, "Taiwan's Policy toward the United States, 1969–1978," in *Normalization of U.S.-China Relations*, ed., Kirby, Ross, and Gong, 245–47.

128. Telegram, Loh I-cheng to the Government Information Office, June 28, 1973, 11-7-2-3-10, IMH.

129. Gallup, *Gallup Poll, 1972–1977*, vol. 1, 40, 129.

130. Gallup, *Gallup Poll, 1972–1977*, vol. 3, 2015; and Gallup, *Gallup Poll, 1972–1977*, vol. 1, 20.

131. A. Doak Barnett, *A New U.S. Policy toward China* (Washington, DC: Brookings Institution, 1971), 126.

132. Ching, "China."

133. "Zhonggong zhongyang guanyu ZhongMei lianhe gongbao de tongzhi (gaiyao)," March 7, 1972, CCRD.

134. Shaanxi Provincial Revolutionary Committee Foreign Affairs Office, "Waishi gongzuo qingkuang fanying [Report on situations in foreign affairs work] 166," November 16, 1972, 196-1-480–15, SPA.

135. John K. Fairbank, "The New China and the American Connection," *Foreign Affairs* 51, no. 1 (1972): 31–43.

2. Trade

1. On the "400 million customers," see Carl Crow, *Four Hundred Million Customers: The Experience—Some Happy, Some Sad of An American in China, And What They Taught Him* (New York: Harper and Brothers, 1937). For US "open door" diplomacy, see George Kennan, *American Diplomacy* (Chicago: University of Chicago Press, 1951); Marilyn Blatt Young, *The Rhetoric of Empire, Making of American China Policy, 1895–1901* (Cambridge, MA: Harvard University Press, 1968); and Thomas McCormick, *China Market, America's Quest for Informal Empire, 1893–1901* (Latham, MD: Ivan R. Dee, 1990).

2. Shu Guang Zhang, *Economic Cold War: America's Embargo against China and the Sino-Soviet Alliance, 1949–1963* (Stanford, CA: Stanford University Press, 2002); Chad Mitcham, *China's Economic Relations with the West and Japan, 1949–1979: Grain, Trade and Diplomacy* (New York: Routledge, 2012); and articles in the special issue of *Modern Asian Studies* 51, no. 1 (2017).

3. William C. Kirby, "China's Internationalization in the Early People's Republic: Dreams of a Socialist World Economy," *China Quarterly* 188 (December 2006): 870–90; and Jason M. Kelly, *Market Maoists: The Communist Origins of China's Capitalist Ascent* (Cambridge, MA: Harvard University Press, 2021).

4. *CBS Reports*, "The U.S. and the Two Chinas."

5. R. R. Kay, "Should United States Trade with Red China?" *The Iron Age*, December 31, 1964, 58.

6. Alexander Eckstein, ed., *China Trade Prospects and U.S. Policy* (New York: Praeger, 1971), x-xi, xxvii.

7. "Free China is Alive and Well," *New York Times*, October 8, 1972; and "Qiaoshang zai Mei sheli shangwu zhongxin tuiguang guohuo [Overseas Chinese business setting up business centers and promoting our products in the United States]," 11-33-2-5-123, IMH.

8. "Lure of Red China Market Is Strong," *Industry Week*, May 10, 1971, 47.

9. William Burr, "'Casting a Shadow' over Trade: The Problem of Private Claims and Blocked Assets in U.S.-China Relations, 1972–1975," *Diplomatic History* 33, no. 2 (2009): 315–49; Min Song, "A Dissonance in Mao's Revolution: Chinese Agricultural Imports from the United States, 1972–1978," *Diplomatic History* 38, no. 2 (2014): 409–30; Kazushi Minami, "Oil for the Lamps of America? Sino-American Oil Diplomacy, 1973–1979," *Diplomatic History* 41, no. 5 (2017): 959–84; and Mao Lin, "More Than a Tacit Alliance: Trade, Soft Power, and U.S.-Chinese Rapprochement Reconsidered," *Journal of American-East Asian Relations* 24, no. 1 (2017): 41–77.

10. Response to NSSM 149, attached to memo, Winthrop G. Brown to Kissinger and Peter M. Flanagan, March 24, 1972, "SRG Meetings NSSM 148–149 3/31/72 [2 of 2]," box H-61, NSC Institutional Files, RNL.

11. Christian Talley, *Forgotten Vanguard: Informal Diplomacy and the Rise of United States-China Trade, 1972–1980* (Notre Dame, IN: University of Notre Dame Press, 2018). The eight National Import and Export Corporations specialized in cereals, oils, and foodstuffs; native produce and animal by-products; light industrial products; textiles; chemicals; machinery; metals and minerals; and technical imports.

12. For US economic diplomacy in earlier decades, see, for example, William Appleman Williams, *The Tragedy of American Foreign Policy* (New York: W. W. Norton, 1959).

13. Henry Giniger, "Allies Clear Sale of U.S. Station to China," *New York Times*, March 4, 1972; "China Purchasing 10 Boeing Liners for $150-Million," *New York Times*, September 11, 1972; and William M. Blair, "China Buys Corn on U.S. Market," *New York Times*, October 28, 1972.

14. Foreign Trade Ministry, "Duiwai huodong jianbao [Digest on foreign affairs activities] 98," April 30, 1975, B170-3-335, SMA.

15. Speech by Secretary of Commerce Frederick Dent, "Annual Meetings Conferences, May 31, 1973 Speeches," box 4, US-China Business Council (USCBC), Gerald Ford Presidential Library (GFL).

16. Mitcham, *China's Economic Relations*, 196, 204, 206.

17. Foreign Trade Ministry, "Guanyu ZhongMei maoyi wenti [On the question of Sino-American trade]," March 22, 1972, 324-2-117-47, GPA.

18. CCP Central Archives and Manuscript Division, ed., *Li Xiannian wenxuan* [Manuscripts of Li Xiannian] (Beijing: Renmin chubanshe, 1989), 302.

19. Stross, *Bulls in the China Shop*, 120–23.

20. Remarks by D. C. Burnham, May 31, 1973, "Annual Meetings Conferences, May 31, 1973 Speeches," box 4, USCBC, GFL.

21. Summary of National Council Meeting in Peking, China, November 7, 1973, and Summary of Meeting with Li Hsien-nien, November 8, 1973, in "Special Report No. 6, The Peking Report," December 12, 1973, "Special Reports #6—The Peking Report," box 158, USCBC, GFL.

22. Fan and Liu, *Huang Zhen zhuan*, 618.

23. "President's Report," June 3, 1974, "Annual Meetings June 3, 1974 Board of Directors Kit," box 4, USCBC, GFL.

24. See, for example, Stross, *Bulls in the China Shop*, 231; and John Kamm, "Reforming Foreign Trade," in *One Step Ahead in China: Guangdong under Reform,* ed. Ezra Vogel (Cambridge, MA: Harvard University Press, 1990), 344–46.

25. "Zhou Enlai zongli shi yue shi san ri tong Jianada zongli Teluduo huitan zhong duiwai maoyi gongzuo de zhishi [Premier Zhou Enlai's instructions on foreign trade during his meeting with Canadian Prime Minister Trudeau on October 13]," October 17, 1973, B200-1-780-42, SMA.

26. Hebei Provincial Revolutionary Committee Foreign Trade Bureau, "Quanguo waimao gongzuo huiyi jingyan jieshao cailiao xuanbian [Compilation of materials to introduce experiences for the national foreign trade work conference]," November 1972, author's personal collection.

27. Zi Ding, *Li Qiang zhuan* [Biography of Li Qiang] (Beijing: Renmin chubanshe, 2004), 431.

28. Foreign Trade Ministry International Trade Research Center, "Waimao diaoyan [Research on foreign trade] 120," February 12, 1974, author's personal collection.

29. Foreign Trade Ministry International Trade Research Center, "Waimao diaoyan 124," March 5, 1974, author's personal collection.

30. Hui He, "Guangjiaohui, ZhongMei maoyi yu Zhongguo de duiwai kaifang [Canton Fair, Sino-American Trade, and China's opening to the world]," *Ershiyi shiji* [21st century], no. 105 (February 2008): 61–70.

31. Warren H. Phillips and Robert Keatley, *China: Behind the Mask* (Princeton, NJ: Dow Jones Books, 1973), 131.

32. "Chinese at Trade Fair Cordial; U.S. Faces Still Competition," *Industry Week*, May 22, 1972, 23–24; and Daniel Tretiak, "The Canton Fair: An Academic Perspective," *China Quarterly*, no. 56 (October-December 1973): 743, 744.

33. Foreign Trade Ministry, "Waimao diaoyan 34," April 7, 1972, author's personal collection.

34. Memorandum of Conversation, February 24, 1972, *FRUS, 1969–1976*, vol. E-13, doc. 93.

35. Response to NSSM 149; Memorandum for the Record, March 31, 1972, *FRUS, 1969–1976*, vol. 17, doc. 218; Central Intelligence Agency, "Communist China: An Overview of the Economy," October 1971, NLN-NSC-847-6-1-8, CIA Electronic Reading Room, accessed April 1, 2020, https://www.cia.gov/library/readingroom/home.

36. Memo, Kissinger to Nixon, June 27, 1972, *FRUS, 1969–1976*, E-13, doc. 147.

37. See, for example, Robert Dernberger, "Prospects for Trade between China and the United States," in *China Trade Prospects*, ed., Eckstein, 248–267; Dwight Perkins, "Is There a China Market?" *Foreign Policy*, no. 5 (Winter 1971–1972): 106.

38. Alexander Eckstein, "U.S. and China: Peking Beckons despite Problems," *New York Times*, March 19, 1972.

39. Song, "A Dissonance in Mao's Revolution," 424–28.

40. Memo, Charles Cooper, Hormats, and Richard Solomon to Kissinger, August 16, 1973, *FRUS, 1969–1976*, vol. 18, doc. 49; and memo, Kurt E. Reinsberg to the Board of Directors, June 3, 1974, "Board of Directors Meetings June 3, 1974 Business," box 1, USCBC, GFL.

41. "Guanyu zhuanda Guowuyuan lingdao tongzhi dui 'Waimao jianbao' pishi de han [Letter on transmitting the leading State Council comrades' instructions on 'Digest on foreign trade']," June 23, 1975, 182-14-513–6, Beijing Municipal Archive (BMA).

42. See, for example, telegram, USLO Peking to Rogers, October 16, 1973, *FRUS, 1969–1976*, vol 18, doc. 54; Alexander Eckstein, "China's Trade Policy and Sino-American Relations," *Foreign Affairs* 54, no. 1 (1975): 154; and Jay Henderson, Nicholas Ludlow, and Eugene Theroux, "China and the Trade Act of 1974," *China Business Review* 2, no. 1 (1975): 10.

43. "Statement of Christopher H. Phillips," April 3, 1974, in *The Trade Reform Act of 1973: Senate Hearings on the Trade Reform Act of 1973 Before the Committee on Finance* (Washington, DC: Government Printing Office, 1974), 1715–38.

44. Resolution adopted by the Executive Committee of the National Council for US-China Trade, April 3, 1975, "Communication with members, 1975 (7)," box 34, USCBC, GFL.

45. Memorandum of Conversation, November 12, 1973, *FRUS, 1969–1976*, vol. 18, doc. 58.

46. Steven Hass, *Impact of MFN on U.S. Imports from the People's Republic of China* (Washington, DC: Office of East-West Trade, Department of State, 1973); and David Denny, *The Effect of*

Normalized Commercial Relations on PRC Exports to the U.S. (Washington, DC: Bureau of East-West Trade, Department of Commerce, 1973).

47. Textiles Meeting at the Chinese Liaison Office, February 9, 1976, "Subject File, PRCLO, Communications with officials, 1974–1976," box 40, USCBC, GFL.

48. Memo, Kissinger to Ford, November 20, 1975, *FRUS, 1969–1976*, vol. 18, doc. 132,

49. Ann Crittenden, "China, Lacking Recognition, Holds Down U.S. Trade," *New York Times*, August 30, 1976.

50. Guangdong Provincial Bureau of Culture, "Guanyu guanche Guowuyuan wenhua zu dui tiaozheng waishi danwei meishu zuopin tongzhi de baogao [Report on implementing the State Council Culture Group's notice on adjusting artworks at foreign affairs units]," May 14, 1974, 214-A1.1-6-137, GPA.

51. Foreign Trade Ministry International Trade Research Center, "Waimao diaoyan 151," July 21, 1975, author's personal collection.

52. Finance and Trade Group, Shanghai Municipal Revolutionary Committee, "Canyue qingkuang [Reference information] 79," July 30, 1976, B248-2-889–17, SMA.

53. Finance and Trade Group, Shanghai Municipal Revolutionary Committee, "Canyue qingkuang 82," August 7, 1976, B248-2-889–27, SMA.

54. Finance and Trade Group, Shanghai Municipal Revolutionary Committee, "Caimao qingkuang [Finance and trade] 210," September 1, 1976, B248-2-889–64, SMA; and Li Qiang, "Shenru kaizhan xue Daqing xue Dazhai de qunzhong yundong yong Daqing Dazhai de geming jinshen ban waimao [Thoroughly promote the mass movement to learn from Daqing and Dazhai, use the revolutionary experiences of Daqing and Dazhai to conduct foreign trade]," in Ministry of Foreign Trade, ed., *Quanguo waimao xue Daqing xue Dazhai jingyan jiaoliuhui wenjian ziliao huibian* [Compilation of documents from the national foreign trade meeting to exchange experiences in learning from Daqing and Dazhai] (Beijing: Zhongguo caizheng jingji chubanshe, 1977), 16.

55. "Guowuyuan pizhuan Waimao bu guanyu guoji shichang huafei jiage mengzhang de jianbao [State Council notice on approving the Foreign Trade Ministry's report on the price hike of chemical fertilizers in the international market]," June 13, 1974, B109-4-364–418, SMA.

56. Foreign Trade Ministry International Trade Research Center, "Waimao diaoyan 124," March 5, 1974, author's personal collection; and Foreign Trade Ministry Administrative Team, "Waimao diaoyan 39," May 10, 1972, author's personal collection.

57. Foreign Trade Ministry Whole Plant Bureau, "Fu Mei hecheng'an shebei jianyanzu zongjie [Summary of the ammonia equipment research group to the United States]," September 10, 1975, SZ142-3-721–1, HPA.

58. Peter E. Hamilton, *Made in Hong Kong: Transpacific Networks and a New History of Globalization* (New York: Columbia University Press, 2021), 227–28. For other local experiments for profit, see Odd Arne Westad, "The Great Transformation: China in the Long 1970s," in Ferguson, Maier, Manela, and Sargent, eds., *Shock of the Global*, 68–71; Frank Dikötter, *The Cultural Revolution: A People's History, 1962–1976* (New York: Bloomsbury Press, 2016), 255–322; and Taomo Zhou, "Leveraging Liminality: The Border Town of Bao'an (Shenzhen) and the Origins of China's Reform and Opening," *Journal of Asian Studies* 80, no. 2 (2021): 337–61.

59. See, for example, Finance and Trade Group, Shanghai Municipal Revolutionary Committee, "Guanyu Shanghai waimao canjia 1974 nian qiuji Guangzhou jiaoyihui qingkuang de baogao [Report on situations of the Shanghai trade office's participation in the Fall 1974 Canton Fair]," December 30, 1974, B248-2-696–21, SMA; and Finance and Trade Group, Shanghai Municipal Revolutionary Committee, "Guanyu Shanghai kou'an canjia 1975 nian chunji Guangzhou chukou shangpin jiaoyihui de qingkuang huibao [Situation report on the Port of Shanghai's participation in the Spring 1975 Canton Fair]," July 4, 1975, B248-2-818–24, SMA.

60. Finance and Trade Group, Shanghai Municipal Revolutionary Committee, "Caimao qingkuang 263," September 28, 1976, B248-2-889–95, SMA.

61. Remarks of Charles W. Freeman, Jr. to the Annual Meeting of the National Council for United States-China Trade, June 3, 1974, "Annual Meetings June 3, 1974—Speeches," box 5, USCBC, GFL; and Lucian Pye, "Current Political Scene in China," June 14, 1974, "Annual Meetings June 14, 1976 Speeches," box 6, USCBC, GFL.

62. William H. Miller, "Where Is U.S.-China Trade Headed?" *Industry Week*, April 29, 1974, 40.

63. Shanghai Municipal Foreign Trade Office Revolutionary Committee, "Jiedai MeiZhong maoyi quanguo weiyuanhui fu lishizhang Theroux [Receiving National Council Vice President Theroux]," May 2, 1975, B170-3-335, SMA; and Ben Baden, "40 Years of US-China Commercial Relation," *China Business Review* 40, no. 1 (2013): 14.

64. Fox Butterfield, "Trade Fair Reflecting Chinese Difficulties," *New York Times*, May 15, 1976.

65. CCP Central Archives and Manuscript Division, ed., *Zhou Enlai nianpu* [Chronology of Zhou Enlai], vol. 2 (Beijing: Zhongyang wenxian chubanshe, 1997), 696.

66. Lei Liu, "China's Large-scale Importation of Western Technology and the U.S. Response, 1972–1976," *Diplomatic History* 45, no. 4 (2021): 794–820.

67. Li Lanqing, trans. Ling Yuan and Zheng Siying, *Breaking Through: The Birth of China's Opening-Up Policy* (New York: Oxford University Press, 2009), 210–11.

68. CCP Central Archives and Manuscript Division, ed., *Mao Zedong nianpu* [Chronology of Mao Zedong], vol. 6 (Beijing: Zhongyang wenxian chubanshe, 2013), 534–35.

69. Summary of Meeting with Li Hsien-nien.

70. Gerd Wilcke, "Kellogg to Build 8 Plants in China," *New York Times*, November 28, 1973.

71. Stephanie Green, "Chinese Technicians in the United States," *China Business Review* 4, no. 6 (1977): 41–43.

72. Leslie Gelb, "Surging Trade with China," *New York Times*, December 2, 1973.

73. Kenneth Lieberthal, *Central Documents and Politburo Politics in China* (Ann Arbor: Center for Chinese Studies, the University of Michigan, 1978), 44–49.

74. Lieberthal, *Central Documents*, 115–54.

75. Cheng Zhongyuan and Xia Xingzhen, *Qianzou: Deng Xiaoping 1975 nian zhengdun* [Prelude: Deng Xiaoping's 1975 readjustment] (Shijiazhuang: Hebei renmin chubanshe, 2009), 269–71.

76. State Planning Commission, "Jinkou chengtao shebei xiangmu jianshe gongzuo huiyi zonghe jianbao [Comprehensive summary of the construction work conference on whole plant equipment import projects]," January 15, 1975, B109-4-442–1, SMA.

77. CCPIT criticism team, "Qingsuan 'Sirenbang' de zuixing, fazhan shehui zhuyi duiwai maoyi [Clearing the Gang of Four's sins, develop socialist foreign trade]," *People's Daily*, January 2, 1977.

78. Zi, *Li Qiang zhuan*, 313–14.

79. Lü Da, "Yi ge jiakuai fubi ziben zhuyi de 'tiaoli'—pipan Deng Xiaoping shouyi paozhi de 'Guanyu jiakuai fazhan gongye de ruogan wenti' [One regulation that accelerates the revival of capitalism—criticize 'Some questions on accelerating industrial development' inspired and concocted by Deng Xiaoping]," *People's Daily*, May 31, 1976, 2; and State Planning Commission Great Criticism Group, "Yi chang cuandang duoquan de fan geming chouju—ping 'si ren bang' dui 'er shi tiao' de 'pipan' [One anti-revolutionary farce of usurping the Party and seizing power—reviewing the Gang of Four's criticism of the twenty points]," *People's Daily*, July 16, 1977, 1–2.

80. CIA, "China: The Steel Industry in the 1970s and 1980s," May 1979, ER79–10245, 3; and State Construction Commission and Foreign Trade Ministry, "Guanyu jiedai ziben zhuyi guojia jishu renyuan gongzuo zhong yi xie wenti he yijian baogao," September 10, 1975, 196-2-102–25, SPA.

81. Alexander Eckstein and Bruce Reynolds, "Sino-American Trade Prospects and Policy," *American Economic Review* 64, no. 2 (1974): 298.

82. James Sterba, "Peking Purchasing U.S. Oil Equipment to Step Up Output," *New York Times*, November 28, 1975.

83. Graham E. Marx, "China's Machine Tool and Metal Working Industries," June 14, 1976, "Annual Meetings June 14, 1976 Speeches," box 6, USCBC, GFL.

84. Jan-Olaf Willums, "The Development of China's Petroleum Industry," June 23, 1976, "Conference on China's Oil Industry and the Prospect for United States Trade, Houston, 6/20/76, Speeches," box 118, USCBC, GFL.

85. "Zhongguo gongchandang zhongyang weiyuanhui zhuxi guowuyuan zongli Hua Guofeng tongzhi zai quanguo gongye xue Daqing huiyi shang de jianghua [Chinese Communist Party Central Committee Chairman and State Council Premier Comrade Hua Guofeng's speech at the national conference on 'Learn from Daqing in industry']," *People's Daily*, May 13, 1977, 1–3.

86. *Zhonghua renmin gongheguo jingji dashiji* [Chronicle of economic events in the People's Republic of China] (Beijing: Beijing chubanshe, 1985), 459–60.

87. Ezra Vogel, *Deng Xiaoping and the Transformation of China* (Cambridge, MA: Belknap Press, 2011), 185, 190.

88. CCPIT Business Meeting, September 8, 1977, "Board of Directors Meetings December 6, 1977 Business," box 125, USCBC, GFL.

89. CCPIT Meeting on the Hill, September 9, 1977, "September 177—CCPIT from China, Notes on Meetings," box 125, USCBC, GFL.

90. Alexander Eckstein, *China's Economic Revolution* (New York: Cambridge University Press, 1977), 276.

91. Holger Hansen's Speech at the National Council's Annual Membership Meeting, June 16, 1977, "Administrative Files: Annual Meetings, June 16, 1977, Phillips, Christopher H. [President]," box 6, USCBC, GFL.

92. Julian M. Sobin, "The Coming Leap Forward in China Trade," *Nation's Business*, July 1977, 56.

93. Steven V. Roberts, "A China Connection for U.S. Companies," *New York Times*, February 26, 1978.

94. Gu Mu, *Gu Mu huiyilu* [Memoirs of Gu Mu] (Beijing: Zhongyang wenxian chubanshe, 2009), 319–26.

95. CCP Central Committee, "Zhonggong zhongyang guanyu jiakuai gongye fazhan ruogan wenti de jueding (cao'an) [CCP Central Committee decisions on some questions on accelerating industrial development (draft)]," April 20, 1978, author's personal collection.

96. Henry Scott-Stokes, "Japanese to Build Giant Steel Mill for Chinese in $2.03 Billion Deal," *New York Times*, December 6, 1978.

97. US Companies and China's Oil (Inserts in Tape Library), August 18, 1978, "Oil Survey Delegation, General (1)," box 126, USCBC, GFL.

98. Willums, "The Development of China's Petroleum Industry."

99. Richard Baum, "A Political Perspective on China's Four Modernizations," *Columbia Journal of World Business* 14, no. 2 (1979): 34; and William H. Miller, "China Flirts with Capitalism," *Industry Week*, August 6, 1979, 38–44.

100. He, *Dangdai ZhongMei minjian jiaoliu shi*, 88.

101. Eckstein, "China's Trade Policy," 150, 154; "Chinese Involvement with Western Technology: Possibilities and Constraints," February 17, 1978, NLC-26-53-5-6-4, RAC, JCL; memo, Juanita M. Kreps to Brzezinski, March 11, 1977, *FRUS*, 1977–1980, vol. 13, doc. 17; and memo, W. Michael Blumenthal to Brzezinski, March 12, 1977, *FRUS*, 1977–1980, vol. 13, doc. 18.

102. Barry Richman, "Sino-American Economic Relations: Constraints, Opportunities, and Prospects," *California Management Review* 21, no. 2 (1978): 16.

103. Foreign Trade Ministry, "Waimao jianbao [Foreign trade digest] 26," April 21, 1978, 235-2-163, GPA.

104. Ambassador Christopher H. Phillips, May 12, 1993, Association for Diplomatic Studies and Training Foreign Affairs Oral History Project, accessed April 1, 2020, https://www.adst.org/OH%20TOCs/Phillips,%20Christopher%20H.toc.pdf?_ga=2.168754401.1118619771.1600874440-10466885.1600874440.

105. Memo, Brzezinski to Carter, June 14, 1977, *FRUS*, 1977–1980, vol. 13, doc. 31; memo, Press to Carter, October 14, 1977, *FRUS*, 1977–1980, vol. 13, doc. 64; and Paper Prepared in Response to Section III of Presidential Review Memorandum 24, undated, *FRUS*, 1977–1980, vol. 13, doc. 67.

106. CCP Central Archives and Manuscript Division, ed., *Deng Xiaoping sixiang nianbian* [Chronicle of Deng Xiaoping Thought] (Beijing: Zhongyang wenxian chubanshe, 2011), 70–71, 105–06, 129–30.

107. Telegram, USLO Peking to Vance, July 12, 1978, 1978PEKING02110, Electronic Telegrams 1978, Central Foreign Policy Files 7/1/1973–12/31/1978 (CFPF), RG 59, NARA, accessed April 1, 2020, https://aad.archives.gov/aad/.

108. Letter, Bergland to Carter, November 22, 1978, *FRUS*, 1977–1980, vol. 13, doc. 156.

109. Memo, Schlesinger to Carter, November 27, 1978, *FRUS*, 1977–1980, vol. 13, doc 157.

110. Memo, Oksenberg to Brzezinski, August 21, 1978, *FRUS*, 1977–1980, vol. 13, doc. 130.

111. "U.S. Executives Demonstrate Growing Trade Interest in People's Republic of China," *Commerce America*, April 24, 1978, 12.

112. "Chinese Trade Could Explode," *Tribune*, November 18, 1978.

113. "Bergland Brings Home More Chinese Trade," *Business Week*, November 27, 1978, 31–32.

114. Fox Butterfield, "U.S. Trade with China Increases As Peking Acts to Lift Economy," *New York Times*, November 23, 1978.

115. Peter T. Kilborn, "But No Quick Gains Expected," *New York Times*, December 19, 1978.

116. "An Interview with W. Michael Blumenthal, Secretary of the Treasury," *China Business Review* 6, no. 1 (1979): 19; and "New Trade Agreements Are Building Bridges to China," *New York Times*, December 24, 1978.

117. Memo, Kreps to Brzezinski, March 11, 1977, *FRUS*, 1977–1980, vol. 13, doc. 17. On export controls, see Hugo Meijer, "Balancing Conflicting Security Interests: U.S. Defense Exports to China in the Last Decade of the Cold War," *Journal of Cold War Studies* 17, no. 1 (2015): 4–40.

118. Memorandum of Conversation, January 31, 1979, *FRUS*, 1977–1980, vol. 13, doc. 209.

119. Minutes of a Policy Review Committee Meeting, January 8, 1979, *FRUS*, 1977–1980, vol. 13, doc. 189; and Jay Mathews, "Jackson Says Peking Dissatisfied about Trade Status," *Washington Post*, August 25, 1979.

120. *Public Papers of the United States: Jimmy Carter, 1979* (Washington DC: Government Printing Office, 1979), 2000–07.

121. Brzezinski, *Power and Principle*, 418

122. Bohdan O. Szuprowicz, "China Fever: Scrambling for Shares in a $600 Million Buying Spree," *Management Review* 68, no. 5 (1979): 9.

123. Department of Commerce, *Doing Business with China* (Washington DC: Government Printing Office, 1979), 6.

124. Chinese People's Institute of Foreign Affairs, "Guanyu jiedai Meiguo Datong Manhadun yinhang dongshizhang Daiwei Luokefeile jihua de qingshi [Request for instruction on receiving David Rockefeller, president of the Chase Manhattan Bank]," June 21, 1973, 196-1-657–12, SPA; and David Rockefeller, *Memoirs* (New York: Random House, 2002), 259.

125. Norman Pearistine and Flora S. H. Ling, "The China Trade: A Note of Caution," *Forbes*, February 5, 1979, 33–34.

126. Paul Marer, "The Future for Trade with China," *Business Horizons* 22, no. 2 (1979): 9.

127. "Guanyu fazhan duiwai maoyi de ji ge wenti [Some problems in developing foreign trade]," October 14, 1977, B252-1-212–95, SMA.

128. "Guanyu jiakuai fazhan Shanghai chukou shangpin shengchan de baogao (taolun gao) [Report on accelerating the production of Shanghai's export commodities (discussion draft)]," November 14, 1977, B252-1-121–66, SMA.

129. "1979 nian di 45 jie (chunji) jiaoyihui qingkuang huibao [Situation report on the 45th (spring) Trade Fair in 1979]," May 27, 1979, B156-2-67–1, SMA.

130. Kazushi Minami, "The Bottleneck of Reform: China's Oil Policy in the 1980s," in Priscilla Roberts, ed., *Chinese Economic Statecraft from 1978 to 1989: The First Decade of Deng Xiaoping's Reforms* (Basingstoke, UK: Palgrave Macmillan, 2022), 297–328.

131. CCP Central Archives and Manuscript Division, ed., *Jianguo yilai Li Xiannian wengao* [Manuscripts of Li Xiannian since the nation's founding], vol. 4 (Beijing: Zhongyang wenxian chubanshe, 2011), 84; and Secretariat, Industry and Transportation Office, Shanghai Municipal Administrative Committee, "Gongjiao qingkuang 323 [Industry and transportation situations]," November 15, 1978, B246-3-525–5, SMA.

132. "Agreement on Trade Relations between the United States and the People's Republic of China," S. Con. Res. 47, November 15, 1979.

133. Elizabeth O'Brien Ingleson, "The Invisible Hand of Diplomacy: Chinese Textiles and U.S. Manufacturing in the 1970s," *Pacific Historical Review* 90, no. 3 (2021): 345–76.

134. Clyde H. Farnsworth, "China, U.S. Set Accord on Textiles," *New York Times*, July 25, 1980.

135. "Guangbo dianshi qingkuang [Situations in television broadcast] 16," May 17, 1978, B285-2-673–178, SMA.

136. Shanghai First Commerce Bureau Revolutionary Committee, "'Yinjin shangpin zhanlanhui' qingkuang huibao [Situation report on 'import product exhibitions']," June 4, 1979, B123-10-922, SMA.

137. Ministry of Light Industry, "Guanyu quanguo qinggongye xin chanping zhanxiaohui qingkuan de baogao [Report on the situations of the national exhibition of new light industry products]," November 29, 1979, B1-9-46–208, SMA.

138. Jay Matthews, "Television: A Symbol of China's Desire for Consumer Goods," *Washington Post*, August 1, 1978.

139. On the continuity of "state consumerism" in Mao's China, see Karl Gerth, *Unending Capitalism: How Consumerism Negated China's Communist Revolution* (New York: Cambridge University Press, 2020).

140. "Trade in Goods with China," Foreign Trade, US Census Bureau.

141. Jonathan Kaufman, "Euphoria on China Yields to Realism at Trade Seminar," *Wall Street Journal*, February 25, 1980.

142. National Bureau of Statistics, *Zhongguo tongji nianjian* [Statistical yearbook of China] *1986* and *1995* (Beijing: Zhongguo tongji chubanshe, 1987 and 1996), 582 and 560.

143. Jim Mann, *Beijing Jeep: The Short, Unhappy Romance of American Business in China* (Boulder, CO: Westview Press, 1997).

144. Niall Ferguson and Moritz Schularick, "Chimerica and the Global Asset Market Boom," *International Finance* 10, no. 3 (2007): 215–39.

145. Telegram, USLO Peking to Vance, June 28, 1977, 26-43-1-6-8, RAC, JCL.

146. Memo, Ludlow to Phillips and Stanley Young, August 15, 1978, "Oil Survey Delegation, General (1)," box 126, USCBC, GFL; and Oral History Project, Phillips, May 12, 1993.

147. Baden, "40 Years," 13–17.

148. Zi, *Li Qiang*, 335–36.

149. "Zhongguo Kexie di yi ju quanweihui di er ci (kuoda) huiyi jianbao [Digest on the second (expanded) meeting of the first plenary conference of the China Association for Science and Technology] 7," November 14, 1978, SZ123-4-3-4, HPA.

150. Jeanne L. Wilson, "'The Polish Lesson:' China and Poland 1980–1990," *Studies in Comparative Communism* 23, no. 3–4 (1990): 263; and Barry Naughton, *Growing Out of Plan: Chinese Economic Reform, 1978–1993* (New York: Cambridge University Press, 1995), 88.

151. Kenneth Lieberthal, "China: The Politics Behind the New Economics," *Fortune*, December 31, 1979, 50. See also Frederick C. Teiwes and Warren Sun, "China's Economic Reorientation After the Third Plenum: Conflict Surrounding 'Chen Yun's' Readjustment Program," *The China Journal*, no. 70 (2013): 163–87.

152. Warren H. Phillips, "China in 2001: Surpassing the U.S.?" *Wall Street Journal*, December 20, 1972, 14–16.

153. Robert J. Samuelson, "A View of the End of China's Isolation," *Washington Post*, January 2, 1979.

154. R. W. Adkins, "Notes on Trip to China," July-August 1977, "Delegation Department Mining Industry Delegation 7/77 Trip Report (1)," box 105, USCBC, GFL.

3. Science

1. Zuoyue Wang, "Transnational Science during the Cold War: The Case of Chinese/American Scientists," *Isis*, 2010, no. 101, 367–77.

2. Letter, John M. H. Lindbeck to Harrison Brown, January 29, 1965, "IR 1965 Pacific Science Board Com on Science Coop: Mainland China," National Academy of Sciences Archives (NAS).

3. The official name "the Committee on Scholarly Communication with Mainland China" was changed to "Committee on Scholarly Communication with the People's Republic of China" in 1970.

4. Zuoyue Wang, *In Sputnik's Shadow: The President's Science Advisory Committee and Cold War America* (New Brunswick, NJ: Rutgers University Press, 2008), 258–310; Kelly Moore, *Disrupting Science: Social Movements, American Scientists, and the Politics of the Military 1945–1975* (Princeton, NJ: Princeton University Press, 2008), 130–89; Audra J. Wolfe, *Competing with the Soviets: Science, Technology, and the State in Cold War America* (Baltimore, MD: Johns Hopkins University Press, 2013), 105–20; Sarah Bridger, *Scientists at War: The Ethics of Cold War Weapons*

Research (Cambridge, MA: Harvard University Press, 2015); and Alyssa Botelho, Daniel S. Chard, and Sigrid Schmalzer, eds., *Science for the People: Documents from America's Movement of Radical Scientists, 1969–1989* (Amherst: University of Massachusetts Press, 2018).

5. Greg Whitesides, *Science and American Foreign Relations since World War II* (New York: Cambridge University Press, 2018), 145–213.

6. *Public Papers: Nixon, 1971*, 338.

7. Telefax, Handler to Bei, December 14, 1972, "IR 1972 CSCPRC: ACLS-NAS-SSRC Visits: Chinese Scientific Delegation," NAS.

8. Sigrid Schmalzer, "On the Appropriate Use of Rose-Colored Glasses: Reflections on Science in Socialist China," *Isis* 98 no. 3 (2007): 571–83; Chunjuan Nancy Wei and Darryl E. Brock, eds., *Mr. Science and Chairman Mao's Cultural Revolution: Science and Technology in Modern China* (Lanham, MD: Lexington Books, 2013); Sigrid Schmalzer, *Red Revolution, Green Revolution: Scientific Farming in Socialist China* (Chicago: University of Chicago Press, 2016); and Marc Andre Matten and Rui Kunze, *Knowledge Production in Mao-Era China: Learning from the Masses* (Lanham, MD: Lexington Books, 2021).

9. Letter, Frederick Seitz to Herman M. Kalckar, August 25, 1967, "IR 1967 Com on Scholarly Communication w People's Republic of China: ACLS-NAS-SSRC," NAS; and Letter, Kalckar to Seitz, October 23, 1967, "IR 1967 Com on Scholarly Communication w People's Republic of China: ACLS-NAS-SSRC," NAS.

10. The English name of this organization was changed to the China Association for Science and Technology in 1980.

11. Seymour Topping, "U.S. Biologists in China Tell of Scientific Gains," *New York Times*, May 24, 1971.

12. Visit by the Scientific Delegation from the People's Republic of China, January 2, 1973, "IR 1973 Com on Scholarly Communication w People's Republic of China: ACLS-NAS-SSRC Activities: Summary," NAS.

13. China Trip Note by Alexander Eckstein, August 1974, fol. 337, box 33, ser. 3, RG 5, FA1187, NCUSCR, RAC.

14. For an overview of Sino-American scientific exchanges in the 1970s, see Kathlin Smith, "The Role of Scientists in Normalizing U.S.-China Relations: 1965–1979," *Annals of the New York Academy of Sciences*, no. 866 (December 1998): 114–36; Zuoyue Wang, "U.S.-China Scientific Exchange: A Case Study of State-Sponsored Scientific Internationalism during the Cold War and Beyond," *Historical Studies in the Physical and Biological Sciences* 30, no. 1 (1999): 249–77; Zhang Jing, "ZhongMei minjian keji jiaoliu de yuanqi, shijian yu xushi (1971–1978) [The China-US science and technology exchanges from 1971–1978: The Origin, practice, and narration]," *Meiguo yanjiu* [American studies], no. 5 (2020): 122–60; and Pete Millwood, "An 'Exceedingly Delicate Undertaking': Sino-American Science Diplomacy, 1966–78," *Journal of Contemporary History* 56, no. 1 (2021): 166–90.

15. Survey on Science Exchange with the People's Republic of China, November 15, 1972, "IR1973 CSCPRC: ACLS-NAS-SSRC Activities: Summary," NAS. On Chinese medicine, see E. Grey Dimond, "Medical Education and Care in People's Republic of China" and "Acupuncture Anesthesia; Western Medicine and Chinese Traditional Medicine," *Journal of the American Medical Association*, no. 218 (December 1971): 1552–57 and 1558–63; and E. Grey Dimond, "Medicine in the People's Republic of China: A Progress Report," *Journal of the American Medical Association*, no. 222 (November 1972): 1158–59.

16. Letter, Handler, Henry Riecken, and Burkhardt to Guo Moruo, May 20, 1971, "IR 1971 CSCPRC: ACLS-NAS-SSRC," NAS.

17. Letter, Keatley to Handler, July 21, 1971, "IR 1971 CSCPRC: ACLS-NAS-SSRC," NAS.

18. Letter, Brown to Guo, August 23, 1971, "IR 1971 CSCPRC: ACLS-NAS-SSRC," NAS.

19. "Zhongguo kexueyuan waishizu zuzhang Pan Chuntong tongzhi yu Meiguo kexuejia xiehui daibiaotuan tanhua jilu [Record of conversation between Comrade Pei Chutong, head of the CAS foreign affairs team, and the FAS delegation]," May 28, 1972, 196-1-512–19, SPA.

20. Memo, Holdridge to Kissinger, August 28, 1972, *FRUS, 1969–1972*, vol. 17, doc. 248.

21. "Report on Exchange Discussions, CSCPRC Visit to China, May 15–June 15, 1973," attached to letter, Keatley to Handler, July 20, 1973, "IR 1973 CSCPRC: ACLS-NAS-SSRC Visits: Com Visit on Scholarly Exchanges," NAS.

22. "The Committee on Scholarly Communication with the People's Republic of China," and "Recent Developments in United States-People's Republic of China Scientific Exchanges," unattributed documents at NAS, courtesy of Janice Goldblum.

23. Memo, CSC Programs Staff Report to the Committee, December 1975, "CSCPRC-JAN 5–6, 1976," box. 4, Albert Feuerwerker (AF), Bentley Historical Library (BHL).

24. Letter, Smith to Kissinger, October 9, 1973, "China: Committee on Scholarly Communication . . . Correspondence: 1973–April 21, 1975," box 1, Alexander Eckstein (hereafter AE), BHL.

25. Memo, Solomon to Kissinger, July 30, 1973, *FRUS, 1969–1976*, vol. 18, doc. 45; and telegram, Kissinger to USLO, September 10, 1973, 1973STATE179901, Electronic Telegrams 1973, CFPF, RG 59, NARA.

26. Memorandum of Conversation, November 11, 1973, "PRC Counterpart Talks on Exchanges (Jenkins) 1971–1973 [2 of 2]," box 87, NSC Henry A. Kissinger (HAK) Office Files, RNL.

27. Memorandum of Conversation, July 9, 1974, "China: National Committee on US-China Relations (NCUSCR): Exchange with the PRC: General: 1972–1974," box 3, AE, BHL.

28. Gloria B. Lubkin, "C. N. Yang discusses physics in People's Republic of China," *Physics Today* 24, no. 11 (1971): 63.

29. Yang Jianye, *Yang Zhenning zhuan* [Biography of Yang Zhenning] (Beijing: Shenghuo-Dushu-Xinzhi san lian shudian, 2011), 437–38.

30. Zhou Peiyuan, "Dui zonghe daxue like jiaoyu geming de yixie kanfa [Some views on the revolution in science education at universities]," *Guangming Ribao* [*Guangming Daily*], October 6, 1972.

31. T. D. Lee, "My Meeting with Mao," *The Sciences* 28, no. 1 (1990): 18.

32. Smith, "The Role of Scientists," 124.

33. Yang, *Yang Zhenning zhuan*, 446.

34. He, *ZhongMei minjian jiaoliu shi*, 206; and Yang Chen-ning, "What Visits Mean to China's Scientists," in *Reflections on Scholarly Exchanges with the People's Republic of China, 1972–1976*, ed., Anne Keatley (Washington, DC: Committee on Scholarly Communication with the People's Republic of China, 1976), 20–21.

35. C. K. Jen, "Science and the Open-Doors Educational Movement," *China Quarterly*, no. 64 (December 1975): 746.

36. John Gardner, "The Gang of Four and Chinese Science," *Bulletin of the Atomic Scientists* 33, no. 7 (1977): 27; Chinese Academy of Sciences, "1976 nian zhi 1985 nian Zhongguo kexueyuan kexue fazhan guihua gangyao [Digest of the CAS science development plan between 1976 and 1985]," March 1975, SZ122-4-192–1, HPA; and "Quanguo kexue jishu gongzuo huiyi jiyao (cao'an) [Summary of the national science and technology work conference]," undated, 135-2-506–2, BMA.

37. For the drafting process of this document, see Lieberthal, *Central Documents*, 35–44. For the English text, see Lieberthal, *Central Documents*, 141–54.

38. *Deng Xiaoping sixiang nianbian*, 37.

39. Zhang Chunqiao, "On Exercising All-Round Dictatorship over the Bourgeoisie," *Peking Review*, April 4, 1975, 5–11.

40. Chinese Academy of Science Great Criticism Group, "Deng Xiaoping yao keji jie dai shenme tou? [What did Deng Xiaoping bring to the science and technology community?]" *People's Daily*, August 7, 1976; and Fang Yi, "Guanche zhuagang zhiguo de zhanlüe juece wei shixian kexue jishu de xiandaihua er nuli fendou [Carry out the strategic decision to grasp the key link in running the country, strive for the realization of scientific and technological modernization]," June 21, 1977, author's personal collection.

41. "Nuli danghao kexue jishu de zhuren [Strive to become a master of science and technology]," undated, C42-3-98–89, SMA.

42. Summary of Exchange Discussion, September 27, 1975, "IR 1975 CSCPRC: ACLS-NAS-SSRC Visits: Chinese Scientific & Technical Assoc Delegation: Meetings," NAS.

43. The Future of Academic Exchange with the People's Republic of China, June 1975, "CSCPRC, July 17, 1975 Meeting with Dept of State," box 4, AF, BHL.

44. Memo, Kissinger to Ford, November 20, 1975, *FRUS*, 1969–1976, vol. 18, doc. 132.

45. Memorandum of Conversation, December 2, 1975, *FRUS*, 1969–1976, vol. 18, doc. 135.

46. Memo, Anne Keatley to Files, January 12, 1976, fol. 334, box 33, ser. 2, RG5, FA1187, NCUSCR, RAC.

47. Letter, Frank Press to Han Hsu, January 8, 1976, "IR 1976 CSCPRC Exchange Agreement: Negotiations," NAS.

48. Letter, Press and Keatley to Chou Pei-yuan, January 23, 1976, "IR 1976 CSCPRC Exchange Agreement: Negotiations," NAS.

49. Discussion of 1976 Exchange Negotiations, January 30, 1976, "IR 1976 CSCPRC Exchange Agreement: Negotiations," NAS.

50. Frank Press, "Scholarly Exchange with the People's Republic of China—Recent Experience," in *Our China Prospects: Symposium on Chinese-American Relations at the Autumn General Meeting of the American Philosophical Society November 12, 1976*, ed., John K. Fairbank (Philadelphia: American Philosophical Society, 1977), 37–43.

51. Mary Brown Bullock, "The CSCPRC and the Social Sciences and Humanities," undated, "CSCPRC–Meeting JAN 31, 1977," box 4, AF, BHL.

52. Victor Li, "Health Services and the New Relationship between China Studies and Visits to China," *China Quarterly*, no. 59 (July-September 1974): 566–79.

53. Mu Shih, "Research Work in Philosophy and Social Sciences Unshackled," *Peking Review*, May 12, 1978, 16–21.

54. China Tourism Enterprise Administration, "Guanyu jiedai Meiguo 'Guanxin Yazhou wenti xuezhe weiyuanhui Xianggang fenhui' shi san min chengyuan fangHua jihua de qingshi baogao [Report on the plan for receiving thirteen members of the US 'Committee of Concerned Asian Scholars Hong Kong branch']," June 12, 1971, 196-1-467–11, SPA; and Chinese Academy of Sciences Foreign Affairs Team, "Jiedai Meiguo kexuejia xiehui daibiaotuan huodong jianbao [Report on activity for receiving the Federation of American Scientists delegation] 5," May 28, 1972, 196-1-512–16, SPA.

55. Memo, Holdridge to Kissinger, August 28, 1972, *FRUS*, 1969–1976, vol. 17, doc. 248, fn. 3.

56. "Report on Exchange Discussions, CSCPRC Visit to China, May 15–June 15, 1973," attached to letter, Keatley to Handler, July 20, 1973, "IR 1973 CSCPRC: ACLS-NAS-SSRC Visits: Com Visit on Scholarly Exchanges," NAS.

57. Memo, CSC Programs Staff Report to the Committee.

58. Reception team, "Jiedai Meiguo you'er fazhan he jiaoyu daibiaotuan qingkuang baogao [Report on the situation of receiving the US early childhood development and education delegation] 4," November 26, 1973, 153-6-42-11, BMA.

59. Ministry of Agriculture, "Waibin qingkuang jianbao [Report on foreign guests], 40," September 6, 1974, 196-2-97-13, SPA.

60. Reception Team at the Chinese Academy of Sciences Foreign Affairs Bureau, "Jiedai Meiguo dizhen daibiaotuan qingkuang jianbao [Report on receiving the US earthquake delegation] 5," October 17, 1974, 196-2-97-15, SPA.

61. Reception team, "Jiedai Meiguo yuyan daibiaotuan qingkuang jianbao [Report on receiving the US language study delegation] 2, 5" October 23 and November 15, 1974, 196-2-97-3, SPA; "The Problems of Dr. Mote, Member of US Linguists Delegation," undated, "Secretary's Visit to Peking Bilateral Issues S/P Mr. Lord Nov 1974 (1 of 2)," box 371, Policy Planning Staff, RG 59, NARA; and Frederick W. Mote, *China and the Vocation of History in the Twentieth Century: A Personal Memoir* (Princeton, NJ: Princeton University Press, 2010), 219-28.

62. Memo, CSC Programs Staff Report to the Committee.

63. Memo, Keatley, November 13, 1975, "China: Committee on Scholarly Communication . . . Memoranda: Nov. 1975-1976," box 1, AE, BHL.

64. Memo, Keatley to Feuerwerker, June 15, 1976, "Feuerwerker, Albert 4, 1973," box 6, National Archive on Sino-American Relations (NASAR), BHL.

65. Shaanxi Provincial Revolutionary Committee Bureau of Agriculture, "Guanyu jiedai Meiguo xiaomai kaochatuan de qingkuang jianbao [Report on receiving the US wheet delegation]," June 10, 1976, 196-1-758-20, SPA.

66. Memo, DOS/CU to CSCPRC, June 17, 1976, "Feuerwerker, Albert 4, 1973," box 6, NASAR, BHL.

67. Journal of a Visit to the People's Republic of China, May-June 1976 by Lloyd E. Eastman, "Eastman, Lloyd E., 1976," box 5, NASAR, BHL.

68. Memo, Keatley to all CSCPRC members, June 18, 1976, "Feuerwerker, Albert 4, 1973," box 6, NASAR, BHL.

69. Memo, Keatley to CSCPRC Members, July 16, 1976, "Feuerwerker, Albert 4, 1973," box 6, NASAR, BHL.

70. Memo, Keatley to Feuerwerker, August 30, 1976, "Feuerwerker, Albert 4, 1973," box 6, NASAR, BHL.

71. Memo, Keatley to CSCPRC Members, September 15, 1976, "Feuerwerker, Albert 4, 1973," box 6, NASAR, BHL.

72. Memo, Tsuchitani to Executive Committee, November 16, 1976, "Feuerwerker, Albert 4, 1973," box 6, NASAR, BHL.

73. State Council, "Guanyu geren jinkou yinshuapin de zanxing guanli banfa [Tentative measure to administer imports of printed items by individuals]," December 6, 1975, SZ139-6-609-6, HPA; and Ministry of Foreign Trade and Foreign Ministry, "Guanyu Meiguo zhuGang jigou xiang wo sanfa shukan chuli wenti de qingshi [Request for instruction on how to deal with US agencies in Hong Kong distributing books and periodicals to us]," October 25, 1975, 196-2-102-52, SPA.

74. Zhou Peiyuan, "'Sirenbang' pohuai jichu lilun yanjiu yong xin zai he ['The Gang of Four' destroys basic theoretical research for what purpose]," *People's Daily*, January 13, 1977; and "Jianjue ba Zhongguo keuxueyuan zhengdun hao jinkuai ba kexue yanjiu gao shang qu [Determined to rectify the CAS, enhance scientific research as soon as possible]," *People's Daily*, March 9, 1977.

75. Gardner, "Gang of Four," 30; and Xu Chi, "Gedebahe caixiang," *Renmin wenxue* [People's literature], no. 1 (1978): 53-68.

76. CAS Theory Group, "Yao zhi song gaojie, dai dao xue hua shi—tuifan 'Sirenbang' dui 'huigao tigang' de wuxian [Only when the snow melts do you realize the beauty of a pine tree—reversing the Gang of Four's false charges against the 'Outline Report']," *People's Daily*, June 30, 1977.

77. Frederic Wakeman, Report on Exchange Discussion in Peking, June 1977, "CSCPRC–1978," box 4, AF, BHL.

78. Philip Handler, "Trip Report: Visit of Delegation of CSCPRC to Peking—June13–19, 1977," undated, "IR 1977 CSCPRC Visits: Com Visit on Scholarly Exchanges," NAS.

79. Letter, Handler and Sheldon to Vance, August 5, 1977, "IR 1977 CSCPRC Exchange Agreement: Negotiations," NAS.

80. Memorandum of Conversation, August 24, 1977, *FRUS*, 1977–1981, vol. 13, doc. 50.

81. Deborah Shapley, "China after Mao: Science Seeks to Be Both Red and Expert," *Science*, August 19, 1977, 740.

82. Memo, Bullock to Handler, October 28, 1977, "IR 1977 CSCPRC General," NAS; and letter, Charles H. Townes to Leo Goldberg, November 30, 1977, "IR 1977 CSCPRC General," NAS.

83. "China's Attempt at a Renaissance," *Science News*, August 13, 1977, 104.

84. CCP Central Archives and Manuscript Division, ed., *Deng Xiaoping nianpu* [Chronology of Deng Xiaoping], vol. 2 (Beijing: Zhongyang wenxian chubanshe, 2004), 177. See also Chenxi Xiong, "Deng Xiaoping's Views on Science and Technology: Origins of the Sino-U.S. Science and Technology Cooperation, 1977–1979," *Journal of American-East Asian Relations* 28, no. 2 (2021): 159–85.

85. "Zhongguo Kexueyuan 1978 nian zhi 1985 nian quanguo jichu kexue fazhan jihua gangyao [CAS national basic science development plan for 1978–1985]," January 1978, B1-9-8-3, SMA.

86. National Science Conference Preparation Team, "Guanyu yingjie quanguo kexue dahui de xuanchuan yaodian [Key points on propaganda to celebrate the national science conference]," August 29, 1977, 229-5-68-29, GPA.

87. Chen Jinhua, "Zai 'Shanghai shi qingshaonian keji huodong zhou' kaimushi shang de jianghuagao [Speech draft for the opening ceremony of 'the Shanghai youth science and technology activity week']," November 7, 1977, B105-9-159–62, SMA.

88. "Dongyuan quan minzu xiang kexue jishu xiandaihua jinjun—quanguo kexue dahui qingkuang huibao tigan [Mobilize all the people to march toward scientific and technological modernization—digest of the situation at the national science conference]," undated, SZ122-4-464–1, HPA.

89. Hua Guofeng, "Tigao zheng ge Zhonghua minzu de kexue wenhua shuiping [Enhancing the standard of scientific culture of the entire Chinese population]," *People's Daily*, March 26, 1978.

90. Guo Rifang, "Zuojin kexue de chuntian [Toward the spring of science]," in *Kexue de chuntian* [The spring of science], ed. Fang Xin (Beijing: Kexue chubanshe, 2008), 31–32.

91. Deng Xiaoping, "Zai quanguo kexue dahui kaimushi shang de jianghua [Speech at the opening ceremony of the national science conference]," *People's Daily*, March 22, 1978.

92. Luo Wei, "Keji tizhi gaige de xumu [Beginning of the scientific system reform]," in *Kexue*, ed., Fang, 20.

93. Guo Moruo, "Kexue de chuntian—zai quanguo kedue dahui bimushi shang de jianghua [Spring of science—speech at the closing ceremony of the national science conference]," *People's Daily*, April 1, 1978.

94. Shanghai Municipal Committee on Science and Technology, "Keji qingkuang [Science and technology situations] 32," June 26, 1978, B247-4-8, SMA.

95. Conversation with Vice-Premier Teng Hiao-ping, October 23, 1977, "NC US-C Relations 7/77," box 131, ADB, CU.

96. Barbara J. Culliton, "China's 'Four Modernizations' Lead to Closer Sino-U.S. Ties," *Science*, August 11, 1978, 512–13.

97. "Recent Developments in United States-People's Republic of China Scientific Exchanges," unattributed, NAS.

98. Mary Brown Bullock, "Beyond Friendship: Scholarly Exchange with the PRC," *Contemporary China* 2 (Spring 1978): 31–38.

99. Memo, Samuel Huntington to Brzezinski, May 11, 1978, *FRUS, 1977–1981*, vol. 13, doc. 100.

100. CIA, "A Report on the National Science Conference in China," June 26, 1978, "Press (Frank) 7/78 Trip to China: Briefing Book [II]: 6/78," box 60, Far East, Brzezinski Material, National Security Affairs (NSA), JCL.

101. CCP Central Archives and Manuscript Division, ed., *Deng Xiaoping wenxuan* [Selected works of Deng Xiaoping], vol. 2 (Beijing: Renmin chubanshe, 1993), 111–12.

102. Letter, Press to Handler, March 7, 1977, "IR 1977 CSCPRC Visits: Com Visit on Scholarly Exchanges," NAS; and letter, Brzezinski to Handler, March 31, 1977, "IR 1977 CSCPRC Visits: Com Visit on Scholarly Exchanges," NAS.

103. Memo, Press to Brzezinski, March 13, 1978, "China (PRC), 2–5/78," box 8, Country Files, Brzezinski Material, NSA, JCL.

104. Telegram, USLO Peking to Vance, July 9, 1978, 1978PEKING02073, Electronic Telegrams 1978, CFPF, RG 59, NARA.

105. Telegram, USLO Peking to Vance, July 12, 1978, 1978PEKING02110, Electronic Telegrams 1978, CFPF, RG 59, NARA.

106. Memo, Press to Carter, October 13 1978, "China (PRC), 9–11/78," box 8, Country Files, Brzezinski Material, NSA, JCL.

107. Presidential Directive 43, November 3, 1978, *FRUS, 1977–1980*, vol. 13, doc. 150.

108. Memorandum of Conversation, Feng and Bullock, August 3, 1978; Memorandum of Conversation, Huang and Bullock, August 3, 1978; and Memorandum of Conversation, Chien and Bullock, August 2, 1978, "IR 1978 CSCPRC General," NAS.

109. Jay Matthews, "Both Chinas Attend Same Conference," *Washington Post*, August 25, 1978.

110. State Science and Technology Commission and the Foreign Ministry, "Guanyu dui ziben zhuyi guojia keji jiaoliu guanli gongzuo de ruogan guiding [Some regulations on administering scientific and technological exchanges with capitalist countries]," November 3, 1978, B242-4-249-13, SMA.

111. E. E. David, Jr., "China: Objectives, Contradictions, and Social Currents," *Science*, February 9, 1979, 512.

112. William Carey, "The Chinese Scene," *Science*, February 9, 1979, 510; and William Carey, "AAAS Board Visit to China—A Brief Report," *Science*, February 9, 1979, 535.

113. Hu Qiaomu, "Zai quanguo zhexue shehui kexue jihua huiyi yubeihui shang de jianghua [Speech at the preparatory meeting for the national planning conference on philosophy and social sciences]," September 13, 1978, A22-4-36–1, SMA.

114. Chinese Academy of Social Sciences Publication Team, "'Sirenbang' shi Makesi zhuyi zhexue shehui kexue de sidi [The 'Gang of Four' is a deadly enemy of Marxist philosophy and social sciences]," *Lishi yanjiu* [Historical research], no. 10 (1978): 3–16.

115. Julian B. Gewirtz, *Unlikely Partners: Chinese Reformers, Western Economists, and the Making of Global China* (Cambridge, MA: Harvard University Press, 2017).

116. Bullock, "Beyond Friendship."

117. Frederic Wakeman Jr., "Historiography in China after 'Smashing the Gang of Four'," *China Quarterly*, no. 76 (December 1978): 891–911; and Frederic Wakeman Jr., "A Conversation with Four Chinese Historians in Nanking," *China Quarterly*, No. 60 (December 1974): 767–72.

118. Jay Matthews, "China Permits U.S. Sociologists to Study Village," *Washington Post*, July 7, 1978; and Edward Friedman, Paul G. Pickowicz, and Mark Selden, eds., *Chinese Village, Socialist State* (New Haven, CT: Yale University Press, 1991).

119. Gu Jiegang, "Bixu chedi pipan 'bang shixue' [We must thoroughly criticize 'national history']," *Guangming Ribao* [*Guangming Daily*] March 11, 1978.

120. *Public Papers: Carter, 1979*, 200–12.

121. Memo, Press to Carter, July 27, 1979, *FRUS*, 1977–1980, vol. 13, doc. 257.

122. David Binder, "Chinese Social Science Means to Study in America," *New York Times*, April 15, 1979.

123. Fei Xiaotong, "FuMei fangxue guangan diandi [Some impressions on the visits to US schools]," in Chinese Academy of Social Sciences Delegation to the United States, *FangMei guangan* [Impressions on the visit to the United States] (Zhongguo shehui kexue chubanshe, 1979), 34.

124. Whitesides, *Science and American Foreign Relations*, 225–27.

125. Paul A. Cohen, *A Path Twice Travelled: My Journey as a Historian of China* (Cambridge, MA: Harvard University Press, 2019), 128–37; Anne F. Thurston and Burton Pasternak, eds., *The Social Sciences and Fieldwork in China: Views from the Field* (New York: Routledge, 1984), 7–19; and Jay Matthews, "Stanford Expels Student Faulted on China Study," *Washington Post*, February 26, 1983.

126. Julian Gewirtz, "The Futurists of Beijing: Alvin Toffler, Zhao Ziyang, and China's 'New Technological Revolution,' 1979–1991," *Journal of Asian Studies* 78, no. 1 (2019): 115–40.

127. Albert Feuerwerker, "Impact on Chinese Studies in the United States," in *Reflections*, ed., Keatley, 13; and A. Doak Barnett, "Exchanges in the Process of 'Normalization': An Academic View," in *Reflections*, ed., Keatley, 46.

128. Interview with Li Mingde, quoted in Smith, "The Role of Scientists," 131.

129. Hunter Rouse, "Impressions of the People's Republic of China—China: A New Land," *Mechanical Engineering* 97 (2): 28–29; and George Bugliarello and Hunter Rouse, "Impressions of the People's Republic of China: Engineering Education," *Mechanical Engineering* 97, no. 4 (1975): 28–29.

130. Letters and Comment, *Mechanical Engineering* 97, no. 5 (1975): 62.

131. Letters and Comment, *Mechanical Engineering* 97, no. 5 (1975): 62

132. Letters and Comment, *Mechanical Engineering* 97, no. 9 (1975): 40.

133. Philip Abelson, "Mainland China: An Emerging Power," *Science*, July 28, 1967, 373.

134. David Jr., "China," 515.

4. Education

1. Jonathan Spence, *To Change China: Western Advisers in China* (New York: Penguin Books, 2002).

2. Arthur H. Smith, *China and America Today: A Study of Conditions and Relations* (New York: Fleming H. Revell, 1907), 214; and Michael H. Hunt "American Remission of the Boxer Indemnity: A Reappraisal," *Journal of Asian Studies* 31, no. 3 (1972): 550.

3. Weili Ye, *Seeking Modernity in China's Name: Chinese Students in the United States, 1900–1927* (Stanford, CA: Stanford University Press, 2001), 11.

4. Li Tao, ed., *Zhonghua liuxue jiaoyu shilu: 1949 nian yihou* [A history of China's study-abroad education after 1949] (Beijing: Gaodeng jiaoyu chubanshe, 2000), 220–224.

5. *Zhongguo jiaoyu nianjian, 1949–1981* [Education yearbook of China, 1949–1981] (Beijing: Zhongguo dabaike quanshu chubanshe, 1984), 965, 966.

6. *Zhongguo jiaoyu nianjian, 1949–1981*, 966; and "15,000 Workers' Colleges," *Peking Review*, July 30, 1976, 4; and Suzanne Pepper, "An Interview on Changes in Chinese Education after the 'Gang of Four'," *China Quarterly*, no. 72 (December, 1977): 816. On the revolution in education, see, for example, Suzanne Pepper, *Radicalism and Education Reform in Twentieth-Century China: The Search for an Ideal Development Model* (New York: Cambridge University Press, 1996), 381–465.

7. See, for example, Andrew Hartman, *Education and the Cold War: The Battle for the American School* (New York: Palgrave Macmillan, 2008).

8. Herbert R. Kohl, *The Open Classroom* (New York: Random House, 1969); Ivan Illich, *Deschooling Society* (New York: Harper and Row, 1971); Jean Piaget, *The Science of Education* (New York: Orion Press, 1970); and Samuel Bowles and Herbert Gintis, *Schooling in Capitalist America: Educational Reform and the Contradictions of Economic Life* (New York: Basic Books, 1976).

9. Ching, "China."

10. Douglas P. Murray, "Exchanges with China?" *International Educational and Cultural Exchange* 7, no. 3 (1972): 6; Report on March 1, 1973 Roundtable on Exchanges, March 1, 1973, fol. 558, box 57, ser. 5, RG 4, FA1186, NCUSCR, RAC; and "Meiguo kexuejia xiehui lishi Sitong yu Zhongguo kexueyuan waishi zu fuzeren Zhu Yonghang tongzhi tanhua jilu [Record of conversation between Chairman of the Federation of American Scientists (Jeremy) Stone and Comrade Zhu Yonghang of the foreign affairs team of the Chinese Academy of Sciences]," May 26, 1972, 1961-1-512-17, SPA.

11. Memo, Solomon to Kissinger, June 9, 1972, *FRUS, 1969–1976*, vol. 17, doc. 229.

12. John Dewey, *Impressions of Soviet Russia and the Revolutionary World: Mexico—China—Turkey* (New York: New Republic, 1929).

13. Committee of Concerned Asian Scholars, *China!* 197–227.

14. Airgram, Hong Kong to State Department, January 19, 1973, "POL CHICOM 8-31-72," box 2178, SNF, RG 59, NARA.

15. "A Month in China: John Lewis Reports," *Stanford Observer*, February 1973, 9.

16. Jan S. Prybyla, "Notes on Chinese Higher Education: 1974," *China Quarterly*, no. 62 (June 1975): 296.

17. Alexander Eckstein, "China Trip Notes," August 1974, fol. 337, box 33, ser. 3, RG 5, FA1187, NCUSCR, RAC; and Memorandum of Conversation, November 21, 1972, "POL CHICOM-US 4-3-72," box 2189, RG 59, SNF, NARA.

18. Memorandum of Conversation, February 16, 1973, "PRC Counterpart Talks on Exchanges (Jenkins) 1971–1973 [2 of 2]," box 87, NSC HAK Office Files, RNL.

19. *Zhongguo jiaoyu nianjian, 1949–1981*, 666, 950.

20. Murray, "Exchanges with China?" 5; William Kovacic, "A Student Reports on Trip to China," *New York Times*, October 22, 1972; "25 at S.I. College Plan China Trip," June 16, 1973, *New York Times*, June 16, 1973; David Louie, "Life at China's 'Big River Commune'," *Washington Post*, July 23, 1973; and C. K. Jen, *Recollections of a Chinese Physicist* (Los Alamos, NM: Signition, 1990), 177.

21. See, for example, letter, William P. Glade to Huang Hua, April 12, 1973, B244-3-551-177, SMA.

22. Impressions of Modern China, undated, "Oksenberg, Michael, 6, 1972," box 11, NASAR, BHL.

23. Report of the Delegation of University and College Presidents to the People's Republic of China, undated, fol. 130, box 17, S3, FA1086, RG 4, RAC.

24. Impressions of Modern China; and "Daxue jiaoyu geming zuotanhui jianbao [Digest on the forum on the revolution in university education] 3," June 30, 1972, B244-1-331–204, SMA.

25. The Price of Freedom, December 14, 1974, "Travel Records: 1974, China & Japan (1)," box 19, Robben Fleming, BHL.

26. Observation on China, December 26, 1974, "Travel Records: 1974, China & Japan (1)," box 19, Robben Fleming, BHL.

27. Transcript of Meeting with Teng Hsiao-Ping, undated, fol. 132, box 17, ser. 3, RG 4, FA1186, NCUSCR, RAC.

28. Letter, Roger W. Heyns to Kissinger, undated draft, fol. 130, box 17, ser. 3, RG 4, FA1186, NCUSCR, RAC.

29. Impressions of Modern China.

30. Telegram, USLO to Kissinger, October 1, 1975, "People's Republic of China—State Department Telegrams: To SECSTATE—NODIS (6)," box 15, NSA, Presidential Country Files for East Asia and the Pacific, 1974–1977, GFL.

31. Memorandum of Conversation, October 22, 1975, "October 19–23, 1975—Kissinger's Trip (4)," box 2, National Security Adviser, Kissinger Reports on USSR, China, and Middle East Discussions, GFL.

32. Anne FitzGerald, Linguistics Delegation to the People's Republic of China, October 16–November 13, 1974, Staff Report, "People's Republic of China, Exchanges [exchange programs] (2)," box 8, NSC East Asian and Pacific Affairs Staff Files, GFL; and Chinese Academy of Sciences Foreign Affairs Office, "Jiedai Meiguo gaoneng wuli xuezhe daibiaotuan qingkuang jianbao [Report on receiving the US high energy physics delegation], 8," September 30, 1974, 196-2-97–8, SPA.

33. Ministries of Education and Foreign Affairs, "Guanyu jiedai Meiguo Niuyue zhouli daxue zongxiao xiaozhang Baoye fangHua jihua [Plan on receiving (Ernest) Boyer, chancellor of the US State University of New York]," May 24, 1975, B105-4-1370–97, SMA.

34. Liu Bing, *Fengyu suiyue: 1964–1976 nian de Tsinghua* [Years of storm and rain: Tsinghua University between 1964 and 1976] (Beijing: Dangdai Zhongguo chubanshe), 175.

35. Suzanne Pepper, "Education and Revolution: The 'Chinese Model' Revised," *Asian Survey* 18 (9): 869–70.

36. State Council Science and Education Group, "Guanyu 1974 nian gaodeng xuexiao zhaosheng gongzuo de qingshi baogao [Request for instruction on enrollment work for higher education schools in 1974]," June 9, 1974, B123-8-1156–1, SMA.

37. David S. Zweig, "The Peita Debate on Education and the Fall of Teng Hsiao-p'ing," *China Quarterly*, no. 73 (March 1978): 140–41; and MacFarquhar and Schoenhals, *Mao's Last Revolution*, 391–92.

38. Zhang Tiesheng, "Yi fen fa ren shen sheng de dajuan [One test sheet that prompts people to reflect deeply]," *Liaoning Ribao*, July 19, 1973, and *People's Daily*, August 10, 1973.

39. Zhu Yan, "Gaige daxue zhaosheng zhidu de shenyuan yiyi [The deep significance of the reform on the university enrollment system]," *Red Flag*, no. 8 (1973): 9–13.

40. Liu, *Fengyu suiyue*, 263–73.

41. Great Criticism Group of Peking University and Tsinghua University, "Jiaoyu geming de fangxiang burong cuangai [The orientation of the revolution in education must not be tampered with]," *Red Flag*, no. 12 (1975): 5–12.

42. Hubei Provincial Revolutionary Committee Bureau of Education, "Jiaoyu geming qingkuang fanying [Report on situations of the revolution in education] 3," May 15, 1974, SZ118-4-286-3, HPA.

43. D. I. Chambers, "The 1975–1976 Debate over Higher Education Policy in the People's Republic of China," *Comparative Education* 13, no. 1 (1977): 5–9.

44. Ann Kent, "Red and Expert: The Revolution in Education at Shanghai Teachers' University, 1975–1976," *China Quarterly*, no. 86 (January 1981): 304–05.

45. Zweig, "Peita Debate," 153.

46. Fox Butterfield, "U.S. Group Detects No Hostility in China," *New York Times*, March 1, 1974.

47. Report of the Delegation of University and College Presidents; and Merle Goldman, Contradictions in China's Higher Education, November 8–29, 1974, "Feuerwerker, Albert 8 8 8 1973," box 6, NASAR, BHL.

48. "Shisan nian lai zhong xiaoxue yingyu jiaocai chengdu jiangdi de qingkuang [Situations of the declining level of English materials at middle-high and elementary schools in the past thirteen years]," undated, B105-9-251-29, SMA.

49. Ministry of Education, "Guanyu banhao waiguoyu xuexiao de ji dian yijian [Some opinions on managing foreign language schools well]," undated, B244-4-379-61, SMA; and National Publication Enterprise Administration and the Ministry of Education, "Guanyu zhaokai Zhongwai yuwen cidian bianxie chuban guihua zuotanhui de qingshi baogao [Request for instruction on convening a forum on planning the compilation and publication of Chinese-foreign language dictionaries]," March 22, 1975, B167-3-302-50, SMA.

50. "Jiaoyu geming qingkuang [Situations of the revolution in education]," May 27, 1971, B105-4-639-1, SMA.

51. "Quanguo jiaoyu gongzuo huiyi jianbao [Digest on the national education work conference] 73," July 3, 1971, SZ118-4-73-33, HPA.

52. "Guanyu Shanghai waiyu xueyuan, Fudan daxue, Shanghai shida sanxiao fahui waiguo zhuanjia zuoyong de qingshi baogao [Request for instruction on utilizing foreign experts at Shanghai Foreign Language Institute, Fudan University, and Shanghai Normal University]," January 7, 1976, B105-4-1547-41, SMA.

53. FitzGerald, Linguistics Delegation.

54. Ross Terrill, *800,000,000: The Real China* (New York: Little Brown, 1972), 73.

55. Edward Friedman, Paul G. Pickowicz, and Mark Selden, eds., *Revolution, Resistance, and Reform in Village China* (New Haven, CT: Yale University Press, 2005), 192.

56. "Guanyu 'Mazhenfu gongshe zhongxue shijian' de diaocha [Investigation on the 'Mazhenfu Commune middle school incident']," *People's Daily*, December 9, 1977.

57. Shanghai People's Radio Station Revolutionary Committee, "Guanyu 'Yeyu yingyu guangbo jiangzuo' de jianghua gao (di yi ke) [Speech draft of 'Radio lectures in amateur English (first lesson)]," 1972, B92-2-1625-22, SMA.

58. Shanghai People's Radio Station Revolutionary Committee, "'Yeyu yingyu guangbo jiangzuo' guangbo hou de qingkuang fanying [Report on situations after broadcasting 'Radio lectures in amateur English']," March 11, 1972, B92-2-1625-14, SMA.

59. Shanghai People's Radio Station Revolutionary Committee, "Yingyu guangbo jiangzuo chuji-ban jinzhan qingkuang jianbao [Report on the progress of radio lectures in elementary English]," September 9, 1972, B92-2-1625-6, SMA; and "'Yeyu waiyu guangbo jiangzuo' qunzhong laixin huibian [Compilation of letters from the masses for 'Radio lectures in amateur foreign languages'] 5," September 1, 1973, B285-2-100-25, SMA.

60. "'Yeyu keji yingyu guangbo jiangzuo' choubei gongzuo xiaojie [Summary of preparatory work for 'Radio lectures in amateur technical English']," July 1, 1977, 198-2-2919–12, TMA.

61. See, for example, Gene Giancarlo, "A China Diary," 12–13; and Susan W. Dryfoos, "China Adventure: Are They Ready for Us?" *New York Times*, November 25, 1973.

62. "Guangbo dianshi qingkuang [Situations in radio and television] 4," February 21, 1978, B285-2-673–38, SMA.

63. Ministry of Education Great Criticism Group, "Mao zhuxi de jiaoyu fangzhen qi rong cuangai—pipan Zhang Chunqiao de yi ge miulun [How can you distort Chairman Mao's education policy—criticize one of Zhang Chunqiao's fallacies]," *Guangming Ribao*, November 23, 1976.

64. *Deng Xiaoping nianpu*, vol. 2, 159–60.

65. *Deng Xiaoping nianpu*, vol. 2, 172–73.

66. Memorandum of Conversation, September 22, 1979, 214-2-842–1, SPA.

67. Jay Mathews, "Education in China," *Washington Post*, June 23, 1978.

68. Chen Yu, *Zhongguo shenghuo jiyi: Jianguo 65 zhounian minsheng wangshi* [Memories of life in China: People's stories at the 65th anniversary of the nation's founding] (Beijing: Zhongguo qinggongye chubanshe, 2014), 291.

69. CCP Central Document no. 37, "Wang Hongwen, Zhang Chunqiao, Jiang Qing, Yao Wenyuan fan dang jituan zuizheng [The crime list of the anti-Party group of Wang Hongwen, Zhang Chunqiao, Jiang Qing, and Yao Wenyuan] 3," September 23, 1977, 1–2; and Ministry of Education Great Criticism Group, "Jiaoyu zhanxian de yi chang da lunzhan—pipan 'Sirenbang' paozhi de 'liang ge guji' [One huge controversy on the education front—criticizing the 'two estimates' fabricated by the Gang of Four]," *Red Flag*, no. 12 (1977): 3–13.

70. Robin Munro, "Settling Accounts with the Cultural Revolution at Peking University 1977–78," *China Quarterly*, no. 82 (January 1980): 333.

71. David M. Lampton, "Thermidor in the Chinese Educational Revolution," *Theory into Practice* 17, no. 5 (1978): 367–74.

72. "Politics in Command of the Curriculum": Education in the People's Republic of China, January 9, 1978, "Anrig, Gregory R. 1977," box 1, NASAR, BHL; and Mary F. Berry and Albert Shanker, "The Politics of Thinking about China," *Change* 10, no. 2 (1978): 39.

73. Berry and Shanker, "Politics," 39, 64; and William Safire, "A Time for Testing," *New York Times*, December 8, 1977.

74. Jay Matthews, "Education in China: Reverting to the Old Way," *Washington Post*, January 17, 1978.

75. National Commission on Excellence in Education, *A Nation at Risk: The Imperative for Educational Reform* (Washington, DC: Government Printing Office, 1983); and Christopher P. Loss, *Between Citizens and the State: The Politics of American Higher Education in the 20th Century* (Princeton, NJ: Princeton University Press, 2012), 227–28.

76. Deng Xiaoping, "Zai quanguo jiaoyu gongzuo huiyi shang de jianghua [Speech at the national education conference]," *People's Daily*, April 26, 1978.

77. "Quanguo jiaoyu gongzuo huiyi zai Jing longzhong kaimu [National education work conference commences in Beijing]," *People's Daily*, April 23, 1978.

78. "1978–1985 nian quanguo jiaoyu shiye guihua gangyao (cao'an) [Outline of the national education program, 1978–1985 (draft)]," May 1978, SZ1-4-820–1, HPA.

79. Transcript of Final Meeting, July 8, 1978, fol. 79, box 10, ser. 3, RG 4, FA1186, NCUSCR, RAC; and Fred Burke's travel journal, undated, "Burke, Dr. Fred G. 1978," box 2, NASAR, BHL.

80. Personal Observations, undated, "Salmon, Paul B. 1978," box 11, NASAR, BHL.

81. "Yingyu bishi [Written test in English]," undated, B105-9-108-8, SMA.
82. Shanghai Municipal Bureau of Education, "Guanyu tigao benshi gelei xuexiao waiyu jiaoyu shuiping de qingshi baogao [Request for instruction on the level of foreign language education at various kinds of schools in this city]," December 1, 1978, B244-4-286-36, SMA; and "Hubei zhongxiaoxue waiyu jiaoxue qingkuang [Situations of foreign language education in elementary and secondary schools in Hubei]," July 6, 1978, SZ118-4-770-1.
83. "Quanguo waiyu jiaoyu zuotanhui jiyao [Summary of the national foreign language education forum]," September 10, 1978, B105-9-251-3, SMA.
84. Ministry of Education "Guanyu yinfa 'Jiaqiang waiyu jiaoyu de ji dian yijian' de tongzhi [Notice of circulation of 'A few opinions on strengthening foreign language education']," March 29, 1979, B243-4-112-40, SMA.
85. Memo, University Team, Shanghai Municipal Bureau of Education, May 25, 1977, B105-9-77-99, SMA; Ministries of Education, Foreign Affairs, and Finance, "Guanyu ban hao waiyu duanxun ban de tongzhi [Notice on administering short-term courses in foreign language]," April 1, 1978, 214-2-802-17, SPA.
86. Central Broadcast Bureau, "Guanyu tingzhi ganrao 'Meiguo zhi yin' de tongzhi [Notice on stopping jamming 'The Voice of America']," October 7, 1978, A22-4-43-13, SMA.
87. CCP Propaganda Department, "Tongzhi [Notice]," January 5, 1979, 306-1-105-2, SPA.
88. Memo, Stanton H. Burnett to John Edward Reinhardt, April 9, 1979, "M-4-79," box 35, Office of Research and Media Reaction (ORMR), RG 306, NARA.
89. Letter, Handler and Sheldon to Zhou, May 4, 1977, "IR 1977 CSCPRC Exchange Agreement: Negotiations," box 11, NAS.
90. Wakeman, Report on Exchange Discussion.
91. Douglas P. Murray, "Visit to Peking University, October 22, morning," October 20, 1977, fol. 98, box 13, ser. 3, RG 4, FA1186, NCUSCR, RAC.
92. Ministries of Education and Foreign Affairs, "Guanyu jiedai Meiguo zhou he difang jiaoyujie fuzeren daibiaotuan de tongzhi [Notice on receiving the US state and local education representative delegation]," October 6, 1977, B105-9-48-1, SMA.
93. Memo, Brzezinski to Carter, June 14, 1977, *FRUS*, 1977–1980, vol. 13, doc. 31.
94. See, for example, *Deng Xiaoping nianpu*, vol. 2, 179.
95. "Jiaoyu bu Yong Wentao fu buzhang zai quanguo jiaoyu shiye jihua zuotanhui zongjie dahui de jianghua [Vice Education Minister Yong Wentao's speech at the concluding session of the national education planning forum]," November 7, 1977, SZ118-4-572-1, HPA.
96. Memo, Bullock to Handler, December 2, 1977, "IR 1977 CSCPRC Visits: General," NAS.
97. "Zhongguo gaodeng jiaoyu daibiaotuan fangMei baogao [Report of the Chinese higher education delegation to the United States]," May 1978, B105-9-250-233, SMA.
98. "1978–1985 nian quanguo jiaoyu shiye guihua gangyao (cao'an)."
99. *Deng Xiaoping nianpu*, vol. 2, 331; and Li Qi, "FuMei tanpan liuxuesheng wenti shimo [The Story of visiting the United States to discuss student exchanges]," *Shenzhou xueren*, June 1998, 14–16.
100. Ministry of Education, "Guanyu zengxuan chuguo liuxuesheng de tongzhi [Notice regarding selecting more study abroad students]," August 4, 1978, in State Education Commission, *Chuguo liuxue gongzuo wenjian huibian, 1978–1991* [Compilation of documents on study abroad, 1978–1991] (Beijing: Qunzhong chubanshe, 1992), 1–4,
101. Memo, Doty and Johnson to Derek Bok, Handler, Press, and Jerome Weisner, July 8, 1978, "China: General MIT Correspondence," box 42, Walter A. Rosenblith Papers (WAR), MIT Archives (MIT).

102. Memo, Pye to Rosenblith, October 4, 1978, "CSCPRC Comm. on Scientific Comm. 4/6," box 43, WAR, MIT.

103. "Report of a Visit to the People's Republic of China by the Stanford International Security and Arms Control Group (July 10–19, 1978)," fol. 358, box 35, ser. 3, RG 5, FA1187, NCUSCR, RAC.

104. *Zhongguo jiaoyu nianjian, 1949–1981*, 675.

105. Interview with Woodcock, quoted in Qian Ning, *Chinese Students Encounter America* (Seattle: University of Washington Press, 2002), 9.

106. Telegram, USLO Peking to Vance, July 12, 1978, 1978PEKING02110, Electronic Telegrams 1978, CFPF, RG 59, NARA.

107. Proposal for Sending American Students to China, Revised Draft, August 9, 1978, "Albert Feuerwerker, CSCPRC-June 1978," box 5, AF, BHL.

108. CSCPRC, "Report of the Meeting on Student Exchanges with China," August 24, 1978, "U.S.-China Student Exchanges, The Interagency Working Group on," box 44, WAR, MIT.

109. Ministry of Education, Foreign Ministry, State Commission on Science and Technology, "Zhuwai shiguan wenhua canzan huiyi taolun paiqian chuguo liuxuesheng gongzuo de qingkuang baogao [Report on the situation in discussion on sending students abroad at the cultural counselors stationed at embassies abroad]," September 29, 1978, SZ118-4-659–18, HPA.

110. Qian Jiang, *1978 liuxue gaibian rensheng: Zhongguo gaige kaifang shou pi fuMei liuxuesheng jishi* [Stories of the first postreform Chinese students to study in the US] (Chengdu: Sichuan renmin chubanshe, 2017), 43.

111. Richard C. Atkinson, "Recollections of Events Leading to the First Exchange of Students, Scholars and Scientists between the United States and the People's Republic of China," December 14, 2006, accessed April 1, 2020, http://www.rca.ucsd.edu/.

112. *Public Papers: Carter, 1979*, 203–04.

113. "52 Chinese Scholars Arrive in U.S. for 2-Year Stay," *New York Times*, December 28, 1978.

114. Alice Bonner, "U.S. and China Soon Begin Exchanging University Scholars," *Washington Post*, October 24, 1978.

115. Guo Chengcai, "Gaige kaifang hou shoupi liuMeisheng de xuanpai ji qi yingxiang [The Selection and impact of the first batch of Chinese students in the United States after Reform and Opening-Up]," *Dangdai Zhongguoshi yanjiu* [Contemporary China History Studies] 12, no. 6 (2005): 73.

116. Letter, Hu to Rosenblith, January 28, 1979, "China: General MIT Correspondence," box 42, WAR. MIT.

117. Memo, CSCPRC to University Centers for Asian Studies, East Asian Studies, and Chinese Studies, October 17, 1978, "CSCPRC Comm. on Scientific Comm. 3/6," box 43, WAR, MIT.

118. "The Pioneers: American Students and Researchers in China—an Update," *China Exchange Newsletter* 7, no. 3 (1979): 1–3.

119. John Pomfret, *Chinese Lessons: Five Classmates and the Story of the New China* (New York: Henry Holt, 2006), 5.

120. David M. Lampton, *A Relationship Restored: Trends in U.S.-China Educational Exchanges, 1978–1984* (Washington, DC: National Academy Press, 1986), 112.

121. Peking University, "Meiguo Jiazhou Bokeli daxue daibiaotuan fanghua qingkuang jianbao [Report on the UC Berkeley delegation] 2," April 18, 1979, B243-4-26–62, SMA.

122. Roger L Geiger, *Research and Relevant Knowledge: American Research Universities since World War II* (New York: Oxford University Press, 1993), 310–20.

123. Patrick G. Maddox and Anne F. Thurston, "Academic Exchanges: The Goals and Roles of U.S. Universities," in *Educational Exchanges: Essays on the Sino-American Experience*, ed., Joyce K. Kallgren and Denis Fred Simon (Berkeley, CA: Institute of East Asian Studies, UC Berkeley, 1987), 127.

124. Maddox and Thurston, "Academic Exchanges," 133.

125. Nien Cheng, *Life and Death in Shanghai* (New York: Grove Press, 1986), 496–97.

126. Institute of International Education, *50 Years of Open Doors*, CD-ROM (New York: Institute of International Education, 2000).

127. "Zhonggong zhongyang guanyu zifei chuguo liuxue ruogan wenti de jueding [CCP Central Committee's decision on some issues regarding self-funded study abroad]," March 31, 1982, in *Chuguo liuxue gongzuo wenjian huibian*, 567–70; and "Education News," *Peking Review*, January 16, 1984, 11.

128. Norton Wheeler, *The Role of American NGOs in China's Modernization: Invited Influence* (New York: Routledge, 2013), 7–27.

129. Greg Rienzi, "An Unlikely Success Story in China," *Johns Hopkins Gazette* 36, no. 37 (2007), accessed April 1, 2020, https://pages.jh.edu/gazette/2007/11jun07/11nanj.html.

130. Qian, *Chinese Students*, 38.

131. Maddox and Thurston, "Academic Exchange," 135–36.

132. Maddox and Thurston, "Academic Exchange," 135, 145.

133. "CPC to Recruit More Intellectuals," *Peking Review*, December 3, 1984, 10.

134. Shanghai Municipal Education Bureau, "Guanyu Shida yi fu zhong deng wu suo xuexiao de waishi jiedai gongzuo qingkuang jianbao [Report on receiving foreigners at five schools such as the First Middle School attached to Shanghai Normal University]," December 21, 1979, B105-9-523–1, SMA.

135. Bureau of Propaganda, Hubei Provincial Committee, "Xuanchuan gongzuo [Propaganda work] 9," May 17, 1979, SZ7-6-337–12, HPA.

136. "Wan yu liuMei Zhonggong xuesheng yi qian duo wei qingqiu bihu [Over a thousand out of some ten thousand Communist Chinese students request asylum]," *Sing Tao Daily*, November 19, 1982.

137. Leo A. Orleans, *Chinese Students in America: Policies, Issues, and Numbers* (Washington, DC: National Academy Press, 1988), 112.

138. Maddox and Thurston, "Academic Exchanges," 144.

139. Richard Bernstein, "Student from China Defects to Establish New Rights Journal" *New York Times*, November 18, 1982.

5. Tourism

1. Samuel Wells Williams, *The Middle Kingdom: A Survey of the Geography, Government, Education, Social Life, Arts, Religion, etc. of the Chinese Empire and Its Inhabitants* (New York: Wiley and Putnam, 1848); and Arthur Henderson Smith, *Chinese Characteristics* (New York: Revell, 1894).

2. Pearl S. Buck, *The Good Earth* (New York: John Day, 1931); and Alice Tisdale Hobart, *Oil for the Lamps of China* (Indianapolis, IN: Bobbs-Merrill, 1933).

3. Agnes Smedley, *China's Red Army Marches* (New York: Vanguard Press, 1934); Agnes Smedley, *China Fights Back: An American Woman with the Eighth Route Army* (London: Victor Gollancz, 1938); Anna Louise Strong, *Red Star in Samarkand* (New York: Coward-McCann, 1929); Anna Louise Strong, *China's Millions: The Revolutionary Struggles from 1927 to 1935* (New

York: Knight Publishing, 1935); and Anna Louise Strong, *One-Fifth of Mankind* (New York: Modern Age Books, 1938).

4. Edgar Snow, *Red Star over China* (New York: Random House, 1937).

5. Theodore H. White and Annalee Jacoby's *Thunder Out of China* (London: Victor Gollancz, 1946); and Jack Belden's *China Shakes the World* (New York: Harpers, 1949).

6. Anne-Marie Brady, *Making the Foreign Serve China: Managing Foreigners in the People's Republic* (Lanham, MD: Rowman and Littlefield, 2003); Julia Lovell, "The Uses of Foreigners in Mao-Era China: 'Techniques of Hospitality' and International Image-Building in the People's Republic, 1949–1976," *Transactions of the Royal Historical Society* 25 (2015): 135–58; and Beverly Hooper, *Foreigners under Mao: Western Lives in China, 1949–1976* (Hong Kong: Hong Kong University Press, 2016). On occasional visits by non-"friend" journalists, see H. Timothy Lovelace Jr., "William Worthy's Passport: Travel Restrictions and the Cold War Struggle for Civil and Human Rights," *Journal of American History* 103, no. 1 (2016): 108; and Max Frankel, "41 Defy Warning, Set off for China," *New York Times*, August 14, 1957.

7. Edgar Snow, *The Other Side of the River: Red China Today* (New York: Random House, 1962); Felix Greene, *Awakened China: The Country American Don't Know* (Garden City, NY: Doubleday, 1961); Felix Greene, *The Wall Has Two Sides: A Portrait of China Today* (London: Jonathan Cape, 1961); and Felix Greene, *A Curtain of Ignorance: How the American Public Has Been Misinformed about China* (Garden City, NY: Doubleday, 1964).

8. "Americans in China," *New York Times*, February 7, 1957; and "Paying the Price," *Washington Post*, June 25, 1957.

9. Susan Sontag, "Project for a Trip to China," *Atlantic Monthly*, April 1973, 77.

10. Bill Shirley, "With Spikes On: How to See China on $0.00 a Day," *Los Angeles Times*, June 3, 1975.

11. Dryfoos, "China Adventure."

12. Fan Tiequan and Wang Sujun, "Lüyou, zhengzhi yu waijiao: xin Zhongguo chengli chuqi de chuguo lüyou, 1956–1965 [Tourism politics and diplomacy: Foreign tourism in early New China, 1956–1965]," *Hebei xuekan*, no. 2 (2018): 78–84; "Peking's 'See China' Program in Trouble?" March 15, 1966, "M-122-66," box. 25, ORMR, RG 306, NARA; and David Oancia, "Chinese Reds Block Newsmen's Reports," *New York Times*, July 24, 1967.

13. "Lüyou ju Yang Gongsu tongzhi zai lüyou gongzuo zuotanhui shang de fayan [Remarks of Comrade Yang Gongsu of the CTEA at the tourism work forum]," March 5, 1975, 63-1-21-15, GMA; and Yang Gongsu, *Cangsang jiushi nian—yi ge waijiao teshi de huiyi* [Great changes in the ninety years of my life—memoirs of a special diplomatic envoy] (Haikou: Hainan chubanshe, 1999), 305.

14. Jessica C. E. Gienow-Hecht, *Transmission Impossible: American Journalism as Cultural Diplomacy in Postwar Germany, 1945–1955* (Baton Rouge: Louisiana State University Press, 1999); Christopher Endy, *Cold War Holiday: American Tourism in France* (Chapel Hill: University of North Carolina Press, 2004); and Dennis Merrill, *Negotiating Paradise: U.S. Tourism and Empire in Twentieth-Century Latin America* (Chapel Hill: University of North Carolina Press, 2009). On Americanization and cultural imperialism, see Jessica C. E. Gienow-Hecht, "*Shame on U.S.?* Academics, Cultural Transfer, and the Cold War: A Critical Review," *Diplomatic History* 24, no. 3, 465–94.

15. Wu, *Radicals on the Road*, 4–5. On orientalism, see Christina Klein, *Cold War Orientalism: Asia in the Middlebrow Imagination, 1945–1961* (Berkeley: University of California Press, 2003).

16. China Tourism Enterprise Administration, "Guanyu lüyou gongzuo dangqian de jiben qingkuang he jinhou fazhan yijian de qingshi baogao (caogao) [Report on current basic situations in tourism work and opinions on future developments (draft)]," January 1975, 196-2-102-6, SPA.

17. Foreign Ministry telegram, "Weida lingxiu Mao zhuxi de zhongyao pishi [Great leader Chairman Mao's important instructions]," December 22, 1970, SZ139-6-235–16, HPA.

18. CTS and CITS usually received tourists of little diplomatic importance and with little specific interest, while CTS tended to host foreigners of Chinese descent. The CPIFA and the CPAFFC both received guests with interest in foreign affairs, but the CPIFA was slightly more inclined to host those of political importance.

19. Shaanxi Provincial Revolutionary Committee Foreign Affairs Office, "Waishi gognzuo qingkuang fanying 68," December 18, 1970, 196-1-410–68, SPA.

20. Shanghai Municipal Revolutionary Committee Foreign Affairs Team, "Waishi jianbao [Digest on foreign affairs] 322," September 23, 1971, B92-2-1501–26, SMA.

21. Ministry of Foreign Affairs, "Sinuo qu Xi'an, Yan'an diqu de caifang tongzhi [Notice on Snow's interviews in Xi'an and Yan'an]," September 16, 1970, 196-1-423–8, SPA.

22. *Mao Zedong nianpu*, vol. 6, 368.

23. Shanghai Municipal Revolutionary Committee Foreign Affairs Team, "Guanche zhongyang waishi gongzuo huiyi jingshen de qingkuang [Situations on carrying out the spirit of the CCP leadership's foreign affairs conference," September 22, 1971, B92-2-1501–14, SMA.

24. James Reston, "Now, about My Operation in Peking," *New York Times*, July 26, 1971.

25. Shanghai Municipal Revolutionary Committee Foreign Affairs Team, "Waishi jianbao [Digest on foreign affairs] 306," September 10, 1971, B92-2-1501–6, SMA.

26. China Tourism Enterprise Administration, "Lüyou qingkuang fanying [Report on situations in tourism] 13," March 27, 1974, B50-4-112–1, SMA; and China Tourism Enterprise Administration, "Lüyou qingkuang fanying 34," June 18, 1974, B50-4-112–17, SMA.

27. Heping Hotel Revolutionary Committee, "Jianbao [Digest]," March 15, 1974, B50-4-112–12, SMA.

28. Shanghai Municipal Revolutionary Committee Foreign Affairs Team, "Guanyu shehui shang de yi xie ren zai tong waibin, lüyouzhe jiechu zhong chuxian de ji ge tuchu wenti de tongbao [Notice regarding some outstanding problems that appeared in the interactions between some people in society and foreign guests and travelers]," November 27, 1979, B285-2-837–8, SMA.

29. Alice Xiang, "'When Ordinary Seeing Fails': Reclaiming the Art of Documentary in Michelangelo Antonioni's 1972 China Film *Chung Kuo*," *Senses of Cinema*, no. 67 (July 2013).

30. Commentary, "Edu de yongxin, beilie de shoufa [A vicious motive, despicable tricks]," *People's Daily*, January 30, 1974; and Wu De, "Cong guowuyuan wenhua zu dao si jie renda [From the State Council Culture Group to the Fourth National People's Congress]," *Dangdai Zhongguoshi yanjiu* 9, no. 1 (2002): 80.

31. Isabel Hilton, "Struggle with Antonioni," October 24, 2012, ChinaFile, accessed April 1, 2020, https://www.chinafile.com/struggling-antonioni.

32. James R. Lilley and Jeffrey Lilley, *China Hands: Nine Decades of Adventure, Espionage, and Diplomacy in Asia* (New York: Public Affairs, 2004), 169–95.

33. Meeting Secretariat, "Lüyou gongzuo zuotanhui jianbao [Digest on the tourism work forum] 7," March 11, 1975, 63-1-21–8, GMA.

34. "Lüyou gongzuo zuotanhui jianbao 12," March 14, 1975, 63-1-21–13, GMA.

35. Bureau of Foreign Experts, "Xinpin waiguo zhuanjia gongzuo zuotanhui jiyao [Summary of the forum on inviting new foreign experts," August 28, 1978, 214-2-767–18, SPA.

36. "Lüyou ju Yang Gongsu tongzhi zai lüyou gongzuo zuotanhui shang de fayan"; and "Lüyou gongzuo zuotanhui jianbao 5," March 11, 1975, 63-1-21–6, GMA.

37. "Lüyou gongzuo zuotanhui jianbao 2," March 4, 1975, 63-1-21–3, GMA.

38. "Lüyou ju Yang Gongsu tongzhi zai lüyou gongzuo zuotanhui shang de fayan."

39. "Lüyou ju Yang Gongsu tongzhi zai lüyou gongzuo zuotanhui shang de fayan"; China Tourism Enterprise Administration, "1976 nian gongzuo zongjie baogao," April 5, 1975, 196-2-116–7, SPA.

40. Yang, *Cangsang*, 304; and "Lüyou gongzuo zuotanhui jianbao 13," March 14, 1975, 63-1-21–14, GMA.

41. Peggy Seeger and Diane Alexander, "Package Tour of Mainland China," *New York Times*, April 13, 1975; and William H. Hinton, *Fanshen: A Documentary of Revolution in a Chinese Village* (New York: Monthly Review Press, 1966).

42. "Luo Qingchang tongzhi zai lüyou gongzuo zuotanhui shang de baogao [Comrade Luo Qingchang's report at the tourism work forum]," March 8, 1975, SZ142-4-417–1, HPA.

43. Foreign Ministry and the Civil Aviation Administration of China, "Guanyu dui jingji kunnan de bufen huaqiao, waiji ren, GangAo tongbao lüxingtuan guonei jipiao jiyu youdai de tongzhi," April 20, 1976, 196-2-120–4, SPA.

44. "Lüyou gongzuo zuotanhui jianbao 5."

45. "Guanyu jinyibu zuohao zhengzhi jiedai gongzuo de ji ge wenti—Zhu Manping tongzhi daibiao zongshe fayan zhaiyao [Some problems for improving political reception work—Summary of Comrade Zhu Manping's speech as the representative of the headquarters]," undated, 1057-1-9-9, Hebei Provincial Archive (HEPA).

46. "Lüyou gongzuo zuotanhui jianbao 7."

47. "Lüyou gongzuo zuotanhui jianbao 5."

48. Klaus Mehnert, *China Returns* (New York: E. P. Dutton, 1971), 9, 11; "Onward to Peking," *Washington Post*, July 17, 1971; and Max Frankel, "Like a Trip to the Moon," *New York Times*, February 20, 1972.

49. Stephen FitzGerald's review of the Committee of Concerned Asian Scholars, *China!*; Jan C. Ting, *An American in China* (New York, Paperback Library, 1972); and William H. Hinton, *Turning Point in China. An Essay on the Cultural Revolution* (New York: Monthly Review Press, 1972) in *Pacific Affairs* 46, no. 1 (1973): 126–28.

50. Unita Blackwell, *Barefootin': Life Lessons from the Road to Freedom* (New York: Crown Publishers, 2006), 207.

51. Dryfoos, "China Adventure."

52. Hearing, Subcommittee on Asian and Pacific Affairs, House Committee on Foreign Affairs, *Newsman's Visit to China: Briefing by William Attwood, Publisher of Newsday* (Washington, DC: Government Printing Office, 1971), 8.

53. Tillman Durdin, "Hearing the Words in Person Makes a Difference," *New York Times*, April 25, 1971.

54. Wassily Leontief, "Socialism in China," *Atlantic Monthly*, March 1973, 74–81.

55. John Kenneth Galbraith, *A China Passage* (Boston: Houghton Mifflin, 1973), 118, 137.

56. James Tobin, "The Economy of China: A Tourist's View," *Challenge* 16, no. 1 (1973): 26.

57. *CBS News Special Report*, "Reston on China: A Conversation with Eric Sevareid," August 31, 1971, LOC.

58. Tillman Durdin, James Reston, and Seymour Topping, *The New York Times Report from Red China* (New York: New York Times, 1972), 246.

59. On 1970s America, see Borstelmann, *1970s*. On US romanticism about China, see, for example, Sigrid Schmalzer, "Speaking about China, Learning from China: Amateur China Experts in 1970s America," *Journal of American-East Asian Relations* 16, no. 4 (2009): 313–52; and Kazushi Minami, "How Could I Not Love You?: Transnational Feminism and U.S.-Chinese Relations during the Cold War," *Journal of Women's History* 31, no. 4 (2019): 12–36. On Galston, Blackwell, and MacLaine, see Arthur W. Galston, with Jean S. Savage, *Daily Life in People's China*

(New York: Crowell 1973); Blackwell, *Barefootin'*, 204–05; and Shirley MacLaine and Claudia Weill, "The Other Half of the Sky: A China Memoir" (1975).

60. David Rockefeller, "From a China Traveler," *New York Times*, August 10, 1973.

61. Tianjin Commune, "Some Lessons of Carrying Out the Work of External Propaganda," undated, SZ142-4-419–5, HPA.

62. Leontief, "Socialism in China," 81.

63. Barbara W. Tuchman, *Notes from China* (New York: Macmillan, 1972), 57, 62.

64. Orville Schell, *In the People's Republic: An American's First-Hand View of Living and Working in China* (New York: Random House, 1977), 237; and Orville Schell, "A China Frontier: Once the Border of Borders," December 3, 2012, ChinaFile, accessed April 1, 2020, https://www.chinafile.com/china-frontier-once-border-borders.

65. Richard Bernstein, "A Bridge to a Love for Democracy," *New York Times*, December 29, 2010; and Jonathan Mirsky, "From Mao Fan to Counter-Revolutionary in 48 Hours," in *My First Trip to China: Scholars, Diplomats and Journalists Reflect on their First Encounter with China*, ed., Kin-ming Liu (Hong Kong: East Slope Publishing, 2012), 24–28.

66. Shanghai Municipal Broadcasting Station Revolutionary Committee, "Jiedai 'Gelunbiya guangbo gongsi' dianshi sheying dui de gongzuo xiaojie [Summary of the work on receiving the CBS television crew]," October 9, 1973, B285-2-35–30, SMA.

67. *CBS Reports*, "Shanghai," March 8, 1974, LOC.

68. Central Broadcasting Administration and the Foreign Ministry, "Tongzhi jiedai waiguo dianshi shiying dui de ji xiang yuanze [Notice on some principles in receiving foreign television crews]," January 10, 1976, 196-2-116–1, SPA.

69. Bill Shirley, "U.S. Visitor: 2 Weeks in China Both Sweet, Sour," *New York Times*, June 14, 1975.

70. "Waldheim Gets Plea on Ousted Newsmen," *New York Times*, February 9, 1972.

71. "China Asks the Times to Bar Pro-Taiwan Ads, but Paper Refuses," *New York Times*, May 17, 1973.

72. Memo, Solomon to Kissinger, February 16, 1974, "China Exchanges November 1, 1973–March 31, 1974 [2 of 4]," box 96, NSC HAK Office Files, RNL.

73. Douglas P. Murray, "Exchanges with the People's Republic of China: Symbols and Substance," *The Annals of the American Academy of Political and Social Science* 424, no. 1 (1976): 40.

74. James Grant, "New China Hands: They Seem as Misguided and Biased as the Old," *Barron's*, no. 57 (January 1977): 7.

75. Review of Bao Ruo-wang and Rudolph Chelminski, *Prisoner of Mao: A Survivor's Account of the State Prison System of the New China* (New York: Coward, McCann and Goeghegan, 1973) in John K. Fairbank, "In Chinese Prisons," *New York Review of Books*, November 1, 1973, 3–7.

76. Sheila K. Johnson, "To China, with Love," *Commentary* 56, no. 6 (1973): 37–45; Stanley Karnow, "China through Rose-Tinted Glasses," *The Atlantic*, October 1973, 73–76; and A. Doak Barnett, "There Are Warts There, Too," *New York Times*, April 8, 1973.

77. Peter Berger, *Pyramids of Sacrifice* (New York: Basic Books, 1975), 160; and Grant, "New China Hands."

78. Jerome Alan Cohen, "U.S.-China Relations," *New York Times*, December 18, 1974. See also, Lucian Pye, "Building a Relationship on the Sands of Cultural Exchanges," in *China and America: The Search for a New Relationship*, ed., William J. Barnds (New York: New York University Press, 1977), 116–23.

79. Edward N. Luttwak, "Seeing China Plain," *Commentary* 62, no. 6 (1976): 27–34.

80. Audrey Topping, "Letters from Readers," *Commentary* 63, no. 3 (1977): 10; and Aubrey Topping, "Farms Are Sprouting on Chinese 'Prairie'," *New York Times*, December 27, 1975.

81. "Letters from Readers," *Commentary* 63, no. 3 (1977): 5.
82. For positive comments, see, for example, "Friendship Has a History: Mao Tsetung," *New China* 3, no. 1 (1977): 8–16.
83. Simon Leys, *Chinese Shadows* (New York: Viking Press, 1977).
84. Jacques Leslie, "Euphoria Has Faded for Some Visitors to China," *Los Angeles Times*, October 9, 1976.
85. John K. Fairbank, "Mao's War on Culture," *New York Times*, August 28, 1977.
86. Fabio Lanza, *The End of Concern: Maoist China, Activism, and Asian Studies* (Durham, NC: Duke University Press, 2017), 143–74.
87. Memo, Oksenberg to Brzezinski, July 11, 1977, "PRC:7–8/77," box 41, Country Files, Brzezinski Material, NSA, JCL.
88. "Dui Beijing lüyou shiye de yi dian yijian [Some suggestions for Beijing's tourism industry]," *Reference News*, November 18, 1977, 4.
89. China Tourism Enterprise Administration, "Guanyu liang nian lai lüyou gongzuo de fazhan qingkuang he jinhou gongzuo yijian de qingshi baogao [Request for instruction on the development of tourism in the past two years and opinions on the future work," April 1, 1977, SZ142-4-443–1, HPA.
90. Hubei Provincial Revolutionary Committee Foreign Affairs Team, "Guanyu lüyou ju zhaokai lüyou gongzuo guihua zuotanhui qingkuang de huibao [Report on the tourism work planning forum held by the China National Tourism Administration," undated, SZ142-4-443–2, HPA.
91. Shen Shoujun, "Dali fazhan lüyou shiye, nuli zengjia lüyou jinianpin, gongyipin de shengchan he xiaoshou, wei jiasu shixian si ge xiandaihua zuochu gongxian [Greatly develop the tourism industry, strive to increase the production and sales of souvenirs and handicrafts, contribute to the acceleration of the four modernizations]," November 20, 1978, author's personal collection.
92. Stanley Carr, "Notes: Chinese Aides Visit U.S. as Tourists," *New York Times*, April 9, 1978.
93. Marie Ridder, "Young Masters of an Old Oriental Custom," *Washington Post*, November 19, 1978; and National Bureau of Statistics, *Zhongguo tongji nianjian 1981* (Beijing: Zhongguo tongji chubanshe, 1982), 394.
94. "Lüyou waibin dui wo fandian gongzuo de yijian he jianyi [Foreign travelers' opinions and suggestions on our hotel work]," undated, SZ142-4-463–3, HPA.
95. Ridder, "Young Masters."
96. State Council Document no. 224 (1978), "Guowuyuan pizhuan quanguo lüyou gongzuo zuotanhui jiyao [The State Council approves and transfers the digest of the national tourism work forum]," October 23, 1978, SZ139-6-809–14, HPA.
97. *Deng Xiaoping sixiang nianbian*, 176–77.
98. Jay Matthews, "American Firm, China Sign Deal for Hotel Venture," *Washington Post*, November 10, 1978; and China National Tourism Administration, "Guanyu tiaozheng 1979 nian guonei touzi he liyong qiao, waizi jianzao lüyou fandian de baogao [Report on building tourist hotels by adjusting domestic investment in 1978 and using foreign and overseas Chinese capital]," April 10, 1979, B1-9-68–8, SMA.
99. "Tourism: The Hotel Deals," *China Business Review* 6, no. 2 (1979): 21–27.
100. *Deng Xiaoping nianpu*, vol. 2, 466.
101. Zhuang Yanlin, "Women gongtong zouguo—huainian xin Zhongguo lüyou shiye dianjiren zhi yi Lu Xuzhang [We have walked together—Remembering Lu Xuzhang, one of the pioneers in New China's tourism industry]," in *Lu Xuzhang jinian wenji* [Commemorative essays

on Lu Xuzhang], ed., CCP Ningbo Municipal Consultative Conference Literature and History Committee (Beijing: Zhongguo wenshi chubanshe), 25.

102. Carter Wiseman, *I. M. Pei: A Profile in American Architecture* (New York: Harry N. Abrams, 1990), 184–207.

103. Ministries of Light Industry, Foreign Affairs, and Commerce, "Guanyu gao hao lüyouye jinianpin gongyepin shengchan he xiaoshou de baogao [Report on establishing production and sales of gifts and artifacts for tourism]," February 21, 1978, SZ142-4-461-5, HPA.

104. Light Industry Ministry, "Guanyu fazhan lüyouye jinianpin gongyepin shengchan he xiaoshou ji ge wenti de qingshi baogao [Request for instruction on some problems in developing the production and sales of gifts and artifacts for tourism]," October 11, 1978, SZ142-4-461-7, HPA.

105. Shaanxi Provincial Revolutionary Committee Foreign Affairs Office, "Waishi qingkuang [Situations in foreign affairs], 31," September 7, 1979, 196-1-878–11, SPA.

106. "Yingguo pengyou Gelin he Meiguo youhao renshi Han Ding tan duiwai xuanchuan [British friend Green and American friend Hinton discuss external propaganda]," undated, SZ42-4-463–1, HPA.

107. "Lüyou waibin dui wo xuanchuan gongzuo de yijian he jianyi [Foreign travelers' opinions and suggestions on our propaganda work]," undated, SZ142-4-463–2, HPA.

108. "Guanyu zuo hao canguan lüyou waibin, Huaqiao deng xuanchuan gongzuo de ruogan yijian (taolun gao) [Some opinions on carrying out propaganda work for foreign travelers, overseas Chinese, and others (discussion draft)]," November 1978, A22-4-438–202, SMA; and CCP Propaganda Department, "Xuanchuan dongtai [Trends in propaganda], 9," April 17, 1979, 1057-8-26, HEPA.

109. Shanghai Municipal Revolutionary Committee Foreign Affairs Office, "Guanyu tingzhi duiwai sanfa he gongying 'Mao zhuxi yulu' de tongzhi [Announcement on the secession of external distribution and supply of 'Quotations from Chairman Mao']," March 8, 1979, B285-2-837–72, SMA.

110. Brendan Jones, "China Trade Welcomed Here," April 19, 1970, *New York Times*; Ching, "China"; and Eric Friedheim, "China Diary: A Final Entry," Travel Agent, fol. 191, box 21, ser. 15, RG 5, FA1187, NCUSCR, RAC.

111. "The Great Pacific and Orient Cruise of the Queen Elizabeth 2," *New York Times*, October 9, 1977; Francis X. Clines, "About New York: To China with Luxury," *New York Times*, February 21, 1978; and William R. Frye, "Cruising the People's Republic," *Washington Post*, June 10, 1979.

112. Nancy L. Ross, "China: The First U.S. Air Tours," *Washington Post*, October 2, 1977.

113. Paul Grimes, "China, 1979: The Ways and Means," *New York Times*, February 4, 1979.

114. *Deng Xiaoping sixiang nianbian*, 176–77.

115. Wallace Turner, "Scheduled Air Service from China to U.S. Resumes," *New York Times*, January 8, 1981.

116. John E. Felber, *American Tourist Manual for the People's Republic of China* (Newark, NJ: International Intertrade Index, 1974); Ruth Lor Malloy, *Travel Guide to the People's Republic of China* (New York: William Morrow, 1975); Arne J. de Keijzer and Frederic M. Kaplan, *JAL Guide to the People's Republic of China* (Tokyo: Japan Air Lines, 1978); John Summerfield, *Fodor's People's Republic of China* (New York: David McKay, 1979); and Hilliard Saunders, *The Complete Travel Guide to China* (Seal Beach, CA: China Publishing, 1979).

117. Nina S. Hyde, "Shop Unlimited, but Beware the Jade That Isn't Jade, Antiques That Aren't Antiques," *Washington Post*, June 10, 1979.

118. "Quanguo lüyou gongzuo huiyi jianbao [Digest of the national tourism work conference] 6," January 26, 1978, SZ142-4-463–14, HPA; and Public Security Bureau, Wuhan Municipal

Revolutionary Committee, "Yinfa 'Guanyu zhengque duidai he tuoshan chuli waiguoren guanfang zhong ruogan wenti jieda' de tongzhi [Notice on issuing 'The answers to correctly treating and properly handling some problems of foreign sightseers]," March 6, 1979, author's personal collection.

119. CCP Hubei Provincial Department of Propaganda, "Xuanchuan dongtai [Trends in propaganda] 37," October 19, 1979, SZ7-6-340–14, HPA.

120. Arthur Miller, "In China," *Atlantic Monthly*, March 1979, 96.

121. David Butler, Holger Jensen, and James Pringle, "Teng's New Deal," *Newsweek*, February 5, 1979, 26; Gail Gregg and A. O. Sulzberger Jr., "The Long Way Home," *New York Times*, July 1, 1979; and David Finkelstein, "Downstairs with the 'Masses'—Hard Class through China," June 1979, Ford Foundation Catalogued Report 6552, Open Vault, RAC.

122. National Bureau of Statistics, *Zhongguo tongji nianjian 1989* (Beijing: Zhongguo tongji chubanshe, 1989), 650.

123. China International Travel Service, *The Official Guidebook of China* (New York: Books New China, 1980), preface.

124. Zhang Haitao, *Meiguo zou ma guan hua ji* [Viewing flowers from horseback in America] (Shanghai: Shanghai renmin chubanshe, 1980); and Wang Ruoshui, "Meiguo yi pie [A Glimpse of America] 1, 2, 3," *People's Daily*, October 17, 1978; October 18, 1978; October 19, 1978.

125. Ru Zhijuan and Wang Anyi, *Munü manyou Meilijian* [Wandering in America] (Shanghai: Shanghai weiyi chubanshe, 1986), 1. See also He, *Dangdai ZhongMei minjian jiaoliu shi*, 162–64; and Yang Yusheng, *Zhongguoren de Meiguo guan: Yi ge lishi de kaocha* [Chinese views of the United States: A Historical observation] (Shanghai: Fudan daxue chubanshe, 1997), 256–98.

126. Harry Harding, "From China, with Disdain: New Trends in the Study of China," *Asian Survey* 22, no. 10 (1982): 934–58; and James Kenneson, "China Stinks," *Harpers*, April 1982, 13–20. For illustrative examples of this literature, see Fox Butterfield, *China: Alive in the Bitter Sea* (New York: Times Books, 1982); Richard Bernstein, *From the Center of the Earth: The Search for the Truth about China* (New York: Little, Brown, 1982); and Steven W. Mosher, *Broken Earth: The Rural Chinese* (New York: Free Press, 1983).

127. A. M. Rosenthal, "Memoirs of A New China Hand," *New York Times*, July 19, 1981.

128. A. M. Rosenthal, "Memoirs of A New China Hand," *New York Times*, July 26, 1981.

6. Sport

1. For the context of this statement, see Carolyn Marvin, "Avery Brundage and American Participation in the 1936 Olympic Games," *Journal of American Studies* 16, no. 1 (1982): 81–105.

2. See, for example, Rider, *Cold War Games*.

3. Gerald R. Ford, "In Defense of the Competitive Urge," *Sports Illustrated*, July 8, 1974, 17.

4. On China's sports diplomacy during the early Cold War, see Wang Guanhua, "'Friendship First': China's Sports Diplomacy during the Cold War," *Journal of American-East Asian Relations* 12, no. 2 (2003): 145–50; Fan Hong and Lu Zhouxiang, "Representing the New China and the Sovietisation of Chinese Sport (1949–1962)" and "Sport, Militarism and Diplomacy: Training Bodies for China (1960–1966)," *International Journal of the History of Sport* 29, no. 1 (2012): 1–29 and 30–52; Amanda Shuman, "Elite Competitive Sport in the People's Republic of China 1958–1966: The Games of the New Emerging Forces (GANEFO)," *Journal of Sport History* 40, no. 2 (2013): 258–83; Amanda Schuman, "From Soviet Kin to Afro-Asian Leader: The People's Republic of China and International Sport in the early 1960s," *Comparativ* 23, no. 3 (2013): 78–98;

Fan Hong and Lu Zhouxiang, "Politics First, Competition Second: Sport and China's Foreign Diplomacy in the 1960s and 1970s," in *Diplomatic Games: Sport, Statecraft, and International Relations since 1945*, ed., Heather L. Dichter and Andrew L. Johns (Lexington: University Press of Kentucky, 2014), 385–407; Steven Huebner, *Pan-Asian Sports and the Emergence of Modern Asia, 1913–1974* (Singapore: National University of Singapore Press, 2016); and Amanda Shuman, "Learning from the Soviet Big Brother: The Early Years of Sport in the People's Republic of China," in *The Whole World Was Watching: Sport in the Cold War*, ed., Robert Edelman and Christopher Young (Stanford, CA: Stanford University Press, 2020),163–74.

5. Deng Liqun, Ma Hong, and Wu Heng eds., *Dangdai Zhongguo tiyu* [Contemporary Chinese sports] (Beijing: Zhongguo shehui kexue chubanshe, 1984), 23; and Fan Hong and Lu Zhouxiang, "Sport in the Great Proletarian Cultural Revolution (1966–1976)," *International Journal of the History of Sport* 29, no. 1 (2012): 53–73.

6. "Jianchi dang de jiben luxian, ba tiyu zhanxian de shehui zhuyi geming jinxing daodi," February 8, 1975, SZ133-2-775–8, HPA; and "A Review on China's Foreign Aid Projects in the Area of Sport," *China Sports Daily*, August 19, 2009, cited in Fan and Lu, "Sport," 62.

7. Xu Guoqi, *Olympic Dreams: China and Sports, 1895–2008* (Cambridge, MA: Harvard University Press, 2008), 49–51.

8. Murray, "Exchanges with the People's Republic of China," 38.

9. See, for example, Damion L. Thomas, *Globetrotting: African American Athletes and Cold War Politics* (Urbana: University of Illinois Press, 2012); and Toby C. Rider and Kevin B. Witherspoon, eds., *Defending the American Way: Sport, Culture, and the Cold War* (Fayetteville: University of Arkansas Press, 2018).

10. William Gildea, "Dribbling through the Bamboo Curtain to Find Good Sports in High Places," *Washington Post*, May 6, 1973.

11. Tim Boggan, *History of U.S. Table Tennis, vol. V: 1971–1972* (Colorado Springs, CO: USA Table Tennis, 2005), 168.

12. "Red China's Sports Surge Perils West's Dominance," *Washington Post*, July 27, 1972.

13. Xu, *Olympic Dreams*, 74; and Andrew D. Morris, *Marrow of the Nation: A History of Sport and Physical Culture in Republican China* (Berkeley: University of California Press, 2004), 32.

14. Zhuang Zedong, "Youyi di yi, bisai di er: tantan canjia san shi yi jie shijie pingpangqiu jinbiao sai de yi dian tihui [Friendship first, competition second: discussing some experiences of attending the 31st table tennis world championship]," June 1971, SZ133-2-673-2, HPA.

15. "1971 nian quanguo tiyu gongzuo huiyi jiyao (cao'an) [Summary of the 1971 national sports work conference (draft)],", July 27, 1971, SZ133-2-672-1, HPA.

16. Yanqiu Zheng, "The Cultural Politics of Chineseness: The US Tour of Taiwan's National Chinese Opera Theatre, 1973–1974," *Twentieth-Century China* 45, no. 1 (2020): 51–52.

17. *Zhou Enlai nianpu*, vol. 3, 520.

18. "Zhuang Zedong tongzhi guanyu wo guo pingpangqiu daibiaotuan fangwen Meiguo de baogao [Comrade Zhuang Zedong's report on our table tennis delegation to the United States]," September 1, 1972, author's personal collection.

19. "Wo guo ping pang qiu daibiaotuan dao Mengfeisi canguan fangwen [Our table tennis delegation visits Memphis]," *People's Daily*, April 25, 1972.

20. Shih Pen-shan, "I Fought in Red China's Sports War," *Readers Digest*, no. 90 (June 1967): 73–78.

21. "Zhao Zhenghong tongzhi guanyu di qi jie Yayunhui qingkuang de baogao [Comrade Zhao Zhenghong's report on the situations in the seventh Asian Games]," undated, SZ133-2-751-1, HPA.

22. "Zhou zongli, Jiang Qing tongzhi zai jiejian qi ge huiyi quanti daibiao shi de jianghua [Talks of Premier Zhou and Comrade Jiang Qing when meeting the seven conference representatives]," July 29, 1971, SZ133-2-672-2, HPA.

23. National Sports Work Conference Office, "Chairman Mao's instructions on sport," December 1977, SZ133-2-891-4, HPA.

24. People's Liberation Army and the State Sports Commission Military Control Committee, "Xiang sheng shi tiwei chuanda Jiang Qing tongzhi zhongyao zhishi dianhua gao [Telephone transcript of conveying important instructions of Comrade Jiang Qing to provinces and municipalities]," January 11, 1972, SZ133-2-691-8, HPA.

25. "Li Desheng tongzhi zai quanguo tiyu gongzuo huiyi shang de jianghua [Comrade Li Desheng's talk at the national sports work conference]," January 22, 1973, SZ133-2-718-6, HPA.

26. "1973 nian quanguo tiyu gongzuo huiyi jiyao [Summary of the 1973 national sports work conference]," January 24, 1973, in *Tiyu yundong wenjian xuanbian, 1949–1981* [Compilation of sports documents, 1949–1981], ed., Sports Commission Policy Research Office, 114.

27. Letter, He Xiangxiang, Sun Hongmei, Jin Haiyin, Chen Yuyin, et al. to the CCP central leadership, November 1973, attached to "Shaanxi tiyu qingkuang [Sports situations in Shaanxi] 1," November 1974, 281-2-203-1, SPA.

28. Shaanxi Provincial Sports Commission, "Tiyu qingkuang fanying [Report on situations in sport] 9," May 15, 1974, 281-5-121-1, SPA.

29. "Zhongguo ticao dui zai Meiguo [Chinese gymnastics team in the United States]," *People's Daily*, June 22, 1973.

30. William Johnson, "And Smile, Smile, Smile," *Sports Illustrated*, June 4, 1973, 76–78.

31. Gerald Eskenazi, "Chinese, U.S. Gymnasts in Friendly Strife," *New York Times*, May 22, 1973.

32. Gymnastics Delegation of China, "Zhongguo ticao dui fangwen Mei, Jia jishu zongjie [Summary of techniques during the Chinese gymnastics team's visits to the United States and Canada]," *Zhongguo tiyu keji* [China sport science and technology], no. 18 (1973): 9–10.

33. Senate Congressional Record, vol. 119, no. 108, July 12, 1973, 23514.

34. Thomas M. Hunt, "Countering the Soviet Threat in the Olympic Medals Race: The Amateur Sports Act of 1978 and American Athletics Policy Reform," *International Journal of the History of Sport* 24, no. 6 (2007): 801–02.

35. John Wilson, *Playing by the Rules: Sport, Society, and the State* (Detroit, MI: Wayne State University Press, 1994), 370.

36. "Amateur Sports Obstacles Hit: Swimmers' Ban Shocks Senator," *Los Angeles Times*, May 24, 1973.

37. Guangdong Provincial Sports Commission, "Jiedai Meiguo nanzi, nüzi lanqiu dui jihua [Plans for receiving the US male and female basketball delegation]," June 10, 1973, 316-A1.2-36-098, GPA.

38. Jan Carol, Berris, "The Evolution of Sino-American Exchanges: A View from the National Committee," in *Educational Exchanges*, ed., Kallgren and Simon, 85.

39. Telegram, USLO to William Rogers, June 20, 1973, 1973PEKING00349, Electronic Telegrams 1973, CFPF, RG 59, NARA.

40. Letter, Zhou Xiyang to Yang Hong, January 1, 2013, accessed April 1, 2020, http://blog.sina.com.cn/s/blog_82ea5291010156ol.html.

41. Dave Anderson, "Basketball Travels with Kevin," *New York Times*, March 12, 1974.

42. William Johnson, "Courting Time in Peking," *Sports Illustrated*, July 2, 1973, 13.

43. Deng Huayao, Zhang Yuntao, and Gao He, eds., *Meiguo lanqiu xunlianfa huibian* (Beijing: Renmin tiyu chubanshe, 1973); and *Meiguo youyong jishu he xunlian* (Beijing: Renmin tiyu chubanshe, 1975).

44. Zhuang Zedong, "Relie huanying YaFeiLa pengyoumen! [Warm welcome to Asian-African-Latin American friends!]" *People's Daily*, August 21, 1973.

45. State Sports Commission Criticism Group, "Zhanduan 'Sirenbang' shen xiang tiyu zhanxian de heishou [Chop off the Gang of Four's black hands extended toward the sports front]," *People's Daily*, January 20, 1977.

46. Yun Li, "Deng Xiaoping zai tiyu zhanxian guchui shenme? [What did Deng Xiaoping preach on the frontier on sport?]," *Red Flag*, no. 5 (1976): 53–56.

47. Nancy Seannell, "China Tour Complicated By NCAA-AAU Argument," *Washington Post*, April 16, 1975.

48. Hunt, "Countering the Soviet Threat," 805–06.

49. *Mao Zedong nianpu*, vol. 6, 577.

50. Letter, Ford to Track-and-Field Team, April 29, 1975, "People's Republic of China—Exchanges [exchange programs] (7)," box 8, NSC East Asian and Pacific Affairs Staff Files, GFL.

51. Howard M. Newburger, "Winning, Losing and Chinese," *New York Times*, May 11, 1975.

52. Irving L. Kintisch, "Friendship First, Competition Second," *Columbia Today* (December 1975): 25.

53. Telegram, USLO to Kissinger, June 17, 1975, 1975PEKING01131, Electronic Telegrams 1975, CFPF, RG 59, NARA.

54. Kintisch, "Friendship First," 25.

55. Sports Science Institute at the Sports Commission, "Guanyu Meiguo tianjing dui lai Hua fangwen jishu diaoyan baogao [Technical research report on the visit to China by the US track-and-field delegation]," August 1975, author's personal collection.

56. Xu, *Olympic Dreams*, 103–4.

57. Richard Baum, "Trip Report: American Track and Field Delegation to the People's Republic of China, May 16–30, 1975," May 1976, fol. 139, box 18, ser. 3, RG 4, FA1186, NCUSCR, RAC.

58. Memo, Arne de Keijzer and Peggy Blumenthal to the Record, June 25, 1975, fol. 389, box 40, ser. 4, RG 4, FA1186, NCUSCR, RAC.

59. Guangdong Provincial Sports Committee Observation Delegation, "Canguan Meiguo tianjing dui lai Hua bisai qingkuang huibao [Report on the situation of watching the games of the visiting US track-and-field delegation]," June 6, 1975, SZ133-2-774–24, HPA.

60. "China Plans a Leap Forward in Track and Field," *New York Times*, June 8, 1975.

61. John Underwood, "What's China's Track?" *Sports Illustrated*, June 16, 1975, 74.

62. Richard Baum, *China Watcher: Confessions of a Peking Tom* (Seattle: University of Washington Press, 2010), 69–70.

63. Telegram, Kissinger to USLO, October 9, 1975, 1975STATE239679, Electronic Telegram 1975, CFPF, RG 59, NARA.

64. Telegram, Kissinger to USLO, September 18, 1976, 1976STATE231774, Electronic Telegram 1976, CFPF, RG 59, NARA.

65. Telegram, Kissinger to USLO, October 15, 1976, 1976STATE256078, Electronic Telegram 1976, CFPF, RG 59, NARA.

66. Telegram, Kissinger to USLO, October 9, 1976, 1976STATE251793, Electronic Telegram 1976, CFPF, RG 59, NARA.

67. Berris, "Evolution of Sino-American Exchanges," 86.

68. Linda Metheny, "China 1976," *International Gymnast* 19, no. 1 (1977): 79.

69. Sports Commission Great Criticism Group, "Jianchi you hong you zhuan, wei zuguo chuangzao youyi chengji [Maintain red and expert, create excellent results for the motherland]," *New Sports*, no. 332 (April 1977): 3–5.

70. Wu Shaozu, "Deng Xiaoping tiyu qingjie [Deng Xiaoping's sports complex]," *News of the Communist Party of China*, undated, accessed April 1, 2020, http://cpc.people.com.cn/GB/85037/85038/7183986.html.

71. Jiang Lianming, "Yao you tiyu kanwu de tedian [Must have the characteristics of a sports journal]," *New Sports*, no. 340 (December 1977): 44.

72. Meeting with Chu Tse, October 21, 1977, fol. 98, box 13, ser. 3, RG 4, FA1186, NCUSCR, RAC.

73. Hunt, "Countering the Soviet Threat," 809.

74. "Wei shixian si ge xiandai hua jiji duanlian shenti [Actively exercise to achieve the 'four modernizations']," *New Sports*, no. 339 (November 1977): 2.

75. "Gao sudu fazhan wo guo tiyu shiye [To Develop the physical culture of our country at a high speed]," *New Sports*, no. 342 (February 1978): 4–6.

76. "1978 nian quanguo tiyu gongzuo huiyi jiyao (caogao) [Summary of the 1978 national sports work conference (draft)]," February 2, 1978, in *Tiyu yundong wenjian xuanbian*, 122–31.

77. China National Table Tennis Team, "Ji yao jianchi zou ziji de daolu, you yao xuexi waiguo xianjin jingyan [We should not only maintain our own way, but also learn modern experiences from foreign countries]," *New Sports*, no. 346 (June 1978): 21–22.

78. "Quanguo tiyu shiye fazhan guihua gangyao (cao'an) '23 nian shexiang (1978–2000), banian guihua (1978–1985)' [Summary of the national physical culture development plan (draft) '23-year projection (1978–2000), eight-year plan (1978–1985)']," January 25, 1978, SZ133-2-893-8, HPA.

79. Shirley MacLaine, *You Can Get There from Here* (New York: Bantam Books, 1975), 121–22.

80. Paul Simon, "China Report," *School Administrator* 36, no. 2 (1979): 18.

81. Ed McGonagle, "Athletes by Millions: Sports Is Serious Business in China, Where Policy Involves Everybody," *Washington Post*, September 22, 1977.

82. Borstelmann, *1970s*, 159–160; and "Television: The Big Daddy of Nearly All Sports," *New York Times*, December 30, 1979.

83. Robert Elias, *The Empire Strikes Out: How Baseball Sold U.S. Foreign Policy and Promoted the American Way Abroad* (New York: The New Press, 2010), 208–11.

84. Robert Edelman and Wayne Wilson, eds., *The Oxford Handbook of Sports History* (New York: Oxford University Press, 2013), 399–400.

85. *Dangdai Zhongguo tiyu*, 212–213. On Ping-Pong diplomacy in 1977 and 1978, see *Zhongguo tiyu nianjian* [Sports yearbook of China], 1977 and 1978 (Beijing: Renmin tiyu chubanshe, 1982 and 1981), 5–6; and 8–9.

86. Jack Bell, "First Nixon, Then Cosmos Go to China," February 25, 2016, North American Soccer League, accessed April 1, 2020, http://www.nasl.com/news/2016/02/25/throwback-thursday—first-nixon-then-cosmos-go-to-china.

87. Xu Yinsheng, "Gan mo shijie gaofeng de laohu pigu [Daring to touch the butt of the tiger of the world standard]," *New Sports*, no. 341 (January 1978): 17.

88. NBC Evening News, October 9, 1977, Vanderbilt Television News Archive.

89. Parton Keese, "Tie Rutgers Men; U.S. Women Win," *New York Times*, November 19, 1978.

90. Central Newsreel and Documentary Film Studio, "ZhongMei lanqiu sai [US-China basketball games]," May 1979, author's personal collection.

91. "Zhi Zhongguo lanqiu aihaozhe [Dear basketball lovers in China]," *New Sports*, no. 357 (May 1979): 11–12; and Sports Science Institute at the Sports Commission, "Meiguo lanqiu jiaolian jiangxue huibian [Compilation of American basketball coaching lessons]," January 1980, author's personal collection.

92. J. Freedom du Lac, "30 Years Later, Visit to China Still Resonates," *Washington Post*, September 13, 2009.

93. Sports Commission, "Tiyu gongzuo qingkuang fanying [Report on sports work situations] 6," June 20, 1978, 235-2-146, GPA.

94. Beijing Municipal Sports and Exercise Committee, "Beijing tiyu jianbao [Beijing sports digest] 35," June 27, 1978, 185-2-43, BMA.

95. Editorial, "Zhongguo yu Aolinpike [China and the Olympics]," *New Sports*, no. 364 (December 1979): 2.

96. Liang Lijuan, *He Zhenliang wu huan zhi lu* [He Zhenliang and the Olympics] (Beijing: Shijie zhishi chubanshe, 2005), 124–25.

97. "1979 nian quanguo tiyu gongzuo huiyi jiyao [Summary of the 1979 national sports conference]," March 9, 1979, in *Tiyu yundong wenjian xuanbian*, 133.

98. Xing Junji and Zu Xianhai, *Bai nian chenfu: Zoujin Zhongguo tiyu jie* [A Century of ups and downs in Chinese sport] (Zhengzhou: Henan wenyi chubanshe, 2000), 346.

99. Xu Guoqi, "Reimagining and Repositioning China in International Politics: The Role of Sports in China's Long 1970s," in *China, Hong Kong, and the Long 1970s*, ed., Roberts and Westad, 120–28; and Joseph Eaton, "Reconsidering the 1980 Moscow Olympic Boycott: American Sports Diplomacy in East Asian Perspective," *Diplomatic History* 40, no. 5 (2016): 854–61.

100. Y. Andrew Hao and Thomas M. Hunt, "Sporting Exchanges between China and the United States, 1980–1984: Inevitable Politics and Excessive Political Strings," *International Journal of the History of Sport* 36, no. 9–10 (2019): 854–75.

101. Susan Brownell, *Beijing's Games: What the Olympics Mean to China* (Lanham, MD: Rowman and Littlefield, 2008), 104.

102. CCP leadership, "1984 nian Zhonggong zhongyang guanyu jin yi bu fazhan tiyu yundong de tongzhi," October 5, 1984, accessed April 1, 2020, http://www.olympic.cn/rule_code/code/2004/0426/26065.html; and Bao Mingxiao, Qiu Xue, Wu Sa, and Zhao Yilong, "Guanyu jiakuai tuijin tiyu qiangguo jianshe de ji ge jiben lilun wenti—ji yu dang de shi jiu da baogao tichu tiyu fazhan quanju de zhanlüexing wenti [Basic theoretical issues on speeding up the construction of sport power—strategic problems for the overall development of sport based on the report at the CCP 19th National Congress]," *Journal of Beijing Sport University* 41, no. 2 (2018): 1.

103. Letter, Manley to IOC, June 29, 1976, *New China* 2, no. 3 (1976): 25.

104. China Football Association, *Zhongguo zuqiu yundongshi* [History of football in China] (Wuhan: Wuhan chubanshe, 1993), 149.

7. Art

1. Ian Shin, "The Chinese Art 'Arms Race': Nationalism in Art Collecting, Scholarship, and Institution Building between the United States and Europe, 1910–1920," *Journal of American-East Asian Relations* 23, no. 3 (2016): 229–56.

2. On US cultural exports, see, for example, Michael L. Krenn, *Fall-Out Shelters for the Human Spirit: American Art and the Cold War* (Chapel Hill: University of North Carolina Press, 2005); Von Eschen, *Satchmo Blows Up the World*; Hiroshi Kitamura, *Screening Enlightenment: Hollywood and the Cultural Reconstruction of Defeated Japan* (Ithaca, NY: Cornell University Press, 2010); and Greg Barnhisel, *Cold War Modernists: Art, Literature, and American Cultural Diplomacy* (New York: Columbia University Press, 2015). On globalization of US culture, see, for example, Richard H. Pells, *Modernist America: Art, Music, Movies, and the Globalization of American Culture* (New Haven, CT: Yale University Press, 2012); and Andrew C. McKevitt, *Consuming Japan: Popular Culture and the Globalizing of 1980s America* (Chapel Hill: University of North Carolina Press, 2017).

3. Philip H. Dougherty, "Chinese Pavilion Revives a Palace," *New York Times*, July 7, 1964.

4. *Selected Works of Mao Tse-tung*, vol. 3, 69–98.

5. Brian James DeMare, *Mao's Cultural Army: Drama Troupes in China's Rural Revolution* (New York: Cambridge University Press, 2015).

6. Josh Stenberg, "Opera Diplomacy: Performers from the People's Republic of China on a 1960 Canada Tour," *Pacific Historical Review* 91, no. 3 (2022): 361–88; Perry Link, "Hand-Copied Entertainment Fiction from the Cultural Revolution," in *Unofficial China: Popular Culture and Thought in the People's Republic*, ed., Perry Link (New York: Routledge, 1989); Matthew D. Johnson, "Beneath the Propaganda State Official and Unofficial Cultural Landscapes in Shanghai, 1949–1965," in *Maoism at the Grassroots: Everyday Life in China's Era of High Socialism*, ed., Jeremy Brown and Matthew D. Johnson (Cambridge, MA: Harvard University Press, 2015), 199–229; and Nicolai Volland, "Clandestine Cosmopolitanism: Foreign Literature in the People's Republic of China, 1957–1977," *Journal of Asian Studies* 76, no. 1 (2017): 185–210.

7. The five operas were *The Legend of the Red Lantern, Shajiabang, Taking Tiger Mountain by Strategy, Raid on the White Tiger Regiment*, and *On the Docks*; the two ballets were *Red Detachment of Women* and *The White-Haired Girl*; and the symphony was *Shajiabang*.

8. Douwe Fokkema, "Creativity and Politics," in *The Cambridge History of China*, vol. 15, part 2, ed., Roderick MacFarquhar and John K. Fairbank (New York: Cambridge University Press, 1991), 594; Barbara Mittler, "Popular Propaganda? Art and Culture in Revolutionary China," *Proceedings of the American Philosophical Society* 152, no. 4 (2008): 466–89; and Barbara Mittler, "'Eight Stage Works for 800 Million People': The Great Proletarian Cultural Revolution in Music—A View from Revolutionary Opera," *Opera Quarterly* 26, no. 2–3 (2010): 377–401. On Cultural Revolution art, see Paul Clark, *The Chinese Cultural Revolution: A History* (New York: Cambridge University Press, 2008); and Barbara Mittler, *A Continuous Revolution Making Sense of Cultural Revolution Culture* (Cambridge, MA: Harvard University Press, 2013).

9. Letter, Dianne Mize to Mao Zedong, March 14, 1972, WHCF, RNL; Richard Nixon, *RN: The Memoirs of Richard Nixon* (New York: Grosset and Dunlap, 1978), 570; and Henry Kissinger, *White House Years* (Boston: Little, Brown, 1979), 779.

10. *Zhou Enlai nianpu*, vol. 3, 460.

11. Henry Kissinger, *Years of Upheaval* (Boston: Little, Brown, 1982), 45.

12. Sheila Melvin and Jindong Cai, *Rhapsody in Red: How Western Classical Music Became Chinese* (New York: Algora Publishing, 2004), 266–67.

13. Roxane Witke, *Comrade Chiang Ch'ing* (Boston: Little, Brown, 1977), 459.

14. Wu, "Cong guowuyuan wenhua zu dao si jie renda," 77.

15. Ching, "China."

16. Chinese People's Institute of Foreign Affairs, "Jiedai jianbao [Digest on reception work] 129," October 24, 1977, 196-1-824–18, SPA.

17. Tracy Ying Zhang, "Bending the Body for China: The Uses of Acrobatics in Sino-US Diplomacy during the Cold War," *International Journal of Cultural Policy* 22, no. 2 (2016): 136.

18. Clive Barnes, "Shenyang Acrobats Dazzle City Center Audience," *New York Times*, January 3, 1973.

19. Interview with Jan Carol Berris, March 31, 2019.

20. Department of State, *Bulletin*, January 1, 1973, 132.

21. Letter, Ministry of Foreign Affairs to the Bureau of Culture, Ministry of Education, March 2, 1972, 11-11-25-4-3, IMH.

22. New York Office, ROC Government Information Office, "Guoxituan fangMei zong jiantao baogao [Summary report on the National Chinese Opera Theater's visit to the United States]," February 12, 1974, 11-11-25-4-3, IMH.

23. Alan M. Kriegsman, "Where East and West Meet," *Washington Post*, November 28, 1973.

24. Nancy I. Ross, "National Chinese Opera Theater: Gongs, Cymbals and More," *Washington Post*, November 25, 1973.

25. London Philharmonic Orchestra Reception Team, "Tuchu wuchan jieji zhengzhi, gaohao jiedai gongzuo—jiedai Lundun aile guanguanxian yuetuan de huibao [Stress proletarian politics, carry out the reception work—Report on receiving the London Philharmonic Orchestra]," March 29, 1973, B172-2-61-76, SMA.

26. Memo, Berris to Murray, May 8, 1973, fol. 126, box 16, ser. 3, RG 4, FA1186, NCUSCR, RAC.

27. Nicholas Platt, *China Boys: How U.S. Relations with the PRC Began and Grew* (Washington, DC: VELLUM, 2010), 187–89; and Francis B. Tenny, "The Philadelphia Orchestra's 1973 China Tour: A Case Study of Cultural Diplomacy during the Cultural Revolution," June 2012, American Diplomacy, accessed April 1, 2020, https://americandiplomacy.web.unc.edu/2012/06/the-philadelphia-orchestras-1973-china-tour/.

28. Memo, Murray to the Record, September 28, 1973, fol. 126, box 16, ser. 3, RG 4, FA1186, NCUSCR, RAC.

29. Harold Schonberg, "Philadelphians a 'Big Success' In Their First Concert in China," *New York Times*, September 15, 1973.

30. Barbara Mittler, "'Enjoying the Four Olds!' Oral Histories from a 'Cultural Desert,'" *Journal of Transcultural Studies* 4, no. 1 (2013): 196.

31. Louise Hood, "China Diary," September 10–23, 1973, fol. 126, box 16, ser. 3, RG 4, FA1186, NCUSCR, RAC.

32. Tenny, "Philadelphia Orchestra's 1973 China Tour."

33. Melvin and Cai, *Rhapsody*, 269.

34. Memo, Murray to the Record, September 28, 1973, fol. 126, box 16, ser. 3, RG 5, FA1186, NCUSCR, RAC.

35. Melvin and Cai, *Rhapsody*, 274.

36. Harold C. Schonberg, "Yin Spoke Only Chinese, Ormandy Only English," *New York Times*, October 14, 1973.

37. Chu Lan, "Criticize the Revisionist Viewpoint in Music," *Peking Review*, March 1, 1974, 18–19.

38. Memo, Solomon to Kissinger, December 31, 1973, *FRUS, 1969–1976*, vol. 18, doc. 65.

39. Melvin and Cai, *Rhapsody*, 278–79.

40. Ellen Johnston Laing, *The Winking Owl: Art in the People's Republic of China* (Berkeley: University of California Press, 1988), 85–87; and Wang Aihe, "Wuming: An Underground Art Group during the Cultural Revolution," *Journal of Modern Chinese History* 3, no. 2 (2009): 183–99.

41. Beijing Teacher's College Revolutionary Committee, "Guanyu shenqing zujie neibu dianying yi fuzhu waiguo wenxue jiaoxue de baogao [Report on application for renting internal films to supplement the teaching of foreign literature]," December 19, 1972, 147-2-376, TMA.

42. Hubei Provincial Revolutionary Committee Bureau of Education, "Jiaoyu geming qingkuang fanying 4," May 15, 1974, SZ118-4-286-4, HPA.

43. "Daxue wenke jiaogai zuotanhui jianbao [Digest on the forum on education reform in college liberal arts and humanities] 2," July 3, 1973, B244-3-571-65, SMA.

44. Paul Clark, "Model Theatrical Works and the Remodelling of the Cultural Revolution," in *Art in Turmoil: The Chinese Cultural Revolution, 1966–76*, ed., Richard King (Hong Kong: Hong Kong University Press, 2010), 185.

45. *Mao Zedong nianpu*, vol 6, 595.

46. Hong Yida, "Henpi Deng Xiaoping, ba yishu jiaoyu geming jinxing daodi [Thoroughly criticize Deng Xiaoping, carry out the revolution in art education to the end]," *People's Daily*, May 6, 1976.

47. Yuan Hong, *Han Xu zhuan: Yi ge waijiaojia de jingli* [Biography of Han Xu: Experiences of a diplomat] (Beijing: Shijie zhishi chubanshe, 2004), 175.

48. Fan and Liu, *Huang Zhen zhuan*, 625.

49. Fan and Liu, *Huang Zhen zhuan*, 628.

50. Cohen, "U.S.-China Relations"; and Bernard Gwertzman, "U.S. Gallery Drops Preview over Demand by China," *New York Times*, December 11, 1974.

51. Memorandum of Conversation, July 9, 1974, "China: National Committee on U.S.-China Relations (NCUSC): Exchanges with the PRC: General: 1972–1974," box 3 AE, BHL.

52. Memo, Murray to the Record, July 23, 1974, fol. 380, box 39, ser. 4, RG 4, FA1186, NCUSCR, RAC.

53. Letter, Murray to Charles W. Yost, August 6, 1974, "Secretary's Visit to Peking Bilateral Issues S/P Mr. Lord Nov 1974 (1 of 2)," box 371, Policy Planning Staff, NARA.

54. Murray, "Exchanges with the People's Republic of China," 36–37; and Proceedings of the Provisional National Steering Committee Conference of the US-China People's Friendship Associations, June 22–23, 1974, "National Board Minutes 1974," box 1, US China People's Friendship Association Records, New York Public Library.

55. Letter, Rosen to Eckstein, March 11, 1975, fol. 385, box 39, ser. 4, RG 4, FA1186, NCUSCR, RAC.

56. Fan and Liu, *Huang Zhen zhuan*, 565–66; Yuan, *Han Xu zhuan*, 177–78.

57. Memo, Rosen to the Files, March 12, 1975, fol. 385, box 39, ser. 4, RG 4, FA1186, NCUSCR, RAC.

58. Memorandum of Conversation, March 20, 1975, "PRC—Liaison Office (1)," box 39, NSC East Asian and Pacific Affairs Staff Files, GFL.

59. Memo, Habib and Lord to Kissinger, March 25, 1975, "WHG 1975 (January-March) PRC-related Papers," box 6, Subject Files of the Office of People's Republic of China and Mongolia Affairs, 1969–78, RG 59, NARA.

60. Statement, undated, fol. 385, box 39, ser. 4, RG 4, FA1184, NCUSCR, RAC.

61. Letter, Eckstein to Rosen, March 20, 1975, fol. 385, box 39, ser. 4, RG 4, FA1186, NCUSCR, RAC.

62. Linda Winer, "Ping-Pong 'Diplomacy' Revisited," *Chicago Tribune*, April 2, 1975.

63. Richard Baum, "The Coming U.S.-China Confrontation," *Los Angeles Times*, April 7, 1975.

64. Foreign Affairs Office of the Shanghai Municipal Revolutionary Committee, "Waishi jianbao [Digest on foreign affairs work] 76," April 8, 1975, B172-3-157-85, SMA.

65. Announced Cancellation of US Conference of Mayors Trip to China, September 8, 1975, fol. 142, box 18, ser. 3, RG 4, FA1186, NCUSCR, RAC

66. Cheng and Xia, *Qianzou*, 236–45.

NOTES TO PAGES 170-173   243

67. Chinese People's Institute of Foreign Affairs, "OuMei qingkuang [Situations in Europe and America] 32," October 10, 1977, 196-1-824-17, SPA; and memo, Jan Beris to the Record, January 19, 1976, "Exchange—General, Memos on the Exchange Process 1976," fol. 334, box 33, ser. 2, RG5, FA1187, NCUSCR, RAC.

68. Ba Jin, "Chu e wu jin, bu liu houhuan [Completely eradicate the evil, to leave no future troubles]," *People's Daily*, December 26, 1977; and Xie Bingxin, "Dui 'wenyi heixian zhuanzheng' lun de liudu bu ke digu [We cannot underestimate the poison of the 'dictatorship of the literary black line' theory]," *People's Daily*, December 4, 1977.

69. Melvin and Cai, *Rhapsody*, 286.

70. Norman Lebrecht, "A New Cultural Revolution," *Standpoint*, September 25, 2013.

71. Kung Yen, "More Musicians for the Future," *China Reconstructs* 27, no. 5 (1978): 42.

72. "Wenhua bu wei da pi shou pohai wenyi gongzuo zhe pingfan [The Ministry of Culture rehabilitated a large group of art and literature workers who underwent suppression]," *People's Daily*, April 21, 1978.

73. Fan and Liu, *Huang Zhen zhuan*, 673-74, 688-97.

74. Harrison E. Salisbury, "Now It's China's Cultural Thaw," *New York Times*, December 4, 1977.

75. Zhu Xuxin, Xu Minhe, and Li Derun, "Da huishi, da shengtao, da jinjun—Zhongguo wenxue yishu jie lianhehui quanguo weiyuanhui kuoda huiyi ceji [Great union, great criticism, great march—a side story of the expanded session of the national committee of the China Federation of Literary and Art Circles]," *People's Daily*, June 8, 1978.

76. Ministry of Culture, "Guanyu peihe zuo hao lüyou gongzuo de tongzhi [Notice on helping conduct tourism work well]," April 28, 1978, SZ142-4-461-8, HPA.

77. Ministry of Culture, "Guanyu yishu yuanxiao shisheng guanmo zhongwai ziliao yao peihe guanmo wenyi yanchu, zhanlan de tongzhi [Notice on the necessity of arranging visits to art performances and exhibits for students and teachers in art schools learning Chinese and foreign materials]," January 15, 1979, 199-2-2050-7, TMA; and Cao Ying, "'Heixian zhuanzheng' lun dui waiguo wenxue gongzuo zaocheng de zainan [Calamity in foreign literature work created by the 'dictatorship of the black line' theory]," *People's Daily*, January 5, 1978.

78. "Bian hou ji [Afterword]," *Shijie wenxue*, no. 1 (1977): 319-20.

79. Richard Curt Kraus, *Pianos and Politics in China: Middle-Class Ambitions and the Struggle over Western Music* (New York: Oxford University Press, 1989), 181-84.

80. Tim Brook, "The Revival of China's Musical Culture," *China Quarterly*, no. 77 (1979): 114, 115.

81. "U.S.-China Arts Exchange Newsletter," vol. 1, no. 1 (1980): 1-2.

82. Fan and Liu, *Huang Zhen zhuan*, 743.

83. Jay Matthews, "A Calmer China One Year After Mao," *Washington Post*, September 11, 1977.

84. Performance Office Secretariat, "Qinzhu Zhonghua renmin gongheguo chengli sanshi zhounian xianli yanchu jianbao [Digest on the performance celebrating the thirtieth anniversary of the founding of the People's Republic of China] 25," April 4, 1979, 199-2-2017-6, TMA.

85. National Art and Craft Exhibit Leading Group, "Quanguo gongyi meishu zhanlanhui jianbao [Digest on the National Art and Craft Exhibit] 6," March 1, 1978, 199-2-1919-2, TMA; Ministry of Foreign Trade, the Ministry of Commerce, and the State Administration of Cultural Heritage, "Guanyu jin yi bu zuo hao yiban wenwu (jiu gongyipin) guanli he chukou gongzuo de qingshi [Request for instruction on doing better at administering and exporting general cultural relics (old crafts)]," October 18, 1978, 199-2-1919-25, TMA; and Di Yin Lu, "From

Trash to Treasure: Salvage Archaeology in the People's Republic of China, 1951–1976," *Modern China* 42, no. 4 (2016): 432–34.

86. Xie Xinhe, "Guanche luoshi yingming lingxiu Hua zhuxi de guanghui tici, wei fazhan wo guo de gongyi meishu chanpin er fendou! [Carry out wise leader Chairman Hua's brilliant inscription, strive for the development of our country's exports of art and craft products]," April 15, 1978, author's personal collection.

87. Letter, Cohen to Rosen, April 14, 1975, fol. 385, box 39, ser. 4, RG 4, FA1186, NCUSCR, RAC.

88. Memo, Rosen to Board Members, May 19, 1976, fol. 412, box 42, ser. 4, RG 4, FA1186, NCUSCR, RAC.

89. Memorandum of Conversation, May 5, 1977, fol. 412, box 42, ser. 4, RG 4, FA1186, NCUSCR, RAC.

90. Alan M. Kriegsman, "A Spectacle from the East," *Washington Post*, July 19, 1978.

91. Jean M. White, "A Taste of America," *Washington Post*, July 19, 1978.

92. Zhou Xiaoyan, "Zai Meiguo renmin youyi de hongliu zhong duguo sishi tian [Spending forty days in the flood of the American people's friendship]," *Renmin yinyue*, no. 1 (1979): 34.

93. Fan and Liu, *Huang Zhen zhuan*, 774–75.

94. ABC Evening News, April 20, 1972, Vanderbilt Television News Archive.

95. Letter, Shanghai Acrobatic Troupe to Deng Xiaoping, Li Xiannian, and Chen Yun, December 15, 1979, B172-7-115, SMA.

96. Jack Anderson, "Dance: Shanghai Acrobatic Theater," *New York Times*, March 27, 1980.

97. Shanghai Municipal Cultural Bureau, "Guanyu zajituan fuMei yanchu de yi xie qingkuang [Some situations on the acrobatic troupe's performances in the United States]," April 30, 1980, B172-7-272, SMA.

98. See, for example, *Zhongguo tongji nianjian 1995* (Beijing: Zhongguo tongji chubanshe, 1996), 648.

99. Melvin and Cai, *Rhapsody*, 287.

100. Harold C. Schonberg, "U.S. Symphony Thrills Chinese in Peking Hall," *New York Times*, March 18, 1979.

101. Harold C. Schonberg, "18,000 Hear Bostonian's Finale in Peking," *New York Times*, March 20, 1979.

102. CBS Report, "The Boston Goes to China," April 20, 1979, fol. 72, box 9, ser. 3, RG 4, FA1186, NCUSCR, RAC.

103. Foreign Broadcast Information Service, Daily Report, People's Republic of China, March 20, 1979, B2.

104. Schonberg, "18,000."

105. Jindong Cai and Sheila Melvin, *Beethoven in China: How the Great Composer Became an Icon in the People's Republic* (Sydney, Australia: Penguin Random House Books Australia, 2015), 4.

106. Isaac W. Stern, *My First 79 Years* (New York: Alfred A. Knopf, 1999), 246.

107. Murray Lerner, *From Mao to Mozart: Isaac Stern in China* (1980).

108. See, for example, Liu Xinwu, "Ban zhuren [Class teacher]," *Renmin wenxue*, no. 11 (1977): 16–29.

109. *Public Papers: Carter, 1979*, 207–09.

110. Stross, *Bulls*, 265–74; and Charles Kraus, "More than Just a Soft Drink: Coca-Cola and China's Early Reform and Opening," *Diplomatic History* 43, no. 1 (2019): 107–29.

111. Fay Kanin, "Academy President's Report: Visit to China," undated, fol. 532, box 54, ser. 4, RG 4, FA1186, NCUSCR, RAC.

112. Ministries of Education, Foreign Affairs, and Culture, and the State Council Foreign Expert Bureau, "Guanyu waiji jiaoshi he waiguo zhuanjia yaoqiu fangying dianying wenti de buchong tongzhi [Supplemental notice on the issue of foreign teachers and engineers requesting film viewings]," December 20, 1979, 199-2-2052–11, TMA.

113. CCP Propaganda Department, "Guanyu jinzhi yinshou waiguo he GangAoTai dianying mingxing de tongzhi [Notice regarding the ban on printing and selling the photographs of foreign and Hong Kongese/Macanese/Taiwanese movie stars]," January 28, 1980, 199-2-2180–14, TMA.

114. Commentary, "Yishu yu minzhu [Art and *minzhu*]," *Shanghai wenyi*, no. 12 (1978): 4.

115. "Hu Yaobang tongzhi zai shikan chaungzuo zuotanhui shang de jianghua (jilu gao) [Comrade Hu Yaobang's speech at the forum on creating poetry periodicals (record draft)]," January 19, 1979, author's personal collection.

116. Fan and Liu, *Huang Zhen zhuan*, 698–701.

117. Fox Butterfield, "Reporter's Notebook: 'Inscrutable' Is a Two-Way Street," *New York Times*, February 6, 1979.

118. Curtis L. Carter, "Avant-garde in Chinese Art," in *Subversive Strategies in Contemporary Chinese Art*, ed., Mary Bitter Wiseman and Liu Yuedi (Leiden, the Netherlands: Brill, 2011), 310–11.

119. James P. Sterba, "U.S. Art Exhibition on View in Peking," *New York Times*, September 2, 1981.

120. Julia F. Andrews and Gao Minglu, *Fragmented Memory: The Chinese Avant-Garde in Exile* (Columbus: Wexner Center for the Arts, Ohio State University, 1993), 8–10; and Gao Minglu, *Total Modernity and the Avant-Garde in Twentieth-Century Chinese Art* (Cambridge, MA: MIT Press, 2011).

121. CCP Propaganda Department, "Guanyu tiaozheng dang de wenyi zhengce fanrong shehui zhuyi wenyi de ruogan yijian (cao'an) [Some opinions on adjusting the Party's cultural policy and fostering socialist culture (draft)]," November 2, 1978, SZ120-4-513–3, HPA.

122. See *Dazhong dianying*, no. 5, 10, and 11, 1979.

123. *Deng Xiaoping wenxuan*, vol. 3, 194–97.

124. Brook, "Revival," 119.

Epilogue

1. Address by President Carter to the Nation, December 15, 1978, *FRUS*, 1977–1980, vol. 1, doc. 104.

2. George H. Gallup, *The Gallup Poll: Public Opinion 1979* (Wilmington: Scholarly Resources, 1980), 14; and "CO 34–2 General 11/1/79–2/28/79," box CO19, Country Files, WHCF, JCL.

3. CCP Shanghai Municipal Committee Department of Propaganda, "Sixiang dongxiang [Trends of thought]," December 25, 1978, A22-4-14–64, SMA; and CCP Shaanxi Provincial Committee Propaganda Department, "Xingshi jiaoyu cankao cailiao [Reference materials on education on situations] 1," January 1979, 306-2-178–1, SPA.

4. Address by President Carter; and editorial, "Lishi xing de dashi [A major event of historical significance]," *People's Daily*, December 17, 1978.

5. Hunt, *Making of a Special Relationship*, 313.

6. Kjeld Erik Brodsgaard, "The Democracy Movement in China, 1978–1979: Opposition Movements, Wall Poster Campaigns, and Underground Journals," *Asian Survey* 21, no. 7 (1981): 747–74.

7. *Public Papers of the Presidents of the United States: Ronald Reagan, 1982* (Washington, DC: Government Printing Office, 1983), 1052–53.

8. "China's New Face: What Reagan Will See," *Time*, April 30, 1984.

9. James Kelly, "East Meets Reagan," *Time*, April 30, 1984, 32–33.

10. Robert Ross, *Negotiating Cooperation: The United States and China, 1969–1989* (Stanford, CA: Stanford University Press,1995), 233–45.

11. Memorandum of Conversation, February 26, 1989, Wilson Center Digital Archive, accessed August 1, 2020, https://digitalarchive.wilsoncenter.org/document/116507.

12. *Public Papers of the Presidents of the United States: George Bush, 1989* (Washington: Government Printing Office, 1990), 669–74.

13. Commentary, "Zhongguo neizheng bu rong ganshe [China brooks no interference in domestic politics]," *People's Daily*, June 14, 1989.

14. George H. Gallup, *The Gallup Poll: Public Opinion 1989* (Wilmington: Scholarly Resources Inc., 1990), 98, 180.

15. Memorandum of Conversation, July 2, 1989, and Letter, Bush to Deng, July 21, 1989, accessed August 1, 2020, https://www.chinafile.com/library/reports/us-china-diplomacy-after-tiananmen-documents-george-hw-bush-presidential-library; and *Deng Xiaoping nianpu*, vol. 2, 1285.

16. Zhang Liang, comp., and Andrew J. Nathan and Perry Link, eds., *The Tiananmen Papers* (New York: Public Affairs, 2001), 445–59.

17. Memo, Lampton to Board of Directors, June 5, 1989, "Board, Committees, Members, Board Minutes and Mailings 1989 (2 of 2)," fol. 562, box 58, ser. 11, RG5, FA1187, NCUSCR, RAC.

18. Annual Report 1989, National Committee on United States-China Relations, undated, fol. 213, box 143, ser. 6, RG 1, FA772, NCUSCR, RAC.

19. Interview with David M. Lampton, March 30, 2020.

20. Robert L. Jacobson, "Uncertainty about Status of Academic Relations between China and United States Puts Plans for Fall Semester in Disarray," *Chronicle of Higher Education*, July 19, 1989, A30–31.

21. The Johnson Foundation News Release, July 9, 1989, fol. 2112, box 141, ser. 5, RG 1, FA772, NCUSCR, RAC.

22. David M. Lampton and Roger Sullivan, "The Price China Has Paid," *Christian Science Monitor*, July 10, 1989.

23. "54th Meeting of the Board of Directors of the National Committee on United States-China Relations, Inc.," August 1, 1989, "Board, Committees, Members, Board Minutes and Mailings 1989 (1 of 2)," fol. 561, box 58, ser. 11, RG5, FA1187, NCUSCR, RAC.

24. Report, David M. Lampton and A. Doak Barnett to the National Committee Board of Directors, undated, fol. 630, box 33, ser. 3, RG 1, FA772, NCUSCR, RAC.

25. *Deng Xiaoping nianpu*, vol. 2, 1289–90.

26. Richard Nixon, *In the Arena: A Memoir of Victory, Defeat, and Renewal* (New York: Simon and Schuster, 1990), 63.

27. Memo, Nixon to Bush, November 5, 1989, fol. 6, box 1, Post-Presidential Correspondence with George H. W. Bush, RNL.

28. Henry Kissinger, "The Caricature of Deng as a Tyrant Is Unfair," August 1, 1989, *Washington Post*; and Henry Kissinger, *On China* (New York: Penguin Books, 2011), 421–34.

29. George Bush and Brent Scowcroft, *A World Transformed* (New York: Alfred A. Knopf, 1998), 157–58.

30. Memorandum of Conversation, December 10, 1989, accessed August 1, 2020, https://www.chinafile.com/library/reports/us-china-diplomacy-after-tiananmen-documents-george-hw-bush-presidential-library.

31. *Deng Xiaoping nianpu*, vol. 2, 1304.

32. On this Dialogue series, see Priscilla Roberts, "'Our Friends Don't Understand Our Policies and Our Situation': Informal U.S.-China Dialogues Following Tiananmen," *Journal of American-East Asian Relations* 27, no. 1 (2020): 58–95.

33. Fourth United States-China Dialogue Discussion on Sino-US Relations, February 26-March 1, fol. 118, box 14, ser. 5, RG 2, FA1184, NCUSCR, RAC.

34. Harry Harding, "Prospects for Sino-American Relations," February 28, 1990, fol. 117, box 13, ser. 5, RG 2, FA1184, NCUSCR, RAC.

35. Washington eased or ended most of the sanctions by mid-1991; Pelosi's efforts resulted in Executive Order 12711 on April 11, 1990 and later the Chinese Student Protection Act of 1991; and Washington and Beijing agreed on Fang's departure to Britain in June 1990.

36. Harry Harding, "Pressure Won't Break This Impasse," *Los Angeles Times*, April 6, 1990; and Raymond P. Shafer and David M. Lampton, "Rebuild China-US Relations," *Christian Science Monitor*, April 18, 1990.

37. Jim Mann, "Shanghai Mayor Tours U.S., Seeks to Revive Goodwill," *Los Angeles Times*, July 14, 1990.

38. David M. Lampton, *Same Bed, Different Dreams: Managing U.S.- China Relations, 1989–2002* (Berkeley: University of California Press, 2001).

39. Zheng Wang, *Never Forget National Humiliation: Historical Memory in Chinese Politics and Foreign Relations* (New York: Columbia University Press, 2014); Sebastian Veg, "The Rise of China's Statist Intellectuals: Law, Sovereignty, and 'Repoliticization'," *China Journal* 82 (2019): 23–45; and Song Qiang, Zhang Zangzang, Qiao Bian et al., *Zhongguo keyi shuo bu—Lengzhanhou shidai de zhengzhi yu qinggan jueze* [China can say no—the political and emotional choice in the post-Cold War era] (Beijing: Zhonghua nonggongshang lianhe chubanshe, 1996).

40. Zheng Bijian, "China's 'Peaceful Rise' to Great-Power Status," *Foreign Affairs* 84, no. 5 (2005): 18–24; and C. Fred Bergsten, *The United States and the World Economy: Foreign Economic Policy for the Next Decade* (Washington, DC: Peterson Institute, 2005), 53–54.

41. See, for example, Kurt M. Campbell and Ely Ratner, "The China Reckoning: How Beijing Defied American Expectations," *Foreign Affairs* 97, no. 2 (2018): 60–70.

42. M. Taylor Fravel, J. Stapleton Roy, Michael D. Swaine, Susan A. Thornton, and Ezra Vogel, "China Is Not an Enemy," *Washington Post*, July 3, 2019.

43. Laura Silver, Kat Devlin, and Christine Huang, "American Fault China for Its Role in the Spread of COVID-19," July 30, 2020, accessed August 1, 2020. https://www.pewresearch.org/global/wpcontent/uploads/sites/2/2020/07/PG_20.07.30_U.S.-Views-China_final.pdf.

44. Orville Schell, "The Death of Engagement," June 7, 2020, *The Wire China*, accessed August 1, 2020, https://www.thewirechina.com/2020/06/07/the-birth-life-and-death-of-engagement/.

45. Interview with Lampton, March 30, 2020. See also David M. Lampton, "Engagement with China: A Eulogy and Reflections on a Gathering Storm," in *Engaging China: Fifty Years of Sino-American Relations*, ed., Anne F. Thurston (New York: Columbia University Press, 2021), 402.

Selected Bibliography

Only primary sources that have been of use in the making of this book—archives, published sourcebooks, digital resources, statistical data, and memoirs and biographies—are listed here. For the last category, I include biographies written or compiled by Chinese authors with access to some classified and unpublished materials. This bibliography is by no means a complete record of all the sources consulted.

Archives

United States

Bentley Historical Library, University of Michigan
Columbia University Rare Books and Manuscript Library
Gerald R. Ford Presidential Library
Harvard University Archives
Jimmy Carter Presidential Library
Library of Congress
Lyndon B. Johnson Presidential Library
MIT Institute Archives and Special Collections
National Academy of Sciences Archives
National Archives and Record Administration
New York Public Library
Richard Nixon Presidential Library
Rockefeller Archive Center

250   SELECTED BIBLIOGRAPHY

China (People's Republic of China)

Beijing Municipal Archive, Beijing
Guangdong Provincial Archive, Guangzhou
Guilin Municipal Archive, Guilin
Hebei Provincial Archive, Shijiazhuang
Hubei Provincial Archive, Wuhan
National Library, Beijing
Shaanxi Provincial Archive, Xi'an
Shanghai Municipal Archive, Shanghai
Tianjin Municipal Archive, Tianjin

Taiwan (Republic of China)

Institute of Modern History Archives, Academia Sinica

Published Sourcebooks

United States

Foreign Relations of the United States
Public Papers of the Presidents of the United States

China

Chuguo liuxue gongzuo wenjian huibian, 1978–1991 [Compilation of documents on study abroad, 1978–1991].
Deng Xiaoping nianpu [Chronology of Deng Xiaoping].
Deng Xiaoping sixiang nianbian [Chronology of Deng Xiaoping thought].
Deng Xiaoping wenxuan [Manuscripts of Deng Xiaoping].
Jianguo yilai Li Xiannian wengao [Manuscripts of Li Xiannian since the nation's founding].
Jianguo yilai zhongyao wenxian xuanbian [Collection of important documents since the nation's founding].
Li Xiannian nianpu [Chronology of Li Xiannian].
Li Xiannian wenxuan [Manuscripts of Li Xiannian].
Mao Zedong nianpu [Chronology of Mao Zedong].
Mao Zedong waijiao wenxuan [Collection of Mao Zedong's diplomatic manuscripts].
Mao Zedong wenji [The Writings of Mao Zedong].
Selected Works of Mao Tse-tung.
Tiyu yundong wenjian xuanbian, 1949–1981 [Compilation of sports documents, 1949–1981].
Zhongguo zuqiu yundongshi [History of football in China].
Zhonghua liuxue jiaoyu shilu: 1949 nian yihou [A History of China's study-abroad education after 1949].

Zhonghua renmin gongheguo jingji dashiji [Chronicle of economic events in the People's Republic of China].
Zhou Enlai nianpu [Chronology of Zhou Enlai].

Digital Resources

American Diplomacy
Association for Diplomatic Studies and Training, Foreign Affairs Oral History Project
Central Intelligence Agency Electronic Reading Room
ChinaFile
Chinese Cultural Revolution Database (*Zhongguo wenhua dageming wenku*)
National Archive, Central Foreign Policy Files, Electronic Telegrams
National Security Archives
US Congressional Record
Vanderbilt Television News Archive
Wilson Center Digital Archive

Statistical Data

Institute of International Education. *50 Years of Open Doors.*
George H. Gallup, *The Gallup Poll: Public Opinion.*
National Bureau of Statistics. *Zhongguo jiaoyu nianjian* [Education yearbook of China].
National Bureau of Statistics. *Zhongguo tiyu nianjian* [Sports yearbook of China].
National Bureau of Statistics. *Zhongguo tongji nianjian* [Statistical yearbook of China].

Memoirs and Biographies

United States

Baum, Richard. 2010. *China Watcher: Confessions of a Peking Tom.* Seattle: University of Washington Press.
Brzezinski, Zbigniew. 1983. *Power and Principle.* New York: Farrar, Straus and Giroux.
Bush, George H. W., and Brent Scowcroft. 1998. *A World Transformed.* New York: Alfred A. Knopf.
Carter, Jimmy. 1995. *Keeping Faith: Memoirs of a President.* Fayetteville: University of Arkansas Press.
Cohen, Paul A. 2019. *A Path Twice Travelled: My Journey as a Historian of China.* Cambridge: MA: Harvard University Press.
Fairbank, John King. 1982. *Chinabound: A Fifty-Year Memoir.* New York: Harper and Row.
Ford, Gerald R. 1979. *A Time to Heal: The Autobiography of Gerald R. Ford.* New York: Harper and Row.

Holdridge, John H. 1997. *Crossing the Divide: An Insider's Account of Normalization of U.S.-China Relations.* Lanham, MD: Rowman and Littlefield.
Jen, C. K. 1990. *Recollections of a Chinese Physicist.* Los Alamos, NM: Signition.
Kallgren, Joyce K., and Denis Fred Simon, eds. 1987. *Educational Exchanges: Essays on the Sino-American Experience.* Berkeley: University of California Press.
Keatley, Anne. ed. 1976. *Reflections on Scholarly Exchanges with the People's Republic of China, 1972–1976.* Washington, DC: Committee on Scholarly Communication with the People's Republic of China.
Kissinger, Henry. 1979. *White House Years.* Boston: Little, Brown.
Kissinger, Henry. 1982. *Years of Upheaval.* Boston: Little, Brown.
Kissinger, Henry. 2011. *On China.* New York: Penguin Books.
Lampton, David M. 1986. *A Relationship Restored: Trends in U.S.-China Educational Exchanges, 1978–1984.* Washington, DC: National Academy Press.
Lilley, James R., and Lilley, Jeffrey. 2004. *China Hands: Nine Decades of Adventure, Espionage, and Diplomacy in Asia.* New York: *Public Affairs*.
Liu, Kin-ming, ed. 2012. *My First Trip to China: Scholars, Diplomats and Journalists Reflect on Their First Encounter with China.* Hong Kong: East Slope Publishing.
Mote, Frederick W. 2010. *China and the Vocation of History in the Twentieth Century: A Personal Memoir.* Princeton, NJ: Princeton University Press.
Nixon, Richard. 1978. *RN: The Memoirs of Richard Nixon.* New York: Grosset and Dunlap.
Nixon, Richard. 1990. *In the Arena: A Memoir of Victory, Defeat, and Renewal.* New York: Simon and Schuster.
Pickowicz, Paul G. 2019. *A Sensational Encounter with High Socialist China.* Hong Kong: City University of Hong Kong Press.
Platt, Nicholas. 2010. *China Boys: How U.S. Relations with the PRC Began and Grew.* Washington, DC: VELLUM.
Pomfret, John. 2006. *Chinese Lessons: Five Classmates and the Story of the New China.* New York: Henry Holt.
Scalapino, Robert A. 2008. *From Leavenworth to Lhasa: Living in a Revolutionary Era.* Berkeley: Institute of East Asian Studies, University of California Press.
Tucker, Nancy Burnkopf, ed. 2001. *China Confidential: American Diplomats and Sino-American Relations, 1945–1996.* New York: Columbia University Press.

China

Chai, Zemin. *ZhongMei jianjiao fengyulu* [Stormy path toward normalization of US-China relations]. 2010. Shanghai: Shanghai cishu chubanshe.
Chinese Communist Party Ningbo Municipal Consultative Conference Literature and History Committee, ed. *Lu Xuzhang jinian wenji* [Commemorative essays on Lu Xuzhang]. 2011. Beijing: Zhongguo wenshi chubanshe.
Fan, Zhonghui, and Liu Haifeng. 2007. *Huang Zhen zhuan* [Biography of Huang Zhen]. Beijing: Zhongyang wenxian chubanshe.

Fang, Xin, ed. 2008. *Kexue de chuntian* [The spring of science]. Beijing: Kexue chubanshe.

Gu, Mu. 2009. *Gu Mu huiyilu* [Memoirs of Gu Mu]. Beijing: Zhongyang wenxian chubanshe.

Huang, Hua. 2007. *Qinli yu jianwen: Huang Hua huiyilu* [Experience and hearsay: Memoirs of Huang Hua]. Beijing: Shejie zhishi chubanshe.

Li, Lanqing. 2009. *Breaking through: The Birth of China's Opening-Up Policy.* Translated by Ling Yuan and Zheng Siying. New York: Oxford University Press, 2009.

Liang, Lijuan. 2005. *He Zhenliang wu huan zhi lu* [He Zhenliang and the Olympics]. Beijing: Shijie zhishi chubanshe.

Liu, Bing. 2010. *Fengyu suiyue: 1964–1976 nian de Tsinghua* [Years of storm and rain: Tsinghua University between 1964 and 1976]. Beijing: Dangdai Zhongguo chubanshe.

Liu, Xiyao. 2000. *Panfeng yu chuanwu: Liu Xiyao huiyilu* [Fog over the mountaintop: Memoirs of Liu Xiyao]. Wuhan: Wuhan daxue chubanshe.

Luo, Yinsheng. 2012. *Qiao Guanhua zhuan: Hongse waijiaojia de beixi rensheng* [Biography of Qiao Guanhua: A Red diplomat's life of joy and sorrow]. Beijing: Wenhua yishu chubanshe.

Luo, Yunyun. 2001. *Li Delun zhuan* [Biography of Li Delun]. Beijing: Zuojia chubanshe.

Qian, Qichen. 2003. *Waijiao shi ji* [Ten stories in diplomacy]. Beijing: Shijie zhishi chubanshe.

Sun, Guowei. 2009. *Qinli ZhongMei jianjiao: Zhongguo shouren zhuMei dashi Chai Zemin zhuan* [Experiencing US-China normalization: Biography of first Chinese ambassador to the United States Chai Zemin]. Beijing: Shejie zhishi chubanshe.

Xiong, Xianghui. 2006. *Wo de qingbao yu waijiao shengya* [My life in intelligence and diplomacy]. Beijing: Zhonggong dangshi chubanshe.

Yang, Gongsu. 1999. *Cangsang jiushi nian—yi ge waijiao teshi de huiyi* [Great changes in the ninety years of my life: Memoirs of a special diplomatic envoy]. Haikou: Hainan chubanshe.

Yang, Jianye. 2011. *Yang Zhenning zhuan* [Biography of Yang Zhenning]. Beijing: Shenghuo-Dushu-Xinzhi san lian shudian.

Ye, Rugeng, ed. 2008. *Fang Yi zhuan* [Biography of Fang Yi]. Beijing: Renmin chubanshe.Yuan, Hong. 2004. *Han Xu zhuan: Yi ge waijiaojia de jingli* [Biography of Han Xu: Experiences of a diplomat]. Beijing: Shijie zhishi chubanshe.

Zhang, Dianyu, ed. 1998. *Yang Zhenning wenji* [The Writings of Yang Zhenning]. Shanghai: Huadong shifan daxue chubanshe.

Zi, Ding. 2004. *Li Qiang zhuan* [Biography of Li Qiang]. Beijing: Renmin chubanshe, 2004.

Index

Page numbers in *italics* indicate figures

acrobatic groups, Chinese, 162–63, 174–75
acupuncture, 119, *120*
Afghanistan, Soviet invasion of, 6
African Americans, 33–34
agriculture, 50, 60–61
airlines, 134–35
All-China Sports Federation, 18, 40–41, 139–40
Amateur Athletic Union (AAU), 144–45, 146–47
Amateur Sports Act, 152
American Association for the Advancement of Science (AAAS), 86
American film week, 177–78
American Friends Service Committee (AFSC), 23
anti-Americanism, popular and revolutionary, 29–32, 38–39
Anti-Rightist Campaign of 1957, 69
Anti-Spiritual Pollution Campaign, 179
Antonioni, Michelangelo: *Chung Kuo (China)*, 120–21
archaeological exhibit, 167–68
arms embargo, 182–83
art: and the Cultural Revolution, 160–61, 162, 170–71, 172; globalization of, 159; modernization of, 18, 161–62, 171–77; in politics, 18, 159–60, 162–72, 178–79.
  See also cultural exchanges
Asian Games, 142, 146–47, 152–53
Asian-African-Latin American Table Tennis Friendship Invitational Tournament, 146–47
asylum requests, 114
athletes: in East-West rivalry, 138–39; and "friendship first," 138–41, 143–45, 146; in the quest for medals, 152, 156–57, 158; in sports exchanges, 18, 138–39; and the triumph of competition, 146–48, 150.
  See also sports diplomacy/sports exchanges
avant-garde movement, China, 178–79

Barnett, A. Doak, 23–24, 42–43, 185
basketball, 145–46, 150–51, 154–56
Baum, Richard, 148–50
Beethoven, Ludwig van, 161–62, 163–66, 170–71, 175–77
Bei Shizhang, 69–70
Beijing People's Radio Station, 100–101
Berris, Jan, 151, 168–69, 184–85
Berry, Mary Frances, 102–3
Black Panther Party, 34, 39
Black Power, 34
Bliss, Anthony, 173–74

Blumenthal, W. Michael, 61
Boston Symphony Orchestra, 175–77
Brown, Edmund, 44–45
Brown, Harold, 7
Brzezinski, Zbigniew, 6, 7, 60–61, 84–85
Buerkle, Dick, 147–48, 150
Bullock, Mary, 81, 85–86
Burger, Warren, 178–79
Burnham, Donald, 47
Bush, George H. W., 147–48, 182–83, 187–88
Butterfield, Fox, 26

Cai Jingdong, 176–77
California, 44–45
Canton Fair (China Export Commodities Fair), 48–49, 52–53, 61, 173
capital: foreign, in trade, 53, 65–66; human, 17–18, 111; overseas Chinese, in building hotels, 132–33
capitalism/anti-capitalism: in educational exchanges, 99–100, 113–14; in foreign language instruction, 99–100; in moral corruption from tourism, 121–22; and scientific exchanges, 83; in Sino-American trade, 52–53, 54, 55–56, 63, 64, 65–66; in tourism, 123–24, 126–27, 131, 132–33
capitalist countries: Chinese need for ties with, 14–15, 16; Chinese trade with, 44–45, 46, 48, 52–53, 54; and scientific exchanges, 85–86
"capitulationism," 170
Carter, Jimmy and administration, 6, 7, 59–62, 84–85, 87–88, 152, 157, 180–81
Center for US-China Arts Exchange, 171–72
Central Broadcasting Administration, 127–28
Central Conservatory of Music, 171
Central Intelligence Agency (CIA), 8, 27, 39–41, 77, 84, 121
Chai Zemin, 186–87
championships/championship mentality, 139–40, 142, 143, 146–47, 150, 151–58
"Chimerica," 64–65
China Can Say No, 188
China Central Philharmonic, 161–62, 164–66, 170–71, 175–76
China Council for the Promotion of International Trade (CCPIT), 17, 45, 47–48, 57–58

China International Travel Service (CITS), 117, 124, 131–32, 229n18; *The Official Guidebook of China*, 136
China Lobby, 21–22, 23–24, 42
China Lobby, new, 22–29
China Quarterly: "Reports from China," 77–78
China Scholar Escort Program, 77–80
"China threat theory," 188
China Tourism Enterprise Administration (CTEA), 117, 121–23, 124, 130–31
China Travel Service (CTS), 117, 123–24, 229n18
Chinese Academy of Social Sciences (CASS), 86–88
Chinese Americans, 42, 72–74, 83–84, 87–88, 116–17, 132–33, 171–72, 185
Chinese Communist Party (CCP): on Chinese freedom, 126–27; in cultural exchanges and politics, 159–60, 178–79; and education, 91–92, 97–98, 101–2; in opening up trade, 58–59, 60; in the origins of people's diplomacy, 29–30, 31–32, 38–39; people's diplomacy institutionalized by, 9; in sports exchanges, 138–39, 142; in tourism policy, 115–16, 118, 130–31
Chinese Nationalist Party (KMT), 21–22, 42, 44–45, 67, 128–29, 138–39, 163. *See also* Taiwan/Taiwan problem
Chinese People's Association for Friendship with Foreign Countries (CPAFFC), 40–41, 118, 229n18
Chinese People's Institute of Foreign Affairs (CPIFA), 36, 40–41, 118, 186–87, 229n18
Chinese Revolution, 2, 16, 31, 91–92, 159–60. *See also* revolution and counterrevolution in education
Chinese Sports Commission. *See* State Physical Culture and Sports Commission
civil rights movement, 14, 33–34
civil society, transnational, 13–14
class, political and socioeconomic: in Chinese science, 82–83, 84; in Chinese tourism, 122–24, 133, 134
class struggle, 32–33, 69, 74–75, 80, 87, 100–101, 146–47, 160–62, 165–66
Cohen, Jerome, 173
Cold War, 2, 8–13, 92–93, 138–39, 152, 159–60, 167–68, 176–77

INDEX

commercialization: of cultural exchanges, 172–77; of sports, 153–54; of tourism, 117–18, 122–23, 134
Committee of Concerned Asian Scholars (CCAS), 39, 77, 94, *128*
Committee of One Million against the Admission of Communist China to the UN, 23–24, 36–37
Committee on Scholarly Communication with China (CSC), 17, 40–41, 68–72, 75–80, 81–82, 87–89, 107, 109–10
communism/anti-communism, 42, 66, 127, 141–42
compensation trade, 53, 62–63
consumer goods, 1–2, 48, 63–64
"containment without isolation" policy, 23–25, 26
Cowan, Glenn, 37–38
Criticize Deng Campaign, 14–15, 53, 97–99
Criticize Lin, Criticize Confucius Campaign, 6–7, 52, 78–79, 165–66
cultural exchanges: model plays in, 160–61; modernization of, 18, 172–77; in opening to the West, 161–62; politics in, 18, 159–60, 162–72, 177–78; return of Beethoven in, 162–68; US as superpower in, 159
Cultural Revolution: in art, 160–61, 162, 170–71, 172; in Chinese participation in international sports, 138–39; in disruptions of the 1970s, 14–15; and educational exchanges, 91–92, 102, 113–14; in normalization of relations, 6–7; and the origins of people's diplomacy, 22, 27, 31–32, 36–37; in scientific exchanges, 69, 73–74, 77; and tourism, 117
culture: American, in the "change China" mentality, 113–14; American consumption of, 159; and bilateral relations, 1–2; and bilateral trade, 59, 64–65; "cultural exports," 133, 173; culture-power relationship, 16; in scientific exchanges, 76–77, 80, 82–83; in student exchanges, 108–10, 113–14, 119–20
Culture, Ministry of, 160, 171–72
curricula, 26, 92–93, 96–97, 100, 103–4, 166–67

David, Edward, 86, 89–90
debt, Chinese, 58–59, 62–63

defense technology transfer, 60
democracy movement, Chinese, 181, 182
Democracy Wall Movement, 181
Deng Xiaoping: and bilateral trade, 55, 60–62; in cultural exchanges and politics, 166–67, 173; in disruptions of the 1970s, 14–16; and education, 96–98, 101–2, 103–4, 106–7; in normalization of relations, 6, 7, 87–88; "Outline Report" by, 74–75, 80–81; in scientific exchanges, 74–75, 80–81, 82–85, 87–88; "Some Questions on Accelerating the Development of Industry" by, 55; in sports exchanges, 146–47, 151–52, 156–57; and the Tiananmen Square Massacre, 182–83, 185–86; and tourism, 132, 137
Dent, Frederick, 45–46
détente, 6, 12–13, 129
diplomatic relations, establishment of. *See* normalization of relations
Du Bois, W. E. B., 33–34
Durdin, Tillman, 38–39, 125

Eagleburger, Lawrence, 182–83, 185–86
Eckstein, Alexander, 36–37, 39–40, 44–45, 50, 56, 58, 168, 169
economics/economic strategy: in disruptions of the 1970s, 13–14; in the opening of trade, 46, 48, 52–53, 55; and tourism, 122–24, 125–26
"economy class" tourism, 122–24
Education, Ministry of, 101–2, 103–4
education/educational exchanges: American application of Chinese revolution in, 92–93; "change China" mentality in, 113–14; egalitarianism in, 17–18, 93–94, 102–4, 112–13; English language in, 94–95, 99–105, 107, 108–9, 111–12; in the origins of people's diplomacy, 25–26, 42–43; progress in negotiations on, 105–12; revolution and counterrevolution in, 91–92, 93–105; and the scientific renaissance, 82. *See also* schools
Eisenhower, Dwight D., 8, 115–16
embargos, 44–45, 46, 159–60, 182–83
energy/energy projects, 55, 60–61, 64–65
engagement, definition of, 189
English language, 94–95, 99–105, 107, 108–9, 111–12, 116–17, 135–36

espionage, 71–72, 121
exports/export commodities, 48–49, 62–63, 173. *See also* imports; trade, bilateral

factories, Chinese, 55–56, 59, 64, 92
Fairbank, John K., 20, 36–37, 43
Fang Yi, 106–7
Federation of American Scientists (FAS), 70–71, 77, 125–26
Fengqing Incident, 55–56
Fifth Symphony (Beethoven), 164–65, 170–71, 175–77
films, 120–21, 127–28, 166–67, 171–72, 177–78
Fleming, Robben, 95–96
Ford, Gerald, 6, 138, 147
Ford Foundation, 20, 25
foreign currency: in bilateral trade, 48, 52–53, 62–63; in cultural exchanges, 162, 173, 174–75; in the economics of tourism, 117, 122–23, 130–36
Foreign Trade, Ministry of, 48, 52–53
foreign trade companies (FTCs), Chinese, 45, 48–49, 52, 53
Foster, William, 32
"four modernizations": in cultural exchanges, 171–72; in Deng's reforms, 14–15; in educational exchanges, 101–2, 110–11; and foreign trade, 54–55, 58, 64; need for foreign currency in, 130–31; in scientific exchanges, 81–82, 86–87; in sports exchanges, 152–53. *See also* agriculture; industry/industrialization; modernization; science/scientific exchanges
Fourth US-China Dialogue, 186–87
freedom, 89, 95–96, 115–16, 126–27, 128–29, 178–79
friends/friendship: in cultural exchanges, 163, 167–68, 170, 174–75; fantasy and reality of, 181–82; in people's diplomacy, 9, 32–35, 37–38, 39, 43; scientific exchanges in, 17, 69–70; in sports exchanges, 138–39, 140–41; and tourism, 115–17
"friendship first, competition second" mantra: in 1970s sports exchanges, 141–46; championship ambitions in abandonment of, 152–57; as the golden rule of Chinese sport, 138–39; and Olympic participation, 158; and sports nationalism, 140–41, 146–52. *See also* sports diplomacy/sports exchanges

From Mao to Mozart (film), 177
Fulbright, J. William, 23–24

Galbraith, John Kenneth, 125–26
Galston, Arthur, 69–70
Gang of Four: on art and cultural exchanges, 167, 170–71, 172; on counterrevolution in education, 97–98; in disruptions of the 1970s, 14–16; and foreign language instruction, 100–101; in normalization of relations, 6–7; in policy on tourism, 122–23, 130–31; on scientific exchanges, 75; in the social science crisis, 80–81; on sports diplomacy and competition, 142, 146–47; in trade, 52–53, 55–56
geopolitics: in normalization of relations, 6, 7–8, 181–82; in Sino-American rapprochement, 5
globalization, 13–14, 68–69, 153–54, 159
Goldwater, Barry, 23–24
Gorbachev, Mikhail, 181–82
Great Leap Forward, 15, 91–92
Greene, Felix, 29, 115–16
Gu Chaohao, 73–74
Gu Mu, 58–59
guides, English-speaking Chinese, 116–17, 118, 120–22, 123–24, *128*, 131–32, 135–36
Guo Moruo, 82–83
gymnastics, 144, 151

Habib, Philip, 168–69
Han Zhongjie, 175, 179
Handler, Philip, 68–69, 81, 105
Harding, Harry, 137, 187–88
Hart-Celler Act, 93
Harvard University, 106
Heyns, Roger, 95, 96
higher education: delegations in, in negotiations on educational exchanges, 95; Deng's reform of, 101–3; and English language instruction, 99–105; revolution and counterrevolution in, 91–93, 94, 95–99, 101–2; and the road to student exchanges, 105–12. *See also* education/educational exchanges
Hilsman, Roger, 20–21
Hilton, Isabel, 120–21
Hinton, William, 133–34

INDEX

Holdridge, John, 39–40, 70–71
Hollander, Paul, 14
hotels for foreign tourists, 132–33
Hu Chengli, 108–9
Hu Na, 157
Hu Yaobang, 74–75, 133–34, 178
Hua Guofeng, 15, 56–57, 102–3, 105, 150–51, 170–71
Huan Xiang, 87–88
Huang Zhen, 47–48, 167, 171–72
Hunt, Michael, 181
Hurok, Sol, 163, 173

ideology: and bilateral trade, 52–53, 65–66; in educational exchanges, 94; in foreign language education, 99–101; in people's diplomacy, 9; and scientific exchanges, 17, 70, 74–75, 80, 83; and the Tiananmen Square Massacre, 183, 185; and tourism, 121–22
imperialism/anti-imperialism: and American tourism, 117–18; in the Chinese meaning of freedom, 126–27; in educational exchanges, 91–92, 111–12; in the origins of people's diplomacy, 22, 29–35, 38–39; in post-Tiananmen rhetoric, 182; in trade, 52–53
imports: of American technology, 17, 54–60; and the China differential, 44; of consumer goods to China, 64; cultural, 162–63, 171–72, 175, 177–78; in trade, 64–65. *See also* exports/export commodities; trade, bilateral
industry/industrialization, 15, 54–58, 61, 64–65, 71–72, 77
International Olympic Committee (IOC), 148, 156–57
Iriye, Akira, 16
isolation of China, 23–26, 28–29, 184–85, 188–89

Jackson-Vanik Amendment, 50–51
James, Edmund, 91
Jenkins, Alfred, 27, 39–40
Jiang Qing, 6–7, 55–56, 120–21, 143, 145, 160–67, 170–71. *See also* Gang of Four
Johnson, Lyndon B., and administration, 22–23, 24–25, 26–27
joint ventures: in education, 112; in tourism, 132–33; in trade, 60–61, 63, 64–66

journalists: in the origin of people's diplomacy, 29, 32–33, 34–35; as tourists, 115–17, 119, 125, 126, 127, 128–30
Judd, Walter, 23–24, 42

Kallgren, Joyce, 119–20
Keatley, Anne, 70–71, 79–80
Kennedy, John F., and administration, 20–21
Kissinger, Henry, 2–3, 11, 13, 37–38, 41, 50, 72, 185–86
Kriegsman, Alan, 163, 174

Lake Placid Olympics, 157
Lampton, David M., 79–80, 184–85, 187–88
Leontief, Wassily, 125–27
Li Delun, 164–65, 166, 170–72
Li Peng, 186–87
Li Qiang, 48, 61–62
Li Xiannian, 46, 47–48, 54–55
Li Zhengdao, 72–74, 80–81, 185
liaison offices, 41, 116–17, 121, 128–29, 150–51, 167–69
Lin Biao, 6–7, 29–30
literature, 161–62, 166–67, 171–72, 177, 178
Liu Bing, 97–98
Liu Xiyao, 103–4
Los Angeles Olympics, 158
Lu Xuzhang, 132–33
Luce, Clare Booth, 22–23
Luo Qingchang, 121, 123
Luttwak, Edward: "Seeing China Plain," 129–30

machine tool industry, *49*, 56
"Made in China," 1–2, 52, 63–64
Madsen, Richard, 14
Major League Baseball (MLB), 153
"make the foreign serve China," 58–59, 146, 152–53
Manley, Michael, 158
Mao Yuanxin, 97
Mao Zedong: and American journalism, 115–16; on art and politics, 159–60; criticism of legacies of, 130; on freedom of artistic expression, 166–67; friendships of, 32–35, 37–38; in the origins of people's diplomacy, 20–21, 32–35, 37–38; *Quotations from Chairman Mao Tse-tung*, 34–35; on the skills of Chinese athletes,

Mao Zedong (*continued*)
    143; on technology imports, 54; *On the Ten Major Relationships*, 15; Three Worlds Theory, 6
Mao Zedong Thought, 48–49, 118–19
markets: American, 48–49, 50; Chinese, 44–46, 47–53, 58–59, 60, 61, 62–63, 64–65. *See also* trade, bilateral
martial arts, Chinese (Wushu), 167
mass organizations, Chinese, 10–11, 36, 124. *See also under name of organization*
Mei Lanfang, 159
MFN (most favored nation) status, 50–51, 61–62. *See also* trade, bilateral
Middle Kingdom, 18, 116–17, 135
Miller, Arthur, 135–36
minzhu (democracy), in art, 178
MIT (Massachusetts Institute of Technology), 106
model plays, 160–61, 166–67, 172
modern art, 178–79. *See also* art; cultural exchanges
modernization: and cultural exchanges, 18, 161–62, 171–77; democratization as, 181; in disruptions of the 1970s, 14–16; and educational exchanges, 17–18, 95, 99, 101–2, 104–5, 110–12, 113; scientific exchanges in, 17, 70, 81–84, 86–87, 89–90; sport in, 152–53; and tourism, 130–31; trade in, 54–62, 64, 65–66; US as agent of, 12–13
Mondale, Walter, 7
Moscow Olympics, 156–57
movies. *See* films
Murray, Douglas, 106, 139–40, 164–65
Museum of Fine Arts, Boston, 178–79
music: in China's opening to the West, 161–62; in cultural politics, 18, 159–60, 165–67, 168–69, 171–72; in modernizing cultural exchanges, 173–74, 175–77; performances of Beethoven, 161–62, 163–66, 170–72, 175–77; in the social science crisis, 77–78

National Academy of Sciences (NAS), 67–69, 107
National Basketball Association (NBA), 153, 156
National Chinese Opera Theater, 163
National Collegiate Athletic Association (NCAA), 144–45, 147

National Committee on US-China Relations: in cultural exchanges, 162, 163–64, 168–69; in educational exchanges, 94–95; in the origins of people's diplomacy, 22–29, 36–37, 39–43; in sports exchanges, 139–40; on the Tiananmen Square Massacre, 183–85, 187–88
National Council for US-China Trade: in cultivating the China market, 17, 65; in economic normalization, 60, 61, 62; and the myth of the great China market, 47–48, 50–51, 53; in opening bilateral trade, 45–46; and technology trade, 54–55
National Science Foundation (NSF), 84–85, 107–8
National Security Council (NSC), 24–25, 36
New Sports (China), 143, 151–53, 154
New York Cosmos, 154–55
NGOs (nongovernmental organizations), 10–11, 25–26. *See also under name of organization*
Nien Cheng, 110–11
Nixon, Richard, and administration, 2–3, 36, 38, 68–69, 185–86
nonstate actors, 3–4, 8, 9–14, 16, 25–26, 183–84
normalization of relations: in bilateral trade, 46–48, 50–51, 59–60, 61–64, 65, 66; in contemporary bilateral relations, 2–8; cultural exchanges in, 162; in educational exchanges, 94–95, 99, 105, 106; people's diplomacy in, 10–13, 22–24, 36–37, 39–40; realism in approval of, 180–81; in scientific exchanges, 71, 75, 81, 83–84, 87–88; sports exchanges in, 139–40; and strategic concerns, 180. *See also* rapprochement, Sino-American
North Korea, 26–27, 139, 156–57
novels, 115, 166–67, 170, 171–72
nuclear weapons/threat, 5, 21–23, 30–31

oil ventures and technology, 55, 56–57, 63–64
Oksenberg, Mickel, 60–61
Olympic Games, 138–39, 147, 148, 156–57, 158
orientalism: and American tourism in China, 18, 126, 130, 134, 136, 137; in cultural exchanges, 159, 163; "radical orientalism," 117–18, 126, 130, 137

Ormandy, Eugene, 163–66
"Outline Report on the Work of the (Chinese) Academy of Sciences," 74–75, 80–81
Ozawa, Seiji, 175–77

paintings, 166–67, 178–79
Pan American World Airlines (Pan Am), 134–35
Paris Peace Accords, 5
Patriotic Education Campaign, 188
Pearson, James, 144–45, 147
Pei, I. M., 132–33
Peking opera, 160, 161–62, 173–74
Pelosi, Nancy, 185–86, 189–90, 247n35
"People of Taiwan, Our Own Brothers," 168–70, 173–74
People's Liberation Army (PLA), 5–6, 30, 91–92, 138–39
performing arts: model plays, 160–61, 166–67, 172; in modernization, 172–77; performing arts troupes, 147, 167, 168–72, 173–75. *See also* acrobatic groups, Chinese; music; Peking opera
Philadelphia Philharmonic Orchestra, 163–66
Phillips, Christopher, 45, 47–48, 56, *57*, 58–59, 63–64, 65
ping-pong diplomacy, 9–10, 37–38, 40, 116, 139–40, 141–42, 146–47. *See also* sports diplomacy/sports exchanges
Press, Frank, 60, 76, 84–85, 106–7
profit, 52–53, 64–65, 122–24, 131–32, 134–35, 153, 172–77
propaganda: in cultural exchanges, 169–70, 178–79; in educational exchanges, 98–99, 102; in the origins of people's diplomacy, 29–35, 38–40; in people's diplomacy, 8, 10–11; in scientific exchanges, 82–83; in sports exchanges, 147–48; and tourism, 18, 115–16, 117–19, 126, 127, 129–30, 133–34
Propaganda Department (CCP), 104–5, 178–79
public opinion: of American tourists on New China, 129–30; on bilateral relations, and sports exchanges, 139–40; on exchanges programs, 12; in the origins of people's diplomacy, 24, 28–29, 38, 42–43; Tiananmen Square Massacre in, 182; US, on China, in 2020, 188–89

Qian Dayong, 72, 168
Qian Ning: *Chinese Students Encounter America,* 112–13
Qiao Guanhua, 94–95
Quakers (Religious Society of Friends), 23
Quotations from Chairman Mao Tse-tung, 34–35, 133–34

racism/racial discrimination, American, 33–34
radio broadcasts in English language instruction, 100–101, 104–5, 111–12
rapprochement, Sino-American, 2–4, 5–8, 11, 36–41, 42–43, 139–40, 150–51. *See also* normalization of relations
Reagan, Ronald and administration, 14, 181–82
recession, global, 50, 63–64
recognition of China, diplomatic. *See* normalization of relations
Red Detachment of Women, 161–62
Red Guard movement, 31
reform, Chinese: in disruptions of the 1970s, 14–16; economic, 64–66; in education, 96–99, 101–3; Reform and Opening-Up, 7, 15–16, 64–66, 185; in science, 74–75, 84, 86–87; in sports and physical education, 151–54
Reischauer, Edwin, 26–28
Ren Zhigong, 73–74
Republic of China. *See* Taiwan/Taiwan problem
"Resist America, Aid Vietnam" campaign, 29
Reston, James, 119, *120,* 126
revisionism, 52, 55–56, 75, 97–98, 146–47, 161–62, 166–67, 171–72
revolution and counterrevolution in education, 92–93, 94–105
Rockefeller, David, 62, 126–27
Rosen, Arthur, 173–74
Rosenthal, A. M., 137
Rouse, Hunter, 89
Rusk, Dean, 20–21
Ryckmans, Pierre: *Chinese Shadows,* 130

sanctions, economic, 182–83, 184–86
Scali, John, 40
Scalpino, Robert, 23, 125
Schell, Orville, 127, 188–89
Schlesinger, James, 60–61
Schonberg, Harold, 164, 165–66

schools: of art and music, 166–67, 171–72; Chinese elementary, physical education in, 153; foreign language, 99–100; revolution and counterrevolution in, 91–93, 98–100, 102–4. *See also* education/educational exchanges
Science and Education Group, China, 92, 96–97
Science and Technology Association of China (STA), 69, 71, 75–77, 78–80, 81, 86, 88–89, 105
Science for the People movement, 68–69
science/scientific exchanges: basic and theoretical research in, 68–69, 71–75, 80–81, 82; debate over nature of, 70–76; history of exchanges in, 67; in Mao's China, 69–70; in modernization, 17, 70, 81–84, 86–87, 89–90; in the renaissance of Chinese science, 82–88; resumption of, as cure for Sino-American relations, 67–69; and the social sciences, 76–82, 86–88
Scowcroft, Brent, 182–83, 185–86
self-reliance/self-sufficiency, principles of, 50, 52–55, 56–59, 69, 81–82
Senate Foreign Relations Committee, 23–24
Shafer, Raymond, 187–88
Shanghai Acrobatic Troupe, 174–75
Shanghai Communiqué, 2–3, 9–10, 38, 43, 45, 168–69
Shanghai Municipal Foreign Trade Office, 52–53
Shanghai Municipal Revolutionary Committee, 169–70
Shanghai People's Radio Station, 100–101
Shanghai Writers Association, 178
Shenyang acrobatic troupe, 162–63
Signer, Ethan, 69–70
Sinicization, 54, 59, 84
sinologists/sinology: on Chinese education, 94; in educational exchanges, 106, 109–10; on the myth of the great China market, 50; in the origins of people's diplomacy, 20, 23–24, 25–26; in scientific exchanges, 76–82; on Sino-American rapprochement, 42–43; as tourists, 129, 130. *See also under name of sinologist*
Sino-Soviet split, 5, 44
Sixth Symphony (Beethoven), 163–65
Smith, Emil, 71, 72
Snow, Edgar, 34–35, 36–37, 115–16, 119

Sobin, Julian, 53, 58
soccer, 154–55, 156–57
social science/scientists, 76–82, 86–88, 106, 107, 110–11
socialism/socialists: and bilateral trade, 44–45; in cultural exchanges, 159–61, 171–72; and educational exchanges, 113–14; as remedy to American social ills, 14; and scientific exchanges, 74–75, 82, 83; in sports exchanges, 149–50, 152–53, 156–57; and tourism, 18, 115–16, 118–19, 120–21, 122–23, 124, 125–29, 133–34
Socialist Education Movement, 30–31
Solomon, Richard, 72, 93, 166
souvenir industry, 133
Soviet Union: Chinese cultural exchanges with, 159–60; Chinese educational exchanges with, 91–92; in opening of Sino-American trade, 50–51, 60–62; in the origins of people's diplomacy, 30–31, 38; and the revolution in education, 94; in Sino-American relations, 5–6, 7, 180–82; Sino-Soviet split, 5, 44; in sports exchanges, 138–39, 152, 157–58
Sports Commission. *See* State Physical Culture and Sports Commission
sports diplomacy/sports exchanges: American reform in amateur sport, 152; championships in, 139–40, 142, 143, 146–47, 150, 151–58; elitism in, 139; nationalism in, 140–41, 146–52, 157–58; in the origins of people's diplomacy, 40; rivalries and respect in, 18, 138–39, 152–57, 158; triumph of competition in, 146–52; winning and losing in, 138, 139, 140, 142–45, 146–58. *See also* "friendship first, competition second" mantra
sports nationalism, 138–39, 140–41, 148–50, 152–57
Stanford University, 106, *109*
State Administration of Cultural Heritage, 173
State Council of China: in cultural politics and exchanges, 160, 166, 173, 174–75; in educational reform, 96–97; in the social science crisis, 80; in tourism, 132–33; on trade, 50, 52–53
State Physical Culture and Sports Commission, 138–39, 143, 148–50, 152–53, 156–57, 158

steel production, Chinese, 55–56
Stern, Isaac, 177
Strategic Arms Limitation Talks (SALT), 5, 6, 61–62
Strong, Anna Louise, 32–33, 115, *128*
students, American, 26, 109–10
students, Chinese: in bilateral relations, 1–2; in educational exchanges, 17–18; English language education for, 94–95, 99–105, 107, 108–9, 111–12; first cohort of exchanges students, 108–9; motivations of, in educational exchanges, 108–9, 111–12
swimming and diving delegation, 144–45, 146

table tennis. *See* ping-pong diplomacy
Taiwan Relations Act, 180–81
Taiwan/Taiwan problem: in bilateral trade, 51, 57–58, 59–60; in contemporary bilateral relations, 189–90; in cultural politics and exchanges, 167, 168–70; in negotiations on educational exchanges, 94–95, 96, 99, 105–6, 107–8; in normalization of relations, 2–3, 6; in the origins of contemporary relations, 2–3; in people's diplomacy, 11; realism on, 180–82; in scientific exchanges, 75, 81; in sports diplomacy, 150–51; "three principles" on, 6, 11, 51, 81; trade with, 44–45. *See also* Chinese Nationalist Party (KMT); "two-China problem"
technology, 17, 54–61, 88. *See also* science/scientific exchanges; trade, bilateral
textile exports, Chinese, 63–64
Theis, Nancy, 144
Theroux, Eugene, 53, 58
Thomas, Cecil, 23, 25
"three competitions" in trade, 53
Three Worlds Theory (Mao Zedong), 6, 122–23, 124, 146–47
Thucydides Trap, 1
Tiananmen Papers, The, 183
Tiananmen Square Incident, April 5, 1976, 15–16
Tiananmen Square Massacre, June 4, 1989, 19, 182–88
Tobin, James, 125–26
tourists/tourism: in bilateral relations, 1–2; Chinese policy on, 116–17, 118–24; as cultural diplomacy, 117–18; foreign currency in driving, 130–36; journalists as, 115–17; in New China, 125–30; politics and economics of, 118–24; scientific, 70–76; socioeconomic class in, 122–24, 133, 134; travelogues, 115, 125–30, 136–37
track and field delegation, 147–50
trade, bilateral: Chinese views on, 65–66; economic normalization in, 60–64; fall of, 50–53; growth of, 46, 47–49; markets in, 44–46, 47–53, 58–59, 60, 61, 62–63, 64–65; in modernization, 54–62, 64, 65–66; in people's diplomacy, 9. *See also* imports
travelogues, 115, 125–30, 136–37
Trump, Donald J., 188–89
Tsinghua University, 97–98
twenty points (Deng), 55–56, 58–59
"two-China problem," 22, 27, 40–41, 150–51. *See also* Taiwan/Taiwan problem

United Nations, 23–24, 38
universities, American: in educational exchanges, 91, 95, 107, 108–9, 110–12, 113; in the origins of people's diplomacy, 25–26; on the revolution in education, 95–96; in scientific exchanges, 67, 76, 81–82, 83–84, 89
universities, Chinese: American perceptions of, 94; in educational exchanges, 92–93, 105–6, 107, 108–9, 110–11; revolution and counterrevolution in, 91–92, 94–99, 100, 101–2, 103–4
US International Communication Agency, 109–10
US-China Joint Commission on Scientific and Technological Cooperation, 87–88
US-China People's Friendship Association (USCPFA), 123, 168, 169
USSR (Soviet Union). *See* Soviet Union

Vance, Cyrus, 81
Vietnam War, 5, 6, 22–23, 29–32, 33–35, 36–37, 141–42
Voice of America (VOA), 104–5, 111–12, 182–83
volleyball delegation, 150–51
Volleyball World Cup, 157–58

Wakeman, Frederic, 76–77, 81, 87
Wang Hongwen, 6–7, 142. *See also* Gang of Four

Wang Meng, 152–53
Wang Yaoting, 47–48, 57–58
Washington Bullets, 156
"Western-Led Leap Forward," 15
White Haired Girl, 160–61, 173–74
Williams, Robert F., 34, *35*
Woodcock, Leonard, 61–62, 106–7, 176–77

xenophobia, Chinese, 121, 161–62
Xi Jinping, 188–89
Xie Qimei, 168–69
Xu Chi: *Goldbach's Conjecture,* 80–81

Yan'an Forum on Literature and Art, 1942, 159–60
Yang Zhenning, 72–74, 80–81
Yao Wenyuan, 6–7. *See also* Gang of Four
Yellow River Piano Concerto, 164–66, 171–72
Yu Huiyong, 161–62, 165–66

Zhang Chunqiao, 6–7, 75, 101–2. *See also* Gang of Four
Zhang Haitao, 136–37
Zhang Jianhua, 51
Zhang Junqiu, 171
Zhang Tiesheng, 97, 102
Zhang Wenjin, 94–95
Zhao Jianjun, 31–32
Zhao Ziyang, 181–82
Zhenbao/Dmansky Island incident, 5
Zhou Enlai: and the counterrevolution in education, 96–97; in cultural politics and art exchanges, 161–62, 165–66; in disruptions of the 1970s, 14–15; on ping-pong diplomacy, 37–38, 143; in the return of tourism, 117; in scientific exchanges, 70–71; on the skills of Chinese athletes, 143; on social sciences, 77; on technology trade, 55
Zhou Peiyuan, 71, 72–73, 78–79, 80–81, 105–6, 107–8, *110*
Zhou Rongxin, 96, 97–98
Zhou Wenzhong, 171–72
Zhou Xiaoyan, 174
Zhu Yonghang, 75, 81, 105
Zhuang Zedong, 37–38, 141–42, 146–47

www.ingramcontent.com/pod-product-compliance
Lightning Source LLC
Chambersburg PA
CBHW021659230426
43668CB00008B/670